Apple II®
Assembly Language

by

Marvin L. De Jong

Howard W. Sams & Co., Inc.
4300 WEST 62ND ST. INDIANAPOLIS, INDIANA 46268 USA

International Standard Book Number: 0-672-21894-1
Library of Congress Catalog Card Number: 82-50015

Edited by: *Jack Davis*
Illustrated by: *Ralph Lund*

Printed in the United States of America.

Preface

Welcome to a world where your vocabulary is limited to 56 three-letter words—words like LDA, STX, EOR, and PLA to mention a few. It is amazing what you can do with this limited vocabulary. You can make a calculator that can compute transcendental functions so fast that you do not realize you are waiting, or you can program the microcomputer to do something so slow and tedious that no human being could possibly stand the boredom. It is the tremendous power and versatility of this simple 56-word vocabulary and the microcomputer that make it so fascinating to human beings.

Without any attempt to detract from the usefulness and beauty of high-level programming languages, the author suggests that studying assembly language programming brings you as close to the microprocessor as you can get without actually building one yourself. Such study will give you a much greater appreciation of computer systems in general. Perhaps some youthful readers will even be inspired to eventually explore the world of symbolic logic, digital electronics, and quantum mechanics that lies hidden from view inside the microprocessor.

It is the author's hope that you will *enjoy* studying 6502 assembly language programming. Read the book for fun. Skip over the difficult parts. There is no need to underscore lines with a magic marker, take notes, memorize, or otherwise engage in mental torture. There will be no examination at the end of the book.

On the other hand, this book is a serious attempt to enable you to become a competent assembly language programmer. If this is your goal, then you must add a mode of study to the one just described. You must spend a lot of time at your computer keyboard with the book at your side, doing the exercises and either writing the programs that are suggested in the book or creating your own programs. You cannot learn to program a computer by simply reading a book about it. You must create, write, execute, and debug programs. In this mode of study the book simply becomes one of several resources that you will use to learn assembly language programming. Your computer is, of course, another important resource, but your most valuable resource is your imagination and your creativity. This mode of learning need not be any less enjoyable than reading the book while lounging on a couch. Allow your curiosity to be a motivating force, do not pressure yourself to succeed, and the process of learning a new programming language will be very rewarding.

Because the assembly language programmer works more closely to the microcomputer hardware than a high-level language programmer, some elementary interfacing techniques and projects have been included throughout the book. In the unlikely event that you find the hardware topics too difficult, simply skip the bothersome sections. There are many challenging problems that require no skill with integrated circuits, circuit diagrams, and wires.

One final note: the machine language versions of all the programs in the book are available, with no documentation, on DOS version 3.3,16 sector diskettes. Write to the author at 103 Hero Drive, Branson, MO 65616, if you are interested in purchasing such a diskette.

MARVIN L. DE JONG

To Three Friends

Contents

CHAPTER 1

The Microcomputer System

OBJECTIVES

At the completion of this chapter you should be able to do the following:

- Identify the major components of a microcomputer system and describe their functions.
- Understand the concept of address space and memory organization.
- Understand read and write operations.
- Comprehend elementary input/output concepts.
- Use the Apple monitor to examine and modify memory locations.
- List machine language and assembly language programs using the Apple monitor.
- Identify the registers in the 6502 microprocessor.

INTRODUCTION

Without any knowledge of the hardware inside a microcomputer or an appreciation of what the microcomputer is doing, it is still possible for you to be an excellent computer programmer if you are using a high-level language such as BASIC or Pascal. The same statement cannot be made if you wish to program the computer in 6502 assembly language. In the latter case you must know something about the structure of a microcomputer system and the architecture of the microprocessor. This knowledge is neither complicated nor difficult to acquire. The purpose of this chapter is to introduce the concepts necessary to proceed quickly to writing assembly language programs.

MICROCOMPUTER SYSTEM COMPONENTS

The terms *microcomputer* and *microprocessor* are frequently used interchangeably in computer literature. We wish to make a clear distinction between these terms. The microcomputer is the entire computer system, probably sitting on a desk nearby. The author's system is shown in Fig. 1–1. The microprocessor, on the other hand, is only a single component in the microcomputer. Typically, a *microprocessor* is a 40-pin integrated circuit, and some of the most popular microprocessors are the 6502, 6809, 8085, 1802, Z80, 8080A, and the 8086. A photograph of the 6502 is shown in Fig. 1–2. If you look inside your Apple you will see many integrated circuits, but the 6502 is easily located. The microprocessor is the brain of the microcomputer system.

(Courtesy Apple Computer, Inc.)

Fig. 1–1. Photograph of a microcomputer.

A typical microcomputer will include the following components:

- A microprocessor such as the 6502.
- A clock circuit that keeps the microprocessor running and synchronizes all the operations that the processor performs. In the Apple the clock circuit uses a 1.023-MHz crystal oscillator circuit.
- *Read/write* memory, sometimes abbreviated R/W memory.

Fig. 1-2. Photograph of a microprocessor.

This kind of memory is frequently called RAM, an acronym for *R*andom *A*ccess *M*emory.

- *Read-only memory* (ROM) that contains programs that must be permanently stored in the computer. The monitor and the BASIC interpreter are two examples of such programs.
- *Input/output* (i/o) devices, such as the keyboard, video monitor, game paddles, disk drive, and any other devices that the computer controls.
- Address decoding circuits.

The components of a microcomputer system are connected by three sets of wires or printed-circuit conductors called *buses*. These are:

- The *address bus* — 16 lines designated AD15–AD0.
- The *bidirectional data bus* — eight lines designated DB7–DB0.
- The *control bus* — variable number of lines.

Each of the conductors in a bus is called a *line*. A block diagram of a typical microcomputer system that is also representative of the Apple II system is shown in Fig. 1–3. This figure illustrates the relationships between the components mentioned thus far. Note that the various memory devices may decode some of the address lines internally, while the highest-order address lines are decoded by the address decoder.

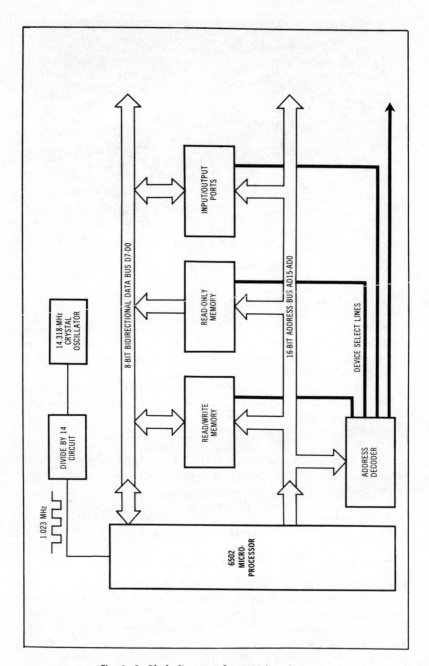

Fig. 1–3. Block diagram of a 6502-based system.

12

ADDRESS SPACE AND MEMORY ORGANIZATION

Sixteen pins on the 6502 are dedicated to *addressing*, that is, they control the two possible logic levels on each of the 16 lines that form the address bus. The logic levels are called "zero" (0) and "one" (1) although electrically they are voltage levels of 0 volts and 5 volts, respectively. The logic 0 or 1 levels on the address bus, AD15, AD14, AD13, . . . , AD0, determine a 16-bit binary number called the *address* of a memory location. The address *names* (or identifies) and *orders* memory locations.

Since there are 2^{16} unique 16-bit binary numbers, the 6502 is capable of addressing 65,536 memory locations. (Readers who are not familiar with binary and hexadecimal numbers and the terms "bit," "byte," and "nibble" are urged to study Appendix A before continuing.) The 16-bit address is frequently discussed in terms of two bytes:

- A high-order byte, called ADH for "address high," whose value is determined by the high-order 8 bits (AD15-AD8) of the address.
- A low-order byte, called ADL for "address low," whose value is determined by the low-order 8 bits (AD7-AD0) of the address.

In turn, each of these two bytes may be represented by two hexadecimal digits, 0–9 and A–F. The entire address is represented by four hexadecimal digits. In this book all hexadecimal numbers will have a "$" prefix. Thus $F9A6 is an example of an address, where $F9 is the ADH and $A6 is the ADL. Each memory location has a 16-bit address, and the *address space* is the total of all memory locations which the microprocessor is capable of addressing.

It is convenient to divide the address space into *blocks*. The smallest block size is called a *page* and consists of 256 (2^8) memory locations. Table 1–1 shows how the address space is divided into pages. The table illustrates that the ADH is the page number, while the ADL gives the memory location within a page. We will see that *page zero*, consisting of memory locations with addresses $0000–$00FF, and *page one*, consisting of memory locations $0100–$01FF, have a special significance in assembly language programming.

The next larger block size after a page is a unit of 1024 (2^{10}) memory locations that is usually referred to as *1K of memory*. Since $2^{10} = 1024$, it will require 10 address bits to uniquely specify each location in a 1K block. This leaves six address bits, AD15–AD10 to identify a 1K block. Six address bits can name

Table 1–1. Dividing the Address Space Into Pages

Address High ADH	Address Low ADL	Address	
(Binary)		(Hexadecimal)	
00000000	00000000	$0000	
00000000	00000001	$0001	
•	•	•	⎫
•	•	•	PAGE ZERO
•	•	•	
•	•	•	
00000000	11111111	$00FF	⎭
00000001	00000000	$0100	
00000001	00000001	$0101	⎫
•	•	•	
•	•	•	PAGE ONE
•	•	•	
•	•	•	
00000001	11111111	$01FF	⎭
•	•	•	
•	•	•	
•	•	•	
•	•	•	
•	•	•	
11111111	00000000	$FF00	⎫
11111111	00000001	$FF01	
•	•	•	PAGE 255$_{10}$
•	•	•	
•	•	•	
11111111	11111111	$FFFF	⎭

2^6, or 64, blocks; thus there are sixty-four 1K blocks of memory in the address space. Note that semiconductor memory (either R/W memory or ROM) is usually sold in "K" units. For example, you can purchase 16K of R/W memory and install it in a 32K Apple II to convert it to a 48K machine. Fig. 1–4 illustrates how various amounts of R/W memory can be installed in an Apple using integrated circuits that store either 4K bits or 16K bits. More recent Apples use only 16K blocks of R/W memory.

Read-only memory (ROM) is also packaged, sold, and installed in "K" units. For example, the Apple monitor comes in a 2K ROM integrated circuit that occupies memory locations with addresses $F800 through $FFFF. Five more 2K ROMs, which could contain a BASIC interpreter for example, can also be plugged into ROM sockets on the Apple circuit board.

Microcomputers, such as the Apple II, that use the 6502 as the microprocessor usually organize the address space so that R/W memory is at the "low end" (addresses $0000 and upward)

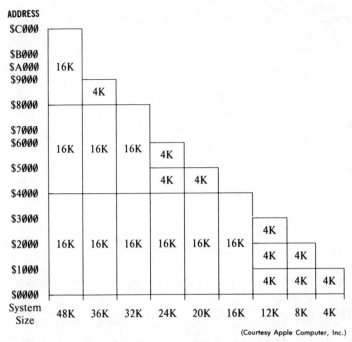

ADDRESS

	48K	36K	32K	24K	20K	16K	12K	8K	4K
$C000									
$B000	16K								
$A000									
$9000		4K							
$8000									
$7000									
$6000	16K	16K	16K	4K					
$5000				4K	4K				
$4000									
$3000							4K		
$2000	16K	16K	16K	16K	16K	16K	4K	4K	
$1000							4K	4K	4K
$0000									

System Size

(Courtesy Apple Computer, Inc.)

Fig. 1—4. R/W memory configurations for the Apple.

of the address space, ROM is at the "high end" (addresses $FFFF and downward), while input/output devices are accessed somewhere in the middle of the address space. A diagram of the organization of the various memory functions in the address space of a microcomputer is called a *memory map*. A memory map for the Apple is shown in Fig. 1–5. Of course, not every Apple will have the full 48K of R/W memory (referred to as RAM in Fig. 1–5) installed, nor is it likely that you will ever need 2K (2048) input/output (i/o) locations that are provided in the Apple's memory organization. In any case, the philosophy behind the memory organization of the Apple and other 6502 based systems will become obvious when you begin to understand some of the characteristics of the 6502 that will be discussed in this book.

READ AND WRITE OPERATIONS

To define the read and write operations we must understand something about the data bus, the $R/\overline{W}$ *line* in the control bus, and memory locations. Eight pins on the 6502 are connected to

System Memory Map		
Page Number:		
Decimal	Hex	
0	$00	
1	$01	
2	$02	
.	.	RAM (48K)
.	.	
.	.	
190	$BE	
191	$BF	
192	$C0	
193	$C1	
.	.	I/O (2K)
.	.	
198	$C6	
199	$C7	
200	$C8	
201	$C9	
.	.	I/O ROM (2K)
.	.	
206	$CE	
207	$CF	
208	$D0	
209	$D1	
.	.	ROM (12K)
.	.	
254	$FE	
255	$FF	

Fig. 1-5. Apple memory map.

(Courtesy Apple Computer, Inc.)

the data bus. The read/write, or R/$\overline{\text{W}}$, pin on the 6502 is connected to a line of the control bus called the R/$\overline{\text{W}}$ line. An *R/W memory* location consists of eight ordered bistable semiconductor devices, each capable of storing one bit of a binary number. The eight data-bus lines and the eight data bits associated with a memory location are *ordered* D7, D6, D5, . . . , D0, from the most significant bit to the least significant bit. Although it is best to think of the eight bits of information stored in a memory location as an *8-bit code*, this information is variously called a *number*, a *word*, or a *byte of data*. Depending on the context, in the course of this book we will use all of the above names.

We are ready now to make two important definitions:

- A *read* operation causes an *8-bit code* (or number) to be transferred over the data bus, *from* the memory location specified by the address on the address bus *to* an 8-bit register in the microprocessor.

- A *write* operation causes an 8-bit code to be transferred over the data bus *from* a register in the microprocessor *to* a memory location specified by the address on the address bus.

The words *load* and *store* are sometimes used synonymously with the words *read* and *write*, respectively.

Because a number is moved in one direction by a read or load operation and in another direction by a write or store operation, the data bus is said to be *bidirectional*. Furthermore, since eight pieces of information are transferred and stored, the 6502 is called an *8-bit microprocessor* and the Apple is an 8-bit microcomputer.

It is the function of the *address decoding circuitry* to *enable*, or activate, the *single* memory location, among the 65,536 possible locations, that is to receive the data in a write operation or to supply the data in a read operation. Special integrated circuits, such as the 74LS138s and other chips in the Apple II, perform some of the decoding by dividing the address space into blocks. The remainder of the decoding is done on the memory chips themselves. The address decoders usually decode the high-order lines (AD15, AD14, . . .) of the address bus to provide *device select lines* that activate a particular block of memory. The memory chips decode the low-order address lines (. . . , AD1, AD0) to *enable* the particular location in that block that has been *selected*. Fig. 1–3 illustrates many of the concepts that have just been described.

At this point it may be worth noting that the write operation is *not* used in connection with ROM, since as the name implies, this memory can only be read. Similarly, the microprocessor only writes to output ports and only reads input ports. Like operations with R/W memory, operations with ROM and i/o ports still involve the transfer of an 8-bit code.

To complete an understanding of read and write operations, we should note that a *register* is an 8-bit storage location in the microprocessor. The register is used to store the data on which the microprocessor is to operate, or it is used to control the operation of the microprocessor itself. Not all of the registers in the 6502 are of interest to the assembly language programmer, and readers who are interested in the internal operation of the 6502 are referred to the *6500 Hardware Manual* published by Rockwell International, Synertek, Inc., or Commodore Business Machines, Inc. The next section introduces and describes only those registers that are used in assembly language programming.

A PROGRAMMER'S VIEW OF THE 6502 ARCHITECTURE

Fig. 1–6 is another block diagram of a 6502-based microcomputer. This diagram emphasizes the five 8-bit registers and the one 16-bit register that are in the 6502 and are used in programming. Brief descriptions of each of the registers follow, although a complete appreciation of these descriptions will not be felt until some programming experience is acquired.

- The *accumulator*, A, is used for data transfers to and from memory. In all arithmetic and logical operations the accumulator contains one of the two numbers involved in the operation.
- The two *index registers*, X and Y, serve similar purposes. Like the accumulator they may be used for data transfers. They can also be used as an 8-bit index (or subscript) to a base address when an indexed addressing mode is used (see Chapter 6). Because the numbers in these registers may be incremented or decremented one unit at a time, they are also used as loop counters.
- The *processor status register* (P register) contains the flags or condition codes that may change with the execution of each instruction in a program. Refer to Chapter 3 for more details.
- The *program counter*, PC, is a 16-bit register that *points* to the address of a location in memory that contains the next byte of the program that is being executed. It is convenient to divide the program counter into two 8-bit parts, called PCH for program counter high-order byte and PCL for program counter low-order byte. If you could watch the program counter during the execution of a program, it would appear to count, except when branches or jumps occur, in which case it would appear to jump forward or backward in its counting.
- The *stack pointer*, S, is an 8-bit register that is used to *point* to a location in page one (addresses $0100–$01FF) of memory. When a read or write operation that references the stack occurs, the high-order byte on the address bus is $01. Thus the stack pointer may be considered to be a 16-bit register whose high-order byte is fixed at $01 and whose low-order byte is the number in the stack pointer. The stack is used to store information required to process

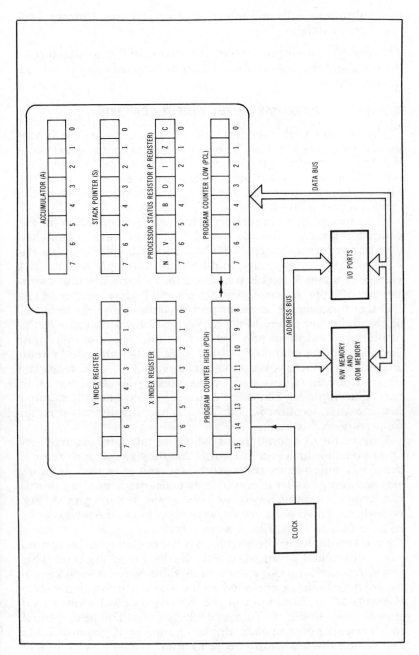

Fig. 1–6. Model of the 6502 microprocessor.

subroutine calls and interrupts correctly. See Chapter 7 for further details.

This completes our preliminary discussion of the architecture of the 6502 and most of our description of the *hardware* found in a microcomputer.

ELEMENTARY INPUT/OUTPUT CONCEPTS

The input/output operations of a microcomputer are fundamental to any application. The most obvious input operation of the Apple is reading the keyboard input port. The most obvious output operation is writing a character to the video monitor. More subtle are those i/o operations that take place when the game i/o port is used.

The purpose of an input port is to provide information for the computer from the outside world. This may be accomplished when an external device, a keyboard for example, controls the voltage levels on (typically) eight pins of an integrated circuit. A voltage of about 5 volts is translated into a logic 1, while a voltage near 0 volts is translated into a logic 0. The integrated circuit that functions as an input port is connected to the data bus of the microcomputer. Refer to Fig. 1-7 for a diagram of the Apple keyboard input port. When the address of the input port is placed on the address bus by the 6502, the integrated circuit controls the logic levels on the data bus, and the 6502 *reads* the binary number represented by the voltage levels at the input port. The Apple keyboard, for example, determines the number that is read at location $C000. We will use this input port rather frequently in this book.

This mode of operation, in which input ports act like any other memory device in the sense that they supply a number to the 6502 only when they are addressed is called *memory mapped* input. As far as the 6502 is concerned, an input port is just another location in its address space. Refer again to Fig. 1-3 where the i/o ports are shown connected to the address bus and the data bus just like memory devices.

Each key on the Apple keyboard is connected to an integrated circuit identified as an MM5740, the keyboard encoder. This keyboard encoder produces a unique 8-bit code for each key on the keyboard. For example, when the A key is pressed, the code $C1 appears at the output of the keyboard encoder integrated circuit. Refer to Fig. 1-7 for a block diagram. The hexadecimal code corresponding to each alphanumeric key is given in Table 1-2. When the keyboard port at location $C000 is read, one of these 8-bit codes will be transferred to the microprocessor.

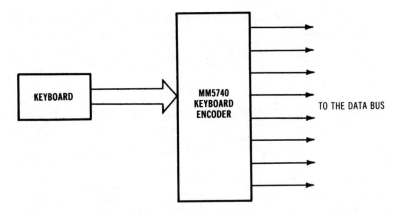

Fig. 1–7. Block diagram of the keyboard input port at location $C000.

The code numbers for most keys have been standardized by the computer industry and collectively they are called the American Standard Codes for Information Interchange (ASCII is the acronym). Thus Table 1–2 gives the ASCII representations of the most commonly used keys. If you are familiar with hexadecimal numbers you will notice that all of the key codes in Table 1–2 correspond to a binary number with a logic 1 in bit seven. It is more common to find ASCII with bit seven having a value of logic 0, but the designers of the Apple chose otherwise, and it will not cause any problems.

Consider output ports next. The purpose of an output port is to provide information from the computer to the outside world. Again, an integrated circuit is connected to the data bus and the address bus. When the 6502 *writes* to this location in the address space, the number stored in the output port controls the voltage levels on the output pins of the integrated circuit. A logic 0 produces a voltage level near 0 volts while a logic 1 produces a voltage level near 5 volts.

This mode of operation, in which the output ports are located in the address space, is called *memory mapped output*. The 6502 does not know if it is writing a number to an R/W location or an output port; only the programmer knows the difference.

To summarize, an input/output port is a location in the address space that can be used to transfer data either from the microprocessor to an external device or from an external device to the microprocessor.

The video output of the Apple operates quite differently from the keyboard input, and we will postpone further discussion of it. Suffice it to point out that writing the code for an al-

Table 1-2. Keyboard Code Table (ASCII)

Key	Code	Key	Code	Key	Code
A	$C1	N	$CE	0	$B0
B	$C2	O	$CF	1	$B1
C	$C3	P	$D0	2	$B2
D	$C4	Q	$D1	3	$B3
E	$C5	R	$D2	4	$B4
F	$C6	S	$D3	5	$B5
G	$C7	T	$D4	6	$B6
H	$C8	U	$D5	7	$B7
I	$C9	V	$D6	8	$B8
J	$CA	W	$D7	9	$B9
K	$CB	X	$D8	SPACE	$A0
L	$CC	Y	$D9	RETURN	$8D
M	$CD	Z	$DA	ESC	$9B

phanumeric character to a certain location in memory causes the character to appear at a certain location on the screen of the video monitor.

The type of input/output operations in which eight bits of information are transmitted *simultaneously* is called *parallel i/o*. Clearly this type of i/o requires at least eight conductors between the microcomputer and the i/o device. When the distance between the computer and the i/o device exceeds several feet, it may be less expensive and more practical to use a type of i/o that uses only two wires and a 1-bit i/o port. This type of i/o, in which an 8-bit code is transmitted one bit at a time, is called *serial i/o*. With serial input (or output), the voltage on a single input pin varies with time. Fig. 1–8 illustrates how one 8-bit code is input in the serial mode. The voltage on the input pin as a function of time is shown in this figure.

Continue to refer to Fig. 1–8. A *start bit,* initiated by a logic 1 to logic 0 transition, signals the microcomputer that an 8-bit code will follow. The eight bits are ordered with the least significant bit first and bit seven arriving last. The code illustrated by the bit stream in Fig. 1–8 is the number $C9. The 8-bit code is frequently followed by a *parity bit* that is used for error detection. The code is completed with a *stop bit.* The next 8-bit code can follow immediately. The reciprocal of the bit time is the bit rate, that is, the number of bits that are transmitted per second. The bit rate is sometimes called the *baud rate,* but it is more accurate to specify either the bit rate or the bit time. A common, but rather slow, rate is 110 bits per second, while a fast rate that is frequently used is 9600 bits per second. Many input/output devices, such as terminals and modems, use a standard serial input/output interface called the RS-232C. Un-

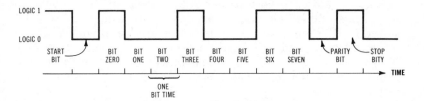

Fig. 1–8. Diagram of a serial i/o bit stream.

fortunately, space does not permit us to discuss these devices further.

THE APPLE MONITOR

A *monitor* is a program stored in ROM. The computer begins to execute this program either when power is first supplied to the computer, or when the RESET key is pressed. Do not confuse the term "monitor" with "video monitor." The monitor has a number of important features in addition to its ability to start the microcomputer running or to restart it after a program has crashed. These features include:

- The ability to input an address on the keyboard in order to see what number is stored in the memory location with that address.
- The ability to modify any number in any R/W memory location using the keyboard; that is, any 8-bit number may be entered into any R/W memory location.
- The ability to list a machine language program on the video monitor or the printer.
- The ability to transfer control of the microprocessor from the monitor to the user's programs that can be stored either in R/W memory or in ROM.
- The ability to display the numbers in the registers of the 6502.

The Apple comes in two varieties and one difference between them is in the monitor. There is a variety with an Autostart Monitor ROM and a variety with an Apple System Monitor ROM. Only the features that are common to both varieties will be used in this book. The exercises at the end of this chapter are designed to familiarize you with the features of the monitor. In the context of this discussion, it is worth pointing out that a program, such as the monitor, that is stored in ROM is frequently called *firmware*.

23

A great deal of the remainder of this book will be devoted to writing assembly language programs. These programs will be stored in R/W memory, and unless they are listed with a printer or stored on a magnetic medium, such as a cassette tape or a floppy disk, they disappear when power is removed from the computer. In this format the assembly language programs are called *software*.

EXERCISES USING THE APPLE MONITOR

The exercises that follow are designed to acquaint you with some of the functions of the Apple monitor, in preparation for using it in the chapters that follow. Keystrokes and responses that you should see on the video monitor are indicated by **boldface type**. We will always assume that a series of keystrokes is followed by a **RETURN**, that is, the specific instructions for you to press the RETURN key will frequently be omitted in the exercises.

Exercise 1–1

a. Turn on the power to your microcomputer. If you have the Autostart ROM, then you will need to get to the monitor by typing **CALL-151**. An asterisk prompt (*) should appear on the screen. If you do not have an Autostart ROM, then you will be in the monitor when power is applied, and the * prompt will appear on the screen.

b. To examine a memory location merely type in the hexadecimal address followed by a return. Type in **F800**. What do you observe?

(The author observed **F800-4A** on the screen, indicating that the number $4A is in location $F800. The computer also returns with a new * prompt on a new line.)

c. Type **RETURN** again. What do you observe?

(The author observed a new line with the numbers **08 20 47 F8 28 A9 0F** representing the contents of locations $F801 through $F807. Note that the monitor does not prefix the hexadecimal numbers with a "$" sign.)

d. Type **RETURN** again. What do you observe?

(The author observed a new line reading **F808- 90 02 69 E0 85 2E B1 26**. $F808 is the address of the location that contains $90. The other hexadecimal numbers are in locations $F809 through $F80F, respectively.)

e. Continue to press the **RETURN** key and analyze for yourself what is happening.

f. How could you examine the contents of page zero of memory with addresses $0000 through $00FF? Try it.

(You could respond to the * prompt by typing **0**, and you would be shown the contents of location $0000. Pressing the **RETURN** key again and again would provide the contents of the entire page.)

Exercise 1–2

a. Respond to the asterisk prompt by typing **0100.017F**. What do you observe?

(The author observed a display of the numbers in the locations $0100 through $017F, neatly arranged in 8 columns by 16 rows corresponding to the 128 ($80) memory locations that are displayed. Every eighth location is identified by its address. You have just produced a *memory dump*. Typing in numbers in the form pqrs.wxyz will display the contents of all the locations from address $pqrs to address $wxyz.)

b. How could you make a memory dump of the monitor ROM?

(Since the ROM starts at $F800 and ends at $FFFF, respond to the * prompt with **F800.FFFF**.)

c. Try it.

d. How would you dump the contents of the entire address space of the Apple? Try it. When you get tired of the numbers flashing in front of you press **RESET**.

Exercise 1–3

a. What number is currently located in memory location $1000? Use the monitor to find this number. Now type **1000:F5**. Next, use the monitor again to find the number in location $1000. What number is there?

(Regardless of what number was first at location $1000, using the : command modifies the contents of this location so it now contains $F5.)

b. How would you put the number $59 in location $0310?

(Type in **0310:59** following the * prompt.)

c. Type **0300:11 22 33 44 55 66 77 88 99 AA BB CC DD EE FF**. Next do a memory dump of locations $0300 through $031E by typing **300.31E**. What do you observe?

(You should observe that you have entered all of the numbers in memory. If you did not succeed, try again. Remember that the spaces between the numbers in the first line in Step *c* are important.)

d. How many numbers can you enter in a single sequence? Try this by typing **1000:01 02 03 04** etc., until something happens.

Exercise 1–4

a. Following the * prompt, type **CTRL E**. That is, first push down the **CTRL** key, then with it held down press the **E** key. Release both these keys, then press **RETURN**. What do you observe?

(You should observe an output on the screen that is similar but not identical to **A=C1 X=00 Y=F9 P=32 S=DC**. This output identifies the numbers in each of the 8-bit registers of the 6502. Again, note that the hexadecimal symbol $ is missing, but the numbers are in hexadecimal.)

b. Following the * prompt after Step *a*, type in **:00 11 22 33 44 66**. Then use the **CTRL E** command. What do you observe?

(You should note that you have succeeded in modifying the contents of these registers with the : command.)

c. Can you modify the number in a single register? Try modifying the number in the X register.

Exercise 1–5

a. Type **F800L**. What do you observe? Compare this with the monitor listings in your *Apple II Reference Manual*.

b. Continue to type in the **L** command and notice the consequences.

(You should observe a machine language listing of the monitor program.)

Exercise 1–6

a. Following the * prompt, load locations $1000 and upward with the hexadecimal codes as follows: **1000:AD 00 C0 10 FB 8D F7 07 8D 10 C0 4C 00 10** and press **RETURN**. Do a memory dump to make sure the numbers are correct.

b. After the * prompt, type **1000G** and then **RETURN**. Now press various keys on the keyboard and notice the lower right portion of the screen. What do you observe?

(You should observe that the character you type on the keyboard appears in the lower right portion of the screen. You have just *loaded* (: command) and executed (**G** command) a machine language program that performs the keyboard input and video monitor output operations described in this chapter. The program inputs a character code from the keyboard and outputs the character to the video monitor.)

Exercise 1–7

a. Turn off the power to the computer, then turn on the power. Examine locations $1000 and upward that you loaded in the previous exercise. What do you find there? What happens to the contents of R/W memory when power is removed?

b. Before going to the next chapter you might try a few mental exercises. First, summarize in your own words the functions of the following monitor commands: **L** , **G** , : , and . , and describe how each is used. Next, write down the main concepts you have learned in this chapter, including a sketch of a microcomputer system. Compare your results with the objectives at the beginning of the chapter. Compare your block diagram with Fig. 1–3.

CHAPTER 2

Writing and Executing Simple Assembly Language Programs

OBJECTIVES

At the completion of this chapter you should be able to do the following:

- Understand the terms *instruction, program, op code, mnemonic, operand, label,* and *symbol.*
- Use the data transfer instructions LDA, STA, LDX, STX, LDY, STY, TAX, TXA, TAY, TYA, and the BRK and JMP instructions in simple programs.
- Understand the format and structure of assembly language programs.
- Be able to write, load, and execute programs using the Apple II.
- Use a single-step mode to execute a program.

INTRODUCTION

Compared with high-level language programs, assembly language programs are concise and fast. There are numerous applications where high-level languages are too slow to operate or control a particular device, require too much memory, or both. By way of example, most of the peripheral cards marketed to operate in one of the eight peripheral card slots in the Apple II come with an assembly language driver *program* in ROM on the card. Applications involving driving printers, fast exchange of data through a serial interface or a modem, analog-to-digital (a/d) converters, and digital-to-analog (d/a) converters often require an assembly language driver. Music or voice synthesis and speech recognition are additional applications where assembly language is absolutely necessary.

Before learning how to write some simple programs, it may be worthwhile to have an overview of the 6502 instruction set. Table 2–1 provides a simple English language description of each instruction in the 6502 instruction set. Reading the complete table will give you a good perspective of the challenge ahead. It will also familiarize you with the capabilities of the 6502, particularly if you have had some previous programming experience.

A second, more concise, description of the 6502 instruction set is given in Table 2–2, the 6502 *instruction set summary*. This table is used so extensively in writing programs that you may wish to purchase a special card with a summary on it. A card that includes the instruction set summary is included with the Apple 6502 Assembler/Editor, a disk-based assembler available from Apple Computer, Inc. In any case, you will often refer to Table 2–2 when writing programs. You are not expected to fully comprehend the instruction set at this time. The purpose of this book is to provide an in-depth understanding of the instructions as you progress through the various chapters that explain and illustrate the instructions with a variety of programs.

MICROCOMPUTER INSTRUCTIONS

The basic elements of microcomputer programs are the instructions. A microcomputer *instruction* is a set of one, two, or three bytes which, when *read* by the microprocessor in the correct sequence, causes it to carry out a specific operation. Three simple examples are:

- *Load* a number from the memory location with the address ADH-ADL into the accumulator, A.
- *Store* the number in the accumulator in a memory location whose address is ADH-ADL.
- *Add* the number stored at the memory location whose address is ADH-ADL to the number in the accumulator. Place the result in the accumulator.

The *first byte* of an instruction always determines the specific operation to be carried out by the processor. In the three examples just given, the *second byte* of the instruction is the low-order byte of the address of the location where the microprocessor is to find the number. The *third byte* of the instruction is the high-order byte of the address of the location where the microprocessor is to find the number.

Table 2–1. English Language Description
of the 6502 Instruction Set*

Mnemonic	Logical Expression	Description
	Data Transfer Instructions	
LDA	M→A	Transfer the contents of a memory location M to the accumulator A.
LDX	M→X	Transfer the contents of a memory location M to the X register.
LDY	M→Y	Transfer the contents of a memory location M to the Y register.
STA	A→M	Transfer the contents of the accumulator to a memory location.
STX	X→M	Transfer the contents of the X register to a memory location.
STY	Y→M	Transfer the contents of the Y register to a memory location.
TAX	A→X	Transfer the contents of the accumulator to the X register.
TXA	X→A	Transfer the contents of the X register to the accumulator.
TAY	A→Y	Transfer the contents of the accumulator to the Y register.
TYA	Y→A	Transfer the contents of the Y register to the accumulator.
	Arithmetic and Logical Operation Instructions	
ADC	A + M + C→A	Add the contents of the accumulator, a memory location, and the carry flag; store the result in the accumulator.
SBC	A − M − $\overline{\text{C}}$→A	Subtract the contents of a memory location from the contents of the accumulator. Also invert and subtract the carry flag; store the result in the accumulator.
AND	A∧M→A	Form the logical AND of the contents of the accumulator and a memory location; store the result in the accumulator.
ORA	A∨M→A	Form the logical OR of the contents of the accumulator and a memory location; store the result in the accumulator.
EOR	A⊻M→A	Form the logical exclusive OR of the contents of the accumulator and a memory location; store the result in the accumulator.
	Test Instructions	
CMP	A − M	Subtract the contents of a memory location from the accumulator; the result is used only to set flags in the P register.
CPX	X − M	Subtract the contents of a memory location from the X register; the result is used only to set flags in the P register.
CPY	Y − M	Subtract the contents of a memory location from the Y register; the result is used only to set flags in the P register.

Mnemonic	Logical Expression	Description
BIT	A · M, $M_7 \rightarrow$ N, $M_6 \rightarrow$ V	Form the logical AND of the contents of the accumulator and a memory location; Use the result to set the Z flag. Transfer bit seven of the memory location to the N flag, and transfer bit six of the memory location to the V flag.

Register Shift and Modify Instructions

Mnemonic	Logical Expression	Description
DEC	$M - 1 \rightarrow M$	Decrement the contents of a memory location by one unit.
INC	$M + 1 \rightarrow M$	Increment the contents of a memory location by one unit.
DEX	$X - 1 \rightarrow X$	Decrement the contents of the X register by one unit.
INX	$X + 1 \rightarrow X$	Increment the contents of the X register by one unit.
DEY	$Y - 1 \rightarrow Y$	Decrement the contents of the Y register by one unit.
INY	$Y + 1 \rightarrow Y$	Increment the contents of the Y register by one unit.
ASL	C←7 0←0	Shift the contents of a location left; 0 into bit zero, bit seven into carry.
LSR	0→7 0→C	Shift the contents of a location right; 0 into bit seven, bit zero into carry.
ROL	C←7 0←	Rotate the contents of a location left; carry into bit zero, bit seven into carry.
ROR	→7 0→C	Rotate the contents of a location right; carry into bit seven, bit zero into carry.

Flag Set and Clear Instructions

Mnemonic	Logical Expression	Description
CLC	$0 \rightarrow C$	Clear the carry flag in the processor status register.
SEC	$1 \rightarrow C$	Set the carry flag.
CLD	$0 \rightarrow D$	Clear the decimal mode flag in the processor status register to do binary arithmetic.
SED	$1 \rightarrow D$	Set the decimal mode flag to do bcd arithmetic.
CLI	$0 \rightarrow I$	Clear the interrupt disable flag to allow $\overline{\text{IRQ}}$ interrupts.
SEI	$1 \rightarrow I$	Set the interrupt disable flag to prevent interrupts from the IRQ pin.
CLV	$1 \rightarrow V$	Clear the overflow flag.

No Operation Instruction

Mnemonic	Logical Expression	Description
NOP		No operation.

Branch Instructions

Mnemonic	Logical Expression	Description
BCC	PC = PC + OFFSET†	If the carry flag is clear, obtain the next instruction at location PC + OFFSET.
BCS	PC = PC + OFFSET	If the carry flag is set, obtain the next instruction at location PC + OFFSET.
BEQ	PC = PC + OFFSET	If the Z flag is set, obtain the next instruction at location PC + OFFSET.
BNE	PC = PC + OFFSET	If the result was not zero, obtain the next instruction at location PC + OFFSET.
BMI	PC = PC + OFFSET	If the N flag is set, obtain the next instruction at location PC + OFFSET.
BPL	PC = PC + OFFSET	If the result is not minus, obtain the next instruction at location PC + OFFSET.

Mnemonic	Logical Expression	Description
BVC	PC = PC + OFFSET	If the arithmetic operation cleared the V flag, obtain the next instruction at PC + OFFSET.
BVS	PC = PC + OFFSET	If the V flag is set, obtain the next instruction at PC + OFFSET.
Stack Operation Instructions		
PHA	$A \rightarrow M_S$, $S - 1 \rightarrow S$	Push the contents of the accumulator on the stack, and decrement the stack pointer.
PLA	$S + 1 \rightarrow S$, $M_S \rightarrow A$	Increment the stack pointer, and pull the accumulator contents from the stack.
PHP	$P \rightarrow M_S$, $S - 1 \rightarrow S$	Push the P register contents on the stack, and decrement the stack pointer.
PLP	$S + 1 \rightarrow S$, $M_S \rightarrow P$	Increment the stack pointer, and pull the P register contents from the stack.
TXS	$X \rightarrow S$	Transfer the contents of the X register to the stack pointer.
TSX	$S \rightarrow X$	Transfer the contents of the stack pointer to the X register.
Jumps, Subroutine Call, Interrupt, and Return Instructions		
JMP	No simple logic.	Jump to a new location to continue program execution. PC is modified.
JSR	No simple logic.	Jump to a subroutine to continue execution. PC is saved.
RTS	No simple logic.	Return to a calling program from a subroutine. PC is restored.
RTI	No simple logic.	Return to a program from an interrupt routine.
BRK	No simple logic.	Force a jump to an interrupt routine with software.

*De Jong, Marvin L., *Microprocessor Handbook*, New York: John Wiley & Sons, Inc., 1982. (*Courtesy John Wiley & Sons, Inc.*)

†OFFSET is the twos complement code of the second byte of any of the branch instructions, and PC is identical with the address of the first operation code following the branch instruction.

In each of the three examples just given, namely the load, store, and add instructions, the microprocessor *operates* on one 8-bit number. The load instruction fetches one number from memory. The store instruction moves one number from the accumulator to a memory location. The add instruction adds a number in memory to a number that is already in the accumulator. These examples lead to an important definition: the *operand* of an instruction is the number transferred or operated on when an instruction is executed.

Since the first byte of an instruction determines the nature of the operation as well as the addressing mode (explained in the next section), it is these 8-bit codes that the user must know in order to program the microprocessor. Because 8-bit codes are difficult to remember and recognize, one seldom sees the binary representation of the instructions. Instead, they are often represented in a hexadecimal format. The hexadecimal equivalent of the first byte of an instruction will be called the *operation code* or *op code*. The op codes for each of the instructions are given in the instruction set summary, Table 2–2. Furthermore, as an aid in programming, each instruction is given a *mnemonic,* which is an abbreviated name suggestive of the operation to be performed. The first column of the 6502 instruction set summary in Table 2–2 gives the mnemonic of each of the instructions.

Two other descriptions of instructions are commonly used. One is the *logical expression* and the other is an *English language description*. In Table 2–1 you will find both a logical expression and an English language description of each instruction. The logical expressions of each instruction are also given in Table 2–2. Refer to Example 2–1 for an illustration of these concepts.

Example 2–1. Illustration of Four Ways of Describing an Instruction

Mnemonic	Logical Expression	Op Code	Description
LDA	M→A	$AD	Transfer the contents of a memory location, M, to the accumulator, A.
STA	A→M	$8D	Move the contents of the accumulator, A, to memory location M.
ADC	A + M + C→A	$6D	Add the contents of the accumulator, a memory location, and the carry flag. Store the result in the accumulator.

In each of these three examples the memory location (M) contains the operand.

ADDRESSING MODES

Examine the instruction set summary in Table 2–2. The first column gives the instruction mnemonic, the second column gives the logical expression, and then there are 13 columns that give the op codes and other information for the various addressing modes. The names of the various addressing modes are found at the heading of each of these 13 columns, for example Immediate, Absolute, Zero-Page, etc. Addressing modes are one of the more confusing concepts for the beginner, and only a simplified explanation will be given at this point. Very briefly, the addressing mode is related to *where* and *how* the microprocessor locates the number on which it operates. That is, the addressing mode is related to how the microprocessor locates the operand of the instruction.

Table 2-2. Instruction Set Summary

MNEMONIC	OPERATION	IMMEDIATE OP	n	#	ABSOLUTE OP	n	#	ZERO PAGE OP	n	#	ACCUM OP	n	#	IMPLIED OP	n	#	(IND, X) OP	n	#	(IND), Y OP	n	#	Z-PAGE, X OP	n	#	ABS, X OP	n	#	ABS, Y OP	n	#	RELATIVE OP	n	#	INDIRECT OP	n	#	Z-PAGE, Y OP	n	#	PROCESSOR STATUS N V · B D I Z C	MNEMONIC
ADC	A + M + C → A (4)(1)	69	2	2	6D	4	3	65	3	2							61	6	2	71	5	2	75	4	2	7D	4	3	79	4	3										N V · · · · Z C	ADC
AND	A ∧ M → A (1)	29	2	2	2D	4	3	25	3	2							21	6	2	31	5	2	35	4	2	3D	4	3	39	4	3										N · · · · · Z ·	AND
ASL	C ← [·]← 0				0E	6	3	06	5	2	0A	2	1										16	6	2	1E	7	3													N · · · · · Z C	ASL
BCC	BRANCH ON C = 0 (2)																															90	2	2							· · · · · · · ·	BCC
BCS	BRANCH ON C = 1 (2)																															B0	2	2							· · · · · · · ·	BCS
BEQ	BRANCH ON Z = 1 (2)																															F0	2	2							· · · · · · · ·	BEQ
BIT	A ∧ M				2C	4	3	24	3	2																															M7 M6 · · · · Z ·	BIT
BMI	BRANCH ON N = 1 (2)																															30	2	2							· · · · · · · ·	BMI
BNE	BRANCH ON Z = 0 (2)																															D0	2	2							· · · · · · · ·	BNE
BPL	BRANCH ON N = 0 (2)																															10	2	2							· · · · · · · ·	BPL
BRK	BREAK													00	7	1																									· · · 1 · 1 · ·	BRK
BVC	BRANCH ON V = 0 (2)																															50	2	2							· · · · · · · ·	BVC
BVS	BRANCH ON V = 1 (2)																															70	2	2							· · · · · · · ·	BVS
CLC	0 → C													18	2	1																									· · · · · · · 0	CLC
CLD	0 → D													D8	2	1																									· · · · 0 · · ·	CLD
CLI	0 → I													58	2	1																									· · · · · 0 · ·	CLI
CLV	0 → V													B8	2	1																									· 0 · · · · · ·	CLV
CMP	A - M	C9	2	2	CD	4	3	C5	3	2							C1	6	2	D1	5	2	D5	4	2	DD	4	3	D9	4	3										N · · · · · Z C	CMP
CPX	X - M	E0	2	2	EC	4	3	E4	3	2																															N · · · · · Z C	CPX
CPY	Y - M	C0	2	2	CC	4	3	C4	3	2																															N · · · · · Z C	CPY
DEC	M - 1 → M				CE	6	3	C6	5	2													D6	6	2	DE	7	3													N · · · · · Z ·	DEC
DEX	X - 1 → X													CA	2	1																									N · · · · · Z ·	DEX
DEY	Y - 1 → Y													88	2	1																									N · · · · · Z ·	DEY
EOR	A ∀ M → A (1)	49	2	2	4D	4	3	45	3	2							41	6	2	51	5	2	55	4	2	5D	4	3	59	4	3										N · · · · · Z ·	EOR
INC	M + 1 → M				EE	6	3	E6	5	2													F6	6	2	FE	7	3													N · · · · · Z ·	INC
INX	X + 1 → X													E8	2	1																									N · · · · · Z ·	INX
INY	Y + 1 → Y													C8	2	1																									N · · · · · Z ·	INY
JMP	JUMP TO NEW LOC				4C	3	3																												6C	5	3				· · · · · · · ·	JMP
JSR	JUMP SUB				20	6	3																																		· · · · · · · ·	JSR
LDA	M → A (1)	A9	2	2	AD	4	3	A5	3	2							A1	6	2	B1	5	2	B5	4	2	BD	4	3	B9	4	3										N · · · · · Z ·	LDA

34

6502 Microprocessor Instruction Set (continued)

Mnemonic	Operation	Immediate OP n #	Absolute OP n #	Zero Page OP n #	Accum OP n #	(Ind,X) OP n #	(Ind),Y OP n #	Z Page,X OP n #	Abs,X OP n #	Abs,Y OP n #	Implied OP n #	Z Page,Y OP n #	Processor Status N V · B D I Z C
LDX	M → X	A2 2 2	AE 4 3	A6 3 2						BE 4 3(1)		B6 4 2	N · · · · · · Z ·
LDY	M → Y	A0 2 2	AC 4 3	A4 3 2				B4 4 2	BC 4 3(1)				N · · · · · · Z ·
LSR	0 → [7...0] → C		4E 6 3	46 5 2	4A 2 1			56 6 2	5E 7 3				0 · · · · · · Z C
NOP	NO OPERATION										EA 2 1		· · · · · · · · ·
ORA	A ∨ M → A	09 2 2	0D 4 3	05 3 2		01 6 2	11 5 2(1)	15 4 2	1D 4 3(1)	19 4 3(1)			N · · · · · · Z ·
PHA	A → Ms S − 1 → S										48 3 1		· · · · · · · · ·
PHP	P → Ms S − 1 → S										08 3 1		· · · · · · · · ·
PLA	S + 1 → S Ms → A										68 4 1		N · · · · · · Z ·
PLP	S + 1 → S Ms → P										28 4 1		(RESTORED)
ROL	(rotate left)		2E 6 3	26 5 2	2A 2 1			36 6 2	3E 7 3				N · · · · · · Z C
ROR	(rotate right)		6E 6 3	66 5 2	6A 2 1			76 6 2	7E 7 3				N · · · · · · Z C
RTI	RTRN INT										40 6 1		(RESTORED)
RTS	RTRN SUB										60 6 1		· · · · · · · · ·
SBC	A − M − C̄ → A	E9 2 2	ED 4 3	E5 3 2		E1 6 2	F1 5 2(1)	F5 4 2	FD 4 3(1)	F9 4 3(1)			N V · · · · · Z(3) C
SEC	1 → C										38 2 1		· · · · · · · · 1
SED	1 → D										F8 2 1		· · · · 1 · · · ·
SEI	1 → I										78 2 1		· · · · · 1 · · ·
STA	A → M		8D 4 3	85 3 2		81 6 2	91 6 2	95 4 2	9D 5 3	99 5 3			· · · · · · · · ·
STX	X → M		8E 4 3	86 3 2								96 4 2	· · · · · · · · ·
STY	Y → M		8C 4 3	84 3 2				94 4 2					· · · · · · · · ·
TAX	A → X										AA 2 1		N · · · · · · Z ·
TAY	A → Y										A8 2 1		N · · · · · · Z ·
TSX	S → X										BA 2 1		N · · · · · · Z ·
TXA	X → A										8A 2 1		N · · · · · · Z ·
TXS	X → S										9A 2 1		· · · · · · · · ·
TYA	Y → A										98 2 1		N · · · · · · Z ·

Symbols:

+	ADD	X	INDEX X
−	SUBTRACT	Y	INDEX Y
∧	AND	A	ACCUMULATOR
∨	OR	M	MEMORY PER EFFECTIVE ADDRESS
⊻	EXCLUSIVE OR	Ms	MEMORY PER STACK POINTER

M7   MEMORY BIT 7
M6   MEMORY BIT 6
n   NO. CYCLES
NO. BYTES

(1) ADD 1 to N IF PAGE BOUNDARY IS CROSSED
(2) ADD 1 TO N IF BRANCH OCCURS TO SAME PAGE
    ADD 2 TO N IF BRANCH OCCURS TO DIFFERENT PAGE
(3) CARRY NOT = BORROW
(4) IF IN DECIMAL MODE Z FLAG IS INVALID
    ACCUMULATOR MUST BE CHECKED FOR ZERO RESULT

(Courtesy Rockwell International)

Take the first three (and the simplest to understand) addressing modes given in Table 2–2, for example, and suppose we are dealing with the LDA instruction. How does the microprocessor locate the operand?

- In the absolute mode, the second and third bytes of the instruction are the ADL and the ADH of the operand. Assume the operand is in location $F97A. Then the complete LDA instruction is specified by the three hexadecimal numbers, in order, AD 7A F9.
- In the zero-page mode, the second byte of the instruction is the ADL of the operand (the ADH of the operand is understood to be $00). Thus, if the operand is in location $007F, then the complete LDA instruction is specified by the two hexadecimal numbers, A5 7F.
- In the immediate mode, the second byte of the instruction *is* the operand. Suppose we want to load the accumulator with $F0. The complete LDA instruction is specified by the two hexadecimal numbers, in order, A9 F0.

Each addressing mode has a *unique* op code, even though the same instruction is involved. This can be seen from the preceding explanation where the LDA instruction had op codes of $AD, $A5, and $A9, depending on the addressing mode.

When, in the process of executing a program, the processor reads the op code, it decodes or interprets that unique bit pattern to determine the nature of the instruction *and* the addressing mode. The meanings of the remaining bytes of the instruction are also determined at the same time. If the processor reads an op code of $AD, it knows that there will be two more bytes in the instruction, and that they will be the ADL and the ADH of the operand, in that order.

It should be clear from Table 2–2 that not all instructions have the same set of addressing modes. For example, the TAX instruction does not have any of the addressing modes described above for the LDA instruction. When executed, the TAX instruction transfers the number in the accumulator to the X register. These registers are *internal* to the 6502, hence they have no address. The op code contains all of the necessary information for the instruction to be executed. This addressing mode is called *implied addressing*, since the instruction itself implies both the source and the destination of the operand. All instructions using the implied addressing modes are single-byte instructions. Other addressing modes will be covered in subsequent chapters.

Refer again to Table 2–2 and observe that in addition to the op code, one can also find the number of bytes (#) in each instruction and the number of clock cycles, n, that each instruction requires for execution. With a clock frequency of 1.023 MHz, each clock cycle is 0.9775 microsecond.

MICROCOMPUTER PROGRAMS

A microcomputer *program* is an *ordered set* of instructions. The program is designed to accomplish an objective. Some examples of program objectives are:

- Multiply two 8-bit numbers.
- Convert the serial data stream from a modem attached to a telephone line to a printed output on a printer.
- Perform a series of a/d conversions of a time-varying voltage from a nerve, store 256 of these conversions, and be able to display them as a graph on the video monitor.
- Read a bar code on an item purchased in a store. Print the name of the item, its price, and update the inventory.
- Convert the Morse code detected on a communications receiver to alphanumeric characters on the video monitor.

The instructions are stored in memory and are *ordered* by their addresses. The *program counter* (PCH-PCL) register in the microprocessor ensures that the instructions are fetched in order. The PC contains the address of the next byte of program data that is to be read. After each byte is read from memory (which takes one clock cycle), the program counter is incremented internally to point to the address at which the next program byte is found. The program counter can jump by more than one unit only when branches, jumps, interrupts, or subroutine calls are executed by the microprocessor.

We begin with a simple illustration. Suppose the object of a program is to transfer a byte of data from location $C000 to location $07F7. A simple program to accomplish this objective is given in Example 2–2. The program requires six bytes of memory, its starting address is $1000, and it requires only two instructions. An LDA instruction is contained in the first three bytes of the program, and the STA instruction is contained in the last three bytes.

Example 2–2. A Simple Data Transfer Program

Location	Contents	Comments
$1000	$AD	Fetch the number in the location whose address
$1001	$00	is $C000 and place that number in the accumulator.
$1002	$C0	

$1003	$8D	Store the number in the accumulator in the
$1004	$F7	memory location whose address is $07F7.
$1005	$07	

If the above program were stored in memory and the program counter were initialized to $1000, then the 6502 will execute the program. As far as the microprocessor is concerned, the actual location of the program or its starting point makes no difference. It is absolutely necessary, however, that each byte of an instruction, and the instructions themselves, be in the proper order.

WRITING ASSEMBLY LANGUAGE PROGRAMS

As a matter of fact, programs are not written in the form illustrated by Example 2–2. The procedure for writing a program is as follows:

- Have the objective clearly in mind and, if necessary, flowchart the steps required to achieve the objective.
- Write an *assembly language* version of the program using *labels* for addresses within the program, *mnemonics* for instructions, and *symbols* for the addresses of locations that contain operands.
- Translate the program into hexadecimal *machine language*.

The assembly language program will be illustrated first. Consider again the program in Example 2–2 whose object was to transfer a byte of data from location $C000 to $07F7. The assembly language version of this program is shown in Example 2–3.

Example 2–3. Assembly Language Data Transfer Program

Label	Mnemonic	Operand Field	Comments
START	LDA	KYBD	Load the number stored at KYBD into A.
	STA	SCREEN	Store the number in A at location SCREEN.

Refer to Example 2–3 and observe that the starting address of the program is *labeled* START. Both instructions are represented by their mnemonics, LDA and STA. Address $C000 is represented by the *symbol* KYBD, and address $07F7 is represented by the *symbol* SCREEN. Since these locations contain the operands, their symbols are in the *operand field* of the program. (The choice of labels and symbols is up to the programmer and they usually contain some meaning.) Almost all assembly language programs are organized in columns like those shown in this example.

To summarize:

- The address of the first byte of any instruction may have a name called a *label*. Labels are found in the first column of an assembly language program.
- The second column contains the instruction *mnemonic*.
- The third column is the *operand field*.
  - It is *empty* if a single-byte instruction using the *implied* addressing mode is involved.
  - It may be a *symbol* for the address of an operand.
  - It may be the *operand* itself if the immediate addressing mode is being used.
  - It may be a *label*, symbolizing a program address.
- The fourth column contains *comments* that interpret or clarify the purpose of the instruction.

Refer again to Example 2–3 where some of these ideas are illustrated. Cases where the operand field is empty and where the operand field contains a label will be illustrated in Examples 2–8 and 2–6, respectively. Example 2–7 will illustrate a case where the operand is in the program.

Step three in writing a program consists of translating the labels, mnemonics, and symbols into their hexadecimal equivalents. The process of translating the assembly language program into hexadecimal bytes is called *assembling*. The translation is called a *machine language* program because it is in the form used to load it into the microprocessor. The machine language program is usually placed directly to the left of the assembly language program. The completed program with which we have been working is given in Example 2–4.

Example 2–4. Completed Data Transfer Program

Location	Instruction	Label	Mnemonic	Operand Field	Comments
$1000	AD 00 C0	START	LDA	KYBD	Load A from KYBD.
$1003	8D 7F 07		STA	SCREEN	Move number in A to SCREEN.

A program that converts labels, mnemonics, and symbols into a machine language program is called an *assembler*. In the writing of this book, extensive use was made of the Apple 6502 Assembler/Editor, and in order to minimize errors in the preparation of the book the printed output of the 6502 Assembler/Editor was submitted to the publisher for printing. In Example 2–5 is illustrated the format of the programs that will be used in this book. The program is identical with the one we have been studying in this chapter. Note the slight differences between the format of Example 2–4 and Example 2–5. In Example 2–5 the format includes line numbers, some of which appear to be missing. The missing line numbers correspond to assembler directives that are not important to explain at this time. We will use the line numbers to identify a particular instruction when discussing a program in the text. For many of the programs in this book, hand assembly using Table 2–2 is almost as practical as assembling a program using an assembler. Do not be concerned if you do not have an assembler at this time.

Up until this point we have neglected the first step in writing an assembly language program, concentrating instead on the details of the program itself. In recent years, largely because of the great expense involved in writing software, a great deal of thought and effort has gone into *software engineering*, the discipline of efficiently developing, documenting, and maintaining computer programs. Space does not permit a lengthy digression into this subject, but it may be worthwhile to point out several steps to take in the process of writing a program.

- *Specify* in words exactly what the program is to do.
- *Analyze* the programming problem:
  - •• What *output* will constitute a solution?
  - •• What data must be *input*?
  - •• Are there special cases to be considered?
- *Repeat* the above steps until you are satisfied with your results.
- *Map* the problem into a series of structures that will solve the programming problem.
- *Write* the assembly language programs to implement each of the structures or modules.
- *Combine* the modules into a completed program after testing the individual modules.

Readers who are interested in an efficient and mature approach to writing programs are urged to obtain a text on *structured programming* techniques, a subject which is beyond the scope of this book.

A minor aid in writing programs is a suitable form. One possible form is shown in Fig. 2–1.

THE JMP AND BRK INSTRUCTIONS

When the microprocessor completes the execution of the program in Example 2–5 it will look for the next op code at location $1006. Assuming that we have loaded this program in R/W

PROGRAM NAME _____ PAGE_____ OF_____
PROGRAMMER _____ DATE _____

ADDRESS	INSTRUCTION B1 B2 B3			LABEL	MNEMONIC	OPERAND	COMMENTS

Fig. 2–1. Sample programming form.

memory in the Apple, the location $1006 will still contain the random data that it obtained during the power-up stage. What the microprocessor will do when it fetches nonsense op codes is not obvious, at least to the author. It seems to wander off, more or less on its own, sometimes destroying pieces of other programs stored in R/W memory. Clearly it would be desirable to know what the microprocessor is doing and to be in control of it.

Example 2–5. Data Transfer Program Using the Absolute Addressing Mode

Object: Transfer the contents of location $C000 to location $07F7.

```
1000:AD 00 C0  6 START    LDA   KYBD    ;TRANSFER THE NUMBER IN KYBD
                                          TO A.
1003:8D 10 C0  7          STA   SCREEN  ;MOVE NUMBER IN A TO SCREEN.
```

For the purposes of this discussion there are at least two ways to prevent the events described in the previous paragraph. We could continually repeat the program by "ending" it with a "JMP START" instruction. This approach makes the program an infinite loop, but at least we know what the processor is doing. The loop can always be broken by pressing the RESET button, which shifts control back to the monitor. In Example 2–6 a JMP instruction has been appended to the program given in Example 2–5. The JMP instruction has the effect of resetting the program counter to the value labeled START. The program will now repeat the LDA KYBD, STA SCREEN, and JMP START instructions continuously and forever, unless the RESET key is pressed or power is removed. The three instructions form a *loop.* The JMP instruction may be used to reset the program counter to any 16-bit number. Note that the *second byte* of the JMP instruction becomes the *new PCL*, while the *third byte* of the JMP instruction becomes the *new PCH*.

Example 2–6. A Program to Illustrate the JMP Instruction

Object: Place the data transfer program in Example 2–5 in an infinite loop to continuously read the Apple keyboard and write the result to a screen location.

1000:AD 00 C0	6 START	LDA	KYBD	;TRANSFER THE NUMBER IN KYBD TO A.
1003:8D F7 07	7	STA	SCREEN	;MOVE NUMBER IN A TO SCREEN.
1006:4C 00 10	8	JMP	START	;GO TO INSTRUCTION LABELLED START.

Another technique that will be used to "end" the demonstration programs in this book is the BRK instruction. In Chapter 7 we will discuss more completely the consequences of this instruction. For the moment we simply note that it will produce a jump to the Apple II monitor and the monitor will cause the contents of each of the 8-bit registers to be displayed on the screen of the video monitor in the form:

$$1008-\ A = 0D\ X = 04\ Y = D8\ P = 30\ S = F0$$

where all the numbers are understood to have a hexadecimal representation. After displaying the contents of the registers, the monitor prompt (*) is given, indicating that control has been transferred to the monitor. The demonstration programs given in the following examples use the BRK instruction to end execution of the programs.

PROGRAMS TO DEMONSTRATE THE DATA TRANSFER INSTRUCTIONS

The purpose of this section is to demonstrate the various data transfer instructions and the immediate, absolute, zero-page, and implied addressing modes in simple programs. Note first that absolute addressing was used in Example 2–6 and all previous examples. Example 2–7 illustrates the immediate addressing mode and the zero-page addressing mode. You should observe that a number symbol (#) is used to prefix the operand in the operand field of the assembly language program to distinguish the immediate addressing mode from other addressing modes. See the LDA instruction in Example 2–7.

Example 2–6 illustrates the situation where the operand field contains a label. Note that the operand field of the JMP instruction contains START, the *destination* of the JMP instruction.

Object: Clear locations $24 and $25.

```
1009:A9 00    6        LDA    #$00      ;"LDA" IN IMMEDIATE MODE.
100B:85 24    7        STA    CURSHO;   ;"STA" IN ZERO-PAGE MODE.
100D:85 25    8        STA    CURSVT
100F:00       9        BRK              ;BREAK TO THE MONITOR.
```

The TAX and TAY instructions are illustrated in Example
2−8. These two instructions use the implied addressing mode,
since the instruction itself identifies the location of the operand,
and consequently no address is necessary.

Example 2−8. Transferring Data from One Register to Another

Object: Clear A, X, and Y.

```
1010:A9 00    4 BEGIN  LDA    #$00      ;"LDA" IN THE IMMEDIATE
                                          MODE.
1012:AA       5        TAX              ;"TAX" USES THE IMPLIED
                                          MODE.
1013:A8       6        TAY              ;"TAY" USES THE IMPLIED
                                          MODE.
1014:00       7 END    BRK              ;"BRK" USES THE IMPLIED
                                          MODE.
```

Example 2−9 illustrates how data transfers can be accomplished without affecting the contents of the accumulator. In
this case the X index register is used to transfer the number $7F
to the location symbolized by INVFLG.

Example 2−9. Using the X Register for a Data Transfer

Object: Store $7F in location $0032 without using the accumulator.

```
1015:A2 7F    5 START  LDX    #$7F      ;"LDX" IN THE IMMEDIATE MODE.
1017:86 32    6        STX    INVFLG    ;"STX" IN THE ZERO-PAGE MODE.
1019:00       7 END    BRK
```

Study these examples, carefully checking the op codes used
in the programs with those given in Table 2−2. The exercises
will give you additional experience with the elementary programming concepts that have been introduced in this chapter.

EXERCISES

Exercise 2−1

a. The program listed below writes the number $00 to several
locations. Use Table 2−2 to fill in the blanks. Assume the following memory assignments: TXTCLR = $C050, MIXCLR =

$C052, HISCR = $C055, and HIRES = $C057. The program has a starting address of $101A.

```
$101A __ 00          LDY #$__        ;"LDY" USING THE IMMEDIATE MODE.
$101_ 8C 50 C0       STY ____        ;CLEAR LOCATION TXTCLR.
$__ __ __ __         STY MIXCLR      ;CLEAR LOCATION MIXCLR.
$1022 8C 57 C0         HIRES         ;CLEAR LOCATION HIRES.
___ __ __ __         STY HISCR       ;CLEAR LOCATION HISCR.
___ __               TYA             ;CLEAR THE ACCUMULATOR.
___ __               BRK             ;RETURN TO THE MONITOR.
```

b. Load the program starting with the first op code at $101A and ending with the last op code at $1029. Use the monitor : command to enter the instructions byte by byte at the proper locations.

c. Run the program by entering **101AG**. What do you observe?

(The writer observed a series of horizontal lines on our black and white video monitor. You have put the Apple into its high-resolution graphics mode (hires) displaying the secondary screen page.)

d. The TYA instruction in this program did not perform a meaningful task, but it did lead to this question: What number will be in the accumulator after the program executes?

(Since the BRK command saves the register contents for display, you can see the answer to this question by pressing the **RESET** key, putting the Apple back into its text mode using the primary screen page.)

e. Which addressing mode was used for the four STY instructions in this program? The first six instructions in the program all had the same value for the operand. What was it?

(The absolute addressing mode was used for the STY instructions. In all of the instructions except the BRK instruction, the value of the byte of data operated on or moved was $00. The operand, therefore, was $00.)

f. Which addressing mode does the TYA instruction use? What happens when this instruction is executed?

Exercise 2–2

a. Load the program listed in Example 2–6. The listing is repeated here for your convenience.

```
1000:AD 00 C0  6 START    LDA    KYBD    ;TRANSFER THE NUMBER IN KYBD TO A.
1003:8D F7 07  7          STA    SCREEN  ;MOVE NUMBER IN A TO SCREEN.
1006:4C 00 10  8          JMP    START   ;GO TO INSTRUCTION LABELED START.
```

It would be wise to save these programs on cassette tape or on a disk. Some of them will be used again, others may make useful subroutines for your own programming purposes.

b. Check the accuracy of the loading process by listing the

program using the monitor L command. Type in **1000L**. Note that the process of converting a machine language in memory to mnemonics is called a *disassemble*. The locations of the operands are not given symbols, only their addresses are shown. In the case of the immediate addressing mode, the actual operand is listed. The writer obtained the listing given below.

```
*1000L
1000–       AD 00 C0        LDA         $C000
1003–       8D F7 07        STA         $07F7
1006–       4C 00 10        JMP         $1000
```

c. Run this program by following the asterisk prompt with **1000G**. You should see a character in the lower right-hand part of your video monitor. Press the **Z** key on the keyboard. What do you observe on the screen? Press several other keys. What does the space bar do? What is the effect of the **CTRL** key? Describe in your own words what this program accomplishes.

(Each symbol on the keyboard is represented by a unique 8-bit code called ASCII, and the keyboard circuitry makes this code available at one location, $C000, in the address space of the microcomputer. Location $C000 is the input port assigned to the keyboard. The program reads this port and stores the 8-bit code it reads at location $07F7. This is one of many locations in a block memory called the *text screen*. Quite independently of the activities of the microprocessor, the video circuitry in the Apple accesses a group of 960 R/W memory locations and maps the 8-bit character codes in these locations into characters displayed on the screen of the video monitor. The 960 locations correspond to the 40 characters on each of 24 lines. Since the LDA KYBD and the STA SCREEN instructions are in an infinite loop, anytime a new key is pressed a new character appears.

d. To break out of the loop, press RESET.

Exercise 2–3

a. Load the program in Example 2–7. It is listed here for your convenience.

```
1009:A9 00     6      LDA    #$00      ;"LDA" IN IMMEDIATE MODE.
100B:85 24     7      STA    CURSHO    ;"STA" IN ZERO-PAGE MODE.
100D:85 25     8      STA    CURSVT
100F:00        9      BRK              ;BREAK TO THE MONITOR.
```

b. Execute the program by typing **1009G**. What do you observe?

(You should observe that the video monitor cursor returns to the upper left-hand corner of the screen. The locations symbolized by CURSHO (cursor horizontal) and CURSVT (cursor vertical) contain the numbers that determine the position of the cursor on the screen of the video monitor. Setting them both to zero has the effect of homing the cursor.)

c. What is the number in the accumulator after the program is executed? The BRK instruction caused a jump to the monitor, which then displays the number in each register on the monitor screen. The answer to the question is there.

d. Experiment with other numbers in the second byte of the program and observe the position of the cursor after the program is executed.

Exercise 2–4

Load and execute the program in Example 2–8. Predict what you will observe on the screen when the numbers in the registers are displayed. The program is listed here.

```
1010:A9 00    4 BEGIN    LDA    #$00      ;"LDA" IN THE IMMEDIATE MODE.
1012:AA       5          TAX              ;"TAX" USES THE IMPLIED MODE.
1013:A8       6          TAY              ;"TAY" USES THE IMPLIED MODE.
1014:00       7 END      BRK              ;"BRK" USES THE IMPLIED MODE.
```

Exercise 2–5

Load the program in Example 2–9. Run it, and describe what you observe. The program is listed here.

```
1015:A2 7F    5 START    LDX    #$7F      ;"LDX" IN THE IMMEDIATE MODE.
1017:86 32    6          STX    INVFLG    ;"STX" IN THE ZERO-PAGE MODE.
1019:00       7 END      BRK
```

(You should observe that *letters* printed on the screen *after* the execution of the program are flashing. Location $32 in page zero of memory controls the format in which the letters are displayed, normally, in the inverse mode (black on white) or flashing. Check your *Apple II Reference Manual* to see how to print inverse characters. Run the program again to accomplish this.)

Exercise 2–6

If you have Integer BASIC in ROM (Monitor ROM), then single-step through each of the programs in Examples 2–6 through 2–9. Pay particular attention to the numbers in the registers that are modified by the instruction just executed. Also observe the program counter very carefully in Example 2–6 to see how it is modified by the JMP START instruction. If you have an Apple II Plus (Autostart ROM) then the single-step mode is not available. In that case you may wish to build the simple single-step circuit in Appendix B. Also given is a program that must be used in conjunction with the circuit to provide single-step capability. Refer to Appendix B for instructions.

Exercise 2–7

Write, load, and execute a program that puts the Apple in the low-resolution graphics mode and displays the secondary page. This requires that you write any data to locations $C050 (TXTCLR), $C052 (MIXCLR), $C056 (LORES), and $C055 (HISCR). You should observe a random graphics display on the screen after running the program.

Although the screen shows graphics, you can still use the monitor but you cannot see what you are doing. Use the : command (and considerable care) to enter **$00, $01, $02, . . . , $0F** in locations $0800 through $080F. If at all possible, try this with a color monitor. Would it be easy to do color graphics using only data transfer instructions? How could you place a picture on the screen using only data transfer instructions?

Exercise 2–8

Here are some very simple programs to try for yourself. Use the instruction set summary in Table 2–2 to obtain the op codes. After you write your program, load it and execute it. You can test the results by using the monitor to examine the memory locations that are modified by the program.

a. Write a program to load locations $03FB, $03FC, and $03FD with the numbers $4C, $00, and $80, respectively.

b. Write a program to transfer the number in location $FFFF to location $0000. Use absolute addressing to fetch the number and zero-page addressing to store the number.

c. Write a program to clear locations (fill with zeros) $3A, $3B, $45, $46, $47, $48, and $49 in page zero of memory. Finish your program with a BRK instruction. Execute it and note the numbers in the various registers after the program executes.

d. Write a program to toggle the Apple speaker. The speaker can be toggled by writing any number to location $C030. Put the instruction in an infinite loop with a JMP instruction. Do you expect to hear the speaker? Why not? Put some dummy instructions (for example, a series of LDA $C000 instructions) between the instruction that toggles the speaker and the JMP instruction. Run your program again. Can you hear the speaker yet? Add some more dummy instructions to take up more time between the instruction that toggles the speaker and the JMP instruction. Is this a practical way to produce a delay? In the next chapter we will find a better way of introducing delays into programs.

CHAPTER 3

Branches and Loops

OBJECTIVES

At the completion of this chapter you should:

- Have an understanding of the function of the processor status register and the flags it contains.
- Be able to use the branch instructions BCC, BCS, BEQ, BNE, BMI, BPL, BVS, and BVC.
- Know how the increment and decrement instructions may be used. These are INC, DEC, INX, DEX, INY, and DEY.
- Be able to utilize some of the subroutines in the Apple monitor.
- Be able to write programs to produce time delays.
- Perform some simple input/output functions with the Apple II keyboard and the game i/o connector.

INTRODUCTION

The ability of the microprocessor to make decisions makes it the powerful tool that it is. Although it may be criticized for its lack of imagination and creative ability, the 6502 is extremely good at handling "if . . . then . . ." *logical* thinking. For example, it can handle a decision of the form "if the logic level on an input pin is 1, then read the keyboard input port." Although each decision is admittedly simple, a set of decisions can be used to monitor or control complex operations. This chapter deals principally with the decision making instructions, called *branch* instructions. The *increment* and *decrement* instructions, as well as the *jump-to-subroutine* instruction will be included to make the programming examples more valuable. Nevertheless, the main emphasis of this chapter is on the branch instructions. Since these instructions are related to specific bit values in the processor status register (the P register), we begin with a detailed study of this register.

THE PROCESSOR STATUS REGISTER

The processor status register, called the P register, is detailed in Fig. 3–1. Although it is an 8-bit register, bit five is not used. Each of the other bits is called a *flag*, a *condition code*, or a *status bit*. Note the following definition:

- If a flag is *set*, then there is a *logic 1* in the corresponding bit in the P register.
- If a flag is *clear*, then there is a *logic 0* in the corresponding bit in the P register.

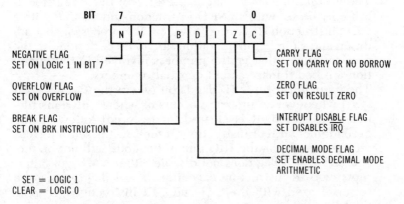

Fig. 3–1. Detail of the processor status register.

The flags or condition codes are modified when instructions are executed or when external events occur. In other words, the condition codes signal a certain course of events as a program executes. A brief description of each flag will be given at this point. Do not be disturbed if you do not completely understand these descriptions. They have been made as complete as possible so they will be valuable for your future reference.

- The *carry* (C) flag is bit zero of the P register. It is set when an addition, shift, or rotate operation generates a carry. It is cleared when a subtraction or a compare operation produces a borrow. The carry flag can also be cleared with a CLC instruction or set with an SEC instruction.
- The *zero* (Z) flag is bit one of the P register. It is set when

the accumulator, index register, or a memory location contains all zeros as the result of an arithmetic, logical, shift, rotate, increment, decrement, or load data operation.

- The *negative* (N) flag is bit seven of the P register. It is set when bit seven of the accumulator, an index register, or a memory location has a logic 1 in its bit seven as the result of the execution of an operation by the microprocessor.

- The *overflow* (V) flag is bit six of the P register. It is set when an addition or subtraction produces a result that is either greater than \$7F (127) or less than \$80 (−128). It is useful in applications involving *signed* numbers. The V flag can also be set with a negative transition on the set overflow (SO) pin on the 6502, it can be cleared with a CLV instruction, and it may be modified as the result of executing a BIT instruction.

- The *decimal mode* (D) flag is bit three of the P register. It can only be set with an SED instruction and cleared with a CLD instruction. It is used to signal the processor that addition and subtraction operations are to be performed in the decimal mode; that is, the numbers involved in the operation are bcd (binary coded decimal) numbers.

- The *interrupt disable* (I) flag is bit two in the P register. It is set whenever an interrupt occurs or when a BRK instruction is executed. It is cleared (or restored) following the execution of an RTI instruction. If the I flag is set, interrupt requests made via the $\overline{\text{IRQ}}$ pin on the 6502 will not be recognized. The I flag does not disable either NMI-type interrupts or BRK instruction execution. The I flag can also be set or cleared with the SEI and CLI instructions, respectively.

- The *break* (B) flag is bit four in the P register. It is set whenever a BRK instruction is executed. The I flag will also be set in this case. Both flags will be cleared when the P register is restored following execution of the RTI instruction.

In addition to introducing some concepts that will not be explained until later in this book, the preceding discussion should have made it clear that execution of certain instructions will modify the flags in the P register. Other flags or condition codes may be set as the result of external events. The particular flags that are affected by an instruction are listed in the Processor Status Codes column (second from the last column) in the instruction set summary in Table 2–2. Example 3–1 illustrates how execution of an LDA instruction affects the flags in the P register.

Example 3–1. The LDA Instruction and the P Register

How does the LDA instruction modify the flags in the P register? What will be the effect on the flags after an LDA instruction is executed if the operand is $8F? What if the operand is $00?

Solution: Referring to the instruction set summary in Table 2–2 we see that the LDA instruction affects only the N flag and the Z flag. If the operand is $8F, the N flag will be set and the Z flag will be cleared because $8F has a logic 1 in bit seven and it is clearly not zero. If the operand is $00, the N flag will be cleared and the Z flag will be set because $00 has a logic 0 in bit seven (and all other bits) and the Z flag is set on "result zero."

It should be clear that during the course of a program the flags are constantly changing. The branch instructions, discussed next, test the flags. It follows that the effect of an LDA instruction on the Z flag cannot be tested with a branch instruction unless the branch instruction *immediately* follows the LDA instruction. Exceptions to this rule occur if no intervening instructions affect the Z flag. Let us conclude this section with one additional example.

Example 3–2. The DEC Instruction and the P Register

How does the DEC instruction modify the flags in the P register?

Solution: The instruction set summary shows that the DEC instruction affects the N flag and the Z flag. If, as a result of executing the DEC instruction, a memory location contains $00, then the Z flag will be set and the N flag will be cleared. If the DEC instruction produces a logic 1 in bit seven (any number between $80 and $FF) then the N flag will be set and the Z flag cleared.

THE BRANCH INSTRUCTIONS

The *branch* instructions *test* the values of specific bits in the processor status register. If the value or condition tested is *met* then the program counter is altered, causing the program to jump to an instruction other than the one following the branch instruction. If the condition is *not met*, the program continues in sequence by executing the instruction immediately following the branch instruction.

The branch instructions are 2-byte instructions. The second byte of a branch instruction is interpreted by the microprocessor as an 8-bit *offset* to be *added* to the program counter *if* the branch condition is met. The offset is interpreted as a twos complement (signed) number, allowing both forward and backward branches. It is *very important* to realize that (because the program counter is incremented after each program byte is fetched) the value of the program counter that is added to the offset is the address of the first op code *following* the branch instruction. The entire sequence is diagrammed in a flowchart in Fig. 3–2. The notation "PC = PC + OFFSET" in Table 2–1 refers to the case where the branch condition is met.

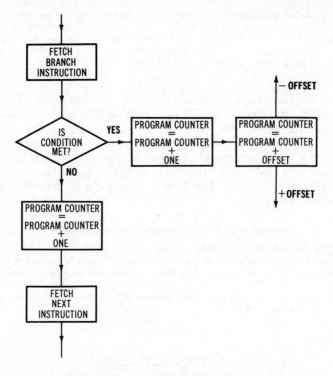

Fig. 3–2. Flowchart of a branch instruction.

It is time to introduce the branch instructions themselves and then illustrate them with some examples. The branch instructions are:

- *BCS* —Branch on Carry Set: The branch occurs if the carry flag in the P register is set (C = 1).
- *BCC* —Branch on Carry Clear: The branch occurs if the carry flag is clear (C = 0).
- *BEQ* —Branch on Result Equal to Zero: The branch occurs if the zero flag in the P register is set (Z = 1).
- *BNE* —Branch on Result Not Equal to Zero: The branch occurs if the zero flag is clear (Z = 0).
- *BMI* —Branch on Minus: The branch occurs if the negative flag in the P register is set (N = 1).

- *BPL*—Branch on Plus (or zero); The branch occurs if the negative flag is clear (N = 0).
- *BVS*—Branch on Overflow Set: The branch occurs if the overflow flag in the P register is set (V = 1).
- *BVC*—Branch on Overflow Clear: The branch occurs if the overflow flag is clear (V = 0).

Let us discuss the branch instruction sequence, illustrated in Fig. 3–2, in terms of a particular example, say the BPL instruction. In a program the BPL instruction might appear as follows:

```
$102A AD 00 C0 OFFSET   LDA   KYBD     ;READ THE APPLE KEYBOARD.
$102D 10 FB             BPL   OFFSET   ;BRANCH ON THE Z FLAG CLEAR.
$102F 8D 10 C0          STA   STROBE   ;WRITE TO LOCATION STROBE.
```

where it is part of some program. The BPL op code is $10, and in this case a value of $FB was chosen for the offset. What happens when the program reaches the LDA KYBD instruction is described as follows:

- If the number stored in the location symbolized by KYBD has a 1 in bit seven then execution of the LDA KYBD instruction will set the N flag. Then the branch condition *is not met*, and program execution will continue with the STA STROBE instruction following the BPL OFFSET instruction.
- If the number stored in location KYBD has a 0 in bit seven then execution of the LDA KYBD instruction will clear the N flag. Then the branch condition *is met*, and program execution will continue with the instruction whose op code is in location $102F + OFFSET, where OFFSET = $FB. As you will see below, this is location $102A, which is labeled OFFSET.

The offset is always *relative* to the location of the op code that follows the branch instruction. This use of the word relative explains why the addressing mode of the branch instructions is called *relative addressing*. As an aid in calculating *backward* branches when the offset is negative as it was above, a table is provided giving the conversion between hexadecimal offsets and signed base 10 numbers in Table 3–1. For example, if the offset is $FB, Table 3–1 shows that this is the same as −5, hence the program will branch backward 5 bytes, which is what our previous example did. In the example just described also note that the effect of the BPL OFFSET instruction is to put the program in a *loop*, where it will wait until the LDA KYBD instruction sets the N flag in the P register. Example 3–3 and Example 3–4 illustrate other cases.

Table 3-1. Hexadecimal Equivalents of Signed Decimal Integers

		Least Significant Hex Digit														
		0	1	2	3	4	5	6	7	8	9	A	B	C	D	E	F
0		0	1	2	3	4	5	6	7	8	9	10	11	12	13	14	15
1		16	17	18	19	20	21	22	23	24	25	26	27	28	29	30	31
2		32	33	34	35	36	37	38	39	40	41	42	43	44	45	46	47
3		48	49	50	51	52	53	54	55	56	57	58	59	60	61	62	63
4		64	65	66	67	68	69	70	71	72	73	74	75	76	77	78	79
5		80	81	82	83	84	85	86	87	88	89	90	91	92	93	94	95
6		96	97	98	99	100	101	102	103	104	105	106	107	108	109	110	111
7		112	113	114	115	116	117	118	119	120	121	122	123	124	125	126	127
8		-128	-127	-126	-125	-124	-123	-122	-121	-120	-119	-118	-117	-116	-115	-114	-113
9		-112	-111	-110	-109	-108	-107	-106	-105	-104	-103	-102	-101	-100	-99	-98	-97
A		-96	-95	-94	-93	-92	-91	-90	-89	-88	-87	-86	-85	-84	-83	-82	-81
B		-80	-79	-78	-77	-76	-75	-74	-73	-72	-71	-70	-69	-68	-67	-66	-65
C		-64	-63	-62	-61	-60	-59	-58	-57	-56	-55	-54	-53	-52	-51	-50	-49
D		-48	-47	-46	-45	-44	-43	-42	-41	-40	-39	-38	-37	-36	-35	-34	-33
E		-32	-31	-30	-29	-28	-27	-26	-25	-24	-23	-22	-21	-20	-19	-18	-17
F		-16	-15	-14	-13	-12	-11	-10	-9	-8	-7	-6	-5	-4	-3	-2	-1

(Leftmost column label, read vertically: Most Significant Hex Digit)

Example 3-3. Calculation of a Forward Branch

When a program reaches $AF25 it must go to $AF5B if the carry flag is set. What instruction should be in locations $AF25 and $AF26?

Solution: A branch on carry set, BCS, instruction is required. The offset is $AF5B − $AF27 = $34. Since the BCS op code is $B0, the instruction is $B0 $34.

A simple rule to find small offsets in the forward direction is to count bytes 0, 1, 2, . . ., beginning with the location of the instruction *following* the branch instruction and ending with the location of the op code to be executed. Then use Table 3-1 to convert this number to hexadecimal. For backward branches count backward: 0, −1, −2, . . ., starting with the op code following the branch instruction to the op code of the instruction to be executed if the branch condition is met. Then use Table 3-1 to convert this number to hexadecimal. If you have an assembler, it will calculate the offset for you.

Example 3-4. Calculation of a Backward Branch Offset

A BNE instruction is stored in locations $AF25 and $AF26. If Z = 0 the program must branch backward to an instruction whose op code is in $AF20. What offset should be used with the branch instruction?

Solution: Counting backward from the byte at $AF27, 0, −1, −2, . . ., to the byte at location $AF20, we get −7. According to Table 3-1, −7 = $F9 in twos complement notation. Thus the offset is $F9.

With practice you can also learn to count forward and backward in hexadecimal as well as add and subtract in hexadecimal, so that calculating offsets by hand is not difficult. The Apple II monitor will add and subtract hexadecimal numbers, making it easy to calculate offsets. If you use an assembler, it will calculate offsets for you.

USING SUBROUTINES

In order to make the programming examples in this chapter more meaningful, a few additional instructions will be introduced. The first of these are the jump-to-subroutine (JSR) instruction and the return-from-subroutine (RTS) instruction. Subroutines will be discussed in more detail in Chapter 7, but since the Apple monitor has several useful subroutines that will make our work easier, we will see how they can be called.

The jump-to-subroutine, *JSR*, instruction is a 3-byte instruction. The first byte, $20, is the op code. The second and third bytes are the ADL and the ADH of the first instruction in the subroutine. As such, they represent the *destination* of the subroutine jump. Example 3–5 illustrates this.

Example 3–5. A Subroutine Call

A subroutine, COUT, is located at $FDED in the Apple monitor. Describe the program line that would call this subroutine.

Solution: The appropriate line is shown below:

```
20 ED FD    JSR    COUT          ;JUMP TO SUBROUTINE COUT AT $FDED.
```

The subroutine itself must end with a return-from-subroutine, *RTS*, instruction. When this instruction is executed, the microprocessor returns to the main program, the program that called the subroutine. Execution of the main program continues with the instruction following the JSR instruction. All of the monitor subroutines end with an RTS instruction.

If you have programmed in BASIC then you are probably familiar with the reasons for using subroutines. Frequently a section of program is used several times during a program. If this section of program code is placed in a subroutine, then it need not be duplicated each time it is needed in the main program. Subroutines also allow a program to be built in terms of modules, namely the subroutines. This is an extremely useful approach to program design. Again, the purpose in introducing the JSR instruction at this point in the book is to allow us to use some of the subroutines that already exist in the monitor. Subroutine COUT at $FDED allows us to output a character to the screen, so we will be able to see the results of some of the programs we write. Subroutine RDCHAR and $FD35 allow us to input a character from the keyboard. For a complete list of useful monitor subroutines see your *Apple II Reference Manual*. The next section will illustrate the use we have for subroutine COUT.

READING THE APPLE KEYBOARD

When a key on the Apple keyboard is pressed, bits zero through six contain the character code (ASCII) corresponding to the key that was pressed. The significance of bit seven of the keyboard input port at location $C000 is different. When a key is pressed, the keyboard circuitry produces a 10-microsecond positive strobe pulse. This pulse is connected to the clock input of a flip-flop. When the strobe pulse occurs, the output of the flip-flop goes to logic 1. (At this point you may well be wondering what a flip-flop is. That bit of intrigue is left for you to unravel. Suffice it to say that it can be flipped to logic 1 by one pulse, and flopped back to logic 0 by another.) The output of the flip-flop is connected to bit seven of the keyboard input port at location $C000.

To summarize, bits zero through six of location $C000 contain the character code corresponding to the last key that was pressed. Bit seven of location $C000 goes to logic 1 when a key is pressed. Refer to Fig. 3–3 for an illustration of the timing of the events that accompany a keystroke. Bit seven of location $C000 is called the keyboard *flag*.

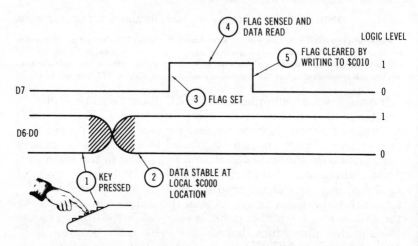

Fig. 3–3. Timing diagram for the events accompanying a keystroke.

After a key is pressed, bit seven of location $C000 stays at logic 1 until the flip-flop is switched to its logic 0 state. In fact, before it can be used as a signal or flag that a key has been pressed again, there must be a way to flip it back to logic 0 after the character has been read. There is. The keyboard flag, bit seven of location $C000, is switched to logic 0 by reading or writing to location $C010. This operation generates a strobe pulse that resets the flip-flop, and bit seven of the keyboard input port returns to logic 0. Refer again to Fig. 3–3.

A short program segment that reads the Apple keyboard and outputs the result to the video monitor is given in Example 3–6. Pay particular attention to the branch instruction and the subroutine call. The first instruction in Example 3–6 reads the keyboard input port. If no key has been pressed, bit seven will be logic 0, and the N flag in the P register will be clear following the LDA KYBD instruction. The BPL WAIT instruction tests the condition of the N flag, and if it is clear then the branch will be taken. The program stays in the WAIT loop until a key is pressed.

Example 3–6. A Routine to Read the Apple Keyboard

Object: Read the keyboard. When a key is pressed output the character to the video monitor.

```
102A:AD 00 C0   7 WAIT   LDA   KYBD     ;READ THE KEYBOARD INPUT PORT.
102D:10 FB      8        BPL   WAIT     ;WAIT IN THIS LOOP FOR A
                                         KEYSTROKE.
102F:8D 10 C0   9        STA   STROBE   ;CLEAR THE FLAG FLIP-FLOP.
1032:20 ED FD   10       JSR   COUT     ;OUTPUT THE CHARACTER.
1035:00         11       BRK
```

When a key is pressed, the N flag will be set, the branch condition is not met, so the program in Example 3–6 continues with the instruction at $102F. Note that at this time the code for the character is in the accumulator, as a result of the LDA KYBD instruction. The instruction at $102F writes to location $C010, which has the effect of resetting the flip-flop, clearing bit seven of the keyboard input port in preparation for reading the next key when it is pressed. The entire process is diagrammed in the flowchart in Fig. 3–4.

The instruction at $1032 is a subroutine call. The program jumps to the subroutine COUT with the ASCII for the key that was pressed in the accumulator. COUT is a monitor subroutine that outputs the character code to the video monitor so that you can see the effect of pressing a key. COUT also advances the cursor, performs an automatic return when the end of a line is reached, and performs scrolling when the bottom of the screen is reached. You will experiment with this program in the exercises at the end of this chapter.

THE INCREMENT AND DECREMENT INSTRUCTIONS

The programs that will be used to illustrate the branch instructions become more meaningful if we can use some additional instructions, namely the increment and decrement instructions. So let us discuss them now.

The logical expression for the INC instruction is $M + 1 \rightarrow M$. Simply stated, the INC instruction *increments* the number in a memory location by one. If the number is $FF and it is in-

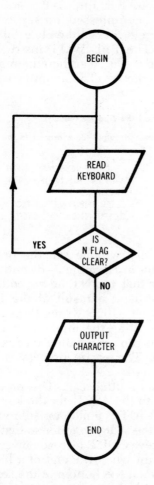

Fig. 3-4. Flowchart of the program in Example 3-6.

cremented, then the new number is $00. All other cases should be obvious. The DEC instruction, whose logical description is M − 1→M, *decrements* the number in a memory location by one each time it is executed. The only unusual case occurs when the number in M is $00 and it is decremented. In that case the new number is $FF. All other cases should be obvious.

Both instructions have the zero-page and absolute addressing modes available, but you might ask yourself why these instructions do not have an immediate addressing mode. The INC and DEC instructions fall into a group of instructions known as *read-modify-write* instructions. In order to increment the number in a certain location, for example, the microprocessor must first *read* the number in that location, then *modify* that number by adding one to it, and finally *write* the new number back to the memory location. Recall that in the immediate addressing mode the operand is in the program. Thus the number to be modified is in the program. If the program is in ROM, it is clearly impossible to modify it by writing a new number back to ROM. In any case it is good programming practice not to write a program that modifies itself since the program will never work in ROM, and the designers of the 6502 have eliminated that option from the INC and DEC instructions.

Having mastered the INC and DEC instructions you will have no difficulty with the INX, DEX, INY, and DEY instructions. The latter instructions operate only on the number in the register that is implied by their mnemonic. That is, the INX instruction increments the number in the X register by one. Thus its logical expression is $X + 1 \rightarrow X$. Since the location of the operand is understood from the instruction itself, these four instructions use only *implied* addressing. The DEX instruction decrements the number in the X register by one. The effect of the INY and the DEY instructions should now be apparent.

TIMING LOOPS

Timing loops are used in many applications. If the Apple speaker is switched on and off (toggled) at intervals, it will produce a tone. The time interval between consecutive "switches" is determined by a delay loop. Refer to our discussion of serial i/o in Chapter 1. To convert the incoming serial bit stream into data bytes, the bit stream is sampled at discrete intervals separated by one bit time. See Fig. 1–8. If the data is arriving at 110 bits/second, then one bit time is approximately 9.09 milliseconds, and a timing loop to produce this delay must be included in the software that is used to receive serial input. As noted earlier, terminals, modems, and printers frequently use serial i/o. Games, data acquisition, and real-time control systems all make use of timing loops. Delay loops also give us a chance to illustrate branch instructions.

The first delay routine is shown in Example 3–7. The X register is loaded with a number stored in $0000, labeled *M*. The number in the X register is decremented with the DEX instruction until it reaches zero. The program is kept in the delay loop with the BNE LOOP instruction. It is important to be able to calculate the delay time produced by a timing loop. We will do this for the set of three instructions, LDX M, DEX, and BNE

LOOP, that make up the loop. Our cycle account proceeds as follows (refer to Table 2–2):

Example 3–7. Simple Delay Loop

Object: Write a program that waits in a loop.

```
1038:A6 00    6         LDX   M        ;LOAD X WITH M.
103A:CA       7 LOOP    DEX            ;DECREMENT X.
103B:D0 FD    8         BNE   LOOP     ;LOOP UNTIL X IS ZERO.
103D:00       9         BRK
```

- LDX instruction = 3 clock cycles.
- DEX instruction = 2 clock cycles, *M* times.
- BNE instruction = 3 clock cycles if the branch is taken, (*M* − 1) times.
- BNE instruction = 2 clock cycles if the branch is not taken.

We have let *M* symbolize the number loaded into the X register, and we are assuming that the branch instructions do not produce a branch across a page boundary.

With these assumptions we can calculate the delay time, *T*. Call T_C the time for 1 clock cycle. Then

$$T = (5M + 2)T_C \qquad (3-1)$$

A flowchart for the simple delay loop in Example 3–7 is shown in Fig. 3–5. Study it, noting in particular the use of the branch instruction, BNE LOOP.

If the loop in Example 3–7 will not provide a sufficiently long delay, then another loop may be nested within the first loop. The program in Example 3–8 and the flowchart in Fig. 3–6 illustrate one solution.

The cycle count for the delay program in Example 3–8 proceeds as follows (assume *M* is the number loaded into X and *N* is loaded into Y):

Example 3–8. Nested Delay Loop Program

Object: Produce a time delay by nesting a delay loop within another loop.

```
103E:A6 00    6          LDX    M       ;LOAD X WITH THE NUMBER IN M.
1040:A4 01    7 LOOPX    LDY    N       ;LOAD Y WITH THE NUMBER IN N.
1042:88       8 LOOPY    DEY            ;DECREMENT THE NUMBER IN Y.
1043:D0 FD    9          BNE    LOOPY   ;IF Y IS NOT ZERO, LOOP BACK TO
                                         LOOPY.
1045:CA       10         DEX            ;DECREMENT THE NUMBER IN X.
1046:D0 F8    11         BNE    LOOPX   ;IF X IS NOT ZERO, LOOP BACK TO
                                         LOOPX.
1048:00       12         BRK
```

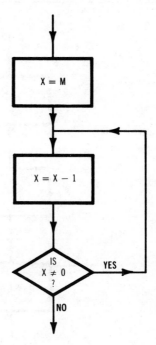

Fig. 3–5. Simple delay loop where M is a number chosen by the programmer to determine the time interval of the delay.

- LDX = 3 cycles.
- LDY = 3 cycles.
- DEY = 2 cycles, N times.
- BNE LOOPY = 3 cycles, $N - 1$ times. $\left.\rule{0pt}{1.5em}\right\}$ M times
- BNE LOOPY = 2 cycles.
- DEX = 2 cycles.
- BNE LOOPX = 3 cycles, $M - 1$ times.
- BNE LOOPX = 2 cycles.

This gives a rather long expression for the number of cycles required for the loop. It is: $3 + 3M + + 2MN + 3M(N - 1) + 2M + 2M + 3(M - 1) + 2$, which simplifies to $M(5N + 7) + 2$. Let T represent the loop time and T_C the time of a clock cycle. Then

$$T = [M(5N + 7) + 2]T_C \qquad (3\text{--}2)$$

is the loop delay time. For the Apple II, $T_C = 0.97779 \times 10^{-6}$ second. If $M = 1$ then an N of 203 gives a delay of 1.0013 milliseconds. In this case M controls the number of 1-millisecond (approximately) intervals.

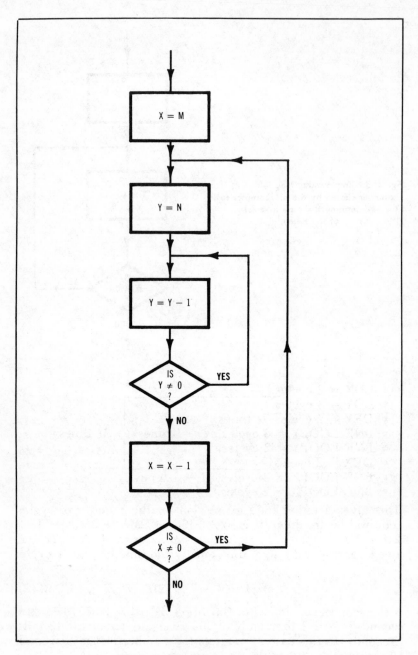

Fig. 3–6. Nested delay loop flowchart.

A MATTER OF NOTATION

Perhaps this would be an appropriate place to clear up a matter of notation that you will encounter in microcomputer literature. Refer to the two previous examples and you will discover that the symbols M and N had two different meanings. In the programs, M and N were *symbols* for locations of numbers, while in the calculations we used M and N as if they were the *numbers* in these locations. In the flowcharts we used the notation "X = X − 1" which really implied "the contents of the X register is replaced with the contents decremented by one".

The confusion is between a symbol representing a *location* or a register and a symbol representing the *number* in that location. In much of the computer literature the bracket notation, [ ], is used to eliminate this double use of a symbol. For example, [X] means *the contents of the* X register, and [KYBD] means *the contents of* the location symbolized by KYBD: To indicate that the contents of the X register are decremented by one, we should write, [X] = [X] − 1. The brackets are read "the contents of . . ."

In the literature associated with the 6502 the bracket notation is conspicuous by its absence, and it will not be used frequently in this book either. There are, however, situations related to indirect addressing where the bracket notation is absolutely necessary to convey the correct meaning, and in those cases we will use it.

TIMING LOOPS AND GAME PADDLES: AN APPLICATION

The Apple uses a timing circuit that may be used in conjunction with a simple delay loop to convert the resistance between two pins in an *external* circuit into an 8-bit number. The two pins are located on the *game i/o connector*, a diagram of which is shown in Fig. 3–7. The pins of interest in this section are the GC0 game controller input and the +5-V pin. Pins GC1–GC3 operate in the same way as the GC0 pin. A photograph of the interior of the Apple, showing a DIP jumper connected to the game i/o connector, is given in Fig. 3–8. The author used a DIP jumper that was 2 feet (100 cm) long to access the game i/o connector for all of the experiments and applications that involve this port. DIP jumpers may be obtained from Priority One Electronics, mentioned earlier, or from JAMECO Electronics, 1355 Shoreway Road, Belmont, CA 94002, (415) 592–8097. The other end of the DIP jumper was connected to an AP Products Super Strip (See Fig. 3–11 for a photograph). The Super Strip is used to mount the components to be interfaced to the game i/o con-

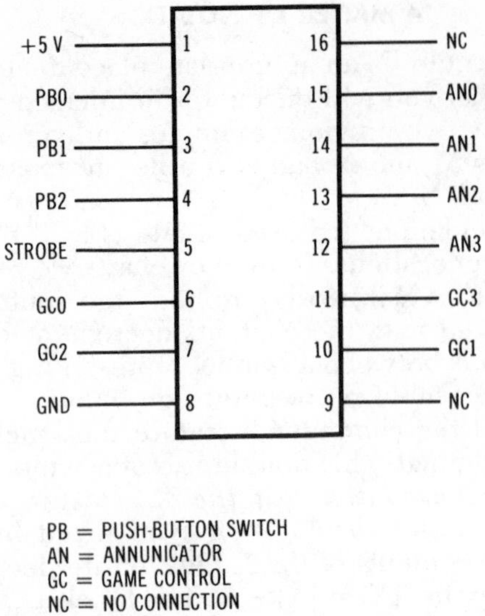

```
    +5 V ———————  1        16  ——————— NC

     PB0 ———————  2        15  ——————— AN0

     PB1 ———————  3        14  ——————— AN1

     PB2 ———————  4        13  ——————— AN2

  STROBE ———————  5        12  ——————— AN3

     GC0 ———————  6        11  ——————— GC3

     GC2 ———————  7        10  ——————— GC1

     GND ———————  8         9  ——————— NC
```

```
PB = PUSH-BUTTON SWITCH
AN = ANNUNICATOR
GC = GAME CONTROL
NC = NO CONNECTION
```

Fig. 3–7. Pin diagram of the game i/o connector.

Fig. 3–8. Photograph of the DIP jumper connection inside the Apple.

nector. Super Strips, or equivalent Global Specialties Proto Boards, are available from Priority One Electronics and JAMECO Electronics. The AP Products Breadboard Jumper Wire Kit is also very useful for breadboarding the circuits that will be described in this book. Needlenose pliers and diagonal cutters will also be useful tools to acquire.

When location $C070 is referenced with either a read or a write operation (LDA $C070 or STA $C070 instructions), the logic levels on bit seven of four locations are set to logic 1 by a 558 quad timer integrated circuit inside the Apple. At this instant four capacitors connected to the 558 begin charging through resistors connected from the +5-V pin on the game i/o connector to the GC0–GC3 pins. Normally these resistors are located in game paddles, but any resistance from 0 ohms to about 150,000 ohms will do. The rate at which the capacitors charge is determined by the resistance. When the voltage on the capacitor reaches two-thirds of +5 V, the logic level on the corresponding bit will flip from logic 1 to logic 0.

The location that must be watched to see how long it takes for the GC0 capacitor to cause its corresponding bit seven to flip to logic 0 is $C064. Locations $C065–$C067 correspond to pins GC1–GC3, respectively. In other words, bit seven of location $C064 is watched to monitor the time it takes the resistor-capacitor combination connected to GC0 to charge to a large enough voltage to flip bit seven.

With a 150,000-ohm resistor connected between +5 V and GC0, it will take about 3 milliseconds from the instant the timer is started until the logic level on bit seven of location $C064 changes to logic 0. Smaller values of the resistance result in shorter times. A sketch of a circuit that uses a 150-kilohm potentiometer is shown in Fig. 3–9. A variable resistor or a potentiometer may be obtained from the electronic parts supply firms mentioned previously.

A program to measure the time interval during which bit seven of location $C064 is at logic 1 is given in Example 3–9. The X register is used to count the number of times the program goes through the timing loop consisting of lines 10–13 of Example 3–9. The loop counter is set to zero in line 8. The LDA CLEAR instruction in line 9 starts the timing cycle by resetting the 558 timer which, in turn, sets bit seven of location $C064 (PAD0) to logic 1. If the LDA PAD0 instruction produces a zero in bit seven corresponding to the completion of the timing interval, then the N flag will be cleared. The BPL OUT instruction tests the N flag, and if it is clear, then the program branches *out* of the timing loop. If the timing interval is not complete, then the N flag will be set by the LDA PAD0 instruction, and the program will *stay* in the timing loop. Each time through the loop the number in the X register is incremented by one.

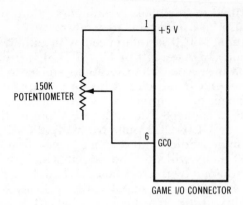

Fig. 3–9. Circuit diagram of the game paddle input.

Example 3–9. Game Paddle Timing Routine

Object: Write a program that measures the time interval during which the game paddle input is at logic 1.

1049:A2 00	8 AGAIN	LDX	#00	;INITIALIZE COUNTER TO ZERO.
104B:AD 70 C0	9	LDA	CLEAR	;START THE TIMER INTEGRATED CIRCUIT.
104E:AD 64 C0	10 WAIT	LDA	PAD0	;READ THE PADDLE PORT.
1051:10 03	11	BPL	OUT	;GET OUT WHEN BIT SEVEN IS ZERO.
1053:E8	12 STAY	INX		;OTHERWISE, INCREMENT THE COUNTER.
1054:D0 F8	13	BNE	WAIT	;TEST THE PADDLE AGAIN.
1056:8A	14 OUT	TXA		;TRANSFER THE COUNTER TO A.
1057:20 DA FD	15	JSR	PRBYTE	;OUTPUT THE NUMBER IN A.
105A:20 8E FD	16	JSR	CROUT	;OUTPUT A CARRIAGE RETURN.
105D:4C 49 10	17	JMP	AGAIN	;REPEAT THE ENTIRE PROCESS.

At the end of the timing interval, after the program branches out of the timing loop, the number in X is transferred to A so the monitor routine PRBYTE can output the result to the video monitor. The subroutine CROUT dresses up the output so it does not fill the screen, but instead it appears on the left side of the screen. The JMP AGAIN instruction was added to put the program just described in an infinite loop so that it will be easier to study the consequences of varying the resistance in the exercises that follow.

An analysis of the timing, similar to the analysis that was carried out for Examples 3–7 and 3–8, shows that the time during which bit seven is at logic 1 is given by the expression

$$T_C(11X - 7) \leq T \leq (11X + 4)T_C \qquad (3-3)$$

where T_C is the time of 1 clock cycle. The uncertainty of the result is a consequence of the fact that it is never clear just where in the timing loop that bit seven switches back to logic 0. That is, the logic level on bit seven is not read *continuously*, but at 11 clock-cycle intervals. The best estimate for the time T is then

$$T = [(11X - 1.5) \pm 5.5]T_C \qquad (3-4)$$

where X is the number in the X register after the BPL OUT instruction is executed, and T_C is the microcomputer's clock period. With the program in Example 3-9, the maximum time interval that can be measured corresponds to X = $FF = 225, in which case T = 2.7 milliseconds. The author found that X = $FF occurred with a resistance of 113 kilohms connected between +5 V and GC0. This agrees very well with the time interval given by Berlin's[1] equation

$$T = 1.1RC \text{ (seconds)} \qquad (3-5)$$

Equation 3-5 gives T = 2.73 milliseconds for an R of 112.9 kilohms and a C of 0.22 microfarad. This suggests that the game paddles might be useful for measuring resistances. These inputs could also be used to measure temperature if thermistors were used instead of resistances.

TIMING LOOPS AND THE SPEAKER OUTPUT

Reading or writing to location $C030 toggles the speaker. If the speaker is toggled at an audio frequency rate, then a tone will be heard. The data read from or written to this location has no consequence. Simply referencing location $C030 with an LDA or STA instruction will switch the speaker output to its opposite logic level, because it is the address decoding circuitry that is responsible for the action of the speaker.

To toggle the speaker at regular intervals, the timing program listed in Example 3-8 is used as a subroutine. The program in Example 3-10 calls the delay subroutine and toggles the speaker. Example 3-10 illustrates an application of timing loops, a subroutine call, and a return from a subroutine. If $CB (203) is in location $0001, then the number in location $0000 controls the number of 1-millisecond intervals. If a logic 1 is put in location $0000 and the program in Example 3-10 is executed, a tone of approximately 500 Hz is used. The frequency of

---

[1]Berlin, Howard M., *The 555 Timer Applications Sourcebook, With Experiments*, Indianapolis: Howard W. Sams & Co., Inc., 1976, p. 17.

the tone is given by the formula $f = 1/T$, where T is the delay loop time.

Example 3–10. A Program to Produce a Tone With the Speaker

Object: Use a delay loop as a subroutine in a program to toggle the speaker at regular intervals.

```
1060:8D 30 C0    7 START     STA   SPKER    ;TOGGLE THE SPEAKER.
1063:20 69 10    8           JSR   TIMER    ;USE THE SUBROUTINE TO DELAY.
1066:4C 60 10    9           JMP   START    ;LOOP BACK TO START.

1069:           11 ;SUBROUTINE TIMER
1069:A6 00      12 TIMER     LDX   M        ;LOAD X WITH THE NUMBER IN M.
106B:A4 01      13 LOOPX     LDY   N        ;LOAD Y WITH THE NUMBER IN N.
106D:88         14 LOOPY     DEY            ;DECREMENT THE NUMBER IN Y.
106E:D0 FD      15           BNE   LOOPY    ;IF Y IS NOT ZERO, LOOP BACK TO
                                             LOOPY.
1070:CA         16           DEX            ;DECREMENT THE NUMBER IN X.
1071:D0 F8      17           BNE   LOOPX    ;IF X IS NOT ZERO, LOOP BACK TO
                                             LOOPX.
1073:60         18           RTS
```

READING THE PUSH-BUTTON SWITCHES

The Apple has three 1-bit input ports located at $C061–$C063. The switches are accessed at the game i/o connector, and they control the logic levels of bit seven at each of the locations just mentioned. If the pins PB0–PB2 are connected to ground, then bit seven in locations $C061–$C063, respectively, will be at logic 0. If, for example, PB2 is connected to +5 V, then bit seven of location $C063 will be at logic 1. Because of the nature of the TTL integrated circuits, the inputs behave as if they are at logic 1 when they are left unconnected, and they will be at logic 0 only if they are connected to ground.

A circuit diagram for a 1-bit input port that is controlled by a switch is given in Fig. 3–10. A photograph of the breadboarding arrangement that was used to construct this circuit is shown in Fig. 3–11. Note the DIP jumper that is used to make the connection to the game i/o connector inside the Apple. Only one of the eight switches on the DIP switch was used. The purpose of the other integrated circuit and the LED will be unveiled presently.

The 1-bit inputs may be tested with the BMI and BPL instructions because reading these input ports will modify the N flag. Recall that N is set if a port with a logic 1 in bit seven is read. Example 3–11 illustrates a simple loop that causes the program to wait until the PB0 switch connects the input pin to ground. Very likely you have a game program that runs on your

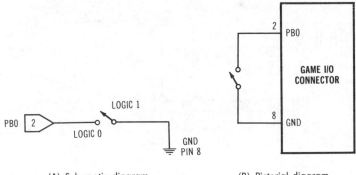

(A) Schematic diagram. (B) Pictorial diagram.

Fig. 3–10. One-bit input port.

Example 3–11. Reading a 1-Bit Input Port

Object: Wait in a loop until push-button switch PB0 is at logic 0.

```
1069:AE 61 C0   5 TEST    LDX  PB0     ;READ THE SWITCH, BIT 7.
106C:30 FB      6         BMI  TEST    ;LOOP UNTIL IT'S LOGIC ZERO,
106E:00         7         BRK          ;THEN DO SOMETHING.
```

Apple, and the switches are used to fire projectiles at enemy tanks or invading star cruisers. What happens in machine language is that the 1-bit input port is tested to see if the switch is closed. If it is, the program branches to a routine that fires a missile or some equally significant event happens when you close the switch.

Why not try to write a program to measure the number of 1-millisecond intervals between the closing of switch PB0 at the beginning and the closing of switch PB1 at the end? The techniques described in this chapter should make this a simple problem, unless you demand much more than stopwatch accuracy.

Next we demand that the input switch control something. That is, when the switch is on it will cause the computer to turn on a device, and when the switch is off, the computer will turn off a device. (The most obvious solution to this problem is to connect the switch to the device and eliminate $1500 worth of computer.) Our purpose here is to illustrate the most simple interfacing techniques and the use of branch instructions to test bits on input ports, so we choose a very elementary device to control, namely a light-emitting diode (LED). The interfacing circuit is shown in Fig. 3–12, and its photograph was given in Fig. 3–11. A program to allow the switch setting to control the LED is given in Example 3–12.

Fig. 3–11. Photograph of the circuit in Fig. 3–12 mounted on a Super Strip.

The logic levels of the annunciator outputs are determined by referencing certain memory locations. For example, to turn annunciator zero (AN0) off, the program must read or write to location $C058. To turn it on, the program must read or write to location $C059.

Annunciators numbered 1 through 3 use locations $C05A through $C05F, in pairs. The first address in a pair turns the annunicator off (0 volts) while the second address in a pair turns the annunciator on (5 volts).

Study the program in Example 3–12. First the switch is read. If it is at logic 0, the BMI instruction will not cause a branch and the STA AN1OFF instruction will turn off the annunciator. Since the LDY PB1 instruction cleared the N flag and the STA AN1OFF instruction *does not* affect any flags, the N flag is still cleared when the BPL AROUND instruction is executed. This branch will be taken, skipping around the instruction that turns on the annunciator. You are left with the problem of analyzing

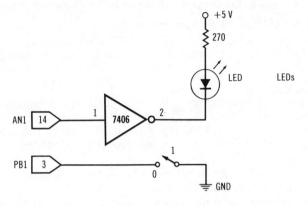

(A) Schematic diagram.

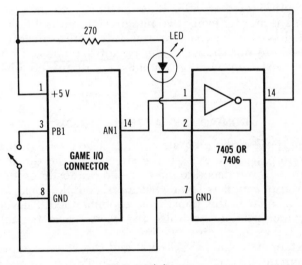

(B) Pictorial diagram.

Fig. 3-12. Annunciator output and push-button input circuit.

what happens if the switch is at logic 1. The entire program has been placed in a loop with the JMP START instruction simply to allow you to experiment with the switch settings without having to restart the program each time.

If you want to control a relay, which in turn can control a more powerful device than an LED, refer to Fig. 10-1 where an annunciator output is used to control a relay that keys a transmitter.

Example 3–12. Controlling an Output Device With a 1-Bit Input

Object: Use PB1 to control the logic level of AN1.

```
106F:AC 62 C0   7 START    LDY   PB1       ;READ THE SWITCH.
1072:30 05      8          BMI   PAST      ;GO TURN ANNUNCIATOR ON.
1074:8D 5A C0   9          STA   AN1OFF    ;TURN ANNUNCIATOR OFF.
1077:10 03     10          BPL   AROUND    ;SKIP TO AROUND.
1079:8D 5B C0  11 PAST     STA   AN1ON
107C:4C 6F 10  12 AROUND   JMP   START     ;LOOP TO RUN PROGRAM AGAIN.
```

An *extremely important practice* in interfacing integrated circuits to a microcomputer is to provide sufficient capacitor bypassing from the supply voltage source *at the integrated circuit* to the *nearest* ground line. A capacitor of approximately 0.1 microfarad is connected between the V_{CC} (+5 V) pin and the nearest ground, in most cases. Thus, in Fig. 3–12B, it is assumed that you will add a 0.1-microfarad capacitor between pin 14 and pin 7 of the 7405. It is customary to have one such bypass capacitor for every two integrated circuits, but it will not hurt to have one capacitor per integrated circuit. These capacitors are not shown in the circuit diagrams, it being understood that they will be included in all the circuits in the book.

CONTROLLING A STEPPER MOTOR*

The purpose of the program and interface circuit described in this section is to allow both the speed and the direction of a stepper motor interfaced to the game i/o connector on the Apple II. This application is somewhat more complex than anything described so far in this book. It is recommended that you study the previous sections and also the exercises in the following section, before beginning this project.

The stepper motor (K82701-P2) and the stepper motor integrated circuit driver (SAA1027) were obtained from AIRPAX, North American Philips Controls, Cheshire, CO 06410, (203) 272–0301. They also publish the *Stepper Motor Handbook*, which will be of considerable use if you wish to incorporate stepper motors in an application.

The interface circuit is shown in Fig. 3–13 where all inputs and outputs on the left of the figure are connections to the game i/o connector on the Apple II. The switch input is the same as that shown in Fig. 3–10. The variable resistor control is identi-

---

*This project is recommended for more advanced experimenters, with some electronics experience.

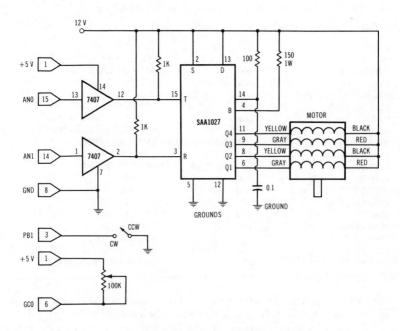

Fig. 3–13. Stepper motor control interface circuit.

cal with that described in the section on timing loops and game paddles. Again, the author used a 24-inch (100-cm), 16-pin DIP JUMPER to a breadboard to construct the circuit. Do *not* attempt to use the 12-V supply on the Apple II to drive the stepper motor and the SAA1027. A separate 12-V power supply, capable of supplying about 1.5 amperes, is required and the minus or ground side must be connected to the ground connection on the game i/o connector. The switch input acts as the clockwise-counterclockwise control, while the variable resistor (potentiometer) controls the rotation rate of the stepper motor.

The program to control the stepper motor circuit is given in Example 3–13. The fact that the program is constructed from the modules or structures found in Examples 3–8, 3–9, and 3–12 suggests a *structured* approach. Compare Example 3–13 with Examples 3–8, 3–9, and 3–12, and you will see that these programs were combined to make the final program with almost no change.

The first five instructions in Example 3–13 (lines 12–16) come from Example 3–12 and their function is to determine whether clockwise or counterclockwise rotation is desired. If

Example 3-13. Stepper Motor Control Program

Object: Write a program to control the direction and speed of a stepper motor.

```
107F:AC 62 C0   12 START    LDY  PB1       ;READ THE SWITCH.
1082:30 05      13          BMI  PAST      ;GO TURN ANNUNCIATOR ON.
1084:8D 5A C0   14          STA  AN1OFF    ;TURN ANNUNCIATOR OFF.
1087:10 03      15          BPL  AROUND    ;SKIP TO AROUND.
1089:8D 5B C0   16 PAST     STA  AN1ON     ;TURN ANNUNCIATOR ON.
108C:AD 58 C0   17 AROUND   LDA  AN0OFF    ;TURN ANNUNCIATOR 0 OFF,
108F:AD 59 C0   18          LDA  AN0ON     ;THEN ON TO STEP MOTOR.
1092:A2 04      19          LDX  #04       ;SET COUNTER TO MINIMUM.
1094:AD 70 C0   20          LDA  CLEAR     ;START THE TIMER.
1097:AD 64 C0   21 WAIT     LDA  PAD0      ;READ THE PADDLE PORT.
109A:10 03      22          BPL  LOOPX     ;GET OUT OF TIMING LOOP.
109C:E8         23 STAY     INX            ;OTHERWISE, STAY IN.
109D:D0 F8      24          BNE  WAIT      ;TEST PADDLE AGAIN.
109F:A0 CB      25 LOOPX    LDY  #$CB      ;SET Y FOR 1 MS LOOP.
10A1:88         26 LOOPY    DEY            ;DECREMENT Y.
10A2:D0 FD      27          BNE  LOOPY     ;LOOP UNTIL Y IS 0.
10A4:CA         28          DEX            ;DECREMENT X.
10A5:D0 F8      29          BNE  LOOPX     ;LOOP UNTIL X IS 0.
10A7:F0 D6      30          BEQ  START     ;REPEAT THE PROGRAM.
```

the PB1 switch is at logic 1, the motor will turn counterclockwise, otherwise it will turn clockwise.

The next two instructions (lines 17–18) toggle the AN0 output off, then on. This in turn causes the stepper motor to rotate one step in the direction selected above.

The next six instructions (lines 19–24) are identical with the instructions in Example 3–9, and they measure the length of time the game paddle output is at logic 1. One difference between this program and Example 3–9 is that the X counter is started at $04 rather than $00. The number in the X register will be used to control the speed of the stepper motor, and an X of $04 prevents it from being driven too fast, causing it to stop.

The value of X found from the game paddle input is used to control the delay between steps. Lines 25–29 in the program are almost identical with the instructions in Example 3–8, the nested delay loop program. In this case, however, the value of X is obtained from the game paddle input, and the value of Y is fixed at $CB. Consequently, X controls the number of 1-millisecond intervals between steps of the stepper motor.

Finally, line 30 causes the program to branch back to the very beginning, and the entire sequence starts over.

Breadboard the circuit, load the program in Example 3–13, and then run it. Turn on the 12-V supply and the stepper should start to turn. Flip the ccw/cw switch and it should change direction. Adjust the potentiometer and it will change speed.

Can you think of applications for stepper motor controllers? Would they work in typewriters or line printers? Why not try a kinetic art project? Can stepper motors be used to construct artificial limbs for handicapped people?

EXERCISES

Exercise 3-1

a. Load the program in Example 3-6. A listing is included here for your convenience. Note that a CLC instruction and a BCC WAIT instruction have been added at the end of the program to put it in an infinite loop. You must supply the op codes and the offset by referring to the instruction set summary in Table 2-2.

102A:AD 00 C0	7 WAIT	LDA	KYBD	;READ THE KEYBOARD INPUT PORT.
102D:10 FB	8	BPL	WAIT	;WAIT IN THIS LOOP FOR A KEYSTROKE.
102F:8D 10 CO	9	STA	STROBE	;CLEAR THE FLAG FLIP-FLOP.
1032:20 ED FD	10	JSR	COUT	;OUTPUT THE CHARACTER.
1035: ⎯⎯⎯	11	CLC		
⎯⎯⎯⎯⎯⎯	12	BCC	WAIT	

b. Run this program. Press various keys on the keyboard and observe the result on the screen. What effect does the shift key have? The space bar? The BELL key?

c. Stop the program and modify the BPL WAIT instruction to be a BMI WAIT instruction. Replace the $10 op code with a $30 op code. Attempt to predict what will happen when you run the program.

d. Run the program with the modified op code. What happens when you press a key? Explain your results.

e. One of the more difficult program bugs to find is an incorrect offset in a branch instruction. Modify the offset in this program to be $BF instead of $FB (digit transposition error). Run the program and describe what you observe?

(The author observed that the program crashed. That is, what was supposed to happen did not, and the only way to recover control of the computer was to perform a RESET.)

Exercise 3-2

This exercise will give you some additional familiarity with calculating offsets. Feel free to use the Apple monitor to perform the subtractions.

a. When a program is at $CFD3 it must go to $D012 if the overflow flag is set. Which instruction should be in locations $CFD3 and $CFD4? Choose the correct branch instruction and calculate the offset.

(The overflow flag is tested with the BVS instruction. The op code is $70. To calculate the offset use the Apple monitor to type **D012-CFD5 RETURN**. Your answer will appear on the screen because the monitor will do hexadecimal addition and subtraction.)

b. How many clock cycles will be required to execute the BVS OFFSET instruction in this case?

(The number of clock cycles required for any instruction is given in the instruction set summary in Table 2–2. Since the branch *is* taken and a page boundary *is* crossed with the branch, the instruction set summary indicates that the instruction requires 4 clock cycles.)

c. When a program is at $167A it must branch to $162F if the Z flag is clear. What instruction must be used? Where will it be located? How many clock cycles are required if the branch is taken? Not taken?

d. What is the longest backward branch (number of bytes) that a program can make? What is the longest forward branch? See Table 3–1 for the largest and smallest decimal numbers represented.

e. A branch instruction, $F0 $80, is located at addresses $FD61 and $FD62. Where will the program branch if the Z flag is clear? If it is set?

Exercise 3–3

a. Load the program in Example 3–7. See the listing below. Run the program. What do you observe?

```
1038:A6 00      6         LDX   M       ;LOAD X WITH M.
103A:CA         7 LOOP    DEX           ;DECREMENT X.
103B:D0 FD      8         BNE   LOOP    ;LOOP UNTIL X IS ZERO.
103D:00         9         BRK
```

(Although this is a delay loop, the delay time is too short for human beings to detect. You will only see the effect of the BRK instruction which returns control to the monitor.)

b. Use the single-step circuit and program in Appendix B or the Apple monitor to put the computer in the single-step mode. Load location $0000 with $05. Single step through the program, observing the value in the X register and the status of the Z flag. When does the Z flag change from logic 0 to logic 1?

(After going through the loop five times the DEX instruction will decrement the number in X to zero. Execution of this instruction *sets* the Z flag. The BNE LOOP instruction *tests* the Z flag and the program exits from the loop.)

c. Change the byte at $0000 to $80. What will be the status of the N flag after executing the LDX instruction? After executing the first DEX instruction? Check by running the program in the single-step mode.

Exercise 3–4

a. Load the program in Example 3–10. It is listed here for your convenience in performing this exercise.

1060:8D 30 C0	7 START	STA	SPKER	;TOGGLE THE SPEAKER.
1063:20 69 10	8	JSR	TIMER	;USE THE SUBROUTINE TO DELAY.
1066:4C 60 10	9	JMP	START	;LOOP BACK TO START.
1069:	11 ;SUBROUTINE, TIMER			
1069:A6 00	12 TIMER	LDX	M	;LOAD X WITH THE NUMBER IN M.
106B:A4 01	13 LOOPX	LDY	N	;LOAD Y WITH THE NUMBER IN N.
106D:88	14 LOOPY	DEY		;DECREMENT THE NUMBER IN Y.
106E:D0 FD	15	BNE	LOOPY	;IF Y IS NOT ZERO, LOOP BACK TO LOOPY.
1070:CA	16	DEX		;DECREMENT THE NUMBER IN X.
1071:D0 F8	17	BNE	LOOPX	;IF X IS NOT ZERO, LOOP BACK TO LOOPX.
1073:60	18	RTS		

b. Execute the program after placing the number $01 in location $0000 and the number $CB in location $0001. What do you observe?

(The author observed a tone whose frequency was approximately 500 Hz.)

c. Single step through the program, noting changes in the P register and the effect of these changes on the branch instructions. Also observe the effect of the branch instructions on the value of the program counter.

d. Some programmers prefer to modify the delay loop program in Examples 3–8 and 3–10 by making the destination of both loops the DEY instruction. That is, they change the BNE LOOPX instruction to a BNE LOOPY instruction. Here is a challenging question. If the above change is made, what is the algebraic expression for the loop time in clock cycles? Make the change, then adjust your timing loop to produce a tone of 500 Hz. For an example of a use of this loop and an explanation of it, refer to Example 10–1, Subroutine TIMER.

Exercise 3–5

a. The purpose of this experiment is to test the game paddle timing program in Example 3–9 and its associated circuit in Fig. 3–9. You will need to assemble some parts, consisting of a 2-foot DIP jumper cable described earlier, a 100,000-ohm or a 150,000-ohm potentiometer, and a breadboard such as a Super Strip. Sources for these parts were mentioned earlier. Of course, if you have game paddles then you will not need these parts.

b. Connect your circuit components to the game i/o connector, double-check all your connections, and turn on the power. Perform the 30-second smoke test; that is, if nothing smokes after 30 seconds, the circuit must be correct. This test should only be conducted *after* you double-check all your work, because it is usually a very expensive test to perform at an early stage in the experiment.

c. Load the program and execute it. Vary the resistor and explain the results.

(With a 100-kilohm variable resistor the author found that the number displayed on the screen varied from $00 at 0 ohms to $DA with 100,000 ohms.)

d. If you increase the resistance above 100 kilohms, the number displayed will eventually reach $FF. What will happen if you increase the resistance even more than that? Try it, you will not hurt anything.

e. Try placing a thermistor between the +5-V pin and the GC0 pin. Run the program and observe the output when you touch the thermistor or blow on it. For further information on temperature measurements see:

- Kershner, Carl J., "A Digital Thermometer for the Apple II," *The Best of Micro*, Vol. 3, p. 149.
- De Jong, Marvin L., "A Simple Temperature Measurement Program and Interface," *The Best of Micro*, Vol. 3, p. 314.

Exercise 3–6

a. Turn off the Apple II and connect the circuit shown in Fig. 3–10. Use the DIP jumper arrangement mentioned in the previous exercise. Load the program in Example 3–11.

b. Put the switch connected to PB0 in the logic 1 position as shown in Fig. 3–10, then run the program. What will happen?

(The program should wait in the BMI TEST loop until the switch is closed, so nothing will happen.)

c. Switch the switch to its logic 0 position. What happens? Explain.

Exercise 3–7

a. Turn off the Apple II and connect the circuit shown in Fig 3–12. Use the DIP jumper arrangement mentioned previously. Load the program in Example 3–12.

b. Run the program. What do you observe?

(You should observe that the switch controls the LED. When the switch is in its logic 1 position the LED glows. Otherwise it is off. You are now the proud owner of a $2000 switch.)

Exercise 3–8

a. Write a delay loop similar to the one in Example 3–8 that does not use either the X or Y registers.

b. Modify the program in Example 3–12 to turn the light off when the switch is in its logic 1 position.

c. Write a 1-second delay loop program. Write a program that produces a 1-minute delay.

d. Write a subroutine that waits in a loop until a key on the keyboard is pressed, then returns to the calling program.

e. Write a program that reads the keyboard and stores the character code in location $0000. Use the program to make a table of character codes. Be sure to include character codes that involve the SHFT, ESC, and CNTRL keys; for example, what is the code associated with the CNTRL E keystroke? Some patterns should emerge.

f. Write a series of steps (in English, not 6502 assembly language) with which one could enter the hexadecimal number $7F in location $0000 by first pressing the 7 key and then the F key. Your objective is to outline a procedure to do this without actually writing the program. It is always worth thinking about the steps needed to accomplish a particular task before writing the program itself.

CHAPTER 4

Logical Operations and Shift and Rotate Operations

OBJECTIVES

At the end of this chapter you should be able to:

- Use these instructions: AND, ORA, EOR, BIT, ASL, LSR, ROL, and ROR.
- Set or clear individual bits in a memory location.
- Complement individual bits with the EOR instruction.
- Understand the concept of masking.
- Test for logic level transitions on input pins.

INTRODUCTION

Two types of instructions will be introduced in this chapter. The first type includes the logic instructions AND, ORA, EOR, and the BIT test. The second type of instruction includes the rotate and shift instructions: ASL, LSR, ROL, and ROR.

The logical operations carried out by a microprocessor are among the most primitive applications of symbolic logic, but the implications of machines performing logical operations and making decisions are far-reaching and profound. Are human thoughts ultimately based in a complex system of logical operations? Is any formal system (logic, for example) capable of representing the entire spectrum of human intellectual activity? Will artificial intelligence become a reality?

We have already reached far beyond the scope of this chapter, and we now quickly return to the simple, safe, and comfortable world of 6502 logic.

LOGICAL OPERATIONS

We will use four logical operations. To describe them, let A and B symbolize 1-bit binary numbers. The four logic operations are:

- The AND operation, symbolized by $A \cdot B$ or $A \wedge B$.
- The OR operation, symbolized by $A + B$ or $A \vee B$.
- The EOR* (exclusive-or) operation, symbolized by $A + B$ or $A \veebar B$.
- The *inversion*, or *complement*, operation, symbolized by $\overline{A}$; that is, the complement of A is $\overline{A}$.

Table 4–1 summarizes the operations with truth tables, and it gives all the possible combinations of the operations for 1-bit numbers. Fig. 4–1 gives the logic circuit symbols for each operation. The dot ($\cdot$) in an AND operation is frequently understood; that is, $A \cdot B = AB$. Although it is possible to confuse the OR ($+$) and the AND ($\cdot$) notation with addition and multiplication, the context of the discussion will indicate the operation that is intended.

Table 4–1. Summary of the Logical Operations

AND			OR			EOR			Complement	
A	B	A·B	A	B	A+B	A	B	A⊕B	A	Ā
1	1	1	1	1	1	1	1	0	1	0
1	0	0	1	0	1	1	0	1	0	1
0	1	0	0	1	1	0	1	1		
0	0	0	0	0	0	0	0	0		
$1 \cdot 1 = 1$			$1 + 1 = 1$			$1 \oplus 1 = 0$			$\overline{1} = 0$	
$1 \cdot 0 = 0$			$1 + 0 = 1$			$1 \oplus 0 = 1$			$\overline{0} = 1$	
$0 \cdot 1 = 0$			$0 + 1 = 1$			$0 \oplus 1 = 1$				
$0 \cdot 0 = 0$			$0 + 0 = 0$			$0 \oplus 0 = 0$				

The symbols $\wedge$, $\vee$, and $\veebar$ frequently replace $\cdot$, $+$, and $\oplus$, respectively. The dot is sometimes understood: $AB = A \cdot B$.

Symbols A and B need not be 1-bit numbers. An 8-bit microprocessor operates on eight bits simultaneously. Any 8-bit logical operation can be performed by doing single-bit operations on corresponding bits. If the eight bits of A are represented by A7, A6, . . . , A0, and the eight bits of B by B7, B6, . . . , B0, and

---

*Textbooks on logic designate the exclusive-or operation by either "XOR" or "EXOR." The EOR notation is used here because it is identical with the 6502 mnemonic for the exclusive-or instruction.

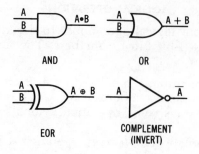

AND

OR

EOR

COMPLEMENT
(INVERT)

Fig. 4–1. Logic symbols for the AND, OR, EOR, and complement operations.

if the answer to A·B is C, then the operation A·B = C is realized by:

$$A7 \cdot B7 = C7$$
$$A6 \cdot B6 = C6$$
$$\cdot \quad \cdot \quad \cdot$$
$$\cdot \quad \cdot \quad \cdot$$
$$\cdot \quad \cdot \quad \cdot$$
$$A0 \cdot B0 = C0$$

Table 4–2 gives 8-bit examples for all four operations. It also suggests that working these logic operations by hand may be made easier if the operation is arranged so that the binary numbers are placed one under the other. Table 4–2 also expresses the numbers and the results in hexadecimal. It is worthwhile to familiarize yourself with the operations and the results in hexadecimal, since this is the form that is frequently used in programs. The exercises in this chapter will provide additional practice.

The logical operations may be summarized as follows:

• The result of an AND is 1 only if both bits are 1.
• The result of an OR is 0 only if both bits are 0.
• The result of an EOR is 1 only if the bits are unlike.
• The complement of a 1 is 0, and vice versa.

These four statements are easy to remember, and with them the truth tables in Table 4–1 may be constructed.

Before turning to the 6502 logic instructions, we note that the instruction set does not include a complement operation. The complement operation may be implemented by performing an exclusive or with a 1. In the general case $A \oplus 1 = \bar{A}$, and in the 8-bit case

$$A \oplus \$FF = \bar{A}$$

Table 4-2. Examples of 8-Bit Logical Operations

AND	OR	EOR
A = 1100 1100 = $CC B = 1010 1010 = $AA	+ A = 1100 1100 = $CC B = 1010 1010 = $AA	⊕ A = 1100 1100 = $CC B = 1010 1010 = $AA
C = 1000 1000 = $88	C = 1110 1110 = $EE **Complement** A = 1100 1100 = $CC $\overline{A}$ = 0011 0011 = $33	C = 0110 0110 = $66

is the formula used to produce the complement of an 8-bit number.

THE LOGIC INSTRUCTIONS IN THE 6502 INSTRUCTION SET

A summary of the logic instructions available to the 6502 follows:

- The AND instruction forms the logical AND operation with a byte of data from memory and the number in the accumulator. The result is stored in the accumulator. Symbolically, $A \cdot M \rightarrow A$.
- The ORA instruction forms the logical OR operation with a byte of data from memory and the number in the accumulator. The result is stored in the accumulator. Symbolically, $A + M \rightarrow A$.
- The EOR instruction forms the EXCLUSIVE-OR operation with a byte of data from memory and the number in the accumulator. The result is stored in the accumulator. Symbolically, $A \oplus M \rightarrow A$.
- The BIT instruction forms the logical AND operation with a byte of data from memory and the number in the accumulator. The result is *not stored*. The logic values of bits seven and six of the memory location accessed by the BIT instruction are transferred to bits seven and six of the P register. Symbolically, $A \cdot M$, $M_7 \rightarrow N$, $M_6 \rightarrow V$.

The summary above should make you aware of the difference between the AND instruction and the BIT instruction. The latter affects only the flags in the processor status register; the number in the accumulator and the number in the memory location are not changed. In any case the examples that follow should clarify the descriptions given above.

To illustrate the logical instructions a very simple program and a simple "pencil and paper" calculation example for each of the instructions will be given. In addition, the exercises at the end of this chapter are designed to give you extensive practice with the logic instructions; a short computer assisted instruction (CAI) program, written in assembly language, is included to allow you to practice with the logical operations. Some uses of the logic instructions will be described in the next section.

In Example 4–1 is a program segment that illustrates the AND instruction. The effect of the first two instructions in this example is to AND the number $7F with the number stored in MEM1. The result is stored in the location symbolized by MEM2. Notice that the AND instruction was used in the zero-page addressing mode. Example 4–2 illustrates how you can find the effect of running this program for one particular number. You can use the program in Example 4–1 to experiment with various numbers in the AND operation, and the answer will be found in the location symbolized by MEM2.

Example 4–1. A Routine to AND Two Numbers

Object: AND $7F with the number in location MEM1.

10A9:A9 7F	6	LDA	#$7F	;PERFORM AN AND OPER-ATION BETWEEN
10AB:25 00	7	AND	MEM1	;$7F AND THE NUMBER IN MEM1.
10AD:8D 0F 10	8	STA	MEM2	;RESULT INTO MEM2.
10B0:00	9	BRK		

Example 4–2. Illustration of an AND Computation

Suppose the number stored in MEM1 is $83. What result would be stored in location MEM2 after executing the program in Example 4–1?
Solution: Form the logical AND of $7F = 0111 1111 with $83 = 1000 0011.

$$\begin{array}{r} \$7F = 0111\ 1111 \\ \$83 = 1000\ 0011 \\ \hline = 0000\ 0011 = \$03 \end{array}$$

Table 4–1 is used to perform the AND operation bit by bit, and the result is converted to hexadecimal. After the program in Example 4–1 is executed, the number $03 will be stored in location MEM2.

Example 4–3 gives a program segment that illustrates the ORA instruction. The effect of the first two instructions in this example is to OR the number stored in MEM1 with the number $80. The result is stored in the location symbolized by MEM2. Notice that the ORA instruction was used in the immediate addressing mode. Example 4–4 illustrates how you can find the effect of running this program for one particular number. You can use the program in Example 4–3 to experiment with various numbers in the OR operation, and the answer will be found in the location symbolized by MEM2.

Example 4–3. A Routine to ORA Two Numbers

Object: OR the number in MEM1 with $80.

10B1:A5 00	6	LDA	MEM1	;PERFORM AN OR OPERATION BETWEEN
10B3:09 80	7	ORA	#$80	;THE NUMBER IN MEM1 AND $80.
10B5:8D 0F 10	8	STA	MEM2	;RESULT INTO MEM2
10B8:00	9	BRK		

Example 4–4. Illustration of an ORA Computation

Suppose the number stored in MEM1 is $16. What result would be stored in location MEM2 after executing the program in Example 4–3?

Solution: Form the logical OR of $16 = 0001 0110 with $80 = 1000 0000.

$$\begin{array}{r} \$16 = 0001\ 0110 \\ +\ \ \$80 = 1000\ 0000 \\ \hline = 1001\ 0110 = \$96 \end{array}$$

Refer to the truth table in Table 4–1 to perform the operation bit by bit. After the program in Example 4–3 is executed, the number $96 will be stored in location MEM2.

In Example 4–5 a program segment illustrates the EOR instruction. The effect of the first two instructions in this example is to EOR the number $FF with the number in MEM1. Recall that forming the EOR of a number with $FF produces the complement of the number. Thus the complement of the number in MEM1 will be stored in location MEM2 at the conclusion of the program. Notice that the EOR instruction was used in the zero-page addressing mode. Example 4–6 illustrates how you can find the result of running the program in Example 4–5 with a pencil and paper calculation. Use the program in Example 4–5 to experiment with various operands in the EOR operation.

Example 4–5. A Routine to EOR Two Numbers

Object: EOR the number $FF with the number in MEM1.

10B9:A9 FF	6	LDA	#$FF	;PERFORM AN EOR OPERATION BETWEEN
10BB:45 00	7	EOR	MEM1	;THE $FF AND THE NUMBER IN MEM1.
10BD:8D 0F 10	8	STA	MEM2	;RESULT INTO MEM2
10C0:00	9	BRK		

Example 4–6. Illustration of an EOR Computation

Suppose the number stored in MEM1 is $0F. What result would be stored in location MEM2 after executing the program in Example 4–5?

Solution: Form the logical EOR of $FF = 1111 1111 with $0F = 0000 1111.

$$\begin{array}{r} \$FF = 1111\ 1111 \\ +\ \ \$0F = 0000\ 1111 \\ \hline = 1111\ 0000 = \$F0 \end{array}$$

Refer to the truth table in Table 4–1 to perform the operation bit by bit. After the program in Example 4–3 is executed, the number $F0 (the complement of $0F) will be stored in location MEM2.

In Example 4–7 is a program segment that illustrates the BIT instruction (often called the BIT test). The effect of the first two instructions in this example is to "BIT" the number $01 with the number stored in MEM2. Recall that one effect of the BIT instruction is to AND the number in A with the number in memory. If this AND operation produces a logic 0, the Z flag in the P register will be set; otherwise it will be cleared. Another effect of the BIT instruction is to set the N flag if the memory location referenced by the BIT instruction has a logic 1 in bit seven; otherwise the N flag is cleared. Finally, the BIT instruction will set the V flag if the location it references has a logic 1 in bit six; otherwise the V flag will be cleared. Example 4–8 illustrates a computation for one particular case. Also note in Example 4–7 that the BIT instruction was used in its absolute addressing mode.

Example 4–7. A Routine to Perform the BIT Test

Object: With $01 in A, perform the BIT test on location MEM2.

```
10C1:A9 01      6      LDA   #$01     ;PERFORM A BIT TEST ON LOCATION
10C3:2C 0F 10   7      BIT   MEM2     ;MEM2 WITH $01 IN A.
10C6:00         8      BRK
```

Example 4–8. Illustration of a BIT Computation

Suppose the number stored in MEM2 is $41. What will be the status of the flags in the P register after executing the program in Example 4–7? What number will be in the accumulator?

Solution: First form the logical AND of $01 = 0000 0001 and $41 = 0100 0001. The result is 0000 0001, which is not logic 0, so the Z flag will be cleared. Next note that bit seven of MEM2 will be transferred to the N flag. Since bit seven is logic 0, the N flag in the P register will be cleared. Finally, recall that bit six of the memory location referenced by the BIT instruction is transferred to the V flag. Since bit six is logic 1 if the number is $41, the V flag in the P register will be set. Since the BIT instruction does not modify the accumulator, the accumulator will still contain the number $01 after the program in Example 4–7 is executed.

USING THE LOGIC INSTRUCTIONS

The logic instructions are used to *set, clear, complement,* or *test* specific bits in a memory location or a register. To illustrate just one situation in which bits must be set or cleared, consider the format of the characters that are displayed on a video monitor connected to the Apple. If the character code obtained from the keyboard, a terminal, or a modem connected to the

Apple has a logic 1 in bit seven, then *normal* characters are displayed. If bit seven is logic 0, a flashing character is displayed. If both bits seven and six are logic 0, an inverse character is displayed. The character code obtained at the keyboard input port will have bit seven at logic 1. To print an inverse character we could AND the character code with $3F, since this number has bits six and seven both logic 0, and the AND operation would produce a result with logic 0 in bits six and seven. On the other hand, the ASCII from a terminal almost always has bit seven logic 0. To print normal characters, we could OR each character code with $80, since this operation would set bit seven to logic 1.

There are many other instances in which it is important to *set, clear, complement,* or *test* bits. We summarize the procedure for the first three of these processes:

- A bit (or a series of bits) in an 8-bit number may be *set* by executing an *ORA* instruction if the operand contains *logic 1s* in the bits to be set and *logic 0s* in the remaining bits. See Example 4–9.
- A bit (or a series of bits) in an 8-bit number may be *cleared* by executing an *AND* instruction if the operand contains *logic 0s* in the bits to be cleared and *logic 1s* in the remaining bits. See Example 4–10.
- A bit (or a series of bits) in an 8-bit number may be *complemented* by executing an *EOR* instruction if the operand contains *logic 1s* in the bits to be complemented and *logic 0s* in the bits to be left unchanged. See Example 4–11.

The process of clearing one or more bits of a given number, leaving the other bits unchanged, is called *masking*. The cleared bits are said to be *masked*. For example, to mask the low-order nibble (lowest 4 bits) of an 8-bit number it must be ANDed with $F0 = 1111 0000. Masking the high-order nibble requires an AND operation with $0F = 0000 1111. How would you mask the odd numbered bits of an 8-bit binary number? Examples 4–9 to 4–11 illustrate the ideas mentioned above.

Example 4–9. Setting a Bit to Logic 1 with the ORA Instruction

Given the binary number 1001 1010 = $9A, modify it to have a logic 1 in bit six, but leave the other bits unchanged.

Solution: The desired effect may be achieved by ORing the given number with the binary number 0100 0000 = $40, since

```
  1001 1010 = $9A
+ 0100 0000 = $40
  ─────────────────
= 1101 1010 = $DA
```

The truth table in Table 4–1 was used to effect the operation. How can you set bit five to logic 1? Bit four? Bit one?

Example 4–10. Clearing a Bit to Logic 0 with the AND Instruction

Show that bit seven in $CA may be cleared without affecting the other bit values by
ANDing it with $7F.
Solution:

```
1100 1010 = $CA
0111 1111 = $7F
= 0100 1010 = $4A
```

How would you clear bit six? But five? Bit one?

Example 4–11. Complementing a Number with the EOR Instruction

Suppose A = $CC = 1100 1100. Then A + $FF is calculated below:

```
     1100 1100 = $CC
 ⊕   1111 1111 = $FF
   = 0011 0011 = $CC = A̅
```

This shows that A ⊕ $FF = A̅. How would you complement bit six? Bit four? Bit one?

The BIT instruction will be illustrated next. You have probably seen this prompt on your computer: PRESS ANY KEY TO
CONTINUE. How can this simple instruction be implemented
with a BIT test, without affecting the number in the accumulator? First refer again to Figs. 3–3, 3–4, and our discussion of keyboard input in Section 3–6. You will recall again that
if a key is pressed then bit seven of the keyboard input port at
location $C000 goes to logic 1. In that case a BIT KYBD in-
struction would transfer the value of bit seven to the N flag,
which could be tested with a BPL or BMI instruction. Example
4–12 illustrates our solution to this problem.

Example 4–12. Using the BIT Instruction

Object: Write a program that waits in a loop until a keystroke occurs.

```
10C7:2C 00 C0   6  WAIT   BIT   KYBD     ;TEST BIT 7. IS IT ZERO?
10CA:10 FB      7         BPL   WAIT     ;YES, THEN WAIT.
10CC:8D 10 C0   8         STA   STROBE   ;CLEAR BIT SEVEN. THEN
                                          CONTINUE.
10CF:00         9         BRK
```

In Example 4–12 the BIT KYBD instruction transfers the
value of bit seven of location $C000 to the N flag in the P regis-
ter. The BPL WAIT instruction tests this flag and holds the program in a loop until the BIT test produces a logic 1 in bit seven.
Finally, the STA STROBE instruction resets the keyboard flip-
flop so bit seven of the keyboard input port is again at logic 0.
The timing diagram for these events was illustrated in Fig. 3–3.

In another illustration of the BIT instruction, suppose our objective is to count pulses on bit zero of an input port. An illustration of the pulses we wish to count is shown in Fig. 4–2.

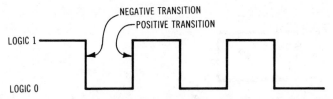

Fig. 4–2. The pulses to be applied to pin 0 of an input port to be detected by the program in Example 4–13.

How can a complete negative pulse, consisting of a logic 1 to logic 0 transition followed by a logic 0 to logic 1 transition be detected? The program in Example 4–13 illustrates the answer, and a flowchart is given in Fig. 4–3. It consists of two loops; the first loop waits for a negative transition in which the logic value of the signal on bit zero of the port changes from 1 to 0, while the second loop waits for a positive transition in which the logic value of the signal on bit zero of the port changes from 0 to 1. The mask byte, which masks bits one through seven, is contained in the accumulator. Can you accomplish the same objective without using the BIT instruction?

Example 4–13. Pulse Detection Routine

Object: Wait in a loop until a complete negative pulse has been detected.

```
10D0:A9 01      5              LDA    #01       ;SET UP THE MASK BYTE.
10D2:2C 61 C0   6  LOOP1       BIT    PORT      ;TEST THE PORT.
10D5:D0 FB      7              BNE    LOOP1     ;WAIT UNTIL BIT 0 IS 0.
10D7:2C 61 C0   8  LOOP2       BIT    PORT      ;TEST THE PORT AGAIN.
10DA:10 FB      9              BPL    LOOP2     ;WAIT UNTIL BIT 0 IS 1.
10DC:00         10             BRK
```

One reason for wanting to be able to count pulses is associated with the fact that a number of transducers produce a pulse output proportional to the physical quantity being measured. There are voltage-to-frequency converters and temperature-to-frequency converters that can be used with the pulse counting logic just described to measure voltage or temperature. We will discuss these circuits in more detail in Chapter 9.

The last illustration of how the logical operations may be used is given in Example 4–14. The objective of that program is to wait in a loop until a logic transition (*either* positive to negative *or* negative to positive) occurs on bit seven of the push-button input on the game i/o connector. The program illustrates the use of an EOR instruction and an AND instruction. Recall that the EOR instruction will set a bit if opposite bit values are involved in the operation. If bit seven *changes* after the LDX

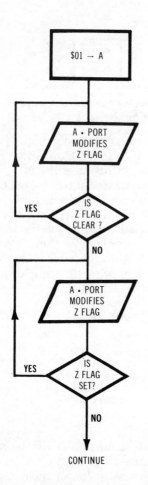

Fig. 4-3. Flowchart of the pulse detection routine in Example 4-13.

Example 4-14. A Program to Detect a Single Transition on Bit Seven

Object: Wait in a loop until the logic level of the PB0 push-button switch input changes.

```
10DD:AE 61 C0   5           LDX   PB0     ;READ THE SWITCH PORT
10E0:8A         6 LOAF      TXA           ;AND SAVE IT IN X. X TO A.
10E1:4D 61 C0   7           EOR   PB0     ;CHECK FOR CHANGE IN BITS.
10E4:29 50      8           AND   #80     ;MASK BITS 0-6.
10E6:10 F8      9           BPL   LOAF    ;WAIT FOR TRANSITION ON
                                            BIT 7.
10E8:00         10          BRK
```

PB0 instruction, the EOR PB0 instruction will produce a logic 1 in the accumulator. The AND #$80 masks the other bits, since only bit seven is of interest. Thus the Z flag is affected only by bit seven, which is tested by the BPL LOAF instruction. Perhaps you could connect the PB0 input to a microswitch on a door in which case jiggling the door would cause the program to drop out of the loop and start a burglar alarm.

THE ROTATE AND SHIFT INSTRUCTIONS

The ASL, LSR, ROL, and ROR instructions will be introduced in this section. The following definitions should be studied in conjunction with their diagrams given in Fig. 4–4 and the examples that follow.

- *ASL*—Arithmetic Shift Left: Each bit of the operand is *shifted* to the *left*. That is, bit zero becomes bit one, bit one becomes bit two, . . . , bit six becomes bit seven, and *bit seven becomes the carry flag*. A logic 0 is shifted into bit zero.

- *LSR*—Logical Shift Right: This instruction is similar to the ASL instruction except that the bits are *shifted right*. A logic 0 is shifted into bit seven, and *bit zero is shifted into the carry flag*.

- *ROL*—Rotate One Bit Left: Each bit of the operand is *shifted* to the *left* as in the ASL instruction, except that the *carry flag is shifted into bit zero*. Since bit seven is shifted into the carry flag, successive ROL instructions simply *rotate* the bits left. A series of nine ROL instructions will leave the operand and the carry flag unchanged (Table 4–3).

- *ROR*—Rotate One Bit Right: The ROR instruction is exactly like the ROL instruction, except the bits are *rotated right*. Bit zero goes into the carry flag, and the carry flag is moved into bit seven.

A very simple program to demonstrate these four instructions is listed in Example 4–15. We shall discuss it in a moment so that you can use it to experiment with rotating and shifting various numbers, but first we must look at an addressing mode that is unique to the rotate and shift instructions. This mode is called *accumulator addressing*. When using the *accumulator addressing mode*, the number in the *accumulator* is shifted or rotated. The accumulator addressing mode is used for the LSR instruction in Example 4–15. Observe that an A is placed in the operand field of the LSR instruction, but also observe that the LSR instruction is a single-byte instruction when the accumulator addressing mode is used. This is also true for the other shift and rotate instructions.

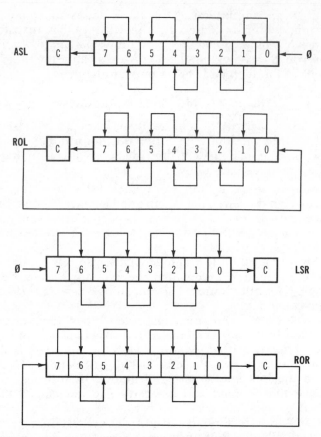

Fig. 4-4. Diagram of the rotate and shift instructions.

Table 4-3. Changing a Number With Successive ROL Instructions

Carry Flag	Number	Number of ROL Instructions
0	0000 0101 = $05	0
0	0000 1010 = $0A	1
0	0001 0100 = $14	2
0	0010 1000 = $28	3
0	0101 0000 = $50	4
0	1010 0000 = $A0	5
1	0100 0000 = $40	6
0	1000 0001 = $81	7
1	0000 0010 = $02	8
0	0000 0101 = $05	9

Example 4–15. A Program to Demonstrate the Shift and Rotate Instructions

Object: Write a program to fetch a number, shift it, and store it in the same location.

10E9:A5 00	4	LDA	MEM1	;GET A NUMBER FROM LOCATION MEM1.
10EB:4A	5	LSR	A	;SHIFT IT RIGHT ONE BIT.
10EC:85 00	6	STA	MEM1	;RETURN IT TO MEM1.
10EE:00	7	BRK		;DISPLAY THE REGISTERS.

Continue to refer to Example 4–15. This program fetches a number from location MEM1, shifts it one bit to the right, and returns the modified number to location MEM1. Since the monitor displays the contents of the accumulator after executing the BRK instruction, you can see the effect of the *successive* shifts by running the program again and again. You can also examine the contents of location MEM1 each time the program is executed, if you want to observe the effect of successive LSR instructions on a number.

To study the other shift and rotate instructions, simply exchange the op code for the LSR instruction ($4A) with the op code of one of the other instructions. They are: ASL with op code $0A, ROL with op code $2A, and ROR with op code $6A. A more elaborate demonstration program will be described in the exercises. Also consider Examples 4–16 and 4–17 listed below.

Example 4–16. Illustration of the ROL Instruction

Suppose the number $05 is stored in a memory location, and it is the operand for successive ROL instructions. What number will be in this same location after one ROL instruction? Two ROL instructions? Nine ROL instructions? Assume the carry flag is clear before any of the ROL instructions are executed.

Solution: Refer to Table 4–3 to observe that successive rotate left operations (ROL) change the number $05 to $0A, $14, $28, $50, $A0, $40, $81, $02, and back to $05 after the ninth ROL operation.

Example 4–17. Illustration of the ROR Instruction

Suppose the number $05 is stored in a memory location, and it is the operand for successive ROR instructions. What number will be in this same location after one ROR instruction? Two ROR instructions? Nine ROR instructions? Assume the carry flag is initially clear.

Solution: Using the same process illustrated in Table 4–3 for the ROL operation, you can find that successive ROR operations change $05 to $02, $81, $40, $A0, $50, $28, $14, $0A, and back to $05 after the ninth ROR instruction.

You are probably wondering how the rotate and shift instructions will be used. If you will recall the multiplication algorithm you learned in elementary school you will remember *shifting* partial products to the left before adding. A modification of that algorithm will be used to construct a multiplication program in the next chapter. The rotate and shift instructions will also be used to perform binary division. So although the programs in this chapter may seem contrived, the techniques will be used many times in subsequent chapters.

Consider some interesting properties of the ASL and LSR instructions illustrated in Examples 4–18 through 4–21. From these examples we conclude:

- A succession of ASL instructions is equivalent to multiplying by 2, 4, 8, 16, . . . , provided no significant bits are shifted out of the location.
- A succession of LSR instructions is equivalent to dividing by 2, 4, 8, 16, . . . , provided no significant bits are shifted out of the location.

Example 4–18. The Effect of One ASL Instruction on a Number

What is \$05 after one ASL instruction?

Solution: \$05 = 0000 0101, which when shifted left once becomes 0000 1010 = \$0A = 10_{10}. Also refer to Table 4–3. Observe that one shift left is equivalent to multiplication by 2.

Example 4–19. The Effect of Two ASL Instructions on a Number

What is \$05 after two ASL instructions?

Solution: \$05 = 0000 0101, shifted twice becomes 0001 0100 = \$14 = 20. Also refer to Table 4–3. Observe that two shifts left is equivalent to multiplication by 4.

Example 4–20. The Effect of One LSR Instruction on a Number

What is \$4A after one LSR instruction?

Solution: 74 = \$4A = 0100 1010, shifted right once, becomes 0010 0101 = \$25 = 37. Observe that one shift right is equivalent to division by 2, provided no logic 1s are shifted out of the number.

Example 4–21. The Effect of Two LSR Instructions on a Number

What is \$4A after two LSR instructions?

Solution: 74 = \$4A = 0100 1010, shifted right twice, becomes 0001 0010 = \$12 = 18. Notice that two shifts right is equivalent to division by 4, but the fractional part (or remainder) of the quotient is lost (a bit value of logic 1 was shifted out of the location), since 74/4 = 18.5, not 18.

In the latter case it should be clear that odd numbers will *always* lose a bit when divided by 2. Also in the latter case, the loss of bits by a series of right shifts destroys only the fractional part of the quotient (the remainder, if you wish), and for certain problems the loss of the fractional part may be acceptable. If it is not, then a ROR instruction can be used to replace the LSR instruction and the bits can be detected as they are shifted into the carry flag. Software can be written to save the fractional part, but this is beyond the scope of the present discussion. Refer once again to Examples 4–18 through 4–21.

We conclude this section with a few simple programming examples that use these instructions. One procedure that is encountered quite often in programming is moving the low-order nibble of a memory location into the high-order nibble of the same location, leaving logic 0s in the four least significant bits. Example 4–22 lists a program to accomplish this procedure. The X register serves as a bit counter. Note that it is initialized to $FC and that Table 3–1 gives −4 as the twos complement equivalent of $FC. Therefore, after X has been incremented four times it will reach zero, and the program will branch out of the loop, having shifted the number in location MEMORY four times to the left. How would you move the high-order nibble of a memory location into the low-order nibble of the same location, leaving zeros in the most significant bits?

Example 4–22. A Program to Shift a Number Four Bits to the Left

Object: Move the low-order nibble in a memory location into the high-order nibble, leaving logic 0s in the four least significant bits.

10EF:A2 FC	5		LDX	#$FC	;X SERVES AS A BIT COUNTER WITH X=−4.
10F1:06 01	6	LOOP	ASL	MEMORY	;SHIFT THE NUMBER ONE BIT LEFT.
10F3:E8	7		INX		;INCREMENT THE BIT COUNTER.
10F4:D0 FB	8		BNE	LOOP	;GO THROUGH THE LOOP FOUR TIMES.
10F6:00	9		BRK		;BREAK TO THE MONITOR.

The program in Example 4–23 is another example of the use of the shift and rotate instructions. The objective of this routine is to transfer a number in one location to another memory location by a series of shift and rotate instructions. Although this sequence of instructions would rarely be used by itself, the general procedure is used quite frequently in multiplication and division programs. Serial output (refer to Chapter 1) uses a variation of the ideas contained in Example 4–23 when a character code in memory is transformed into a serial bit stream by shifting it out one bit at a time at intervals separated by one bit-time. A flowchart of the program in Example 4–23 is given in Fig. 4–5. Study Example 4–23 in connection with its flowchart. What number will be in location LOC1 after the program has executed? Could you accomplish the same objective with LSR and ROR instructions? Try it. What would happen if you replaced the ASL LOC1 instruction with an ROL instruction?

Example 4–23. A Program to Move a Number from One Location to Another Using the Shift and Rotate Instructions

Object: Shift the number in location $01FF into location $01FE.

```
1200:A0 08    6          LDY  #08      ;Y CONTAINS NUMBER BITS
                                        TO BE SHIFTED.
1202:0E FF 10 7 BRANCH ASL LOC1        ;SHIFT BIT 7 INTO CARRY.
1205:2E FE 10 8          ROL  LOC2     ;ROTATE CARRY INTO
                                        LOC2.
1208:88       9          DEY           ;DECREMENT THE BIT
                                        COUNTER.
1209:D0 F7    10         BNE  BRANCH   ;LOOP UNTIL 8 BITS
120B:00       11         BRK           ;HAVE BEEN SHIFTED.
```

EXERCISES

The purpose of these exercises is to familiarize you with the instructions introduced in this chapter. Before you can *see how* an instruction might be used in a program, you must have a good understanding of what it does. A program has been written to provide computer assisted learning in connection with the logical instructions and the rotate and shift instructions in this chapter and the arithmetic instructions in the next chapter. A complete listing of the program, with comments, is given in Example B–2 in Appendix B. For the purposes of this chapter, you need only load the program into memory and to that end a memory dump of the program is given in Chart 4–1. You will probably want to save it, either on cassette tape or on a disk. Load the program using the monitor : command, then save it. We will discuss how to use it in connection with the exercises below.

Exercise 4–1

a. Make sure the CAL (computer assisted learning) program listed in Chart 4–1 is stored in memory.

b. Load the program listed below.

```
120C:20 4F 11 9 AGAIN   JSR  GETBYTS   ;INPUT THE TWO OPERANDS.
              10 ****************

120F:A5 01    12         LDA  OPA      ;FETCH ONE NUMBER.
1211:25 02    13         AND  OPB      ;AND IT WITH ANOTHER
                                        NUMBER.
1213:85 03    14         STA  RESULT   STORE THE ANSWER.
```

```
            16 ****************
1215:20 5D 11  17      JSR   TEST      ;INPUT YOUR OWN
                                       ANSWER.
1218:4C 0C 12  18      JMP   AGAIN     ;TRY ANOTHER PROBLEM.
```

c. Refer to the program listed in Step *b*. The part of the program delineated by asterisks is of particular importance to the content of this chapter. Note that this part of the program fetches a number from location OPA (for Operand A) in location $0001, ANDs it with a number in OPB (for Operand B) in location $0002, and stores the result in RESULT in location $0003.

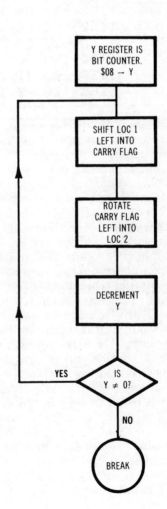

Fig. 4–5. Flowchart of the program in Example 4–23.

Chart 4–1. Memory Dump of the CAL Program Used in the Exercises

```
*1100.1167

1100-   20  16  11  0A  0A  0A  0A  85
1108-   00  20  16  11  05  00  85  00
1110-   20  8E  FD  A5  00  60  20  0C
1118-   FD  20  ED  FD  29  7F  C9  40
1120-   B0  04  29  0F  10  02  E9  37
1128-   60  85  45  48  08  08  68  85
1130-   48  8A  48  A2  07  66  45  A9
1138-   00  69  B0  9D  10  05  CA  10
1140-   F4  66  48  A9  00  69  B0  8D
1148-   0E  05  68  AA  28  68  60  20
1150-   58  FC  20  00  11  85  01  20
1158-   00  11  85  02  60  20  29  11
1160-   20  00  11  45  03  D0  F9  60
```

By simply modifying one op code, the AND instruction on line 13 may be changed to either an ORA instruction or an EOR instruction.

The remainder of the program calls various subroutines in the CAL program. The first subroutine call allows you to input two 2-digit hexadecimal numbers. These are the numbers to be ANDed by the AND instruction. The JSR TEST instruction allows you to see the result of the logic instruction on line 13. The result is displayed in binary on the screen of the video monitor. The carry flag contents are also displayed, but this is of no concern in the present context. The carry flag will be significant when the rotate and shift instructions are used and in the next chapter when we add and subtract numbers. After the result is displayed on the screen, the program will wait for you to input your own answer (two hexadecimal digits) to the AND operation. If it is correct then the program returns from the TEST routine and the program begins again at AGAIN. If your answer is not correct, then you will continue to input hexadecimal numbers until you obtain the correct answer. Run the program listed in Step *b* and make sure it operates as advertised.

d. Use the program to AND the following pairs of numbers: (00, FF), (00, 7F), (00, 37). What do you conclude is the result of ANDing a number with $00?

e. Use the program to AND the following pairs of hexadecimal numbers: (FF, 7F), (FF, 30), (FF, 55). What do you conclude is the result of ANDing a number with $FF?

f. Here are some *mask* bytes: $F0, $0F, $80, $40, $20, $04. What bits will they mask (or clear) when ANDed with another byte? You can use a test byte of $FF and the CAL program to check your answers.

g. How would you clear bit zero of a memory location? Bit one? Bit two? Bit three?

Exercise 4—2

a. With the CAL program loaded and the program in Step *b* of Exercise 4–1 loaded, change the byte at location $1211 (the AND op code) to $05. What instruction will be demonstrated with this op code?

b. Use these programs to ORA the following pairs of hexadecimal numbers: (00, F0), (00, 0F), (00, 55). What is the effect of ORing a number with $00? Can you write a theorem to represent this result?

(The theorem may be expressed as A + $00 = A.)

c. What will be the result of ORing a number with $FF? Try some problems to convince yourself. Can you express this result with a theorem?

(The theorem is A + $FF = $FF.)

d. What number would you pick for an OR operation if you wish to set bit seven of another number? Bit six? Bit one? Bit zero? Use the CAL program to test your hypothesis. Use $00 for the test byte to see what bits you are setting.

e. Suppose you OR a number with its complement. What do you expect for a result? Try these numbers in the CAL program: (7F, 80), (33, CC), (A1, 5E), (EE, 11)? Write a theorem to describe your results.

(The theorem is A + $\bar{A}$ = $FF.)

Exercise 4—3

a. Change the op code in the program in Step *b* of Exercise 4–1 so that an EOR instruction will be demonstrated.

b. As in the previous exercises, use the program to operate on these pairs of numbers: ($FF, $00), ($FF, $55), ($FF, $C8), ($FF, $81). What do you observe is the result of EORing a number with $FF?

(You should find that A $\oplus$ $FF = $\bar{A}$.)

c. What do you get when you EOR a number with its complement? Try these numbers: ($C3, $3C), ($44, $BB), ($A5, $5A), ($82, $7D). Can you write a theorem to describe your results?

(The theorem is A $\oplus$ $\bar{A}$ = $00.)

d. Use pencil and paper and the demonstration program to

demonstrate that $FF - A = \$FF \oplus A$. You can also use the Apple II monitor to check the subtractions.

e. Here is another theorem to demonstrate: $A - B = A + \bar{B} + 1$. In this theorem the minus sign means a subtraction and the plus sign means an addition. Use the demonstration program to find $\bar{B}$ by EORing B with \$FF. Then use the Apple monitor to perform the additions and the subtractions. Try these numbers where the first is A and the second is B: (\$7F, \$33), (\$63, \$2D), (\$EC, \$E3).

Exercise 4—4

a. Load the program in Example 4–12. Run it. Does it do what it was intended to do?

b. Load the program in Example 4–14. Connect a switch to the PB0 input on the game i/o connector. Refer to Fig. 3–10 for a diagram of the switch connection. Does this program do what it was intended to do? What happens when you change the switch setting? Does it detect both positive and negative transitions?

Exercise 4—5

a. Load the CAL program from Chart 4–1.

b. Load the program listed below. Its purpose is to demonstrate the rotate and shift instructions.

```
121B:20 58 FC   10          JSR   HOME      ;HOME THE CURSOR:
                                              CLEAR SCREEN.
121E:20 00 11   11          JSR   RDBYTE    ;GET A 2-DIGIT HEXADECIMAL
                                              NUMBER.
1221:18         12          CLC             ;CLEAR THE CARRY BEFORE
                                              STARTING.
1222:20 29 11   13 AGAIN    JSR   DISPLAY   ;DISPLAY IT.
                14 ***************************

1225:0A         16          ASL   A         ;SHIFT OR ROTATE IT.

                18 ***************************
1226:2C 00 C0   19 WAIT     BIT   $C000     ;"PRESS ANY KEY TO
                                              CONTINE" ROUTINE.
1229:10 FB      20          BPL   WAIT      ;WAIT FOR KEYSTROKE.
122B:8D 10 C0   21          STA   $C010     ;CLEAR FLIP-FLOP.
122E:30 F2      22          BMI   AGAIN
```

c. The program listed in Step b will demonstrate the ASL instruction using several of the routines in the CAL program. With it a number is entered on the keyboard, and this number is displayed, in binary, on the screen. Each time a key is pressed, the ASL instruction is executed and the results can be observed on the screen.

d. Execute the program listed in Step *b.* Enter a $01 on the keyboard when the flashing cursor appears in the upper left-hand corner. You should observe that the contents of the accumulator are displayed in binary on the screen; that is, a 0000 0001 appears on the screen, and the carry flag contains a logic 0. The carry flag is displayed just to the left of the number in the accumulator.

e. Now press any key to continue. What do you observe?

(The logic 1 is shifted from bit zero to bit one, exactly what would be expected from an ASL A instruction.)

f. Continue pressing keys. Describe what happens. What happens after the logic 1 gets in the carry flag and then a key is pressed? Why?

g. Start the program over and enter another number. Experiment with the program until you have a good understanding of the ASL instruction.

Exercise 4–6

a. In Exercise 4–5 replace the ASL A instruction on line 16 with an ROL A instruction. Run the program.

b. Enter a $01 on the keyboard. You should observe that a logic 1 appears in the bit zero location on the display.

c. Continue to press a key on the keyboard until you understand the difference between the ASL and the ROL instructions. Explain in your own words how bits zero and seven are altered by an ROL instruction and an ASL instruction.

d. Replace the ASL A instruction on line 16 with an LSR A instruction in Exercise 4–5. Run the program.

e. Enter a $80 from the keyboard, and press any key. Describe what happens and explain your result. Experiment with other numbers until you are sure you understand the LSR instruction, then try the same program with an ROR instruction instead of the LSR instruction.

Exercise 4–7

a. Load the program in Example 4–22. Load location $01 with the number $0F. That is, place the number $0F in the location symbolized by MEMORY. Execute the program, then examine location MEMORY to see if the low-order nibble was shifted into the high-order nibble.

b. Load the program in Example 4–23. Put one number in location LOC1 and a different number in LOC2. Execute the program and examine these two locations to make sure the program works as it is intended to work.

Exercise 4–8

Here are some programming problems you may want to try:

- Use the LSR and ROR instructions to rotate and shift a number from one location to another.
- Write a program that detects (and counts) positive pulses.
- Write a program that moves the high-order nibble in a memory location into the low-order nibble, leaving logic 0s in the high-order nibble.
- Write a program that combines the high-order nibble in location A with the low-order nibble in location B and stores the result in location C.
- Write a program that clears bit seven of a location symbolized by CODE. Write a program that sets bit seven of a location symbolized by EDOC.
- Here is a very challenging problem. Write a program to move a dot horizontally across the high-resolution graphics (hires) screen. Insert a delay loop between each shift of the dot so that you can see it move.

CHAPTER 5

Arithmetic Operations

OBJECTIVES

At the completion of this chapter you should be able to:

- Use the following instructions: ADC, SBC, CMP, CPX, CPY, CLC, SEC, CLD, SED, and CLV.
- Add, subtract, multiply, and divide binary numbers.
- Understand multibyte arithmetic.

INTRODUCTION

To someone who is either unfamiliar with microprocessors or has used only high-level languages for programming, one of the most surprising facts is that the 6502 can only add and subtract. It is certainly not a calculator chip. All multiplication and division operations must be programmed by the user. Some microprocessors that have recently appeared on the market incorporate multiply and divide instructions in their instruction sets. Nevertheless, the mathematical operations normally done by an electronic calculator require extensive programming. The large amount of programming involved in arithmetic, trigonometric, logarithmic, and exponential operations is one of the reasons why the BASIC interpreter in your Apple II requires about 8000 bytes of memory. The purpose of this chapter is to introduce you to the fundamental arithmetic operations.

FLAG MODIFICATION INSTRUCTIONS

The processor status register (P register) and its flags were introduced in Chapter 3. Two of its flags will be of particular interest to us in this chapter on arithmetic operations. These flags are the carry flag and the decimal mode flag, and their functions will become obvious as the chapter develops. The overflow flag is also used in performing signed number arithmetic, a topic we reserve for Chapter 8. In any case, the carry flag (C), the decimal flag (D), and the overflow flag (V) must usually be set or cleared *before* an arithmetic operation is begun. The Z and N flags will also be used, but their values only become significant *after* a certain operation is performed.

The instructions that set or clear the C, D, and V flags are summarized in Table 5–1. They are all single-byte instructions that use the *implied* addressing mode because their only effect is to change flags in the P register. The circumstances under which these instructions are used will become apparent from the examples and programs, although any intuitive idea you may have about the meaning of the carry flag is very likely correct.

Table 5–1. Descriptions of the CLC, SEC, CLD, SED, and CLV Instructions

Mnemonic	Operation	Logical Description
CLC	Clear the carry flag	V D C P — 0
SEC	Set the carry flag	V D C P — 1
CLD	Clear the decimal mode flag	V D C P — 0
SED	Set the decimal mode flag	V D C P — 1
CLV	Clear the overflow flag	V D C P — 0

THE ADC INSTRUCTION

The truth table in Table 5–2 summarizes the binary addition operation for two single-bit numbers. The sum produces a result, R, and a carry, C. Carry C is zero unless two binary 1s were added. If 8-bit operations are being carried out, as in the case of the 6502, then the carry must be added to the next most significant bit. Refer to Fig. 5–1 for a pictorial representation of an 8-bit addition that demonstrates this carry concept. Observe in particular that *the carry from the seventh bit appears in the carry flag.* If there is a carry from the bit seven, then the C flag in the P register is set. Otherwise it is cleared.

Table 5-2. Truth Table for Binary Addition (R is result, C is Carry)

A	B	R	C	A + B = R	
0	0	0	0	0 + 0 = 0	[C] = 0
0	1	1	0	0 + 1 = 1	[C] = 0
1	0	1	0	1 + 0 = 1	[C] = 0
1	1	0	1	1 + 1 = 0	[C] = 1

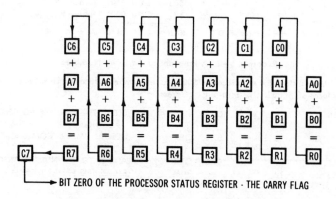

BIT ZERO OF THE PROCESSOR STATUS REGISTER - THE CARRY FLAG

Fig. 5-1. Demonstration of an 8-bit addition.

The ADC (add with carry) instruction is defined as follows:

- The ADC instruction *adds* the operand of the instruction, the number in the accumulator, and the carry flag. The result is stored in the accumulator. The carry flag is added to the least significant bit.
- Symbolically, the ADC instruction is written A + M + C→A, where A and M contain 8-bit numbers, but C is a 1-bit number.
- If the result of the operation exceeds $FF (= 255_{10}), then the carry flag is set; otherwise it is cleared.
- The Z, N, and V flags are also modified by the ADC instruction.

The process of adding two binary numbers is illustrated in Example 5-1. The content of the carry flag before the operation is indicated on the first line, while the content of the carry flag after the operation is indicated to the left of the result.

A program to demonstrate a simple addition in assembly language is given in Example 5-2. Observe that the carry flag was cleared by the first instruction *before* performing the addition. Zero-page addressing was used for the ADC instruction in

Example 5–2. We will use this program in conjunction with an input and display program to provide additional practice in binary addition when we reach the exercises at the end of the chapter.

Example 5–1. Adding Two Binary Numbers

Add $85 and $21. Assume the carry flag is clear.

		0	previous carry
+	$85 = 1000 0101		memory M
+	$21 = 0010 0001		accumulator A
new carry = 0	$A6 = 1010 0110		A + M + C

Example 5–2. A Program to Add Two Numbers

Object: Add the number in location $0001 to the number in location $0002 and store the sum in location $0003. Use zero-page addressing.

1230:18	7	CLC		;CLEAR THE CARRY FLAG BEFORE ADDING.
1231:A5 01	8	LDA	OPA	;GET A NUMBER FROM LOCATION OPA.
1233:65 02	9	ADC	OPB	;ADD IT TO THE NUMBER IN OPB.
1235:85 03	10	STA	SUM	;STORE THE RESULT IN SUM.
1237:00	11	BRK		

Example 5–3 introduces a new complication. The answer to the problem posed in Example 5–3 should be $153, not $53. The fact that the carry flag is set indicates that the answer exceeded the range of numbers that can be represented by eight bits. More than one byte is necessary to represent the answer. All is not lost, however, because the carry bit can be added to a second byte. The program in Example 5–4 illustrates this. It is a simple extension of the program in Example 5–2. Study it carefully because it introduces at least two new concepts. The decimal mode flag was cleared before performing any addition to make sure the processor adds the numbers as binary numbers. Decimal addition will be discussed shortly, but for the time being we want the processor in the binary mode rather than the decimal mode. Also notice that the immediate addressing mode was used for the ADC instruction in line 14. After executing the program you will find the result of any carry from the first addition in the location SUMHI. Try this program with the numbers in Example 5–3. That is, load ADDEND1 with $93 and ADDEND2 with $C0. After executing the program you will find the low byte of the sum, $53 in SUMLO, and the carry from this sum, $01, in location SUMHI.

How would you add the numbers $1234 and $05D2? This is shown in Example 5–5. Clearly each number needs two bytes to represent it, and the answer will also be represented by two bytes. In the event that the numbers to be added require more than one byte to represent them, or if the answer cannot be represented with a single byte, then multiple-byte arithmetic is required. When two bytes are used to represent the numbers involved in an arithmetic operation, we call this *double-precision arithmetic*. If three bytes are used to represent the numbers, then we are using *triple-precision arithmetic*.

A program to perform double-precision addition is given in Example 5–6. Notice how it differs from the program in Exam-

Example 5–3. Adding Two Binary Numbers When the Sum Exceeds $FF

Add $93 and $C0. Assume the carry flag is clear.

$$
\begin{array}{rll}
 & & 0 \quad \text{C} \\
+ & \$93 = 1001\ 0011 & \text{M} \\
+ & \$C0 = 1100\ 0000 & \text{A} \\
\hline
\text{new carry} = 1 & \$53 = 0101\ 0011 & \text{A} + \text{M} + \text{C}
\end{array}
$$

Example 5–4. A Program to Add Two Binary Numbers and Save the Carry Flag

Object: Add the numbers stored in two zero-page locations and save the carry from this addition in another location.

1238:D8	8	CLD		;CLEAR THE DECIMAL MODE FLAG.
1239:18	9	CLC		;CLEAR THE CARRY FLAG.
123A:A5 01	10	LDA	ADDEND1	;GET THE FIRST NUMBER.
123C:65 02	11	ADC	ADDEND2	;ADD IT TO THE SECOND.
123E:85 03	12	STA	SUMLO	;STORE IT HERE.
1240:A9 00	13	LDA	#00	;CLEAR THE ACCUMULATOR.
1242:69 00	14	ADC	#00	;ADD: $00 + $00 + C; THAT IS, ADD C.
1244:85 04	15	STA	SUMHI	;STORE RESULT IN SUMHI.
1246:00	16	BRK		

Example 5–5. Adding Two-Byte Numbers

Add $1234 and $05D2. Assume the carry flag is clear.

$$
\begin{array}{rll}
 & & 0 \quad \text{C} \\
\text{first sum} \left\{ + \right. & \$D2 = 1101\ 0010 & \text{M} \\
\left. + \right. & \$34 = 0011\ 0100 & \text{A} \\
\hline
\text{new carry} = 1 & \$06 = 000\ 0110 & \text{A} + \text{M} + \text{C}
\end{array}
$$

$$
\begin{array}{rll}
 & & 1 \quad \text{C} \\
+ & \$05 = 0000\ 0101 & \text{M} \\
+ & \$12 = 0001\ 0010 & \text{A} \\
\hline
\text{new carry} = 0 & \$18 = 0001\ 1000 & \text{A} + \text{M} + \text{C}
\end{array}
\right\} \text{second sum}
$$

Then $1234 + $05D2 = $1806.

Example 5–6. A Double-Precision Addition Program

Object: Write a program that adds double-precision numbers.

```
1247:18      10      CLC                 ;CLEAR THE CARRY FLAG.
1248:A5 01   11      LDA  ADD1LO         ;GET LSB OF #1.
124A:65 03   12      ADC  ADD2LO         ;ADD TO LSB OF #2.
124C:85 05   13      STA  SUMLO          ;RESULT IS LSB OF SUM.
124E:A5 04   14      LDA  ADD1HI         ;GET MSB OF #1.
1250:65 02   15      ADC  ADD2HI         ;ADD TO MSB OF #2.
1252:85 06   16      STA  SUMHI          ;RESULT IS MSB OF SUM.
1254:00      17      BRK
```

ple 5–4, and observe that the carry flag *is not* cleared after the first addition because we want to include any carry from the first addition in the second addition. The CLD instruction was omitted from the program in Example 5–6 because the same program can be used in either the binary mode or the decimal mode. It is up to the user to select the desired mode with either a CLD or an SED instruction. Thus far we have assumed that we are doing binary rather than decimal additions in all of the examples. A diagram of a triple-precision or 3-byte sum is shown in Fig. 5–2. We leave the implementation of this sum as an exercise.

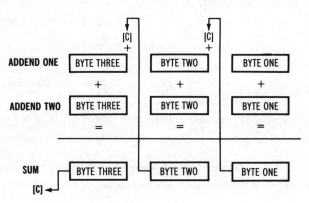

Fig. 5–2. A diagram of a triple-precision sum.

THE SBC INSTRUCTION

The SBC instruction is summarized as follows:

- The SBC instruction *subtracts* the operand from the number in the accumulator. The *complement* of the carry flag is also subtracted from the number in the accumulator. The result, or difference, is placed in the accumulator.

- Symbolically the SBC instruction is expressed as A − M − C̄→A.
- If the result of the subtraction is less than zero, then the carry flag is cleared; otherwise it is set.
- The Z, N, and V flags are also modified when the SBC instruction is executed.

As the summary just given indicates, the carry flag is used not only for performing addition operations, but it is also used when performing subtraction. In the case of subtraction the carry flag is used to *borrow* when it is necessary. We may call the *complement* of the carry flag a borrow flag. In other words:

- C = 1, C̄ = 0 produces *no* borrow. The carry flag is normally set with an SEC instruction before subtraction begins.
- C = 0, C̄ = 1 produces a borrow.
- C will be set whenever a smaller number is subtracted from a larger number.
- C will be cleared whenever a larger number is subtracted from a smaller number, indicating the necessity for a borrow.

Examples 5–7 and 5–8 illustrate these concepts.

A simple program to perform the same subtraction that is illustrated in Example 5–7 is given in Example 5–9. The program subtracts $67 from $8D and outputs the result to the video monitor screen using the monitor subroutine PRBYTE, which prints a byte. The decimal mode flag was cleared before beginning the arithmetic operation to ensure that the processor was operating in the binary mode. To ensure that no borrow would occur with the subtraction, the carry flag was set prior to performing the subtraction. Of course, the program in Example 5–9 is not very useful since it only works for the two numbers supplied in the program (immediate addressing). To make it more general you could modify the instructions on lines 7 and 8 to reference either locations in zero-page (zero-page addressing) or some other memory location (absolute addressing). The exercises at the end of the chapter will provide you with additional practice.

Example 5–7. Subtracting Two Binary Numbers

Subtract $67 from $8D. Assume the carry flag is set: C̄ = 0.

$$\begin{array}{rllll}
 & \$8D & = & 1000\ 1101 & A \\
- & \$67 & = & 0110\ 0111 & M \\
- & & & 0 & C \\
\hline
 & \$26 & = & 0010\ 0110 & A - M - \bar{C}
\end{array}$$

new carry = 1
C = 0

Example 5–8. Subtracting a Larger Number from a Smaller Number

Subtract $8D from $67. Assume the carry flag is set: $\overline{C} = 0$.

$$\$67 = 0110\ 0111 \quad A$$
$$-\ \$8D = 1000\ 1101 \quad M$$
$$-\quad\quad\quad\quad\ \ 0 \quad \overline{C}$$

$$\text{new carry} = 0 \quad \$DA = 1101\ 1010 \quad A - M - \overline{C}$$
$$\overline{C} = 1$$

Example 5–9. A Program to Subtract Two Numbers

Object: Subtract $67 from $8D.

1255:D8	5	CLD		;OPERATE IN BINARY, NOT DECIMAL.
1256:38	6	SEC		;SET THE CARRY BEFORE SUBTRACTING.
1257:A9 8D	7	LDA	#$8D	;PUT $8D INTO THE ACCUMULATOR.
1259:E9 67	8	SBC	#$67	;SUBTRACT $67 FROM $8D.
125B:20 DA FD	9	JSR	PRBYTE	;OUTPUT THE RESULT TO THE SCREEN.
125E:00	10	BRK		

Double-precision subtraction is similar to double-precision addition, except the carry flag is *set* before the first subtraction. Example 5–10 illustrates a double-precision subtraction routine.

Example 5–10. A Double-Precision Subtraction Routine

Object: Write a program to subtract 2-byte numbers.

1260:38	10	SEC		;CLEAR THE BORROW FLAG.
1261:AD 01 10	11	LDA	MINLO	;GET THE LSB OF THE MINUEND.
1264:ED 03 10	12	SBC	SBTLO	;SUBTRACT LSB OF THE SUBTRAHEND.
1267:8D 05 10	13	STA	DIFFLO	;STORE THE LSB OF THE DIFFERENCE.
126A:AD 02 10	14	LDA	MINHI	;GET THE MSB OF THE MINUEND.
126D:ED 04 10	15	SBC	SBTHI	;SUBTRACT MSB OF THE SUBTRAHEND.
1270:8D 06 10	16	STA	DIFFHI	;STORE THE MSB OF THE DIFFERENCE.
1273:00	17	BRK		

DECIMAL MODE ARITHMETIC

The 6502 is also capable of adding and subtracting decimal (base-10) numbers when it is operated in the *decimal mode*. The decimal mode is set by executing an SED instruction which sets the decimal mode flag. The decimal mode is cleared by executing a CLD instruction. In the decimal mode each digit

Table 5–3. Representing Decimal Numbers With Binary Coded Decimal

Decimal Digit	BCD Representation
0	0000
1	0001
2	0010
3	0011
4	0100
5	0101
6	0110
7	0111
8	1000
9	1001

of a number is represented by four bits according to the conversion scheme shown in Table 5–3. Using four bits to represent a base-10 digit is commonly referred to as *binary coded decimal*, or *bcd*. Since each decimal digit requires four bits and we are dealing with 8-bit numbers, a single byte of data represents *two* decimal digits. Thus the numbers 0–99 may be represented by a single byte. Two-byte numbers can represent the decimal numbers between 0 and 9999. For example, 43 is represented by 0100 0011 and 9876 is represented by two bytes, 1001 1000 and 0111 0110.

To summarize decimal mode arithmetic (addition and subtraction):

- The D flag must be set prior to the operation by using an SED instruction.
- The conversion scheme in Table 5–3 is used to represent the numbers.
- The carry flag is set if a single-byte sum exceeds 99; otherwise it is cleared.
- The carry flag is cleared if a larger number is subtracted from a smaller number.

It should be clear from the last two points that the carry flag operates in exactly the same way for decimal mode addition and subtraction as it does in binary arithmetic. It is set if the sum exceeds 99 and it is cleared if the difference is less than zero, and it is useful in performing multiple-precision operations. One minor point: the Z flag is invalid in the decimal mode.

All of the programs that are listed in this chapter can be adapted to perform addition and subtraction in the decimal mode by simply adding an SED (set the decimal mode) before doing the arithmetic operations. Example 5–11 illustrates a simple decimal mode addition program. Since the sum exceeds

99 in this case, the carry will be set after the program is executed.

Example 5–11. Adding Numbers in the Decimal Mode

Object: Add 83 and 35.

1274:F8	4	SED		;SET THE DECIMAL MODE FLAG.
1275:18	5	CLC		;CLEAR THE CARRY FLAG.
1276:A9 83	6	LDA	#83	;LOAD A WITH THE DECIMAL NUMBER 83.
1278:69 35	7	ADC	#35	;ADD THE DECIMAL NUMBER 35.
127A:8D 7F 03	8	STA	HERE	;STORE THE RESULT HERE.
127D:00	9	BRK		

We conclude this section by pointing out that the SED and CLD instructions affect *only* the way in which the ADC and the SBC instructions are performed. No other instructions are affected by these flags.

THE COMPARISON INSTRUCTIONS

Closely related to the subtraction instruction are the comparison instructions CMP, CPX, and CPY. These instructions are very similar, and their function is to test to see if one number is *greater than, equal to,* or *less than* another number. Their value should be obvious to anyone who has written a computer program.

The comparison instructions work by *performing a subtraction;* that is, the operand of the instruction is subtracted *from* a number in *a 6502 register.* In the case of the CMP instruction the 6502 register is the accumulator. In the case of the CPX and the CPY instructions the registers involved are the X register and the Y register, respectively. Note that the 6502 register always contains the *minuend* of the subtraction operation, while some location in memory contains the *subtrahend.* Such a subtraction has three possible consequences:

- If the number in the register is *larger* than the operand, the carry flag is set and the Z flag is cleared.
- If the number in the register is *equal* to the operand, the Z flag is set and the carry flag is set.
- If the number in the register is *less* than the operand, the carry flag is cleared and the Z flag is cleared.

Just as in the case of the BIT instruction, the *only register* modified by a comparison instruction is the processor status register. The numbers in the registers and the memory location referenced by a comparison instruction are not affected.

We will describe the comparison instruction CMP in detail, and the other two (CPX and CPY) by analogy. Here is the definition of CMP:

- CMP means compare the number in the accumulator with a number in memory (the operand).
- If [A] ≥ [M], then C is set; otherwise it is cleared.
- If [A] = [M], then Z is set; otherwise it is cleared.

(Recall that the brackets ([ ]) are read "the contents of . . .") The CPX and CPY instructions are identical with the CMP instruction in all respects except that they compare the numbers in the X and Y registers, respectively, with their operands. Example 5-12 illustrates a CMP operation; Example 5-13 illustrates a CPX operation.

You will see an example of the use of a comparison instruction later in this chapter when we discuss a program to divide two 8-bit numbers. We turn next to multiplication.

Example 5-12. Illustration of a CMP Operation

Assume $CF is in the accumulator and $3E is the operand in memory, M. Which flags will be set by the CMP instruction?

Solution: Since $CF > $3E, the C flag will be set and the Z flag will be cleared. Since the logical expression for the CMP operation is A − M, and since $CF − $3E = $91, the result has a binary 1 in bit seven, so the N flag will also be set. This latter point is not of great interest except when performing operations with signed numbers.

Example 5-13. Illustration of a CPX Operation

Assume the X register contains $80 and M contains $A0. Which flags will be modified by the CPX instruction?

Solution: Since $80 < $A0, the C flag will be cleared and the Z flag will be cleared. Since $80 − $A0 = $E0, the subtraction produces a binary 1 in bit seven; therefore the N flag will be set. In general, the N flag is of little interest when doing comparisons.

A 4-BIT MULTIPLICATION PROGRAM

If there is a turning point in this book, it is here. Most of our programs and program segments thus far have consisted of only a few lines. Of course, that situation cannot last, and since you have mastered most of the 6502 instruction set, the programs will begin to become more complex. The compensation for working with more complex concepts and programs is the fact that they become more meaningful and useful. With some effort toward understanding the programs that follow, you will make the transition between the simple programs we have considered so far and the more complex routines that follow, and become a fine programmer in the process.

We begin simply by considering a program to multiply two 4-bit numbers. Many *algorithms* (an algorithm is a computational *procedure* to accomplish a specific objective) are discovered by first doing the task with pencil and paper and then converting the steps into computer language. Multiplication is no exception. There is a close structural similarity between a 6502 assembly language program and your recollection of elementary decimal multiplication done with pencil and paper. Thus we begin with a simple example of binary multiplication shown in Example 5–14.

Example 5–14. A 4-Bit Binary Multiplication Calculator

Multiply $A by $9.

$A	=	1010	multiplicand
$9	=	1001	multiplier
$5A		1010	
		0000	
		0000	partial products
		1010	
$5A	=	1011010	product

Several important observations can be made by examining the work shown in Example 5–14. First you might guess that the product of two 4-bit numbers will never exceed an 8-bit number. That is, in fact, the case. The largest number than can be represented by four bits is $F = 15. The largest product is, therefore, $15 \cdot 15 = 225$. Since 225 is less than 255, the largest 8-bit number, a product of two 4-bit numbers, will always fit into an 8-bit memory location.

Another important observation to make in the calculation of Example 5–14 is that the multiplicand appears *once* in the set of partial products for each *binary 1* in the multiplier. This suggests a procedure of *shifting* the multiplier one bit at a time into the carry flag. If the carry flag is set after such a shift, then an *appropriate version* of the multiplicand will be added. If the carry flag is clear, no addition is necessary.

What is the appropriate version of the multiplicand that should be added? Notice in the partial products that the multiplicand is *shifted to the left* after forming the previous partial product. The appearance of the left-shifted multiplicands suggests using the ASL (arithmetic shift left) instruction.

Taken collectively, these observations suggest an algorithm for performing multiplication with a computer program.

1. Clear the memory location or register to be used for the product.
2. Shift the *multiplier right* into the carry flag.

3. Is the carry flag clear? Yes, go to 5. No, go to 4.
4. Add the multiplicand to the product.
5. Is the multiplier zero? Yes, go to 7. No, go to 6.
6. Shift the *multiplicand left*; go to 2.
7. Quit.

A flowchart is shown in Fig. 5–3, and a 4-bit multiplication program is given in Example 5–15. The multiplication program is a subroutine.

In the multiplication subroutine the multiplicand is symbolized by MCND and the multiplier by MLTP. The accumulator is used to collect the partial products until the total product is obtained. The subroutine returns with the product in the accumulator. Study the subroutine in connection with the algorithm listed above and the flowchart in Fig. 5–3. How does the program know when it is finished? If Step 2 in the algorithm clears the carry and sets the Z flag, then clearly there are no more binary 1s in the multiplier, so the program branches to the RTS instruction. The BNE RPEAT instruction is a subtle way to force a jump back to the LSR MLTP instruction, since it is clear that it will take five or more shifts to clear the multiplicand compared to no more than five shifts to clear the multiplier.

Example 5–15. A 4-Bit Multiplication Program

Object: Write a routine that multiplies one 4-bit number by another and returns the product in the accumulator.

1280:D8	7	MULTPLY	CLD		;CLEAR THE DECIMAL MODE.
1281:A9 00	8		LDA	#00	;CLEAR THE PRODUCT LOCATION, A.
1283:46 01	9	RPEAT	LSR	MLTP	;SHIFT MULTIPLIER TO CHECK FOR ZERO
1285:90 03	10		BCC	ARND	;OR ONE IN THE CARRY FLAG.
1287:18	11		CLC		;IF C=1, THEN ADD MULTIPLICAND.
1288:65 02	12		ADC	MCND	;ADD MULTIPLICAND.
128A:F0 04	13	ARND	BEQ	QUIT	;MLTP HAS BEEN SHIFTED TO ZERO.
128C:06 02	14		ASL	MCND	;SHIFT MULTIPLICAND.
128E:D0 F3	15		BNE	RPEAT	;GET ANOTHER PARTIAL PRODUCT.
1290:60	16	QUIT	RTS		;THAT'S ALL.

Another observation may be made from the problem in Example 5–14, namely that shifting the multiplicand *left* after each addition is equivalent to shifting the partial product *right* after each addition. In the 8-bit multiplication program described in the next section, it is more convenient to leave the multiplicand stationary and let the partial product move. In both the 4-bit multiplication program and the 8-bit multiplication program which follows, the partial products are summed as

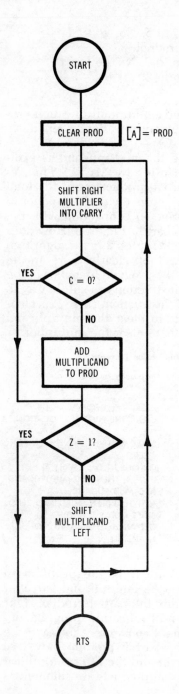

Fig. 5-3. Flowchart of the 4-bit multiplication subroutine.

116

they are calculated. This is the most significant difference between the programs and the pencil and paper calculation in Example 5-14, where the *sum* of all the partial products is calculated *after* all the partial products have been obtained.

Do not fail to note the use of the shift instruction on line 9, the CLC instruction on line 11, and the ADC instruction on line 12. You are just beginning to see how some of these instructions are used in more complex programs. Be sure to study the flowchart in Fig. 5-3.

AN 8-BIT MULTIPLICATION PROGRAM

An 8-bit multiplication program is listed in Example 5-16. Since multiplying two 8-bit numbers can produce a number as large as 16 bits, two locations (PRODLO and PRODHI) are used to store the answer. In this program you should observe how the rotate instructions are used to rotate the number in the accumulator, which contains the most significant byte of the sum of the partial products, into the location PRODLO, which contains the least significant byte of the sum of the partial products. Do you recall doing a similar program in Example 4-23? In any case the 8-bit program should be simple to understand since you have mastered the 4-bit program. The basic difference is that the partial products are shifted right while the multiplicand is left stationary.

Example 5-16. An 8-Bit Multiplication Program

Object: Write a program that multiplies two 8-bit numbers and stores the 16-bit result.

1290:A2 08	8		LDX	#08	;X SERVES AS A BIT COUNTER.
1292:A9 00	9		LDA	#00	;CLEAR THE MSB OF THE PRODUCT.
1294:46 01	10	BR1	LSR	MLTP	;SHIFT MULTIPLIER INTO CARRY.
1296:90 03	11		BCC	BR2	;IF C=0, THEN SKIP ADDITION.
1298:18	12		CLC		;CLEAR CARRY FOR ADDITION.
1299:65 02	13		ADC	MCND	;COLLECT THE SUM OF THE PRODUCTS
129B:6A	14	BR2	ROR	A	;IN THE ACCUMULATOR. ROTATE IT
129C:66 03	15		ROR	PRODLO	;INTO LSB OF THE PRODUCT.
129E:CA	16		DEX		;DECREMENT THE BIT COUNTER
129F:D0 F3	17		BNE	BR1	;UNTIL 8 BITS HAVE BEEN COUNTED.
12A1:85 04	18		STA	PRODHI	;STORE MSB IN PRODHI.
12A3:60	19		RTS		

DIVISION

Just as in the case of multiplication, a program to perform a division of one 8-bit binary number by another is developed by first studying binary division with pencil and paper. It will also help to recall decimal division from the pre–electronic-calculator era. Example 5–17 illustrates one case as an aid to our thinking.

Example 5–17. Illustration of a Binary Division Problem

Divide $FA by $05, where $FA = 1111 1010 and $05 = 0000 0101.

```
              0011 0010
       101   1111 1010
             101
              101
              101
              ‾‾‾‾
                101
                101
                ‾‾‾
                  0
```

Refer to Example 5–17 and see first of all that the leading zeros of the divisor are not considered; that is, 0000 0101 is treated as 101. Next observe that the divisor is compared with the most significant bit of the dividend. Since the divisor, 101, is larger than the most significant bit, a 0 is placed in the quotient, above this bit of the dividend. The divisor is then compared to the *two* most significant bits of the dividend. The divisor is still larger, so another zero is placed in the quotient. The divisor is then compared with the *three* most significant bits. This time the divisor is equal to or less than this much of the dividend, so a subtraction is performed, and a 1 is placed in the quotient above the third most significant bit.

We could do this much of the division on a computer by shifting the dividend left into another location, call it the partial dividend, and comparing the partial dividend to the divisor. If it is equal to or greater than the divisor, a 1 is placed in the quotient, otherwise a 0 is placed in the quotient. Also, if it is equal to or greater than the divisor, then the divisor is subtracted from the partial dividend, and the process begins over, until all eight bits have been shifted out of the dividend. These observations form the basis for our algorithm:

1. Set up a counter to count eight bits.
2. Clear a location for the partial dividend.
3. Shift the dividend left into the partial dividend.
4. Is the divisor greater than the partial dividend? Yes, go to 6. No, go to 5.
5. Subtract the divisor from the partial dividend, and set the carry.
6. Rotate the carry into the quotient.
7. Decrement the counter. Go to 3 if it is not zero; otherwise quit.

Fortuitously, the comparison instruction that implements Step 4 in the algorithm modifies the carry flag so it sets correctly for either Step 5 or 6. Also, it is possible to use the same location for the quotient that is used for the dividend. As the dividend is rotated left into the partial dividend, the quotient is rotated left into the dividend. In fact, Step 6 in the algorithm is used to shift the dividend left and the carry into the quotient, so that in the actual program the loop returns to Step 4 rather than Step 3.

A program to divide two 8-bit numbers is given in Example 5–18. Again, it is designed as a subroutine. Note how each of the steps in the algorithm is accomplished with 6502 assembly language. The accumulator is used to hold the partial dividend, and the location DIVD is used to hold both the dividend and the quotient. The program begins with the divisor in location DVSOR and it returns with the quotient $0002. The remainder is in the accumulator. In this program you should note in particular the use of a comparison instruction (CMP DVSOR) which compares the partial dividend with the divisor to see which is larger.

Example 5–18. A Program to Divide Two 8-Bit Numbers

Object: Divide one 8-bit number by another. Store the quotient in memory, and return from the subroutine with the remainder in the accumulator.

12A4:D8	6	DIVIDE	CLD	;CLEAR THE DECIMAL MODE.
12A5:A9 00	7		LDA #00	;CLEAR THE PARTIAL DIVIDEND.
12A7:A2 08	8		LDX #08	;X IS A BIT COUNTER.
12A9:06 02	9		ASL DIVD	;SHIFT DIVD INTO CARRY,
12AB:2A	10	HERE	ROL A	;AND CARRY INTO PARTIAL DIVIDEND.
12AC:C5 01	11		CMP DVSOR	;COMPARE IT WITH THE DIVISOR.
12AE:90 02	12		BCC PAST	;DO NOT SUBTRACT.
12B0:E5 01	13		SBC DVSOR	;SUBTRACT FROM PARTIAL DIVIDEND.
12B2:26 02	14	PAST	ROL DIVD	;ROTATE CARRY INTO QUOTIENT.
12B4:CA	15		DEX	;DECREMENT THE BIT COUNTER.
12B5:D0 F4	16		BNE HERE	;GO BACK FOR ANOTHER BIT.
12B7:60	17		RTS	

The arithmetic routines described in this chapter were designed to operate with whole numbers (the nonnegative integers). The multiplication and division routines have the additional restriction of being applicable only to 8-bit numbers. All of the routines, however, are easily modified for multiple-precision arithmetic when indexed addressing modes have been mastered. These modes are discussed in the next chapter. The extension of the routines to handle negative integers will be mentioned in Chapter 8.

ASCII-TO-HEXADECIMAL CONVERSION

Because it illustrates several of the concepts introduced in this chapter and in previous chapters, and because it is a useful routine, we conclude this chapter with a description of a program that converts a character code input from the Apple keyboard to a hexadecimal digit. Recall that pressing a key on the keyboard places a character code at the keyboard input port whose location is $C000. The character codes for letters and numbers were given in Table 1–2. In this case we are interested only in the character codes for the hexadecimal digits 0, 1, 2, . . . , A, B, C, D, E, and F. The character codes for these 16 characters are listed in Table 5–4. The first column is the symbol for the hexadecimal digit, the second column is the standard ASCII for the symbol on its left, and the last column is the code that appears at the Apple keyboard input port. It is the same as ASCII, but with bit seven at logic 1. The last column, therefore, represents the codes that are read at the input port, and our objective is to convert the character code to its corresponding hexadecimal digit and place it in a memory location.

Table 5–4. ASCII Representations of Hexadecimal Digits

Hexadecimal Digit	ASCII Representation (Hexadecimal)	Apple II ASCII (Hexadecimal)
0	$30	$B0
1	$31	$B1
2	$32	$B2
3	$33	$B3
4	$34	$B4
5	$35	$B5
6	$36	$B6
7	$37	$B7
8	$38	$B8
9	$39	$B9
A	$41	$C1
B	$42	$C2
C	$43	$C3
D	$44	$C4
E	$45	$C5
F	$46	$C6

Study the table for some time and you will begin to see a pattern emerge that will allow an easy conversion. The author arrived at the following algorithm to convert an Apple character code to a hexadecimal digit:

1. AND the character code with $7F to convert it to ASCII; that is, mask bit seven.
2. If the result of (1) is greater than or equal to $40 then the

character stands for a hexadecimal digit from $A to $F; branch to (4).

3. The result of (1) was less than $40, so the character stands for a hexadecimal digit between $0 and $9. It can be converted from a character code to a digit by masking the high-order nibble. AND with $0F and branch around (4).
4. To convert a character code for the digits $A to $F to the digit itself, subtract $37. (Try it, it works.)
5. Return with the digit in the accumulator.

The program to accomplish this is given in Example 5–19. Each step should be obvious from the preceding description of the algorithm. It is assumed that the character code is in the accumulator at the beginning of the routine. A subroutine call to our keyboard input routine in Example 3–6 would allow us to fetch a character code in the accumulator. The routine in Example 5–19 would convert the code to a hexadecimal digit.

Example 5–19. An ASCII-to-Hexadecimal Conversion Routine

Object: Convert a character code in the accumulator to a hexadecimal digit.

```
111C:29 7F    15        AND    #$7F    ;MASK BIT 7 OFF.
111E:C9 40    16        CMP    #$40    ;DIGIT OR LETTER?
1120:B0 04    17        BCS    ARND
1122:29 0F    18        AND    #$0F    ;DIGIT, MASK HI-NIBBLE.
1124:10 02    19        BPL    PAST    ;BRANCH PAST LETTER.
1126:E9 37    20 ARND   SBC    #$37    ;LETTER, SUBTRACT $37.
1128:60       21 PAST   RTS            ;RETURN WITH DIGIT IN A.
```

To make this routine more useful, suppose we wish to expand it to give us the capability of reading one byte of data and storing it. In other words, we wish to input *two* hexadecimal digits, the most significant digit first, and return with a byte of data in the accumulator. For bells and whistles (additional effects) we will also print the digits on the video monitor and output a carriage return.

Clearly we must first get a character code and convert it to hexadecimal with a variation of the routine in Example 5–19. The first digit that is input is the most significant digit. Therefore, before fetching the second digit, we should shift the first digit four bits to the left, putting it in the most significant place. Next we get another character code, convert it to hexadecimal, and combine it with the first, forming a complete byte of data. The two routines that accomplish this are given in Example 5–20. They are a portion of the computer assisted learning (CAL) program given in Appendix B. This program was used to demonstrate the instructions in the last chapter, and it will be used again in the exercises at the end of this chapter. In Example 5–20 be sure to observe how many of the instructions that have been introduced so far in this book are being used. This example makes an excellent illustration of a variety of programming techniques, and you should study it carefully. Example 5–20, in addition to being useful rather than contrived, illustrates the following instructions: AND, ORA, ASL, CMP, SBC, BCS, BPL, JSR, RTS, as well as simple LDA and STA instructions. Monitor subroutines are used to perform input and output functions.

Example 5–20. Routines to Input One Byte of Data

Object: Input two hexadecimal digits from the keyboard and return with the byte of data in the accumulator.

```
1100:            12 * SUBROUTINE RDBYTE

1100:20 16 11    14        JSR    ASHEX     ;GET NIBBLE.
1103:0A          15        ASL    A         ;SHIFT TO HIGH NIBBLE.
1104:0A          16        ASL    A
1105:0A          17        ASL    A
1106:0A          18        ASL    A
1107:85 00       19        STA    TEMP      ;STORE NIBBLE.
1109:20 16 11    20        JSR    ASHEX     ;GET THE SECOND NIBBLE.
110C:05 00       21        ORA    TEMP      ;COMBINE WITH FIRST NIBBLE.
110E:85 00       22        STA    TEMP      ;SAVE ENTIRE BYTE.
1110:20 8E FD    23        JSR    CROUT     ;OUTPUT A RETURN.
1113:A5 00       24        LDA    TEMP      ;GET BYTE BACK.
1115:60          25        RTS              ;RETURN.


1116:            27 * ASCII-TO-HEX ROUTINE

1116:20 0C FD    29 ASHEX  JSR    RDKEY     ;GET A CHARACTER.
1119:20 ED FD    30        JSR    COUT      ;DISPLAY IT.
111C:29 7F       31        AND    #$7F      ;MASK BIT 7 OFF.
111E:C9 40       32        CMP    #$40      ;DIGIT OR LETTER?
1120:B0 04       33        BCS    ARND
1122:29 0F       34        AND    #$0F      ;DIGIT, MASK HI-NIBBLE.
1124:10 02       35        BPL    PAST      ;BRANCH PAST LETTER.
1126:E9 37       36 ARND   SBC    #$37      :LETTER, SUBTRACT $37.
1128:60          37 PAST   RTS              ;RETURN WITH DIGIT IN A.
```

The algorithm for the routines in Example 5–20 follows:

1. Get a character code for a hexadecimal digit from the keyboard.
2. Display the character on the screen of the video monitor.
3. Convert the character code to its corresponding hexadecimal digit.
   a. AND the character code with $7F to convert it from Apple ASCII to standard ASCII.

b. If the previous result is greater than or equal to $40 then the character stands for a digit from $A to $F; branch to (3d).

   c. The result was less than $40, so the character stands for a digit between $0 and $9. It can be converted from a character code to a digit by masking the high-order nibble. AND with $0F and branch to (4).

   d. To convert a character code for the digits $A to $F to the hexadecimal digit, subtract $37.

4. Move this digit from the low-order nibble to the high-order nibble, where it becomes the most significant digit in the number.

5. Get another character code and display it.

6. Convert the character code to its corresponding hexadecimal digit. Refer to Steps 3a to 3d above.

7. Combine this number, the least significant digit of the two-digit number, with the previous nibble to form the complete two-digit number in the accumulator.

An analysis of a problem similar to the outline of the algorithm just given is a more powerful technique than flowcharting. It is also easier to use, especially with pencil and paper, because it does not require special symbols and because it contains more information. This approach also seems to be more compatible with a structured approach to programming than the more familiar flowchart approach.

Before turning to the exercises, it is worth emphasizing that the programs given in this chapter and in the other chapters of this book are intended to be used to *understand* programming. They are not intended to be the best and fastest approach to any problem, nor are they intended to become part of a library of routines. Try to understand the significance of each instruction in a program before proceeding further, even when you are tempted to move ahead quickly.

EXERCISES

Exercise 5-1

   a. This exercise will familiarize you with the ADC instruction and the SBC instruction. Load the CAL program listed in Appendix B, Example B-2. You should have this program either on cassette tape or disk.

   b. Load the program listed below. It is almost identical with the program in Example 5-2, but it includes instructions to input numbers, display the result, and test your own ability to add hexadecimal numbers. The sequence of instructions that are the most important in the present context have been delineated by asterisks.

```
12B8:20 4F 11   9 AGAIN   JSR   GETBYTS   ;INPUT TWO 2-DIGIT HEX
                                            NUMBERS.
               10 ****************************

12BB:D8        12         CLD             ;CLEAR THE DECIMAL MODE.
12BC:18        13         CLC             ;CLEAR THE CARRY FLAG.
12BD:A5 01     14         LDA   OPA       ;FETCH A NUMBER.
12BF:65 C2     15         ADC   OPB       ;ADD IT TO ANOTHER NUMBER.
12C1:85 03     16         STA   RESULT    ;STORE THE ANSWER.

               18 ****************************
12C3:20 5D 11  19         JSR   TEST      ;INPUT YOUR OWN ANSWER.
12C6:4C B8 12  20         JUMP  AGAIN     ;TRY ANOTHER PROBLEM.
```

c. Execute the program. Try adding these pairs of hexadecimal numbers: (02, 03), (0F, 01), (FF, 01), (FF, FF), (80, 20).

d. Which of the above pairs produce a carry?

e. What do you get when you add a number to its complement with the carry flag set? Change the CLC instruction in the program in Step *b* to an SEC instruction. Then add these numbers: (7F, 80), (33, CC), (A1, 5E). What do you conclude?

(A theorem that describes these results is $A + \bar{A} + 1 = 0$.)

f. Change the CLD instruction to an SED instruction to set up the 6502 to operate in the decimal mode. Add these pairs of numbers: (01, 09), (08, 08), (10, 75), (19, 01), (99, 01), (77, 33), (83, 99). Which pairs produce a carry? Be sure to interpret the number that is displayed as a bcd number when you read the answer.

g. Change the SED instruction back to a CLD instruction, and change the CLC instruction to an SEC instruction. We will use the program to study the SBC instruction, so also change the ADC instruction to an SBC instruction.

h. Execute the program. Subtract the numbers listed in Step *c* or think of your own numbers to subtract. Remember that the second number entered will be subtracted from the first. Describe in your own words the conditions under which the carry flag is set after a subtraction and the conditions under which it is cleared.

i. Replace the SBC instruction with a CMP instruction. Try different numbers to observe the conditions under which the carry flag is set and cleared when a CMP instruction is executed. Do the SED and CLC instructions have any effect on the result obtained from a CMP instruction?

(The answer to the last question is no.)

j. How would you modify the program in Step *b* to perform decimal subtraction?

(Change the CLD instruction to an SED instruction. Change the CLC instruction to an SEC instruction. Change the ADC instruction to an SBC instruction.)

k. Try subtracting some decimal numbers. Under what circumstances is the carry flag (borrow flag) modified?

(The carry flag should be cleared whenever a larger number is subtracted from a smaller.)

Exercise 5–2

a. Load the program in Example 5–6. How would you use it to add $1E03 to $72F3?

(Place $03 in location $0001 and place $1E in location $0002. Place $F3 in location $0003 and place $72 in location $0004. The least significant byte (lsb) of the answer will be found in location $0005, and the most significant byte of the answer will be found in location $0006.)

b. Load the program in Example 5–10. How would you use it to subtract $72F3 from $1E03?

(The number $72F3 is the subtrahend, so its lsb must be stored in SBTLO at $0003 and its msb ($72) must be stored in SBTHI at $0004. The number $1E03 is the minuend, so its lsb must be stored in MINLO at $0001 and its msb ($1E) must be stored at MINHI at $0002. The difference will be found in DIFFLO and DIFFHI in the order lsb, msb, respectively.)

c. How would you modify the programs in Example 5–6 and Example 5–10 to add and subtract, respectively, decimal numbers?

(You must preface each of the programs with an SED instruction to set the decimal mode.)

d. Try this. Then add the numbers 1299 and 8201. Also subtract 1234 from 9102. Do you find the correct decimal (bcd) answers in the two locations that contain the result?

Exercise 5–3

a. Once again load the CAL program in Example B–2 in Appendix B. We will use it to study the multiplication routine in Example 5–15, so load the program in Example 5–15 also.

b. Load the following program. It calls the multiplication routine as a subroutine.

```
12B8:20 4F 11   10 AGAIN   JSR   GETBYTS   ;INPUT TWO 2-DIGIT HEX
                                            NUMBERS.
         11 ***************************
```

```
12BB:20 80 12   13        JSR   MULTPLY   ;CALL THE MULTIPLICATION
12BE:85 03      14        STA   RESULT    ;ROUTINE. STORE THE ANSWER.

                16   ****************************
12C0:20 5D 11   17        JSR   TEST      ;INPUT YOUR OWN ANSWER.
12C3:4C B8 12   18        JMP   AGAIN     ;TRY ANOTHER PROBLEM.
```

c. Try your luck at multiplying hexadecimal numbers. For example, try the 4-bit numbers (01, 02), (0F, 0F), (02, 04), (05, 02) and (08, 04).

Exercise 5–4

a. Use the division routine to divide the following pairs of numbers: (80, 10), (FE, 02), (7F, FF), (01, 00), where the first number is to be divided by the second. You will need to modify the program in Example 5–18 to end with a BRK instruction.

b. Pay careful attention to the last pair of numbers. What should you get when you divide by zero?

(Division by zero is undefined. The program does not flag undefined divisions; it assumes you know what you are doing.)

c. Try dividing zero by zero. Try to predict what the program will do before running it. What answer does it give?

(Zero divided by zero is also not defined. The program does not flag this condition, instead it gives an answer of $FF.)

d. How could you modify the program so that it would not attempt a division if zero were entered for a divisor?

Exercise 5–5

Devise a means to test the programs (subroutines) in Example 5–20. Test the programs to make sure they operate correctly.

Exercise 5–6

Here are some programming problems to try:

- Write a program to add the number in location $03FD to the number in location $03FE and store the result in location $03FF.
- Write a program to subtract the 4-digit bcd number in locations $03FE and $03FF (assume the lsb is in $03FE) from the 4-digit number in locations $03FC and $03FD (assume the lsb is in $03FC). Store the difference in locations $0000 and $0001.
- Write a program to divide one 16-bit number by another.
- Write a program to do a 16-bit multiplication.

CHAPTER 6

Addressing Modes: Indexed Addressing

OBJECTIVES

At the completion of this chapter you should be able to:

- Understand the full complement of 6502 addressing modes.
- Use the following addressing modes in programs: *absolute indexed, zero-page indexed, indexed indirect,* and *indirect indexed.*
- Do multibyte arithmetic using indexed addressing.
- Use indexed addressing in code conversion programs.
- Use indexed addressing in working with tables and lists.

INTRODUCTION

You have mastered the majority of the 6502 instruction set, and no new instructions will be introduced in this chapter. However, the most powerful addressing modes have not yet been explained. These are the so-called indexed addressing modes and the indirect addressing modes. These modes give the 6502 the popularity it has earned in the microprocessor world. They allow the 6502 to handle large amounts of data with great speed and they ensure that multibyte arithmetic and code conversion programs execute quickly and are simple to write.

The instruction set summary first given Table 2–2 is reproduced in Table 6–1 for your convenience. The addressing modes that we will study in this chapter have the column headings ABS, X; ABS, Y; Z-PAGE, X; Z-PAGE, Y; (IND, X); and (IND), Y. The addressing modes that have already been learned have the

Table 6–1. The 6502

MNEMONIC	OPERATION	IMMEDIATE OP # c	ABSOLUTE OP # c	ZERO PAGE OP # c	ACCUM OP # c	IMPLIED OP # c	(IND, X) OP # c	(IND), Y OP # c	Z-PAGE, X OP # c	ABS. X OP # c	ABS. Y OP # c	RELATIVE OP # c	INDIRECT OP # c	Z-PAGE, Y OP # c	STATUS N V • B D I Z C
ADC	A + M + C → A (4)(1)	69 2 2	6D 3 4	65 2 3			61 2 6	71 2 5	75 2 4	7D 3 4	79 3 4				N V • • • • Z C
AND	A∧M → A (1)	29 2 2	2D 3 4	25 2 3			21 2 6	31 2 5	35 2 4	3D 3 4	39 3 4				N • • • • • Z •
ASL	C ← [7...0] ← 0		0E 3 6	06 2 5	0A 1 2				16 2 6	1E 3 7					N • • • • • Z C
BCC	BRANCH ON C = 0 (2)											90 2 2			• • • • • • • •
BCS	BRANCH ON C = 1 (2)											B0 2 2			• • • • • • • •
BEQ	BRANCH ON Z = 1 (2)											F0 2 2			• • • • • • • •
BIT	A∧M		2C 3 4	24 2 3											$M_7 M_6$ • • • • Z •
BMI	BRANCH ON N = 1 (2)											30 2 2			• • • • • • • •
BNE	BRANCH ON Z = 0 (2)											D0 2 2			• • • • • • • •
BPL	BRANCH ON N = 0 (2)											10 2 2			• • • • • • • •
BRK	BREAK					00 1 7									• • • 1 • 1 • •
BVC	BRANCH ON V = 0 (2)											50 2 2			• • • • • • • •
BVS	BRANCH ON V = 1 (2)											70 2 2			• • • • • • • •
CLC	0 → C					18 1 2									• • • • • • • 0
CLD	0 → D					D8 1 2									• • • • 0 • • •
CLI	0 → I					58 1 2									• • • • • 0 • •
CLV	0 → V					B8 1 2									• 0 • • • • • •
CMP	A − M	C9 2 2	CD 3 4	C5 2 3			C1 2 6	D1 2 5	D5 2 4	DD 3 4	D9 3 4				N • • • • • Z C
CPX	X − M	E0 2 2	EC 3 4	E4 2 3											N • • • • • Z C
CPY	Y − M	C0 2 2	CC 3 4	C4 2 3											N • • • • • Z C
DEC	M − 1 → M		CE 3 6	C6 2 5					D6 2 6	DE 3 7					N • • • • • Z •
DEX	X − 1 → X					CA 1 2									N • • • • • Z •
DEY	Y − 1 → Y					88 1 2									N • • • • • Z •
EOR	A∀M → A (1)	49 2 2	4D 3 4	45 2 3			41 2 6	51 2 5	55 2 4	5D 3 4	59 3 4				N • • • • • Z •
INC	M + 1 → M		EE 3 6	E6 2 5					F6 2 6	FE 3 7					N • • • • • Z •
INX	X + 1 → X					E8 1 2									N • • • • • Z •
INY	Y + 1 → Y					C8 1 2									N • • • • • Z •
JMP	JUMP TO NEW LOC		4C 3 3										6C 5 3		• • • • • • • •
JSR	JUMP SUB		20 3 6												• • • • • • • •
LDA	M → A (1)	A9 2 2	AD 3 4	A5 2 3			A1 2 6	B1 2 5	B5 2 4	BD 3 4	B9 3 4				N • • • • • Z •

Instruction Set Summary

Mnemonic	Operation		Flags (N V · · · Z C)
LDX	M → X		N · · · · Z ·
LDY	M → Y		N · · · · Z ·
LSR	0 → ☐☐☐☐☐☐☐☐ → C		0 · · · · Z C
NOP	NO OPERATION		· · · · · · ·
ORA	A ∨ M → A		N · · · · Z ·
PHA	A → Ms S − 1 → S		· · · · · · ·
PHP	P → Ms S − 1 → S		· · · · · · ·
PLA	S + 1 → S Ms → A		N · · · · Z ·
PLP	S + 1 → S Ms → P		(RESTORED)
ROL	☐☐☐☐☐ C		N · · · · Z C
ROR	☐☐☐☐☐ C		N · · · · Z C
RTI	RTRN INT		(RESTORED)
RTS	RTRN SUB		· · · · · · ·
SBC	A − M − C̄ → A		N V · · · Z (3)
SEC	1 → C		· · · · · · 1
SED	1 → D		· · · 1 · · ·
SEI	1 → I		· · · · 1 · ·
STA	A → M		· · · · · · ·
STX	X → M		· · · · · · ·
STY	Y → M		· · · · · · ·
TAX	A → X		N · · · · Z ·
TAY	A → Y		N · · · · Z ·
TSX	S → X		N · · · · Z ·
TXA	X → A		N · · · · Z ·
TXS	X → S		· · · · · · ·
TYA	Y → A		N · · · · Z ·

Notes

(1) ADD 1 to N "IF PAGE BOUNDARY IS CROSSED"

(2) ADD 1 TO N "IF BRANCH OCCURS TO SAME PAGE"
    ADD 2 TO N "IF BRANCH OCCURS TO DIFFERENT PAGE"

(3) CARRY NOT = BORROW

(4) IF IN DECIMAL MODE, Z FLAG IS INVALID
    ACCUMULATOR MUST BE CHECKED FOR ZERO RESULT

Legend

X	INDEX X
Y	INDEX Y
A	ACCUMULATOR
M	MEMORY PER EFFECTIVE ADDRESS
Ms	MEMORY PER STACK POINTER
+	ADD
−	SUBTRACT
∧	AND
∨	OR
∀	EXCLUSIVE OR
M₇	MEMORY BIT 7
M₆	MEMORY BIT 6
n	NO. CYCLES
#	NO. BYTES

column headings IMMEDIATE; ABSOLUTE; ZERO-PAGE; ACCUM; IMPLIED; and RELATIVE.

The fundamental difference between the addressing modes that we have used thus far in this book and the addressing modes still to be learned is the use of an index. Note that the indexed addressing modes have column headings in Table 6–1 that contain either an X or Y index. The *absolute indexed by X* addressing mode, for example, has the column heading ABS, X. Since the addressing mode is related to where the operand of the instruction is located in memory, it should be clear that the indices (X or Y) will be used to identify the location of the operand. With this brief preview, we turn to an analysis of absolute indexed addressing.

ABSOLUTE INDEXED ADDRESSING

To provide some motivation for learning about absolute indexed addressing, suppose we wish to draw a straight horizontal line across the screen of the video monitor using the low-resolution graphics mode. This requires that we store $0F in locations $0528 through $055F, giving a white line approximately in the middle of the screen. The following program will do this:

```
START    LDA #$0F
         STA $0528
         STA $0529
           •
           •
           •
         STA $055F
END      BRK
```

If you restrict yourself to the addressing modes you have learned, then this is the only way you could accomplish the objective. Clearly such a program is extremely long, particularly when you consider the simple objective. It is fortunate that the same thing can be done with a much shorter program that uses absolute indexed addressing.

To illustrate *absolute indexed addressing*, first consider the STA instruction in the absolute addressing mode. In assembly language the instruction

STA TABLE

means store the number in the accumulator in the location symbolized by TABLE. Thus, TABLE symbolizes a 16-bit address consisting of a low-order byte (ADL) and a high-order byte (ADH). Each byte is, of course, eight bits.

The address, TABLE, may be *indexed* by the number in the X register using the addressing mode called "absolute indexed by X" or, more simply, "ABS, X." In assembly language the instruction is written

STA TABLE, X

which means that the number in the accumulator is to be stored at a location whose address is the *sum* of the 16-bit address symbolized by TABLE and the number in the X register. TABLE symbolizes a 16-bit address which consists of a low-order address (BAL for Base Address Low) and a high-order address (BAH for Base Address High). The actual 16-bit address, ADH-ADL, at which the number in the accumulator is to be stored is given by the expression:

ADH-ADL = BAH-BAL + X.

where BAL and BAH are the second and third bytes, respectively, of the STA TABLE, X instruction.

In other words, the microprocessor *adds* the number in the X register to the second byte of the instruction to find the ADL. Any carry from this addition is added to the third byte of the instruction to find the ADH. The number in the accumulator is then stored at the location ADH-ADL. Example 6–1 illustrates these ideas and Fig. 6–1 diagrams the concepts.

Example 6–1. Illustration of the Absolute Indexed Addressing Mode

What is the address of the operand referenced by the LDA instruction in this program segment?

```
0200 A2 2D      LDX #$2D
0202 BD 00 03   LDA TABLE, X
```

Solution: BAL = $00 and BAH = $03, so the base address is $0300. The X register contains $2D, so the operand is at location $0300 + $2D = $032D.

Return now to think about the problem of drawing a horizontal line across the low-resolution graphics screen. Example 6–2 illustrates how this can be done using absolute indexed addressing. The important instructions have been delineated by asterisks. Lines 11–15 merely set up the Apple so that it is in the low-resolution graphics mode with a clear screen. You should concentrate on the instructions in lines 18–22, since it is these lines that write $0F to locations $0528 through $055F, creating a white line across the screen. Notice that the STA TABLE, X instruction uses a base address of $0528. The function of the loop is to write $0F t₀ locations $0528 + X, where the loop causes X to vary from $27 to $00. Indexed addressing

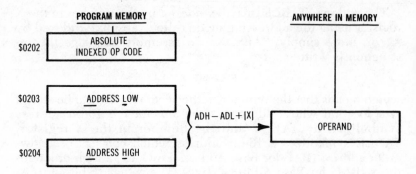

Fig. 6-1. Diagram of the absolute indexed addressing mode, where quantities in the boxes represent the *contents* of those memory locations and quantities outside the boxes refer to the addresses of the boxes. The program bytes were assumed to be in locations $0202-$0204, although they could be anywhere in memory.

would be perfectly useless without the structure of a loop to increment or decrement the index. Notice that we chose to fill the highest location first and decrement the index until the lowest location was loaded with $0F. We could have started with X = $00, incremented it until it was $27, and then used a CPX instruction to branch. The approach used in Example 6–2 requires one less instruction because a CPX instruction is not required. Study this example carefully.

In Example 6–2 we could have used the Y register as an

Example 6–2. A Program to Illustrate the Absolute Indexed Addressing Mode

Object: Write a program that draws a horizontal line on the low-resolution graphics screen. Load locations $0528–$055F with $0F.

```
137C:8D 50 C0   11           STA    SS1       ;SET SCREEN SOFT SWITCHES
137F:8D 52 C0   12           STA    SS2       ;FOR LOW RESOLUTION
1382:8D 54 C0   13           STA    SS3       ;GRAPHICS MODE.
1385:8D 56 C0   14           STA    SS4       ;LORES GRAPHICS MODE IS SET.
1388:20 32 F8   15           JSR    CLRSCR    ;SUBROUTINE TO CLEAR SCREEN.
                16    ****************************

138B:A2 27      18           LDX    #$27      ;START INDEX AT $27 = 39.
138D:A9 0F      19           LDA    #$0F      ;NUMBER TO BE STORED IN TABLE
                                                INTO A.
138F:9D 28 05   20  LOOP     STA    TABLE,X   ;A INTO TABLE LOCATION.
1392:CA         21           DEX              ;DECREMENT THE INDEX.
1393:10 FA      22           BPL    LOOP      ;BRANCH TO LOOP UNTIL X < 0.

                24    ****************************
1395:4C 95 13   25  HERE     JMP    HERE      ;INFINITE LOOP TO OBSERVE
                                                RESULT.
```

index in the ABS, Y addressing mode. It works exactly like the ABS, X addressing mode except the number in the Y register becomes the index.

There are two zero-page indexed addressing modes, called "Z-PAGE, X" and "Z-PAGE, Y," respectively. Zero-page indexed addressing is quite similar to absolute indexed addressing except that the location referenced will always be in page-zero of memory. The second byte of an instruction using either Z-PAGE, X or Z-PAGE, Y addressing is the address low (BAL) of a zero-page memory location. The operand of the instruction is found in the zero-page location whose ADL is the sum of BAL and the number in the X register. That is,

$$ADL = BAL + [X]$$
$$ADH = \$00$$
$$operand = [ADH\text{-}ADL]$$

implying that the operand is the contents of the location whose zero-page address is the sum of the second byte of the instruction and the contents of the X register. This addressing mode is diagrammed in Fig. 6–2, and Example 6–3 illustrates a calculation to locate the operand.

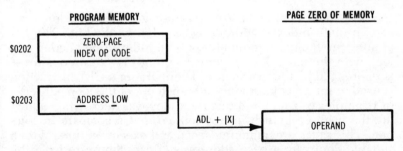

Fig. 6–2. Diagram of the zero-page indexed by X addressing mode, where quantities inside the boxes represent the *contents* of those memory locations and quantities outside the boxes refer to the addresses of the boxes.

It is very important to realize that any *carry* resulting from the second byte of the instruction and the number in the X register *is ignored*. That is, if the second byte of the instruction using the Z-PAGE, X addressing mode is $F0 and the number in the X register is $20, then the location referenced by the instruction is $0010, *not location $0110*. This behavior of this addressing mode is loosely described as "wrapping around." That is, as the index increases until location $00FF is referenced by an instruction, the next increment in the index will cause the instruction to wrap around to the beginning of page zero (location $0000) to fetch the operand. An example of this feature is illustrated in the program in Example 6–4. The object of this program is to load locations $00F0 to $00FF and locations $0000 to $000F with zeros. The program also illustrates the STA instruction in the Z-PAGE, X addressing mode.

Example 6–3. Illustration of the Zero-Page Indexed Addressing Mode

Identify the location of the operand of the ADC instruction in the following program segment.

```
0200 A2 35     LDX #$35
0202 75 20     ADC TABZ, X
```

Solution: The ADC instruction uses Z-PAGE, X addressing. The base address of TABZ is $0020. Adding the X index gives $0020 + $35 = $0055 as the location of the operand.

Example 6–4. A Program that Illustrates Z-PAGE, X Addressing

Object: Load locations $00F0 to $00FF and locations $0000 to $000F with binary 0s.

```
1398:A9 00     5          LDA  #00       ;LOAD A WITH ALL ZEROS.
139A:A2 1F     6          LDX  #$1F      ;$1F IS STARTING VALUE OF INDEX.
139C:95 F0     7 LOOP     STA  TABZ,X    ;LOAD THIS LOCATION WITH ZEROS.
139E:CA        8          DEX            ;DECREMENT THE INDEX TO POINT
                                           TO THE
139F:10 FB     9          BPL  LOOP      ;NEXT LOCATION. IF X > 0,
13A1:00        10         BRK            ;THEN BRANCH BACK.
```

A few more comments about zero-page indexed addressing and absolute indexed addressing may be worthwhile. The beginning programmer frequently puts an indexed instruction in a loop with the index X or Y *increasing* until the desired address is referenced by the instruction. Then CPX or a CPY instruction is used to set a flag to produce a branch out of the loop. Observe in Examples 6–2 and 6–4 that the index was decreasing, allowing the use of a branch instruction *without* a compare instruction. This saves programming space and execution time. With a suitable choice of a base address, you can choose to have the index either increase or decrease, whichever is more convenient. Finally, an examination of the instruction set summary will show you that the Z-PAGE, Y addressing mode is available to only two instructions, the LDX and STX instructions. Needless to say, this mode is not used very often.

INDEXED ADDRESSING PROGRAM EXAMPLES

The indexed addressing modes just introduced add considerable power to the instructions that have been already introduced in this book. The next few paragraphs will be used to give some programming examples that will illustrate the absolute and zero-page indexed addressing modes. The programs or program segments were chosen for their usefulness in illustrating these modes. Many other examples might have been selected. Leo Scanlon's book *6502 Software Design* (published by Howard W. Sams & Co., Inc., 1980) and Lance Leventhal's book *Assembly Language Programming: 6502* (published by Osborne/ McGraw-Hill, Inc., 1979) provide numerous additional examples.

The absolute indexed addressing mode and the zero-page indexed addressing mode are extremely useful when operations involve numbers that are too large to be represented by one byte and must be represented by several bytes. We will refer to these operations either as "multiple-byte" or "multiple-precision" operations. The next few examples illustrate this type of use of the indexed addressing modes for multiple-precision operations.

A 4-Byte Subtraction Routine

A program that subtracts one 4-byte number from another 4-byte number is listed in Example 6–5. The minuend is located at addresses $0019 to $001C and the subtrahend is located at addresses $0011 to $0014, with their *most significant bytes* in the locations with the *smallest addresses*. Actually, the program will handle any number of bytes for either the minuend or the subtrahend simply by changing the initial value of X in line 10 of the program. In general, then, the minuend is located from $0019 to $0019 + X, and the subtrahend is located from $0011 to $0011 + X, where X is the initial value stored in the X register by the LDX instruction on line 10. The difference, or result of the subtraction, is stored in locations $0009 to $0009 + X, with the least significant byte in location $0009. Of course, the difference could also be stored in either the locations assigned to the minuend or the subtrahend if it is not necessary to keep these numbers intact and if zero-page storage space is scarce. Observe that the subtraction routine uses zero-page indexed by X addressing for three instructions, LDA, SBC, and STA. Note that the carry flag is set before the first subtraction. The program goes through the loop labeled "LOOP" *four* times, once for each byte involved in the *4-byte* subtraction. To operate in the decimal mode, simply change the CLD instruction on line 8 to an SED instruction. Some computers, the Apple included, use four bytes to store numbers when the floating-point BASIC interpreter is being used.

Example 6–5. A 4-Byte Subtraction Program

Object: Subtract one 4-byte number from another 4-byte number.

13A2:D8	8		CLD		;CLEAR DECIMAL MODE.
13A3:38	9		SEC		;SET CARRY FOR NO BORROW.
13A4:A2 04	10		LDX	#04	;X CONTAINS NUMBER OF BYTES.
13A6:B5 18	11	LOOP	LDA	MINUND,X	;GET BYTE FROM MINUEND.
13A8:F5 10	12		SBC	SBTHND,X	;SUBTRACT SUBTRAHEND FROM MINUEND.
13AA:95 08	13		STA	DIFF,X	;STORE THE RESULT HERE.
13AC:CA	14		DEX		;DECREMENT THE BYTE COUNTER.
13AD:D0 F7	15		BNE	LOOP	;CONTINUE UNTIL BYTE COUNTER IS ZERO.
13AF:60	16		RTS		

A Decimal Mode Multiple-Precision Addition Program

A program to add one 3-byte number to another 3-byte number is listed in Example 6–6. Refer to Fig. 5–2 for an illustration of a triple-precision sum. In Example 6–6, one of the addends is located at addresses $0011 to $0011 + [Y], where Y is the initial value in the Y register set by the LDY instruction on line 10. The other addend is located at addresses $0019 to $0019 + [Y], while the sum is located at $0081 to $0081 + [Y]. Clearly the program can be modified to handle any number of bytes merely by changing the value of Y initialized by the LDY instruction on line 10. Moreover, the same program can be used to add binary numbers rather than bcd numbers by replacing the SED instruction with a CLD instruction on line 8. The most significant bytes of the addends and the sum are in the locations with the lowest addresses, just as in the case of the subtraction program described earlier. These bytes are added the last time through the loop when the index is one.

Observe that although the zero-page indexed by Y addressing mode is not available for the LDA, ADC, and STA instructions used in Example 6–6, it is possible to reference zero page with a Y-indexed instruction; see lines 11, 12, and 13 of Example 6–6. However, the absolute indexed addressing mode must be used, and there is no savings either in program bytes or execution time by using zero-page locations for the addends and the sum.

Example 6–6. A Multiple-Precision Addition Program

Object: Add one 3-byte number to another using the decimal mode.

13B0:F8	8		SED		;SET DECIMAL MODE.
13B1:18	9		CLC		;CLEAR CARRY FOR FIRST SUM.
13B2:A0 03	10		LDY	#03	;Y CONTAINS # BYTES TO BE ADDED.
13B4:B9 10 00	11	LOOP	LDA	ADD1,Y	;GET BYTE FROM FIRST ADDEND.

```
13B7:79 18 00    12        ADC   ADD2,Y    ;ADD BYTE FROM SECOND
                                             ADDEND.
13BA:99 80 00    13        STA   SUM,Y     ;RESULT INTO SUM.
13BD:88          14        DEY             ;DECREMENT BYTE COUNT.
13BE:D0 F4       15        BNE   LOOP      ;CONTINUE UNTIL ALL BYTES HAVE
                                             BEEN
13C0:60          16        RTS             ;ADDED.
```

A Routine to Find the Largest Number in a Table

The program in Example 6–7 is a subroutine that finds the largest entry in a table. The subroutine returns with this number in the accumulator. It illustrates the CMP and LDA instructions in their absolute indexed by X addressing modes. The table extends from $0300 to $037F in this example, but the program could be easily modified to search any table up to one page of memory in length, that is, 256 locations. The highest address in the table is determined by the value of X that is initialized in line 7 of the program. The smallest address in the table is the base address of the table; see line 10 of the program. You should realize that the largest value may be present in several locations of the table. This program only finds the largest value. Moreover, it does not note where it (they) is (are) or how many of them there are.

Example 6–7. A Program to Find the Largest Number in a Table

Object: Find the largest number in a table located from $0300 to $037F.

```
13C1:A9 00       6         LDA   #00       ;START WITH SMALLEST POSSIBLE
                                             NUMBER.
13C3:A2 7F       7         LDX   #$7F      ;INDEX HIGHEST LOCATION IN
                                             TABLE.
13C5:DD 00 03    8 BR1     CMP   TABLE,X   ;IS A > # IN TABLE?
13C8:B0 03       9         BCS   BR2       ;YES, THEN DO NOT REPLACE A.
13CA:BD 00 03    10        LDA   TABLE,X   ;NO, THEN REPLACE A WITH
                                             NUMBER
13CD:CA          11 BR2    DEX             ;FROM THE TABLE. DECREMENT X.
13CE:10 F5       12        BPL   BR1       ;SEARCH COMPLETE?
13D0:60          13        RTS             ;YES.
```

A Routine to Increment a 3-Byte Number

The program in Example 6–8 illustrates how zero-page indexed addressing can be used to increment a 3-byte counter. There are many applications involving counting in which a single byte number cannot contain the count. With a single byte, a count as large as 255 may be stored. With two bytes a count as large as 65,535 may be stored, and with three bytes the count may go as high as 16,777,215. If the subroutine in Example 6–8 is called each time a count is detected, the subroutine can count from 0 to 16,777,215 before starting over. It is important to know that the least significant byte (lsb) of the count is in location $00FD and the most significant byte is in location $00FF.

Example 6–8. A Routine to Increment a 3-Byte Number

Object: Increment (by one) the 3-byte number located at $00FD, $00FE, and $00FF with the most significant byte in $00FF.

13D1:A2 FD	5		LDX	#$FD	;X CONTAINS 2's COMPLEMENT OF THE
13D3:F6 00	6	BACK	INC	CNTR,X	;# OF BYTES IN THE COUNTER.
13D5:D0 03	7		BNE	OUT	;QUIT UNLESS INCREMENT GIVES ZERO.
13D7:E8	8		INX		
13D8:D0 F9	9		BNE	BACK	;INCREMENT ANOTHER BYTE.
13DA:60	10	OUT	RTS		;RETURN.

A Routine to Complement a 3-Byte Number

The program in Example 6–9 complements a 3-byte number. Multiple-precision complementation is sometimes performed when doing floating-point arithmetic. In any case, the program illustrates the EOR instruction in its absolute indexed by Y addressing mode and another example of absolute indexed addressing.

Example 6–9. A Routine to Complement a 3-Byte Number

Object: Complement the 3-byte number located at $0383, $0382, and $0381.

13DB:A0 03	5		LDY	#03	;Y SERVES AS BYTE COUNTER.
13DD:A9 FF	6	LOOP	LDA	#$FF	;A EOR $FF IS "NOT A."
13DF:59 80 03	7		EOR	NUMB,Y	;COMPLEMENT THE NUMBER.
13E2:99 80 03	8		STA	NUMB,Y	;AND STORE IT IN THE SAME LOCATION.
13E5:88	9		DEY		;DECREMENT THE BYTE COUNTER.
13E6:D0 F5	10		BNE	LOOP	
13E8:60	11		RTS		

A Program to Shift and Rotate One 4-Byte Number Into Another

The program in Example 6–10 illustrates the LSR and ROR instructions in their zero-page indexed by X addressing mode. Note that it makes use of a bit counter (the Y register) to count the number of bits that have been shifted, and a byte counter (the X register) to index the bytes in the multiple-precision number being rotated. These types of operations are encountered in multiple-precision multiplication and division routines as well as in binary-to-bcd conversion routines.

Example 6–10. A Program to Shift and Rotate One 4-Byte Number into Another

Object: Rotate the number in locations $0001 through $0004 into locations $0011 through $0014, respectively.

```
13E9:A0 20     6           LDY    #32          ;Y IS THE # OF BITS TO ROTATE.
13EB:A2 04     7 LOOPY     LDX    #04          ;X IS # OF BYTES IN THE NUMBER.
13ED:56 00     8 LOOPX     LSR    NUMA,X       ;SHIFT A RIGHT INTO CARRY.
13EF:76 10     9           ROR    NUMB,X       ;ROTATE CARRY INTO B.
13F1:CA        10          DEX                 ;DECREMENT BYTE COUNTER.
13F2:D0 F9     11          BNE    LOOPX        ;ROTATE ANOTHER BYTE.
13F4:88        12          DEY                 ;DECREMENT BIT COUNTER.
13F5:D0 F4     13          BNE    LOOPY        ;DO ANOTHER BIT.
13F7:60        14          RTS
```

A Program to Increment a 3-Byte BCD Number

This program might be used in the same kind of applications as the program in Example 6–8. It is frequently more convenient to work with bcd numbers than binary numbers in counting and timing applications. However, the increment instruction cannot be used because it does not produce a carry when the sum reaches 9, 99, 999, 9999, etc. Consequently the program in Example 6–11 must be used. Note that the carry was set before the addition. This has the effect of adding one each time the routine is called. The decimal mode is set at the beginning of the routine and cleared at the end. The author believes this is good practice: only set the decimal mode when you need it and clear it when you are finished.

Example 6–11. A Program to Increment a 3-Byte BCD Number

Object: Increment the 3-byte number located at $0001 to $0003 with the most significant byte in location $0001.

```
1400:F8        3           SED                 ;SET THE DECIMAL MODE.
1401:38        4           SEC                 ;SET THE CARRY TO ADD 1.
1402:A2 03     5           LDX    #03          ;X IS THE BYTE COUNTER.
1404:A9 00     6 HERE      LDA    #00          ;CLEAR ACCUMULATOR.
1406:75 F0     7           ADC    BCD,X        ;ADD CARRY TO THE NUMBER.
1408:95 F0     8           STA    BCD,X        ;STORE IT.
140A:CA        9           DEX                 ;DECREMENT THE BYTE COUNTER.
140B:D0 F7     10          BNE    HERE         ;LOOP BACK FOR ANOTHER BYTE.
140D:D8        11          CLD                 ;CLEAR THE DECIMAL MODE BEFORE
140E:60        12          RTS                 ;RETURNING TO THE MAIN
                                                   PROGRAM.
```

A Checksum Routine

We have already discussed using parity to detect errors when sending and receiving data through a serial i/o. Another scheme to help detect errors that may be introduced into the data stream by noisy telephone lines or faulty circuitry is a checksum. There are several types of checksums. One type forms either an 8-bit or 16-bit sum of all the characters sent, disregarding any overflow from the sum. The checksum is the last piece of information sent. At the receiving end of this communications link, the computer adds all the information sent and forms its own checksum. The two checksums are then compared, and if they are not the same, an error message is displayed, and another attempt at sending the same block of data may be made. This type of checksum is used in several cassette tape i/o operations.

Another kind of checksum is formed by EORing all the character codes in the block of data to be sent (or received). Since we have already had a number of examples involving addition, this is the checksum we chose to illustrate in Example 6–12. The character codes are assumed to reside in a table called BUFFER located in page $08 of memory. The length of the table in bytes is stored in a location symbolized by LENGTH. If the number stored in length is L, then the character codes occupy locations from $0800 to $0800 + (L − 1). To reference these locations the index must range from 0 to L − 1. The checksum will be stored at the "top" of the table, address $0800 + L. Refer to the listing in Example 6–12 for further details.

Example 6–12. A Program to Form an Exclusive-Or Checksum

Object: Form the checksum of the character codes in a table in page $08 of memory. Store the checksum at the top of the table. The length of the table, in bytes, is found at location $000A.

0582:A4 0A	4		LDY	LENGTH	;GET TABLE LENGTH INTO Y.
0584:88	5		DEY		;Y INDEX IS # OF BYTES MINUS ONE.
0585:A9 00	6		LDA	#00	;CLEAR THE ACCUMULATOR.
0587:59 00 08	7	LOOPY	EOR	BUFFER,Y	;EOR ALL THE NUMBERS
058A:88	8		DEY		;IN THE TABLE.
058B:D0 FA	9		BNE	LOOPY	
058D:A4 0A	10		LDY	LENGTH	;SET UP INDEX FOR CHECKSUM STORAGE.
058F:99 00 08	11		STA	BUFFER,Y	;CHECKSUM INTO TOP LOCATION.
0592:60	12		RTS		

An ASCII-to-Morse Code Conversion Routine

One important use of indexed addressing that has not yet been mentioned is in code conversion. That is, when you want to convert one kind of character code to another kind of character code, it is possible to use the first *code* as an *index* to look up the second code in a table. We will illustrate this concept with a program that converts ASCII to Morse code.

There are numerous other examples where this technique is used. How does the monitor disassembler convert an op code to a mnemonic? A table of Fahrenheit temperatures could be used to index a table of memory locations containing the corresponding Celsius temperatures to perform a Fahrenheit-to-Celsius conversion. Hexadecimal numbers could be used to index a table containing corresponding bcd numbers to effect a fast hex-to-bcd conversion. The example to be described should give you enough information to start to program your own conversions.

The motivation for an ASCII-to-Morse code conversion is the desire to use a microcomputer to send Morse code by keying a commercial or amateur (ham) transmitter. A complete program to do this is described in Chapter 10. Our attention at this point focuses on the problem of taking an ASCII character from the keyboard input port and converting it to a Morse code character in the accumulator.

When you think of Morse code you think of dots and dashes, not binary 1s and 0s. A problem that must be faced immediately is how to represent dots and dashes with an 8-bit character code. Table 6–2 summarizes one approach. Each dash will be represented by a 1, each dot by a 0.

Morse code is also a variable length code. That is, A is represented by *two* elements (a dot and a dash), while B is represented by *four* elements (a dash and three dots). Refer to Table 6–2. There must be some means, therefore, to indicate the "length" of a character in a memory location. To do this, the binary character code representing the Morse code is *left-justified*; that is, it is contained in the most significant bits of the memory location. A 1 placed just to the right of the Morse character signals the completion of the character. How can this 1 be distinguished from a dash? The answer lies in how the code is transmitted. Morse code is transmitted in a serial fashion, one element at a time. To transmit a Morse code character, the character is shifted to the left one bit at a time. A dot is transmitted if a zero is shifted into the carry flag, and a dash is transmitted if a one is shifted into the carry flag. The *process is terminated when the last 1 is shifted out of the location containing the character*, that is, when the shift instruction sets the Z flag. This leaves the 1 in the carry flag, which is disregarded.

The program to accomplish the conversion is listed in Example 6–13. A memory dump of the lookup table is shown in Chart 6–1. The program uses an LDX KYBD instruction to get the Apple ASCII character in the X register. This character is the last column in Table 6–2. The character in the X register is then used as an index to find the appropriate binary Morse character (column three of Table 6–2) in the lookup table. The

Table 6-2. Morse Code Representations of Letters and Numbers

Character	Morse Code	Binary Morse	Hex Morse	Apple ASCII (Hex)
A	. −	0110 0000	60	C1
B	− . . .	1000 1000	88	C2
C	− . − .	1010 1000	A8	C3
D	− . .	1001 0000	90	C4
E	.	0100 0000	40	C5
F	. . − .	0010 1000	28	C6
G	− − .	1101 0000	D0	C7
H	. . . .	0000 1000	08	C8
I	. .	0010 0000	20	C9
J	. − − −	0111 1000	78	CA
K	− . −	1011 0000	B0	CB
L	. − . .	0100 1000	48	CC
M	− −	1110 0000	E0	CD
N	− .	1010 0000	A0	CE
O	− − −	1111 0000	F0	CF
P	. − − .	0110 1000	68	D0
Q	− − . −	1101 1000	D8	D1
R	. − .	0101 0000	F0	D2
S	. . .	0001 0000	10	D3
T	−	1100 0000	C0	D4
U	. . −	0110 0000	30	D5
V	. . . −	0001 1000	18	D6
W	. − −	0111 0000	70	D7
X	− . . −	1001 1000	98	D8
Y	− . − −	1011 1000	B8	D9
Z	− − . .	1100 1000	C8	DA
1	. − − − −	0111 1100	7C	B1
2	. . − − −	0011 1100	3C	B2
3	. . . − −	0001 1100	1C	B3
4	. . . . −	0000 1100	0C	B4
5	. . . . .	0000 0100	04	B5
6	−	1000 0100	84	B6
7	− − . . .	1100 0100	C4	B7
8	− − − . .	1110 0100	E4	B8
9	− − − − .	1111 0100	F4	B9
0	− − − − −	1111 1100	FC	B0

Example 6-13. An ASCII-to-Morse Code Conversion Routine

Object: Use a lookup table to convert ASCII to Morse Code.

```
1487:AE 00 C0    7          LDX   KYBD      ;CHARACTER CODE IN X
148A:BD 00 08    8          LDA   CODE,X    ;INDEXES MORSE CODE IN TABLE.
148D:0A          9 DOTDASH  ASL   A         ;SHIFT CODE CHARACTER INTO
                                              CARRY.
148E:D0 01      10          BNE   SEND      ;BRANCH TO SEND ROUTINE.
1490:60         11          RTS
1491:EA         12 SEND     NOP             ;DUMMY INSTRUCTION ILLUSTRATES
                                              BRANCH.
1492:B8         13          CLV             ;CLEAR THE OVERFLOW FLAG.
1493:50 F8      14          BVC   DOTDASH   ;FORCE A BRANCH TO DOTDASH.
```

Chart 6–1. A Memory Dump of the ASCII-to-Morse Code Table

```
*08B0.08DA

08B0-  FC 7C 3C 1C 0C 04 84 C4
08B8-  E4 F4 00 00 00 00 00 00
08C0-  00 60 88 A8 90 40 28 D0
08C8-  08 20 78 B0 48 E0 A0 F0
08D0-  68 D8 F0 10 C0 30 18 70
08D8-  98 B8 C8
```

LDA CODE, X instruction performs that task in the program. Those two instructions are the basis of any code conversion program using lookup tables. The next few instructions are included to hint at the means by which the Morse character is sent. The ASL A instruction shifts the left-most bit into the carry flag. If this clears the accumulator, then the "end" bit is in the carry flag, the accumulator is clear, so the program returns to the calling program with the RTS instruction. On the other hand, if the ASL A instruction does not clear the accumulator, then a character bit is in the carry flag. The BNE SEND instruction will be executed, causing a branch to SEND. A NOP instruction (the NOP instruction is a perfectly legitimate instruction whose only function is to do nothing except take up program space and execution time) was put at this point where a rather complex set of instructions to send the character should be. This set of instructions would include testing the carry flag to determine whether to send a dot or a dash. See Chapter 10 for further details. In any case, the set of instructions to send a dot or a dash terminates, and the CLV and BVC DOTDASH instructions force a jump back to the ASL A instruction to get the next dot or dash or the end of the character.

Why not use a JMP DOTDASH instruction in place of the CLV and the BVC DOTDASH pair of instructions? Note that the JMP instruction contains the address of the destination of the JMP. If this program is *relocated*, that is, moved to another place in memory, then the JMP instruction must be changed to reflect the change in the address of DOTDASH. On the other hand, the branch instruction contains *no reference* to the address of DOTDASH. Relocating the program will require no modifications to the program. Such a program is called *relocatable*. A relocatable program will have no JMP instructions in the absolute addressing mode. Relocating subroutines also requires that the calling program be modified. Programs without subroutines are easier to relocate than programs with subroutines. It is good programming practice to make programs relocatable.

INDIRECT INDEXED ADDRESSING

The essential idea in indirect indexed addressing is that the zero-page location whose address is the second byte of the instruction *does not* contain the operand. Instead, the zero-page location referenced by the instruction *contains the low-order byte of an address*. Call this low-order byte BAL for *base address low*. The *high-order byte* of this address, call it BAH for *base address high*, is contained in the next successive (higher) zero-page location. If the number in the Y register is zero, then the operand is in BAH-BAL. In general, the address ADH-ADL of the operand is given by adding the number in the Y register to BAL, and adding any carry from that sum to BAH. That is,

$$ADL = BAL + [Y]$$
$$ADH = BAH + C$$

where C is the carry from the first sum, *not* the value of the carry flag.

We can summarize this all quite neatly as follows:

- Let IAL symbolize the second byte of an instruction using the indirect indexed addressing mode. IAL is the low-order *address* of a zero-page location. IAL + 1 is the low-order address of the next zero-page location.
- The zero-page locations IAL and IAL + 1 contain an *address*, BAH-BAL; that is, BAH = [IAL + 1] and BAL = [IAL].
- The address of the operand is found by adding the number in the Y register to BAH-BAL; that is, ADH-ADL = BAH-BAL + [Y].

We can eliminate the terms BAH and BAL and express this even more concisely by

$$ADL = [IAL] + [Y]$$
$$ADH = [IAL + 1] + C$$
$$operand = [ADH\text{-}ADL]$$

Example 6–14 illustrates these concepts, and Fig. 6–3 is a diagram of the indirect indexed addressing mode.

Example 6–14 also illustrates the assembly language format of an indirect indexed instruction. The symbol in the operand field, MEM in the case of Example 6–14, is placed in parentheses followed by a comma and the Y index.

Éxample 6-14. Locating the Operand With the Indirect Indexed Addressing Mode

Calculate the address of the operand of the LDA instruction in the following program segment. Assume location $00F0 contains $67 and location $00F1 contains $03; that is, [$00F0] = $67 and [$00F1] = $03.

```
$0200 A0 23    LDY #$23
$0202 B1 F0    LDA (MEM), Y
```

Solution: Observe that IAL = $F0 and its contents are $67. Also note that IAL + 1 = $F1 and its contents are $03. Therefore BAH-BAL = $0367. Adding the contents of the Y register, $23, to BAL gives $8A. There is no carry from this sum, so BAH = $03. The operand is in location $038A. That is, the number in location $038A will be placed in the accumulator when the LDA (MEM), Y instruction in the program segment is executed.

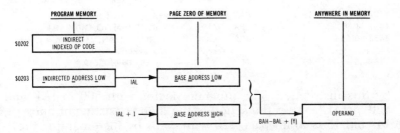

Fig. 6-3. Diagram of the indirect indexed addressing mode, where quantities inside the boxes represent the *contents* of those memory locations and quantities outside the boxes refer to the addresses of the boxes.

The instruction set summary symbolizes the indirect indexed addressing mode with the symbolism "(IND), Y." Note that this mode *does not* ever use the X index. See Table 6-1, the instruction set summary.

To illustrate the value of this addressing mode, consider the problem of clearing the Apple II high-resolution (hires) screen locations. The primary page consists of locations $2000 to $3FFF, and we would like to place zeros in all these locations to produce a blank screen, to be filled later with more meaningful information. A less than desirable solution would be to use the program given in Example 6-4 to clear each location in each of the $20 pages of the primary picture buffer. That would require recoding Example 6-4 32 times or, alternatively, putting it in some kind of subroutine to be called 32 times. Fortunately, the indirect indexed addressing mode makes this clumsy approach unnecessary. The solution is given in Example 6-15.

The program in Example 6-15 uses the STA instruction in the indirect indexed addressing mode: see the STA (IAL), Y instruction on line 13. Since the accumulator is initialized to zero, the STA (IAL), Y will place zeros in all the locations referenced

Example 6–15. A Subroutine to Clear the Hires Primary Picture Buffer

Object: Fill the locations from $2000 through $3FFF with zeros.

```
14A6:              6 ;SUBROUTINE CLEAR
14A6:A0 00         7 CLEAR   LDY   #00        ;INITIALIZE Y TO ZERO.
14A8:A9 00         8         LDA   #00        ;ZEROS INTO THE ACCUMULATOR.
14AA:85 FE         9         STA   IAL        ;SET UP BASE ADDRESS LOW, BAL.
14AC:A2 20        10         LDX   #$20       ;BAH = $20.
14AE:86 FF        11         STX   IAL+1      ;SET UP BASE ADDRESS HIGH, BAH.
14B0:A2 3F        12         LDX   #$3F       ;SET UP ENDING PAGE NUMBER.
14B2:91 FE        13 LOOP    STA   (IAL),Y    ;CLEAR A LOCATION.
14B4:C8           14         INY              ;INCREMENT Y FOR THE NEXT
                                                 LOCATION.
14B5:D0 FB        15         BNE   LOOP       ;LOOP BACK UNTIL A PAGE IS
                                                 CLEARED.
14B7:E6 FF        16         INC   IAL+1      ;GO TO THE NEXT PAGE.
14B9:E4 FF        17         CPX   IAL+1      ;IS IT TIME TO QUIT?
14BB:B0 F5        18         BCS   LOOP       ;NO, FILL ANOTHER PAGE WITH
                                                 ZEROS.
14BD:60           19         RTS              ;YES, THEN QUIT.
```

by this instruction. The program begins with $00 in IAL and $20 in IAL + 1, so the action of the loop consisting of lines 13, 14, and 15 is to fill page $20 with zeros by incrementing the Y index from $00 to $FF. When this loop is completed, the INC IAL + 1 instruction on line 16 increments the page number from $20 to $21, and the loop is repeated. This process continues until the number in IAL + 1 exceeds $3F, the number of the last page to be filled with zeros: see lines 16–18 of the program in Example 6–15. That completes the objective.

Having cleared the hires picture buffer we could flip the so-called soft switches (locations $C050 to $C057) to display a blank screen in the high-resolution mode. How could we put something on the screen? There is room for 53,760 dots on the screen, in a matrix 280 dots across by 190 dots down. Each dot corresponds to a certain bit in the hires picture buffer that extends from locations $2000 to $3FFF, the block of memory cleared by executing the CLEAR subroutine in Example 6–15. If a bit is at logic 1, the dot is "on"; otherwise it is "off." (This discussion will not be concerned with color. Refer to the *Apple II Reference Manual* for details on how to color your dots.) Fig. 6–4 is a memory map of the hires graphics screen. The problem we pose is: how can we select and turn on any one of the 53,760 dots?

The answer is not particularly simple. To begin, how should we identify a dot? The simplest approach to the problem of identifying a dot appears to be giving it two coordinates; a horizontal coordinate (x) and a vertical coordinate (y). The

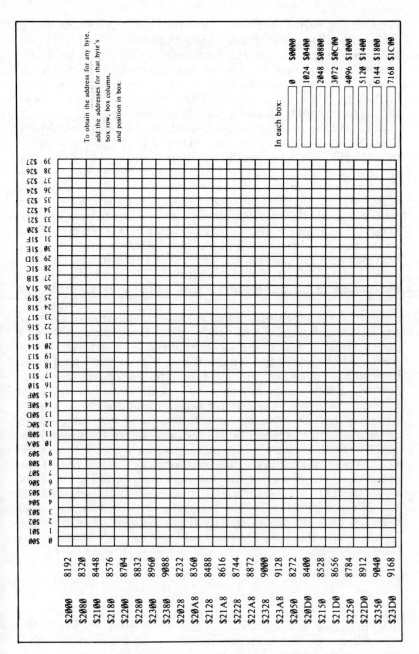

(Courtesy of Apple Computer, Inc.)

Fig. 6-4. A map of the hires graphic screen.

x-coordinate varies from 0 to 279 with 0 being at the left side of the screen. The y-coordinate varies from 0 to 191 with 0 being at the top of the screen. The horizontal position of a dot on the screen is determined by the address of a memory location and the bit position in that location. Refer to Fig. 6–4, the memory map of the hires picture buffer. The vertical position of a dot on the screen is determined by an address only.

Consider the problem of specifying the dot's horizontal position. We must convert a number between 0 and 270 to a logic 1 in a specific bit in a specific memory location. The horizontal space on the screen is divided into 40 ($28) bytes. For example, the *top line* is in the domain of memory locations $2000 to $2027. Seven of the eight bits of these locations are displayed on the screen; the most significant bit of each byte is not displayed. The least significant bit of location $2000 corresponds to $x = 0$. The next bit, bit one, of location $2000 corresponds to the next dot with $x = 1$. The dot with $x = 7$ is the least significant bit in location $2001. The dot with $x = 279$ is controlled by the logic value of bit six, the next-most-significant bit, in location $2027.

Suppose the y-coordinate that we specify determines the base address of each line. For example, if $y = 0$, we are specifying a base address of $2000, the location of the left-most byte on the screen, *at the top* of the screen. If $y = 191$, we are specifying a base address of $3FD0, the location of the left-most byte *on the bottom* of the screen. Given a base address for the left-most byte on the screen, the *Y index register* could serve to specify which of the $28 bytes we wish to modify to turn on a dot. In other words, we propose to use indirect indexed addressing to specify which location in the picture buffer we wish to modify. The IAL of our indirect indexed instruction will contain the low-order byte of one of the 192 addresses of left-most bytes, while the IAL + 1 location will contain the high-order byte of one of these addresses. The Y register will contain a number between $00 and $27 to specify the horizontal offset from the addresses on the left. Thus we will use an instruction of the form

STA (IAL), Y

to turn on a dot. Refer again to Fig. 6–4.

Given an x-coordinate, how can we find the number to be placed in the Y register? The answer is simple: divide the x-coordinate by 7. Furthermore, the remainder from this division is related to the bit that we want to set to turn on a dot. That is, the quotient of the division $x/7$ is the number to be put in the Y register to access the proper byte. The remainder of the division is used to shift a logic 1 from the bit zero position to the proper bit position, with the number of shifts equal to the remainder.

(If this seems complicated you can consider yourself a normal human being. It took the author a *long* time to figure it all out. However, the worst is yet to come.)

The x-coordinate has been converted to a bit position, now the y-coordinate must be converted to one of the 192 base addresses corresponding to the left-most positions on the screen. In hexadecimal, the y-coordinate lies between \$00 and \$BF. To discover a relationship between the y-coordinate, in hexadecimal or binary, and the base addresses, a table containing the coordinate and the address was made. One legal pad and several hours later two logical-arithmetic expressions were found that gave the correct BADH (base address high) and BADL (base address low) for a specific y-coordinate. The uppercase "Y" in the expressions should not be confused with the number in the Y register. Y in the expressions is the Y coordinate in hexadecimal that ranges from \$00 to \$BF. Also, we will use the logic symbols $\wedge$ and $\vee$ for AND and OR, while $+$, $/$, and $\cdot$ are arithmetic symbols. The expressions follow:

$$\text{BADH} = [(Y \wedge \$30)/16] \vee (\$20) + (Y \wedge \$07) \cdot 4$$
$$\text{BADL} = [(Y \wedge \$C0)/2] \vee [(Y \wedge \$C0)/8] + [(Y \wedge \$08)/8] \cdot \$80$$

Given a y-coordinate Y, BADL and BADH are calculated and stored in IAL and IAL $+$ 1, respectively, where IAL is the second byte of an indirect indexed instruction. The instruction can then reference any byte, hence any bit, in the hires picture buffer illustrated in Figure 6–5. In the expressions for BADH and BADL, the AND operations serve to isolate certain bits in the 8-bit number for the y-coordinate, Y. The divide-by-2, divide-by-8, and divide-by-16 operations are accomplished with right shifts, while the times-4 operation is accomplished with two left shifts. The last term in the expression for BADL is essentially a decision whether or not to add \$80. If bit three in Y is logic 1, then \$80 will be added; otherwise it will not be added.

The culmination of these efforts is subroutine PLOT listed in Example 6–16. It takes an 8-bit number in location \$0001 (XPOS) and converts it to an x position on the screen. It takes an 8-bit number in location \$0002 (YPOS) and converts it to a y position on the screen. Note that by confining ourselves to an 8-bit number for the x-coordinate we waste 24 points on the right side of the screen. To avoid this we would have to do a

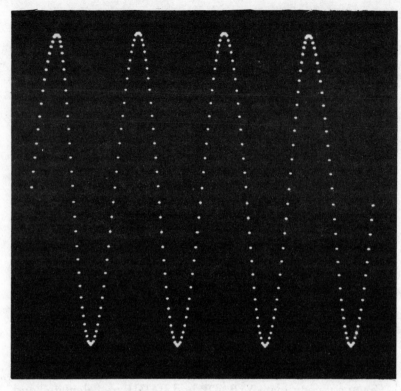

Fig. 6–5. A photograph of four cycles of a sine function plotted on the screen of the video monitor using the PLOT subroutine.

Example 6–16. A Subroutine to Plot a Point on the Hires Screen

Object: Convert two coordinates to a dot on the hires graphics screen.

```
14BE:           8 ;SUBROUTINE PLOT
14BE:A5 02      9 PLOT   LDA   YPOS        ;GET Y-COORDINATE OF DOT.
14C0:29 30     10        AND   #$30        ;ISOLATE BITS 4 AND 5.
14C2:4A        11        LSR   A           ;DIVIDE BY 16.
14C3:4A        12        LSR   A
14C4:4A        13        LSR   A
14C5:4A        14        LSR   A
14C6:09 20     15        ORA   #$20        ;SET BIT FIVE.
14C8:85 04     16        STA   IAL+1       ;LOCATION OF BASE ADDRESS
                                            HIGH.
14CA:A5 02     17        LDA   YPOS        ;GET Y-COORDINATE AGAIN.
14CC:29 07     18        AND   #$07        ;ISOLATE BITS ZERO, ONE, AND
                                            TWO.
14CE:0A        19        ASL   A           ;MULTIPLY BY FOUR.
14CF:0A        20        ASL   A
14D0:65 04     21        ADC   IAL+1       ;ADD PREVIOUS RESULT.
```

```
14D2:85 04      22          STA    IAL+1     ;STORE HERE.
14D4:A5 02      23          LDA    YPOS      ;START CALCULATION OF ADDRESS
                                                LOW.
14D6:29 C0      24          AND    #$C0      ;ISOLATE BITS SEVEN AND SIX.
14D8:4A         25          LSR    A         ;DIVIDE BY TWO.
14D9:85 03      26          STA    IAL       ;LOCATION OF BASE ADDRESS
                                                HIGH.
14DB:4A         27          LSR    A         ;DIVIDE BY TWO AGAIN.
14DC:4A         28          LSR    A         ;AND AGAIN TO GET DIVIDE-BY-8.
14DD:05 03      29          ORA    IAL       ;OR WITH PREVIOUS RESULT.
14DF:85 03      30          STA    IAL       ;RESULT INTO BASE ADDRESS LOW.
14E1:A5 02      31          LDA    YPOS      ;ADD $80?
14E3:29 08      32          AND    #$08      ;DEPENDS ON BIT THREE.
14E5:F0 06      33          BEQ    PAST      ;NO.
14E7:A9 80      34          LDA    #$80      ;YES, ADD $80.
14E9:65 03      35          ADC    IAL
14EB:85 03      36          STA    IAL
14ED:A9 00      37 PAST     LDA    #00       ;WORK WITH THE X-COORDINATE.
14EF:A2 08      38          LDX    #08       ;DIVISION STARTS HERE.
14F1:06 01      39          ASL    XPOS      ;REFER TO EXAMPLE 5-13.
14F3:2A         40 BR1      ROL    A
14F4:C9 07      41          CMP    #07
14F6:90 02      42          BCC    BR2
14F8:E9 07      43          SBC    #07
14FA:26 01      44 BR2      ROL    XPOS
14FC:CA         45          DEX
14FD:D0 F4      46          BNE    BR1
14FF:AA         47          TAX              ;REMAINDER INTO X. QUOTIENT IN
                                                XPOS.
1500:38         48          SEC              ;CARRY CONTAINS BIT TO BE SET.
1501:A9 00      49          LDA    #00       ;CLEAR ACCUMULATOR.
1503:2A         50 BR3      ROL    A         ;# OF SHIFTS = REMAINDER+1.
1504:CA         51          DEX              ;DECREMENT REMAINDER
1505:10 FC      52          BPL    BR3       ;UNTIL IT IS ZERO.
1507:A4 01      53          LDY    XPOS      ;QUOTIENT BECOMES Y INDEX.
1509:11 03      54          ORA    (IAL),Y   ;SET THE DESIRED BIT WITHOUT
150B:91 03      55          STA    (IAL),Y   ;AFFECTING THE OTHERS.
150D:60         56          RTS              ;THAT'S IT, FOLKS.
```

16-bit division. We chose to trade 24 points for simplicity in our programming effort.

Subroutine PLOT should be studied in connection with the expressions for BADH and BADL. BADH is calculated in lines 9–22. BADL is calculated in lines 23–36. The division-by-7, mentioned earlier, is performed in lines 37–46. The quotient is stored in XPOS and the remainder is transferred to the X register to shift a logic 1 into the correct bit. Finally, in line 53 the accumulator, containing a single logic 1 in the appropriate bit, is ORed with the chosen location in the hires picture buffer, and the result is stored in the picture buffer. The dot designated by the x and y coordinates will be turned on; all other dots will be unaffected. *Note in particular the use of the indirect indexed addressing modes in lines 54 and 55 of subroutine PLOT in Example 6–16.*

A program to test and demonstrate subroutine PLOT is listed in Example 6–17. It allows you to input two 2-digit hexadecimal numbers from the keyboard, x-coordinate first, y-coordinate second, and it plots the designated point on the screen of the video monitor. The program calls subroutine CLEAR described in Example 6–15, subroutine PLOT described in Example 6–16, and subroutine RDBYTE described in Example 5–20. Note that it sets the Apple II soft switches so that the microcomputer is in the mixed high-resolution graphics and text mode. The program does not illustrate any new instructions or addressing modes, so it will not be discussed in any more detail.

Example 6–17. A Program to Demonstrate the Plot Subroutine

Object: Plot the dot corresponding to two 8-bit numbers input from the keyboard.

```
150E:D8          14        CLD             ;CLEAR DECIMAL MODE.
150F:20 A6 14    15        JSR   CLEAR     ;CLEAR THE HIRES SCREEN.
1512:8D 53 C0    16        STA   SS1       ;SET THE SOFT SWITCHES
1515:8D 50 C0    17        STA   SS2       ;FOR HIRES GRAPHICS
1518:8D 57 C0    18        STA   SS3       ;MIXED WITH TEXT.
151B:8D 54 C0    19        STA   SS4
151E:20 00 11    20 BR6    JSR   RDBYTE    ;GET THE X COORDINATE.
1521:85 01       21        STA   XPOS      ;STORE IT HERE.
1523:20 00 11    22        JSR   RDBYTE    ;GET THE Y COORDINATE.
1526:85 02       23        STA   YPOS      ;STORE IT HERE.
1528:20 BE 14    24        JSR   PLOT      ;PLOT THE POINT ON THE HIRES
                                             SCREEN.
152B:18          25        CLC             ;FORCE A JUMP TO GET ANOTHER
                                             POINT.
152C:90 F0       26        BCC   BR6
```

The PLOT subroutine has great potential in a variety of applications. With an analog-to-digital converter collecting data, the PLOT subroutine could be used to graph the data on the screen, making a digital storage oscilloscope. If the game paddles are used to input x and y coordinates, you can sketch a figure on the hires screen. The PLOT subroutine has potential for drawing circuit diagrams, particularly if the basic circuit symbols could be stored in memory and placed at a particular coordinate on the screen. The PLOT subroutine is the nucleus of a large variety of graphics applications.

We conclude this section with a program to use the PLOT subroutine to graph the contents of one page of memory. The program is listed in Example 6–18. The numbers stored in locations $0F00 to $0FFF become the y-coordinates, while the low-order byte of the address (ADL) is the *x*-coordinate. The absolute indexed by X addressing mode is used. Note that since this routine and subroutine PLOT both use the X register, it must be saved before the subroutine call and restored after the subroutine call. A program to generate four cycles of a sine function and store them in page $0F is given in Example 6–19. Execute Example 6–19 first, then run the program in Example 6–18. The results are shown in Fig. 6–5, a photograph of the video monitor screen.

Example 6–18. A Program to Plot the Contents of a Table

Object: Plot the contents of page $0F of memory. The number in a memory location will be the *y*-coordinate, and the ADL of the location will be the *x*-coordinate. Plot all 256 points.

152E:AD 52 C0	15		LDA	SS1	;SET SOFT SWITCHES
1531:AD 50 C0	16		LDA	SS2	;FOR ALL HIRES GRAPHICS.
1534:AD 57 C0	17		LDA	SS3	
1537:AD 54 C0	18		LDA	SS4	
153A:20 A6 14	19		JSR	CLEAR	;CLEAR THE HIRES SCREEN.
153D:A2 00	20		LDX	#00	;INITIALIZE X INDEX TO ZERO.
153F:BD 00 0F	21	LOOP	LDA	GRAPH,X	;GET GRAPH DATA FROM TABLE.
1542:85 02	22		STA	YPOS	;DATA INTO Y-COORDINATE.
1544:86 01	23		STX	XPOS	;X INTO X-COORDINATE.
1546:86 FF	24		STX	TEMP	;SAVE INDEX.
1548:20 BE 14	25		JSR	PLOT	;PLOT THE POINT.
154B:A6 FF	26		LDX	TEMP	;RESTORE INDEX.
154D:E8	27		INX		;GET ANOTHER POINT?
154E:D0 EF	28		BNE	LOOP	;YES.
1550:F0 FE	29	INFIN	BEQ	INFIN	;NO, LOOP HERE FOREVER.

Example 6–19. A BASIC Program to Place Four Periods of a Sine Function in Page $0F of Memory

Object: Write a program to make a table of the sine function.

```
10 FOR I = 0 TO 255
20 Y = 95 * SIN (2 * I * 3.14159
   / 64)
30 Y = 95 − Y
35 PRINT I,Y
40 POKE 15 * 256 + I,Y
50 NEXT I
60 END
```

INDEXED INDIRECT ADDRESSING

This addressing mode is used less often than any of the addressing modes in the 6502 instruction set. It is similar but not identical with the indirect indexed addressing mode just described. Symbolize the second byte of an instruction using the indexed indirect addressing mode by IAL. The number in the X register is added to IAL to give an 8-bit number that is the low-order byte of a zero-page location that contains the ADL of the operand. The ADH of the operand is in the next zero-page location. In symbols

$$ADL = [IAL + [X]]$$
$$ADH = [IAL + [X] + 1]$$
$$operand = [ADH\text{-}ADL]$$

where any carry is ignored. The assembly language symbolism for this addressing mode is

LDA (IAL,X)

and the instruction set summary designates this addressing mode with the notation (IND,X). Only the X register may be used as an index. Example 6–20 illustrates a calculation, and the addressing mode is diagrammed in Fig. 6–6.

Example 6–20. Calculating the Address of the Operand When Indexed Indirect Addressing Is Used

Find the address of the operand referenced by the indexed indirect instruction in the following program segment. Assume [$0017] = $FF and [$0018] = $A0.

```
$0200 A2 14    LDX #$14
$0202 E1 03    SBC (MEM,X)
```

Solution: The location of the ADL is $03 + $14 = $17. Location $0017 contains $FF and location $0018 contains $A0, so the location referenced by the SBC (MEM,X) instruction is $A0FF, and the operand will be found there.

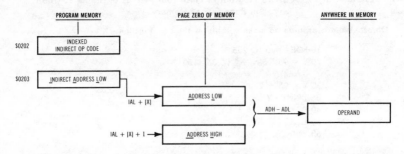

Fig. 6–6. Diagram of the indexed indirect addressing mode, where quantities inside the boxes represent the *contents* of those memory locations and quantities outside the boxes refer to the addresses of the boxes.

A program to illustrate the indexed indirect addressing mode is listed in Example 6–21. The instructions that are of particular interest in the present context have been delineated by asterisks. The function of the program is to allow the user to select, from the Apple keyboard, one of three graphs to be displayed by the PLOT subroutine. Each graph occupies 256 locations, or one page of memory. In Example 6–21 the addresses of these pages, $0F00, $0E00, and $0D00, are loaded into six zero-page locations to be referenced by the LDA (IAL,X) instruction. Clearly, more graphs, and hence more pages of memory, could also be included in the program. The user enters a number from zero to two ($00, $01, or $02) using the RDBYTE subroutine, and the program displays the data in page $0F, $0E, or $0D, respectively. (This program leaves the writer with an uneasy feeling that it might be simpler if we were not trying to illustrate the indexed indirect addressing mode.)

Example 6–21. A Program to Select One of Three Graphs to be Displayed

1552:AD 53 C0	17	LDA	SS1	;SET SOFT SWITCHES FOR MIXED
1555:AD 50 C0	18	LDA	SS2	;HIRES GRAPHICS
1558:AD 57 C0	19	LDA	SS3	;AND TEXT.
155B:AD 54 C0	20	LDA	SS4	
155E:A9 00	21	LDA	#00	;SET UP ADDRESS TABLE.
1560:85 E0	22	STA	IAL	
1562:85 E2	23	STA	IAL+2	
1564:85 E4	24	STA	IAL+4	
1566:A9 0F	25	LDA	#$0F	
1568:85 E1	26	STA	IAL+1	
156A:A9 0E	27	LDA	#$0E	
156C:85 E3	28	STA	IAL+3	
156E:A9 0D	29	LDA	#$0D	
1570:85 E5	30	STA	IAL+5	
1572:20 A6 14	31	JSR	CLEAR	;CLEAR SCREEN.
1575:20 00 11	32 NEWX	JSR	RDBYTE	;GET AN 8-BIT NUMBER.
1578:85 0A	33	STA	TEMPX	;SAVE A.
157A:20 A6 14	34	JSR	CLEAR	;CLEAR SCREEN.
157D:A5 0A	35	LDA	TEMPX	;RESTORE A.
157F:AA	36	TAX		;PUT IT IN THE X REGISTER.
1580:0A	37	ASL	A	;DOUBLE IT.
1581:A8	38	TAY		
	39	**************************		
1582:A1 E0	40 LOOP	LDA	(IAL,X)	;GET DATA FROM THE TABLE.
1584:85 02	41	STA	YPOS	;PUT IT IN THE Y-COORDINATE.
	42	**************************		
1586:B9 E0 00	43	LDA	IAL,Y	
1589:85 01	44	STA	XPOS	
158B:84 0B	45	STY	TEMPY	;SAVE Y.
158D:86 0A	46	STX	TEMPX	;SAVE X.
158F:20 BE 14	47	JSR	PLOT	;PLOT THE POINT.
1592:A4 0B	48	LDY	TEMPY	;RESTORE Y
1594:A6 0A	49	LDX	TEMPX	
1596:38	50	SEC		
1597:B9 E0 00	51	LDA	IAL,Y	

```
159A:69 00        52              ADC    #$00
159C:99 E0 00     53              STA    IAL,Y
159F:D0 E1        54              BNE    LOOP
15A1:F0 D2        55              BEQ    NEWX      ;GRAPH A NEW TABLE.
```

EXERCISES

Exercise 6–1

To review the new concepts in this chapter you should load each of the programs, save them on tape or diskette, and test each one by executing it. Use simple input values and check the programs with pencil and paper calculations if necessary. Make a serious attempt to understand how each program works.

Exercise 6–2

To become more familiar with the absolute indexed addressing mode, write a program that calculates the addition checksum of all the data in page three ($0300–$03FF) of memory. This checksum should be a 2-byte sum of all the character codes located from $0300 to $03FF. An answer is given in Example 6–22.

Exercise 6–3

The purpose of this exercise is to become familiar with indirect index addressing. Write a program to move the data in the hires primary picture buffer (locations $2000 to $3FFF) to the secondary picture buffer (locations $4000 to $5FFF). One solution is given in Example 6–23.

Example 6–22. A Program to Calculate a 2-Byte Checksum

```
15A3:A9 00        9               LDA    #00
15A5:D8           10              CLD
15A6:85 0A        11              STA    CHKSMLO
15A8:85 0B        12              STA    CHKSMHI
15AA:A2 FF        13              LDX    #$FF
15AC:BD 00 03     14 LOOP         LDA    $0300,X
15AF:18           15              CLC
15B0:65 0A        16              ADC    CHKSMLO
15B2:85 0A        17              STA    CHKSMLO
15B4:A9 00        18              LDA    #00
15B6:65 0B        19              ADC    CHKSMHI
15B8:85 0B        20              STA    CHKSMHI
15BA:CA           21              DEX
15BB:10 EF        22              BPL    LOOP
15BD:60           23              RTS
```

Example 6–23. A Program to Move an 8K Block of Data

```
15CE:A9 00        5               LDA    #00
15D0:85 10        6               STA    $10
```

```
15D2:85 12        7           STA    $12
15D4:A9 20        8           LDA    #$20
15D6:85 11        9           STA    $11
15D8:A9 40       10           LDA    #$40
15DA:85 13       11           STA    $13
15DC:A0 00       12           LDY    #00
15DE:B1 10       13  LOOPY    LDA    ($10),Y
15E0:91 12       14           STA    ($12),Y
15E2:C8          15           INY
15E3:D0 F9       16           BNE    LOOPY
15E5:E6 11       17           INC    $11
15E7:E6 13       18           INC    $13
15E9:A5 11       19           LDA    $11
15EB:C9 40       20           CMP    #$40
15ED:D0 EF       21           BNE    LOOPY
15EF:60          22           RTS
```

Exercise 6–4

Generalize the program in Exercise 6–3 to move a block of data starting with address $WXYZ and ending with $PQRS to another starting location, $ABCD. Assume $YZ, $WX, $RS, $PQ, and $AB represent hexadecimal numbers stored in locations $0010 through $0015. The writer's answer is given in Example 6–24.

Example 6–24. A General-Purpose Block-Move Program

```
15F0:D8           5           CLD
15F1:E6 12        6           INC    $12
15F3:D0 02        7           BNE    BR0
15F5:E6 13        8           INC    $13
15F7:A0 00        9  BR0      LDY    #00
15F9:B1 10       10  LOOP     LDA    ($10),Y
15FB:91 14       11           STA    ($14),Y
15FD:E6 10       12           INC    $10
15FF:D0 02       13           BNE    BR1
1601:E6 11       14           INC    $11
1603:E6 14       15  BR1      INC    $14
1605:D0 02       16           BNE    BR2
1607:E6 15       17           INC    $15
1609:A5 10       18  BR2      LDA    $10
160B:C5 12       19           CMP    $12
160D:A5 11       20           LDA    $11
160F:E5 13       21           SBC    $13
1611:90 E6       22           BCC    LOOP
1613:00          23           BRK
```

Exercise 6–5

Write a program to read the keyboard, convert the ASCII code to Morse code (see Tables 6–2 and 6–3) and store the result in page nine of memory. Each entry on the keyboard should be added to the table. Use indexed indirect addressing to fill the table, and use absolute indexed by X addressing to do the code conversion. The author's answer is given in Example 6–25.

Example 6–25. A Program to Store Morse Code Characters in a Buffer

```
1487:A0 00        10          LDY    #00
1489:84 00        11          STY    IAL
148B:A9 09        12          LDA    #$09
148D:85 01        13          STA    IAL+1
148F:2C 00 C0     14  WAIT    BIT    KYBD
1492:10 FB        15          BPL    WAIT
1494:AD 00 C0     16          LDA    KYBD
1497:8D 10 C0     17          STA    STROBE
149A:AA           18          TAX
149B:BD 00 08     19          LDA    CODE,X
149E:91 00        20          STA    (IAL),Y
14A0:E6 00        21          INC    IAL
14A2:18           22          CLC
14A3:90 EA        23          BCC    WAIT
```

Exercise 6–6

Ultimately, the only way to learn to program is to try programming problems until you succeed. You cannot learn to play a piano by reading about it in a book, nor can you become a good programmer without struggling through the process of writing programs. Here are some programs to try if you cannot think of some programming problems for yourself.

a. Write a program to count the number of negative numbers (bit seven is logic 1) in a table from $0500 to $057F.

b. Write a program to find the smallest entry in a table from $0080 to $00FF.

c. Write a program to shift a number represented by four bytes one bit to the left.

d. Write a program to clear the secondary page ($4000–$5FFF) of the hires graphics screen.

e. Write a program that inputs six 2-digit hexadecimal numbers from the keyboard and outputs them in reverse order to the screen.

f. Write a program that plots a point on the low-resolution graphics screen.

g. Write a program that uses the game paddle inputs to control the position of a dot on the screen.

h. Write a program that multiplies one 16-bit number by another 16-bit number and stores the 32-bit result.

i. Write a program that divides a 16-bit number by an 8-bit number.

j. Write a subroutine that multiplies a 4-byte binary number by ten.

k. Write a subroutine that divides a 4-byte binary number by ten.

l. Write a program to order the elements in a table from the smallest to the largest.

m. Write a program that inputs two bcd numbers, multiplies them, and outputs the result in bcd.

CHAPTER 7

Subroutines, the Stack, and Interrupts

OBJECTIVES

At the completion of this chapter you should be able to:

- Use subroutines in writing programs and understand how the microprocessor handles the JSR and RTS instructions.
- Understand how interrupts are produced and how the microprocessor handles the interrupt signals.
- Use these instructions: CLI, SEI, BRK, JSR, RTS, RTI, PHA, PHP, PLA, PLP, TXS, TSX, and NOP.
- Understand the importance of the stack and how it operates.

INTRODUCTION

You have already been exposed to the idea of a subroutine, the JSR instruction, and the RTS instruction. Furthermore, if you have programmed in BASIC or another high-level language, the purpose of subroutines will be evident. This chapter will deal with subroutines at a slightly different level than before, and it may be worthwhile to quickly review the importance of subroutines.

Many of the programs in this book, which were written to illustrate the 6502 instruction set, would generally be part of larger programs with more elaborate objectives. The programs in this book have generally been referred to as *routines*. A *routine* is simply a program segment designed to implement a particular objective, for example, the bcd-to-binary conversion routine. Long programs can frequently be divided into groups of simpler programs, each of which is usually referred to as a routine.

If the same routine is used in several different places in the program, then it is usually advantageous to use a subroutine call to the routine, *rather than duplicating* the routine at each place in the program where it is required. This affords a great savings in the amount of memory required for a particular program. A subroutine is written and stored once. The program can *jump to* the subroutine whenever it is needed, followed by a *return* to the main program. The price for this technique of saving program space and programming effort is the time it takes the microprocessor to process the JSR and RTS instructions. In unusual cases it may be necessary to use *straight-line code,* avoiding the extra time required to process a subroutine call.

Another reason for using subroutines is that they allow a *modular* approach to program design. That is, a series of routines might be used to accomplish a particular objective, where each of the routines has a much more limited objective. The *sub*routines that make up the entire program can be developed one at a time, perhaps even by different programmers, and then combined to accomplish the major objective of the program. The main program will consist mainly of subroutine calls. Some monitors are written in this way, and any monitor, including the Apple II monitor, is a good place to look for extensive use of subroutines.

The 6502 microprocessor has two, quite different, ways of jumping to and returning from a routine. We have just discussed one of these ways, namely by means of the JSR and RTS instructions. The other way of jumping to a routine is through the use of *interrupts.* In this case a circuit that is external to the microprocessor signals it with an appropriate voltage change on one of its 40 pins and thereby *requests* that the microprocessor *interrupt* what it is doing and proceed directly to process a particular routine called an *interrupt routine.* A large portion of this chapter will be devoted to a more complete description of the interrupt concept, and we will not elaborate further at this point.

Finally, it will become obvious that, in order to *return* from either a subroutine or an interrupt, a place to store the *return address* and other important information is necessary. This place turns out to be page one of memory (locations $0100–$01FF), and it is referred to as the *stack*. The stack will also be discussed in detail in this chapter.

SUBROUTINES

A program segment or routine that is used at several points in a program through the use of the JSR instruction is called a *sub-*

routine. Like a program, a subroutine has a specific objective, such as multiplying two 8-bit numbers. Once designed as a subroutine, it cannot be used by itself. The program that contains the JSR instruction that uses or calls the subroutine is called the *main program*. The main program can call the subroutine at any point by means of the JSR instruction. On the other hand, the subroutine signals the main program that it has completed its task by means of an RTS instruction. The main program then continues execution at the instruction *following* the JSR instruction. In this way the instructions in the subroutine have been "inserted" in the main program, between the JSR instruction and the one that follows it.

The JSR instruction is a 3-byte instruction. The first byte is the op code ($20), the second byte is the ADL of the location of the first byte in the subroutine, and the third byte is the ADH of the location of the first byte in the subroutine. Consider the program excerpt shown in Example 7–1. The STA, LDA, and LDX are "dummy" instructions used to illustrate the fact that the JSR instruction is usually found somewhere in a main program. In Example 7–1 we also assume that there are many instructions in the subroutine, only the first and last of which have been shown.

Example 7–1. Illustration of a Subroutine Call and a Return From Subroutine

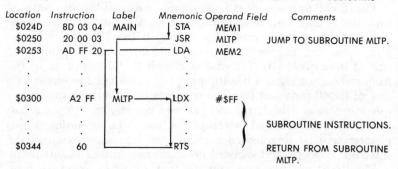

Location	Instruction	Label	Mnemonic	Operand Field	Comments
$024D	8D 03 04	MAIN	STA	MEM1	
$0250	20 00 03		JSR	MLTP	JUMP TO SUBROUTINE MLTP.
$0253	AD FF 20		LDA	MEM2	
$0300	A2 FF	MLTP	LDX	#$FF	
					SUBROUTINE INSTRUCTIONS.
$0344	60		RTS		RETURN FROM SUBROUTINE MLTP.

Refer to Example 7–1. The JSR MLTP instruction results in a jump to the subroutine labeled MLTP, and the op code of the first instruction in subroutine MLTP is located at address $0300. The instruction located at this address will be executed immediately following execution of the JSR MLTP instruction. Subsequent instructions in the subroutine will be executed until an RTS instruction is encountered. Execution of this instruction will result in the next op code being fetched from the location immediately following the last byte of the JSR instruction, address $0253 in Example 7–1.

Although the JSR instruction contains the information necessary to locate the subroutine, it should be obvious that the single-byte RTS instruction does not contain any *return address*. How could it? As indicated above, a jump to a subroutine may occur *anywhere* in the main program, and therefore there would be a number of different return addresses.

How does the microprocessor know where to fetch the next instruction after an RTS instruction? Before the microprocessor jumps to the subroutine it stores the *address of the location of the third byte* of the JSR instruction in a special section of read/write memory called the *stack*. When the RTS instruction is executed, this address is fetched from the stack and stored in the program counter. The program counter is then automatically incremented by one, as it normally is during each clock cycle, to identify the address at which the op code immediately following the JSR instruction is stored.

Refer again to Example 7–1. In this example the address of the "$03" byte is stored on the stack. That is, the numbers $52 and $02 are stored on the stack. When the RTS instruction is executed, the number $0252 is placed in the program counter after being read from the stack. The program counter is incremented to $0253, and the next op code is fetched from location $0253.

Since both subroutines and interrupts, to be described in a subsequent section of this chapter, make use of the stack, we now turn to an explanation of the stack.

THE STACK

The stack is a series of read/write (RAM) memory locations in page one of memory (addresses $0100–$01FF). It is sometimes called a *push-down* stack because locations are filled from the top location downward, and are emptied (loosely speaking) from the bottom upward. It could better be called a *first-in, last-out* (filo) memory, because the *first* byte placed on the stack by the microprocessor is the *last* byte taken off the stack.

All stack operations make use of a 6502 internal register called the *stack pointer, S*. It is an 8-bit register that contains the low-order address of the *next available* location on the stack. The high-order address of this location is, of course, $01. In other words, the stack pointer *points* to a location in page one of memory that the microprocessor may use to store information.

The information stored in the case of a subroutine call is the *return address;* that is, the address of the third byte of the JSR instruction. The operation of the stack and the stack pointer in this case is illustrated in Chart 7–1. In particular, this chart refers to the case outlined in Example 7–1. Assume that before the JSR instruction the value $A9 was in the stack pointer. (A method to set the stack pointer will be described below.) During execution of the JSR instruction the ADH of the return address is first stored at location $01A9 by placing the contents of the stack pointer on the low-order eight lines of the address bus and $01 on the high-order eight lines of the address bus. The high-order byte of the return address is placed on the data bus. Thus the microprocessor *writes* the number $02 into location $01A9.

Chart 7–1. Stack Parameters During the Subroutine Call Illustrated in Example 7–1

Page One Address	Page One Contents		Stack Pointer Contents
	Before JSR	After JSR	During JSR
$01A9	XX*	$02	$A9
$01A8	XX	$52	$A8
$01A7	XX	XX	$A7
	Before RTS	After RTS	Stack Pointer Contents During RTS
$01A9	$02	XX	$A9
$01A8	$52	XX	$A8
$01A7	XX	XX	$A7

*XX means "don't care."

Continue to refer to Example 7–1 and Chart 7–1. The next effect of the JSR instruction is to decrement the stack pointer, and the low-order byte of the return address is stored on the stack at location $01A8. The return address is now on the stack, and the JSR instruction concludes execution by decrementing the stack pointer once more, so that it always points to an *available* or unused location.

The execution of the RTS instruction reverses the action of the stack pointer. It is first incremented and the ADL of the return address is *read* from the stack. The stack pointer is incremented again and the ADH of the return address is read from the stack. The stack pointer is now pointing to the same location it identified before the JSR instruction was encountered. The ADH-ADL go into the program counter, the program counter is incremented, and execution continues with the first instruction following the JSR instruction in the main program. Study Chart 7–1.

The JSR instruction produces two decrements in the number

in the stack pointer, while the RTS instruction produces two increments. Before continuing our discussion of the stack we are now in a position to briefly summarize the JSR and RTS instructions, as follows:

- JSR—Push the *address* of the third byte of the JSR instruction on the top of the stack in the order ADH, ADL. Place the second and third bytes of the JSR instruction into the PCL and PCH, respectively. Continue execution.
- RTS—Pull the top two bytes off the stack and place them in the program counter in the order PCL, PCH. Increment the program counter and continue execution.

It is clear that the JSR and RTS instructions require the microprocessor to perform several operations, and, consequently, one would expect that these instructions take a lot of time. They do. An examination of the instruction set summary in Table 2–2 shows that they each take 6 clock cycles, whereas the shortest instructions only take 2 clock cycles. As pointed out earlier, in applications where time is critical it may be necessary to avoid subroutines.

When power is applied to the microcomputer the stack pointer has a random number in it; that is, there is no way to predict what number will be in the stack pointer after power-up. Generally this is no problem since the stack will "wrap around" $00. That is, if the stack pointer is $00 and it is decremented by a subroutine call, for example, then its new value is $FF, and there are no problems that arise when it goes through $00. Sometimes situations occur where it is desirable to be able to set the stack pointer. This is accomplished by first using the LDX instruction to get the desired number and then using the TXS (transfer the number in the X register to the stack pointer, S) instruction to put the number in the S register. Such situations will not arise in this book.

Another potential problem arises when subroutines are *nested*. If one subroutine calls another, the second is said to be "nested" in the first. For example, a subroutine to read the Apple keyboard might call a subroutine to convert the character code into a hexadecimal number. In this case the ASCII-to-hex conversion routine is nested in the keyboard-input routine. When the main program calls the keyboard-input routine, it in turn calls the ASCII-to-hex routine. Note that each subroutine requires two positions on the stack, so a subroutine nested within another subroutine will use a total of four positions on the stack. It should be clear that since there are only 256 locations on the stack, we could have subroutines nested 128 deep.

Such a program is extremely unlikely, but if it were written and execution were attempted, what would happen? If the 128th subroutine called a 129th subroutine, the 129th subroutine would use the same stack locations as the first subroutine, and it would therefore destroy the possibility of ever *returning* to the main program. Although this event is unlikely, situations can arise where data in the stack are destroyed and the program returns to never-never land. Usually this occurs in the testing stage of a program, when an *odd* number of stack operations has accidentally been placed in a program.

STACK OPERATIONS AND USE OF THE STACK FOR STORAGE

A program that makes use of the X register, for example, may call a subroutine that also requires the use of this register. If this subroutine is called by a JSR instruction that is in a loop that is using the X register as a counter, then the count will be modified by the subroutine call. Since that is more often the case than not, it would be desirable to have a technique to save the contents of the 6502's internal registers so that after a subroutine uses these registers, the registers may be restored to the same value they had prior to the subroutine call. Failure to *save* and *restore* registers produces unusual and typically undesirable effects, whose cause is difficult to determine because the program and the subroutine may be essentially correct except for the fact that they are both using the same register for different purposes.

The approach taken by the programmers who wrote the Apple II monitor is illustrated by two monitor subroutines, IOSAVE at $FF4A and IOREST at $FF3F. The subroutine IOSAVE *saves* the contents of the 6502's 8-bit registers (A-X-Y-P-S) in zero-page locations $45 through $49, respectively. The subroutine IOREST *restores* all five registers from these locations. Consult your *Apple II Reference Manual* for details.

A different, but equally valid, approach to the same problem is to use the stack for temporary storage using the so-called stack operations. We will illustrate this technique shortly, but first we summarize the principal stack operations. In the summary that follows, let S stand for the number in the stack pointer and M_S symbolize a memory location in page one of memory whose address-low is the number in the stack pointer, S.

- PHA—Push the accumulator on the stack: place the number in the accumulator on the stack, then decrement the stack pointer. The logical expressions for this operation are $A \rightarrow M_S$, $S - 1 \rightarrow S$. See Fig. 7-1.

- PHP—Push the P register on the stack: place the contents of the processor status register on the stack, then decrement the stack pointer. Logically, $P \rightarrow M_S$, $S - 1 \rightarrow S$. See Fig. 7–2.
- PLA—Pull accumulator from the stack: increment the stack pointer, then load the accumulator with the number on the stack. The logical expressions for this operation are, $S + 1 \rightarrow S$, $M_S \rightarrow A$. See Fig. 7–3.
- PLP—Pull the P register from the stack: increment the stack pointer, then load the P register with the contents of the stack. Logically, $S + 1 \rightarrow S$, $M \rightarrow P$. See Fig. 7–4.

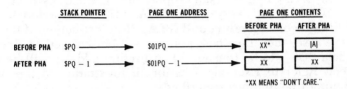

Fig. 7–1. Diagram of the PHA instruction, where [A] symbolizes the contents of the accumulator and PQ symbolizes any 2-digit hexadecimal number.

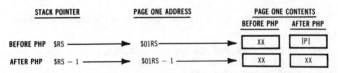

Fig. 7–2. Diagram of the PHP instruction, where [P] symbolizes the contents of the processor status register and RS symbolizes any 2-digit hexadecimal number.

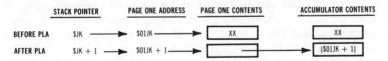

Fig. 7–3. Diagram of the PLA instruction, where JK symbolizes any 2-digit hexadecimal number and [$01JK + 1] symbolizes the contents of the location whose address is $01JK + 1.

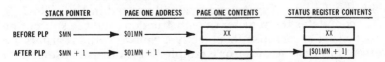

Fig. 7–4. Diagram of the PLP instruction, where MN symbolizes any 2-digit hexadecimal number and [$01MN + 1] symbolizes the contents of the location whose address is $01MN +1.

We will now see how the 6502's registers may be saved during a subroutine call and restored after the call. Assume that the contents of the accumulator and the P register are to be preserved during a subroutine call. *Before* the JSR instruction one would place a PHA and a PHP instruction. *After* the JSR instruction, still in the main program, one would have a PLP and a PLA instruction, *in that order*. Remember, the accumulator was "first in" so it will be "last out." It is very important to keep track of the *order* in which the registers were saved, because they must be restored in *reverse order*. It is also very important that the stack operation instructions occur in *pairs*. That is, for every push (PHA, PHP) instruction there should be a corresponding pull (PLA, PLP) instruction. If this is not the case, then the stack pointer will not correctly point to the data that is to be transferred or a return address will be incorrect. Refer to Example 7–2 for an illustration of the programming example just described.

Example 7–2. Saving A and P Before a Subroutine Call and Restoring A and P After a Subroutine Call

Show how the A and P registers may be saved and restored with instructions in the main program.

Solution: The program segment in the main program would appear as follows:

⋮

PHA	SAVE THE CONTENTS OF THE ACCUMULATOR ON THE STACK.
PHP	SAVE THE P REGISTER CONTENTS ON THE STACK.
JSR SUB	JUMP TO THE SUBROUTINE.
PLP	PULL THE P REGISTER FROM THE STACK (RESTORE P).
PLA	PULL THE NUMBER FOR THE ACCUMULATOR FROM THE STACK (RESTORE A).

⋮

It is more common to perform the register save and restore functions in the subroutine itself. Assume that we want to save the accumulator, the X register, and the Y register during a subroutine call. Example 7–3 illustrates the technique. First the number in the accumulator is saved on the stack with a PHA instruction. The accumulator is now free, and the number in the Y register is transferred to A with a TYA instruction, and then this number is placed on the stack with a second PHA instruction. Next X is transferred to A and A is transferred to the stack with the TXA PHA instruction pair illustrated in Example 7–3. This completes the register save instructions and the subroutine proceeds to accomplish its objective. Note how the registers are restored in reverse order in Example 7–3, and also observe that there is an *even* number of stack operations, with the number of "pushes" equal to the number of "pulls."

We conclude this section with another example of a subroutine that reads the Apple keyboard. Most keyboard-read sub-routines *wait* for a key to be pressed before returning to the calling program. In certain applications it is more desirable to have the microcomputer scan the keyboard at regular intervals to see if a key has been pressed, but rather than wait in a loop for a key to be pressed, the microcomputer continues executing the calling program after scanning the keyboard. The microcomputer can continue to process information or control a device without being stalled in a loop. It *polls* the keyboard to see if a key has been pressed. If a key has been pressed the subroutine returns to the main program with the character code in the accumulator and the V flag in the P register set. Otherwise the V flag is clear.

Example 7–3. Saving A, X, and Y During a Subroutine Call

Show how the A, X, and Y registers may be saved with stack operations placed in the subroutine.

Solution: The subroutine would appear as follows:

```
PHA        TRANSFER A TO THE STACK. FIRST INSTRUCTION IN THE SUBROUTINE.
TYA        TRANSFER Y TO A.
PHA        PUSH A ON THE STACK.
TXA        TRANSFER X TO A.
PHA        PUSH A ON THE STACK.
:          SUBROUTINE INSTRUCTIONS.
:
PLA        PULL A FROM THE STACK.
TAX        TRANSFER IT TO X.
PLA        PULL A FROM THE STACK.
TAY        TRANSFER IT TO Y.
PLA        PULL A FROM THE STACK.
RTS        RETURN TO THE CALLING PROGRAM. LAST INSTRUCTION IN SUBROUTINE.
```

The routine is given in Example 7–4, and it illustrates several of the ideas mentioned thus far in this chapter. Example 7–4 also includes a calling program that *simulates* the real program that might call this subroutine. Focus your attention on the sub-routine. Recall that if bit seven of the keyboard input port, KYBD at location $C000, is clear then a key has not been pressed, and the subroutine returns with the V flag clear. If a key has been pressed, then bit seven of the input port is set, the V flag will be set with the LDA KYBD instruction, and execution will continue with the STA $C010 instruction. This instruction merely resets bit seven of the keyboard input port to zero. To indicate that a character has been input, the character code is put on the video screen by the monitor output sub-routine OUTPUT at location $FDED. In other words, the sub-routine echoes or mimics the input to the output.

Example 7-4. A Subroutine to Poll the Keyboard

```
C000:            3 KYBD     EQU   $C000
─────NEXT OBJECT FILE NAME IS EXAMPLE 7-4.
16A2:            4          ORG   $16A2

16A2:            6 ;MAIN PROGRAM
16A2:20 A8 16    7 MAIN     JSR   INPUT      ;FETCH A CHARACTER.
16A5:4C A2 16    8          JMP   MAIN       ;LOOP BACK.

                10 ***************************
16A8:           11 ;SUBROUTINE INPUT
FDED:           12 OUTPUT   EQU   $FDED
16A8:AD 00 C0   13 INPUT    LDA   KYBD       ;READ THE KEYBOARD PORT.
16AB:10 0A      14          BPL   OUT        ;HAS A KEY BEEN PRESSED?
16AD:8D 10 C0   15          STA   $C010      ;YES, CLEAR THE STROBE.
16B0:48         16          PHA              ;SAVE THE ACCUMULATOR ON THE
                                              STACK.
16B1:08         17          PHP              ;SAVE THE P REGISTER ON THE
                                              STACK.
16B2:20 ED FD   18          JSR   OUTPUT     ;ECHO THE CHARACTER TO THE
                                              MONITOR.
16B5:28         19          PLP              ;PULL THE P REGISTER FROM THE
                                              STACK.
16B6:68         20          PLA              ;RESTORE THE ACCUMULATOR.
16B7:60         21 OUT      RTS              ;NO. RETURN TO MAIN PROGRAM.
```

The OUTPUT subroutine, which is *nested* in the INPUT subroutine, modifies both the accumulator and the P register. Since it is a monitor subroutine it is impossible to modify it to save A and P. Therefore we include in our own subroutine four stack operations. Two of these save A and P on the stack before OUTPUT is called, and two of these stack operations restore A and P after OUTPUT is called. Try running the program to see how it works. Study Example 7-4 in connection with Fig. 7-5, a flowchart of the INPUT subroutine.

INTERRUPTS

Suppose you are using your Apple microcomputer to balance your checkbook, study stock market trends, learn assembly language programming using this book, and you are writing a novel using one of the word processors written for the Apple. Suppose, in addition, you want to make temperature measurements at specific time intervals at various points around your house as part of an effort to minimize energy losses. How can you do both general computing tasks and the temperature measurements? One possible solution is to *interrupt* the general computing whenever a temperature measurement must be made. Frequently it is possible to do this with no noticeable

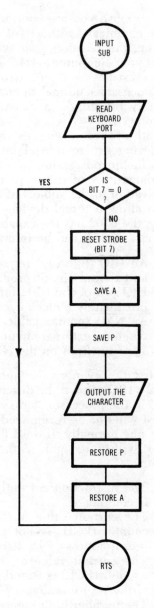

Fig. 7–5. Flowchart of the keyboard INPUT subroutine.

effects on the general use of the computer. You shall learn how interrupts work in a moment.

For another example of a situation where interrupts are useful, suppose you are controlling some process, such as a complex chemical synthesis of some substance. If anything goes wrong, the reaction goes wildly exothermic for example, you want your computer to take immediate steps to stop the process. You must have a "gone wrong" sensor that *interrupts* the microprocessor's normal operation and starts it on another task, namely bringing the situation under control or sounding an alarm.

Both of these examples are intended to motivate you for the following explanation of interrupts. Interrupts are a powerful tool in the possession of a programmer who understands the fundamentals of interrupt operation. We now turn from the motivation to the subject at hand.

To allow external devices to exert control over the program flow, the 6502 has the capability of being *interrupted* by external circuitry. It can be interrupted in either of two ways:

- An $\overline{IRQ}$ (interrupt request) type of interrupt occurs when an external circuit produces a logic 0 voltage *level* on the $\overline{IRQ}$ pin of the 6502 for a time duration equivalent to approximately 8 clock cycles. See Fig. 7–6.
- An $\overline{NMI}$ (nonmaskable interrupt) type of interrupt occurs when an external circuit produces a logic 1 to logic 0 voltage *transition* on the $\overline{NMI}$ pin of the 6502. See Fig. 7–6.

First the events subsequent to an interrupt request on the 6502's $\overline{IRQ}$ pin will be described. If the I flag (interrupt disable flag) in the processor status register is *set* then the interrupt request will *not* be recognized and execution of the program will continue normally. If the I flag is *cleared* then the interrupt request will be recognized and the following sequence of events occurs:

- The instruction currently being executed by the processor is completed.
- The current value of the high-order byte of the program counter (PCH) is stored on the stack. This is half of the return address. The stack pointer is decremented.
- The current value of the low-order byte of the program counter (PCL) is stored on the stack. This is the other half of the return address. The stack pointer is decremented.
- The number in the processor status register, P, is stored on the stack and the stack pointer is decremented.
- The I flag is *set* to disable further interrupt requests.
- The 6502 reads the number in the location whose address is $FFFE. This number becomes the *new* PCL.

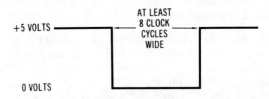

(A) Signal applied to the $\overline{\text{IRQ}}$ pin to produce an interrupt request.

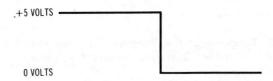

(B) Signal applied to the $\overline{\text{NMI}}$ pin to produce a nonmaskable interrupt.

Fig. 7–6. Signals to produce interrupts.

- The number in location $FFFF becomes the *new* PCH.
- Execution continues with the op code whose address is in PCH-PCL.

In terms that neglect some of the more subtle events described above, an interrupt, *produced by an external event*, causes the program to *jump* to another location, where it continues executing instructions. The address of the *new* location is stored in locations $FFFE and $FFFF. The jump is similar to a jump to a subroutine, since the return addresses are placed on the stack, the return address being, in this case, the location of the op code following the instruction that was interrupted.

The set of instructions starting at the location whose address is in $FFFE and $FFFF is called the *interrupt routine*. Just as a subroutine ends with an RTS (return from subroutine) instruction, an interrupt routine *ends* with an RTI (return from interrupt). The RTI instruction produces the following sequence of events:

- The stack pointer is incremented and the P register is pulled from the stack; thus the P register is restored to the value it had at the completion of the interrupted instruction.
- The stack pointer is incremented and PCL is pulled from the stack.
- The stack pointer is incremented and PCH is pulled from the stack.

- Execution continues at the first instruction following the interrupted instruction.

This completes the entire interrupt request sequence. You should observe the similarities between an interrupt request and a subroutine call. You should also note the differences. A diagram showing the activity of the program counter and the stack pointer during an interrupt request is shown in Chart 7–2. Study this in connection with the previous description and the illustrations given in Example 7–5 and Example 7–6.

Chart 7–2. Diagram of the Program Counter and Stack Pointer Changes During an Interrupt Request

Memory			Remarks
Address		**Contents**	
	Name	*Value*	
	.	.	
	.	.	
.	.	.	
$0150			$50 = [STACK POINTER] after IRQ but before RTI.
$0151	P		P Register stored here during the interrupt.
$0152	PCL	$03	PCL is stored here during the interrupt.
$0153	PCH	$02	PCH is stored here during the interrupt.
.	.	.	
.	.	.	$53 = [STACK POINTER] before IRQ and after RTI.
.	.	.	
.	.	.	
.	.	.	
$0200	LDA	$AD	Somewhere in the main program.
$0201	ADL	$98	Interrupt occurs here.
$0202	ADH	$7F	The "LDA" instruction will be completed.
$0203	BEQ	$F0	The main program continues here after
$0204	THERE	$76	the interrupt routine is completed.
.	.	.	
.	.	.	
.	.	.	
$0380	LDA	$AD	Start of the interrupt routine.
.	.	.	
.	.	.	
$039B	RTI	$40	End of the interrupt routine.
.	.	.	
.	.	.	
.	.	.	
$FFFE	IRQL	$80	Location of interrupt vector low.
$FFFF	IRQH	$03	Location of interrupt vector high.

STACK POINTER

PROGRAM COUNTER

Example 7–5. Tracing the Stack Pointer After an Interrupt Request

Describe how the stack pointer and the contents of the stack change as a result of an interrupt request in the following program segment. Assume the interrupt request occurs during execution of the LDA MEM instruction.

```
0200 AD 98 7F    LDA MEM
0203 F0 76        BEQ LOOP
```

Solution: Assuming the stack pointer was $53 before the interrupt, the number $02 representing the PCH will be stored on the stack at location $0153, and the stack pointer will be decremented to $52. Next, the number $03, representing the PCL at the completion of the LDA instruction, will be stored on the stack at location $0152. The stack pointer will be decremented again, and the contents of the P register at the completion of the LDA instruction will be stored on the stack at the location whose address is $0151. The stack pointer will be decremented a third time to $50.

Example 7–6. Tracing the Stack Pointer Subsequent to an RTI Instruction

Describe how the stack pointer and the numbers on the stack are used as a result of a return from the interrupt described in Example 7–5.

Solution: The stack pointer is first incremented to $51 and the number in location $0151 is transferred to the P register. The number in location $0152 is transferred to the PCL, and the number in location $0153 is transferred to the PCH with suitable increments in the stack pointer. The stack pointer will again be $53 after the RTI instruction is executed, and the program will continue at PCH-PCL = $0203 with the fetch of the BEQ op code.

Before turning to the $\overline{\text{NMI}}$ type of interrupt, it is important to realize that the interrupt disable flag (I flag) in the P register is *set* when an interrupt occurs, and that this prevents any further interrupts *via the* $\overline{\text{IRQ}}$ pin until that flag is cleared. Since the P register is restored during an RTI instruction, the I flag will be cleared after the RTI instruction is executed. This flag can also be set with an SEI (set interrupt flag) instruction to prevent interrupt requests in any program segment where they are not wanted. The flag can be cleared with a CLI (clear interrupt flag) instruction to allow interrupt requests to be recognized. The I flag does not disable or mask $\overline{\text{NMI}}$-type interrupts, described next.

One final note about terminology: the number stored in locations $FFFE and $FFFF is called the *interrupt request vector*. It *points* to the starting location of the interrupt request routine.

A *nonmaskable interrupt* differs from an interrupt request in the following ways:

- The $\overline{\text{NMI}}$ pin on the 6502 is *edge sensitive* rather than *level sensitive*; that is, it responds to a voltage transition rather than a voltage level. An $\overline{\text{NMI}}$ interrupt occurs when a logic 1 to logic 0 voltage transition on the $\overline{\text{NMI}}$ pin is produced by external circuitry.
- The nonmaskable interrupt is recognized and processed *no*

matter what the status is of the interrupt disable flag, I. That is why it is called "nonmaskable."

- The nonmaskable interrupt vector is fetched from locations $FFFA and $FFFB. That is, these locations contain the starting address of the nonmaskable interrupt routine.

The setting and clearing of the interrupt disable flag (I flag) occurs in exactly the same way with an NMI-type interrupt as with an IRQ-type interrupt. Although an NMI *sets* the I flag, this only prevents interrupt requests on the IRQ pin. The interrupt disable flag does not prevent an NMI. The stack operations are identical for both types of interrupts, and the RTI operation is the same. A nonmaskable interrupt can interrupt an IRQ-type interrupt, but an IRQ cannot interrupt an NMI unless the I flag is cleared during the interrupt routine. Thus the nonmaskable interrupt has a higher priority than an IRQ-type interrupt, an important consideration for any decision involving the use of interrupts in an application.

We will take a detailed look at how the Apple II handles interrupts but you must first understand the relationship of the BRK instruction to an interrupt request made on the IRQ pin. The *BRK* instruction is a single-byte instruction which, when executed in a program, forces a jump to the IRQ routine, just as if external circuitry has produced the appropriate signal on the IRQ pin. The only way that the processor distinguishes between the execution of a BRK instruction and an interrupt request on the IRQ pin is in setting the B (break) flag in the processor status register. We have been using the BRK instruction at the end of our programs to force a jump to the monitor when the program is completed. This is part of the interrupt handling structure built into the Apple monitor, and we shall describe it below. No further explanation of the BRK instruction is necessary, but two important details about this instruction should be noted. First, the BRK instruction is not disabled by the I flag, whereas a signal on the IRQ pin is ignored if the I flag is set. The BRK instruction is never ignored. Second, when the BRK instruction is executed, the program counter is incremented by *two*. This means that when the processor returns from the interrupt request routine, it will ignore the program byte immediately following the BRK op code. There should be one "dummy" byte of program separating the BRK op code and the op code of the instruction to be executed on returning from the interrupt routine. If the BRK op code is in location ADH-ADL, then the next instruction to be executed after the interrupt routine must be in location ADH-ADL + 2.

In our use of the BRK instruction to terminate a program, its execution forced a jump to the monitor. The monitor avoids using an RTI instruction so the program *never* returns from the monitor. Since the monitor saves all the 6502's internal register's contents and displays them, this is frequently a useful way to terminate a program segment to see if it is working. The BRK instruction is used to debug programs by inserting it at various places in the program to check the operation of the program to that point.

THE APPLE II'S INTERRUPT HANDLING STRUCTURE

Although the 6502 microprocessor always responds in the same way to interrupt signals on its $\overline{\text{NMI}}$ or $\overline{\text{IRQ}}$, program designers handle the programming aspects of an interrupt in different ways. Thus the Apple II has its own unique way of responding to an interrupt request. Its $\overline{\text{NMI}}$ interrupt handling structure is the simplest of the two, and we will discuss it first.

Recall that the numbers in locations $FFFA and $FFFB are the ADL and the ADH of the first instruction in the $\overline{\text{NMI}}$-type interrupt routine; that is, these numbers are the $\overline{\text{NMI}}$ interrupt vector that points to the interrupt routine. In the Apple II these addresses correspond to *read only memory* (ROM) locations, so we turn to the Apple monitor listings to see what is there.

Location $FFFA contains $FB and location $FFFB contains $03. Thus the $\overline{\text{NMI}}$ interrupt vector is $03FB, and the first instruction in the interrupt routine must be stored at this location. But this location is in read/write memory, so we are free to start the $\overline{\text{NMI}}$ interrupt routine at location $03FB with any instruction that we choose to put in this location. Now location $03FB is only a few locations short of page four (locations $0400 to $04FF) and page four is used for the text shown on the video monitor. So the interrupt routine cannot extend from location $03FB upward. Furthermore, the $\overline{\text{IRQ}}$ interrupt routine uses locations $03FE and $03FF, as you will shortly see, which leaves us with only three locations in page three. This is just enough for a JMP instruction, *so locations $03FB, $03FC, and $03FD should contain a jump to the remainder of the interrupt routine*. If the remainder of this routine is located at $8000 and upward, for example, then a 4C 00 80 instruction should be in locations $03FB–$03FD. The $\overline{\text{NMI}}$ interrupt structure is illustrated in Chart 7–3, and the behavior of the program counter during an $\overline{\text{NMI}}$ interrupt request is illustrated in Example 7–7.

We turn next to the somewhat more complex structure of an $\overline{\text{IRQ}}$ interrupt request on the Apple. This structure is illustrated

Chart 7–3. The Apple II Nonmaskable Interrupt Structure

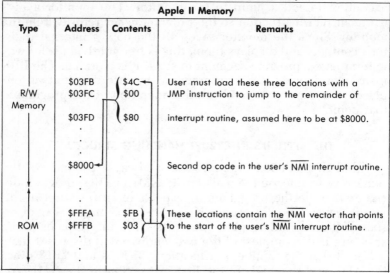

Apple II Memory			
Type	Address	Contents	Remarks
	• • •		
R/W Memory	$03FB $03FC $03FD	$4C $00 $80	User must load these three locations with a JMP instruction to jump to the remainder of interrupt routine, assumed here to be at $8000.
	• • •		
	$8000		Second op code in the user's NMI interrupt routine.
	• • •		
ROM	$FFFA $FFFB	$FB $03	These locations contain the NMI vector that points to the start of the user's NMI interrupt routine.
	• • •		

Example 7–7. Tracing the Program Counter After an NMI-Interrupt Request

Assume that the locations $03FB–$03FD have been loaded with a jump to $8000 where the remainder of the NMI interrupt routine is found, and assume that the NMI line on the Apple II is brought from logic 1 to logic 0 by some external circuit. Trace the history of the program counter subsequent to this signal on the NMI pin of the microprocessor.

Solution: After finishing the instruction that was executing at the time of the interrupt, the program counter and the microprocessor behave as described in the following sequence: (Refer also to Chart 7–3 which describes the Apple NMI interrupt structure.)

PC	Microprocessor Activity
$FFFA	FETCH THE LOW-ORDER BYTE OF THE NMI VECTOR, $FB.
$FFFB	FETCH THE HIGH-ORDER BYTE OF THE NMI VECTOR, $03.
$03FB	FETCH THE JUMP OP CODE, $4C.
$03FC	FETCH THE ADL OF THE JUMP, $00.
$03FD	FETCH THE ADH OF THE JUMP, $80.
$8000	FETCH THE SECOND OP CODE (4C WAS THE FIRST) IN THE NMI ROUTINE.
⋮	CONTINUE EXECUTING THE NMI ROUTINE UNTIL THE RTI INSTRUCTION,
⋮	THEN RETURN TO THE INSTRUCTION FOLLOWING THE INTERRUPTED INSTRUCTION.

in Chart 7–4, and you may wish to refer to Chart 7–4 during the discussion that follows. This chart contains that part of the IRQ interrupt request routine that is found in the Apple II monitor. The interrupt routines in both the Autostart ROM monitor and the older monitor are identical, except for the starting addresses. The Autostart ROM monitor starts the interrupt routine at location $FA40 (see Chart 7–4) while the older monitor starts

Chart 7-4. The Apple II IRQ Interrupt Routine Structure

Location	Contents	Mnemonic	Remarks
			Apple II Memory
.			
.			
.			
$03FE	→$00 ⎫		User must load these locations with the address
$03FF	$0E ⎬		of the start of the user's IRQ routine, assumed
			here to be at $0E00.
.			
.			
.			
$0E00	◄──		Start of the user's interrupt routine.
.			
.			
.			
$FA40	85 45	STA $45 ◄──	Save number in A when interrupt occurred.
$FA42	68	PLA	These two instructions move the number in P
$FA43	48	PHA	into A, and then back on the stack. Since
$FA44	0A	ASL A	P was mapped into A, these shift instructions
$FA45	0A	ASL A	will move the value of the B flag into bit
$FA46	0A	ASL A	seven. If B was clear, then bit seven will
$FA47	30 03	BMI $03	be zero, the branch will not be taken, and
$FA49	└6C FE 03	JMP ($03FE)	this indirect jump will be executed.
$FA4C	28	PLP	Otherwise the program branches here to execute
.			the BREAK routine.
.			
.			
$FFFE	$40 ⎫		⎧These locations contain the IRQ vector that
$FFFF	$FA ⎬		⎨points to the start of the IRQ interrupt routine.

its interrupt routine at $FA86. Consequently the interrupt vectors stored at locations $FFFE and $FFFF are also different. These differences have no effect on the user.

If an interrupt request is made on the IRQ pin of the 6502, the starting address of the interrupt routine is fetched from locations $FFFE and $FFFF. The interrupt vector points to a location in the Apple ROM space. The first instruction here is a STA $45 instruction whose purpose is to *save* the number in the accumulator in this zero-page location. Note that the stack is not used to store the number in the accumulator. Recall that the P register is the last item placed on the stack when an interrupt occurs, so the PLA and PHA instructions which follow the STA $45 instruction have the effect of pulling the P register off of the stack and placing it in the accumulator (the PLA instruction), and then pushing it back on the stack (the PHA instruction).

The net effect of these instructions is to leave the stack intact, while the number in the P register at the time of the interrupt is now also in the accumulator.

The purpose for doing this is to discriminate between an interrupt caused by a BRK instruction and an interrupt caused by a signal on the 6502's IRQ pin. Recall that when a BRK instruction is executed, the B flag in the processor status register is set. The B flag is bit four in the P register, and at this point in the interrupt routine it is also bit four in the accumulator. The three shift-left instructions that are next in the interrupt routine move the B flag logic value into bit seven of the accumulator. If the B flag were set, then the N flag will be set by the last shift-left instruction, and the program branches to the monitor program that handles the BRK instruction. If the B flag were clear, the BMI $03 branch will *not* be taken, and the indirect jump to location $03FE will be executed. Consequently, the user loads locations $03FE with the low-order byte of the starting address of the routine the user has written and stored in R/W memory, and location $03FF is loaded with the high-order byte of this routine. Thus the user's interrupt routine may be located anywhere in memory. Chart 7–4 illustrates each of these steps.

Finally, in order to use interrupts you will need some way to access the interrupt pins on the 6502. Both the NMI pin and the IRQ pin are connected to bus lines that run to all eight of the peripheral card slots inside the Apple. Consult your *Apple II Reference Manual* for details about these card slots. The NMI line is connected to pin 29 of each card slot, while the IRQ bus line is connected to pin 30. To make connections to these pins we use the Vector 4609 Plugboard mentioned in Appendix B in connection with the single-step circuit. Wire-wrap posts can be soldered to the printed-circuit pads that connect to pins 29 and 30, and then you can wire wrap a connection to the interrupt bus lines. Refer to the description of the single-step circuit described in Appendix B and illustrated in Fig. B–1.

AN INTERRUPT CONTROLLED KEYBOARD INPUT

To illustrate the use of interrupts in some programming problems we will write a program to read a keyboard on an interrupt basis and a program to keep time. The 24-hour clock program is described in the next section. In this section we describe the interrupt controlled keyboard.

The *motivation* for reading the Apple keyboard on an interrupt basis will become more obvious in Chapter 9, where we will discuss an application program that converts characters typed in on the keyboard to Morse code, allowing an individual to send Morse code without really knowing the code. Although this program is of particular interest to amateur radio operators, the programming techniques that it illustrates can be applied in a large number of situations. In any case you may wish to skim Chapter 9 to examine the features of the finished program.

In order to write a good program it is necessary to have the objectives specified clearly and in careful detail. Time spent in writing crystal clear specifications before starting to write the program is time well spent. Let us carefully detail what our interrupt controlled keyboard input program is to accomplish.

Objective: Whenever a key on the Apple II keyboard is pressed, the program currently being executed must be interrupted, the keyboard input port must be read, the character code representing the key must be stored in a table of character codes comprising one page of memory, the character must be displayed on the monitor, and control then returned to the interrupted program. The contents of the accumulator, status register, X register, and the Y register must be saved during the interrupt routine. Write programs that will do this on the Apple II for either an $\overline{\text{NMI}}$ interrupt or an $\overline{\text{IRQ}}$ interrupt.

Example 7–8 is our program for the $\overline{\text{NMI}}$ interrupt, and a flowchart for this program is given in Fig. 7–8. Example 7–9 is our solution to this programming problem if $\overline{\text{IRQ}}$-type interrupts are required. The minor differences between these programs is a reflection of the differences in the interrupt structures of the two types of interrupts in the Apple II monitor. Note that neither program stores the P register on the stack because this is automatically done when an interrupt occurs. The comments should make the programs clear, except perhaps for a few points. In order to work, the $\overline{\text{NMI}}$ interrupt routine in Example 7–8 requires that locations $03FB–$03FD be loaded with a jump to the starting address of the $\overline{\text{NMI}}$ routine, namely a $4C $B8 $16 instruction. On the other hand, the $\overline{\text{IRQ}}$ routine in Example 7–9 requires that locations $03FE–$03FF contain the ADL and the ADH of the starting address of the $\overline{\text{IRQ}}$ routine, namely $D4 $16.

The most important difference between the two routines is the way in which the number in the accumulator is saved and restored. In the case of the $\overline{\text{NMI}}$ routine our program saves A on the stack, and restores A from the stack. In the case of the $\overline{\text{IRQ}}$ routine our routine does not save A: this has already been done by the program segment in the Apple monitor. The Apple monitor saves A in zero-page location $45. Therefore all our program has to do is restore A from this location at the comple-

tion of the interrupt routine, which it does with the next to the
last instruction in the routine.

Example 7–8. An NMI-Type Interrupt Routine to Read the Keyboard

```
C000:          3 KYBD    EQU    $C000
0010:          4 PNTR    EQU    $0010          ;PNTR CONTAINS ADL OF TABLE.
0000:          5                               ;PNTR +1 CONTAINS ADH OF
                                                 CHARACTER TABLE.
-----NEXT OBJECT FILE NAME IS EXAMPLE 7-8.
16B8:          6          ORG    $16B8

16B8:          8 ;KYBD    INTERRUPT ROUTINE
               9 ****************************

16B8:48       11 NMIRTN  PHA                   ;SAVE THE ACCUMULATOR.
16B9:98       12         TYA                   ;Y INTO A,
16BA:48       13         PHA                   ;A ONTO STACK. Y IS SAVED.
16BB:8A       14         TXA                   ;X INTO A,
16BC:48       15         PHA                   ;X ONTO STACK. X IS SAVED.
16BD:AD 00 C0 16         LDA    KYBD           ;READ THE KEYBOARD.
16C0:10 11    17         BPL    RETURN         ;RETURN WITHOUT KEY.
16C2:A0 00    18         LDY    #00            ;Y=0 FOR INDIRECT INDEXED
                                                 MODE.
16C4:91 10    19         STA    (PNTR),Y       ;STORE THE CHARACTAER.
16C6:E6 10    20         INC    PNTR           ;INCREMENT THE POINTER.
16C8:20 ED FD 21         JSR    $FDED          ;OUTPUT THE CHARACTER TO THE
                                                 SCREEN.
16CB:8D 10 C0 22         STA    $C010          ;CLEAR THE KEYBOARD STROBE.
16CE:68       23         PLA                   ;RESTORE X.
16CF:AA       24         TAX
16D0:68       25         PLA                   ;RESTORE Y.
16D1:AA       26         TAX
16D2:68       27         PLA                   ;RESTORE A.
16D3:40       28 RETURN  RTI                   ;RETURN TO INTERRUPTED
                                                 PROGRAM.
```

Example 7–9. An IRQ-Type Interrupt Routine to Read the Keyboard

```
C000:          3 KYBD    EQU    $C000
0010:          4 PNTR    EQU    $0010          ;PNTR CONTAINS ADL OF TABLE.
0000:          5                               ;PNTR +1 CONTAINS ADH OF
                                                 CHARACTER TABLE.
-----NEXT OBJECT FILE NAME IS EXAMPLE 7-9.
16D4:          6          ORG   $16D4

16D4:          8 ;KYBD INTERRUPT ROUTINE
               9 ****************************

16D4:98       11 IRQRTN  TYA                   ;Y INTO A,
16D5:48       12         PHA                   ;A ONTO STACK. Y IS SAVED.
16D6:8A       13         TXA                   ;X INTO A,
16D7:48       14         PHA                   ;X ONTO STACK. X IS SAVED.
16D8:AD 00 C0 15         LDA    KYBD           ;READ THE KEYBOARD.
16D8:10 12    16         BPL    RETURN         ;RETURN WITHOUT KEY.
16DD:A0 00    17         LDY    #00            ;Y=0 FOR INDIRECT INDEXED MODE.
```

16DF:91 10	18		STA	(PNTR),Y	;STORE THE CHARACATER.
16E1:E6 10	19		INC	PNTR	;INCREMENT THE POINTER.
16E3:20 ED FD	20		JSR	$FDED	;OUTPUT THE CHARACTER TO THE SCREEN.
16E6:8D 10 C0	21		STA	$C010	;CLEAR THE KEYBOARD STROBE.
16E9:68	22		PLA		;RESTORE X.
16EA:AA	23		TAX		
16EB:68	24		PLA		;RESTORE Y.
16EC:AA	25		TAX		
16ED:A5 45	26		LDA	$45	;RESTORE THE ACCUMULATOR.
16EF:40	27	RETURN	RTI		;RETURN TO INTERRUPTED PROGRAM.

A final consideration is the source of the appropriate interrupt signal. The best source for this signal would be the negative-going 10-microsecond strobe pulse that is available from the keyboard circuitry at pin 6 of U1, the 7400 NAND gate that inverts the strobe pulse from the MM5740 keyboard decoder. This pulse occurs only when a key is pressed, and by referring to Fig. 7–6 you will see that it has the appropriate characteristics. Refer to your *Apple II Reference Manual* if you wish to modify your Apple to make this connection. It will require some hardware work.

Another way in which $\overline{\text{NMI}}$-type interrupts may be generated from circuitry on the Apple is through the use of the 60-Hz square wave generated for the video output. A 60-Hz square wave is available at pin 4 of the 74LS32 integrated circuit C14 near the lower right-hand side of the main circuit board (Fig. 7–8). You can remove the chip, slip a No. 30 wire-wrap wire in the pin 4 socket, and replace the chip. Connect this wire to a switch mounted on the Vector 4609 Plugboard, and connect the other pin of the switch to a wire-wrap post connected to pin 29. Turn the switch on when you want $\overline{\text{NMI}}$ interrupts every sixtieth of a second. Although this approach reads the keyboard more often than is necessary, an examination of the listing in Example 7–8 and the flowchart in Fig. 7–7 indicates that if a key is not pressed, then the program simply returns to the interrupted program and no character codes are recorded. This is the approach to generating interrupts that we took, since it requires no hardware modifications and you do not have to remove any of the circuit boards to access this connection. The only disadvantage is that it cannot be used for $\overline{\text{IRQ}}$ interrupts, because the signal stays at logic 0 for half of each cycle, causing interrupt after interrupt. The $\overline{\text{NMI}}$ pin, being edge sensitive rather than level sensitive, produces only one interrupt per 60-Hz cycle. It would have been helpful if the designers of the Apple had made the keyboard strobe signal more accessible. Refer to Fig.

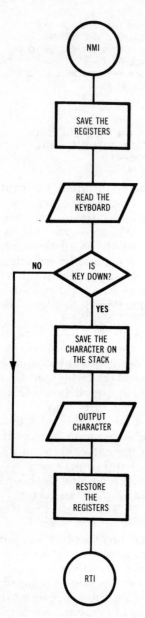

Fig. 7–7. Flowchart of the program in Example 7–8, an interrupt routine to read the keyboard input port.

7–8 for further details about the connections that are necessary to produce $\overline{\text{NMI}}$ interrupts at a 60-Hz rate. You should always have the main program executing before closing the slide switch, and the interrupt routine should be in memory.

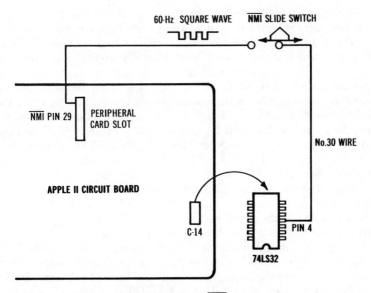

Fig. 7—8. The 60-Hz source of $\overline{\text{NMI}}$-type interrupts.

A 24-HOUR CLOCK

The availability of a 60-Hz signal makes the implementation of a 24-hour clock an attractive example of the use of interrupts. Our objective is to keep time in hours, minutes, and seconds using the 60-Hz clock signal on the Apple II, and to display this time continually on the video monitor screen. We may outline the general approach to an interrupt controlled clock as follows:

- Interrupts occur 60 times per second. Increment the number in a memory location until it reaches 60. If it is not 60, then RTI.
- Each time this number reaches 60, increment the number in another location (the seconds location) until it reaches 60. If it is not 60, then RTI.
- Each time the seconds number reaches 60 increment the number in another location (the minutes location) until it reaches 60. If it is not 60, then RTI.
- Each time the minutes number reaches 60 increment the number in another location (the hours location) until it reaches 24. If it is not 24, then RTI.
- When the hours reach 24, zero the time and start over.

This rather coarse analysis of the problem is sufficient to sketch in our minds what the program must do and, moreover, it gives us a chance to refine our thinking about the program before we start writing it. For example, should we keep time in the three locations using hexadecimal or bcd numbers? Using hexadecimal numbers will undoubtedly make the interrupt routine shorter, but they will have to be converted to bcd numbers before sending them to the output routine because no one wants to read the time in hexadecimal. Furthermore, even the bcd numbers must be converted to an ASCII representation before they can be handled by the output routine, COUT, on the Apple. Why not try to keep time with ASCII, rather than hexadecimal or bcd numbers? In other words, why not have one location that represents units (ones) of seconds using ASCII. A second location could represent tens of seconds, and so on for minutes and hours. This approach would simplify the output routine, and it only requires six locations for the time instead of three if we keep time in hexadecimal or bcd.

Suppose we assign location $047F to be our count-to-60 location. Also let $047E contain the ASCII representation of units of seconds, $047D will contain the code for tens of seconds, $047C has the code for units of minutes, $047B has the code for tens of minutes, and so on. The ASCII representations of the digits 0 through 9 are the numbers $B0 through $B9. Thus the units location of the seconds and minutes must be incremented (at the appropriate time, of course) from $B0 to $B9. The tens locations of the seconds and minutes must be incremented from $B0 to $B6 ($B6 corresponds to 6 in the tens place). The hours locations are slightly different. The units of hours use the character codes from $B0 to $B3, while the tens place will use character codes $B0 to $B2.

Finally, let us update the display once every second. To update the display we must transfer the character codes from their locations $047E–$0479 to the text page of memory where the video circuitry will transfer the character code in memory to a character on the screen. The upper right-hand corner of the screen seems like an appropriate out-of-the-way place, so we will use locations $0422 to $0427.

The program that satisfies the above specifications is given in Example 7–10. It consists of an initialization program that sets up the NMI vector and then breaks to the monitor. Once the clock is set and running, you can continue to work either in BASIC or assembly language and watch the time fly. What you cannot do with this clock routine is either cassette tape or disk input/output operations because the interrupt routine changes the timing parameters for these operations.

Here is how you can start your clock. Run the initialization program which will return control to the monitor. Suppose you wish to start timing at 15 hours, 13 minutes, and 42 seconds. Load $B1, $B5, $B1, $B3, $B4, and $B2 into locations $0479 through $047E, respectively. Load $3C (60) into location $047F. When the clock on the wall strikes 15 13 42, switch the $\overline{\text{NMI}}$ interrupt switch in Fig. 7–8 to the ON position.

Example 7–10. A 24-Hour Clock $\overline{\text{NMI}}$-Type Interrupt Routine

```
-----NEXT OBJECT FILE NAME IS EXAMPLE 7-10.
16F0:            3          ORG    $16F0

16F0:            5 ;INITIALIZATION ROUTINE
16F0:A9 4C       6          LDA    #$4C        ;SET UP NMI JUMP INSTRUCTION.
16F2:8D FB 03    7          STA    $03FB       ;NMI INTERRUPT ROUTINE
16F5:A9 00       8          LDA    #00         ;STARTS AT $1700,
16F7:8D FC 03    9          STA    $03FC       ;SO WE JUMP
16FA:A9 17      10          LDA    #$17        ;TO THAT ADDRESS.
16FC:8D FD 03   11          STA    $03FD
16FF:00         12          BRK                ;JUMP TO THE MONITOR.

1700:           14 ;NMI CLOCK ROUTINE STARTS HERE.
                15 ****************************
1700:48         16          PHA                ;SAVE A.
1701:98         17          TYA                ;SAVE Y
1702:48         18          PHA                ;ON THE STACK.
1703:8A         19          TXA                ;SAVE X
1704:48         20          PHA                ;ON THE STACK.
1705:CE 7F 04   21          DEC    $047F       ;DECREMENT THE COUNT-TO-60
                                                 COUNTER.
1708:D0 64      22          BNE    OUT         ;GET OUT UNLESS IT REACHES 60.
170A:A9 3C      23          LDA    #$3C        ;RELOAD THE COUNTER.
170C:8D 7F 04   24          STA    $047F
170F:A9 B0      25          LDA    #$B0        ;ASCII "0" INTO A.
1711:A2 BA      26          LDX    #$BA        ;UPPER LIMIT FOR ASCII DIGITS.
1713:A0 B6      27          LDY    #$B6        ;ASCII "6" INTO Y.
1715:EE 7E 04   28          INC    $047E       ;INCREMENT SECONDS UNITS.
1718:EC 7E 04   29          CPX    $047E       ;COMPARE WITH UPPER LIMIT.
171B:D0 46      30          BNE    DISPLAY     ;BRANCH TO DISPLAY, THEN GET
                                                 OUT.
171D:8D 7E 04   31          STA    $047E       ;CLEAR SECONDS UNITS.
1720:EE 7D 04   32          INC    $047D       ;INCREMENT TENS OF SECONDS.
1723:CC 7D 04   33          CPY    $047D       ;COMPARE WITH "6".
1726:D0 3B      34          BNE    DISPLAY     ;REFRESH DISPLAY.
1728:8D 7D 04   35          STA    $047D       ;CLEAR TENS OF SECONDS.
172B:EE 7C 04   36          INC    $047C       ;INCREMENT MINUTES UNITS.
172E:EC 7C 04   37          CPX    $047C       ;COMPARE WITH UPPER LIMIT.
1731:D0 30      38          BNE    DISPLAY     ;DISPLAY TIME, THEN GET OUT.
1733:8D 7C 04   39          STA    $047C       ;CLEAR MINUTES UNITS.
1736:EE 7B 04   40          INC    $047B       ;INCREMENT TENS OF MINUTES.
1739:CC 7B 04   41          CPY    $047B       ;COMPARE WITH "6".
173C:D0 25      42          BNE    DISPLAY     ;DISPLAY TIME.
173E:8D 7B 04   43          STA    $047B       ;CLEAR TENS OF MINUTES.
1741:A0 B2      44          LDY    #$B2        ;ASCII "2" INTO Y.
```

```
1743:EE 7A 04    45              INC   $047A        ;INCREMENT HOURS UNITS.
1746:EC 7A 04    46              CPX   $047A        ;COMPARE WITH UPPER LIMIT.
1749:D0 06       47              BNE   TEST         ;WHEN IS TIME= 24 00 00?
174B:8D 7A 04    48              STA   $047A        ;CLEAR HOURS UNITS.
174E:EE 79 04    49              INC   $0479        ;INCREMENT TENS OF HOURS.
1751:CC 79 04    50 TEST         CPY   $0479        ;IS IT 2?
1754:D0 0D       51              BNE   DISPLAY      ;BRANCH TO DISPLAY.
1756:A2 B4       52              LDX   #$B4         ;ASCII "4" INTO X.
1758:EC 7A 04    53              CPX   $047A        ;COMPARE WITH HOURS UNITS.
175B:D0 06       54              BNE   DISPLAY      ;BRANCH TO DISPLAY.
175D:8D 79 04    55              STA   $0479        ;CLEAR TENS OF HOURS.
1760:8D 7A 04    56              STA   $047A        ;CLEAR HOURS UNITS.
1763:A2 05       57 DISPLAY      LDX   #05          ;DISPLAY DATA BY TRANSFERRING
1765:BD 79 04    58 BRANCH       LDA   $0479,X      ;ASCII CHARACTERS
1768:9D 22 04    59              STA   $0422,X      ;FROM MEMORY TO THE
176B:CA          60              DEX                ;SCREEN PAGE FOR THE VIDEO
                                                     MONITOR,
176C:10 F7       61              BPL   BRANCH       ;USING ABSOLUTE INDEXED MODE.
176E:68          62 OUT          PLA                ;RESTORE X
176F:AA          63              TAX                ;FROM THE STACK.
1770:68          64              PLA                ;RESTORE Y
1771:A8          65              TAY                ;FROM THE STACK.
1772:68          66              PLA                ;RESTORE A FROM THE STACK.
1773:40          67              RTI                ;RETURN TO INTERRUPTED
                                                     PROGRAM.
```

USING BASIC AND 6502 ASSEMBLY LANGUAGE

It is possible to use an assembly language subroutine in a
BASIC program. For example, you might wish to collect data on
a time varying voltage using an analog-to-digital converter controlled by an assembly language subroutine. The assembly language routine would allow the data to be collected much more
rapidly than a BASIC program. On the other hand, the analysis
of the data, doing a Fourier transform for example, might be
much simpler with a high-level language, such as BASIC. The
BASIC program would call the assembly language routine to
collect the data, and then control would return to the BASIC
program.

The USR function, which takes the form

$$210 \ Z = USR(23)$$

in a BASIC program, causes a JSR $000A to be performed (210
is simply an arbitrary choice for a BASIC statement number,
and the argument, 23, is simply an arbitrary choice for an argument). Thus the start of the user's subroutine is location $000A.
No one wishes to continue a program in page zero, so in locations $000A through $000C one places a JMP to the location of
the actual subroutine. Suppose you wish to call your subroutine
at $14BE. In locations $000A–$000C you would place the JMP

188

instruction, $4C $BE $14. An RTS instruction placed at the end of your subroutine will return control to the BASIC program that called it. The argument of the USR function is placed in the BASIC interpreter's floating-point accumulator. For further details about the argument, consult your *Applesoft II BASIC Programming Reference Manual*. Our main concern here is *getting to* the subroutine.

Passing parameters between the BASIC program and the assembly language subroutine is handled easily with POKEs and PEEKs. That is, if you wish to pass a number to the subroutine, POKE it in some location, and the subroutine can access this location to use the number. To pass a number back to the BASIC program from the assembly language subroutine, the subroutine should store the number someplace in memory, and the BASIC program can PEEK in this location to obtain the number.

These concepts are illustrated in Example 7–11. The program consists of a BASIC program that generates a relatively complex polar coordinate graph similar to those generated by a Spiralgraph game that was popular several years ago. This function is calculated in statement 40 of the BASIC program. The X and Y coordinates are calculated in lines 50 and 60. These coordinates are passed to the PLOT subroutine, described in Example 6–16, with the POKE statements in line 70. The subroutine jump is implemented with the Z = USR(0) statement. Note that we are interested neither in the argument of this function nor the value of Z. All we wish to do is produce a subroutine call to our PLOT subroutine. Note also that the very first instruction in the BASIC program sets up locations $000A–$000C with the JMP to our subroutine at $14BE ($BE = 190 and $14 = 20, while $4C = 76). The HGR instruction clears the hires screen and puts the Apple in a mixed text and hires graphics mode. The parameter 79 was chosen to keep the graph on the screen. Load the PLOT subroutine and this program, then RUN it. It is fun to watch the results appear on the screen. Change statement 40 to R = 79*COS (ANG/3) and rerun the program. If you happen to teach trigonometry or analytic geometry you will see some educational value in this. Otherwise think of it as fun. Figs. 7–9A through 7–9C illustrate the output from this program.

If you have done a lot of programming with BASIC and you have used the hires graphics capability of Applesoft, you may wonder what advantage there is to using subroutine PLOT as opposed to HPLOT X,Y command in BASIC. In many instances there is no advantage. However, animation may well require the speed of assembly language, while complex graphics can make good use of BASIC. In any case the HPLOT X,Y command will use some kind of assembly language routine to implement it. If you will pardon a personal reference, of the two best graphics programs the writer has seen in his teaching fields, one used assembly language and could not have been done in BASIC, while the other was done in BASIC and would have been exceedingly difficult to program using assembly language. The programmer who knows both languages has the freedom to choose the language that is best suited to accomplish the programming objective.

Example 7-11. A BASIC Program That Calls a Machine Language Subroutine

```
10 POKE 10,76: POKE 11,190: POKE
   12:20
20 HGR
30 ANG = 0
40 R = 79 * SIN (4 * ANG)
50 X = 79 + R * COS (ANG)
60 Y = 79 + R * SIN (ANG)
70 POKE 1,X: POKE 2,Y
80 Z = USR (0)
90 ANG = ANG + 3.14159 / 180
100 GOTO 40
```

EXERCISES

Exercise 7-1

The purpose of this exercise is to familiarize you with the operation of the stack during a subroutine call. Refer to the program segment below for the questions. This program is identical with Example 7-4.

```
16A2:              6 ;MAIN PROGRAM
16A2:20 A8 16      7 MAIN    JSR    INPUT     ;FETCH A CHARACTER.
16A5:4C A2 16      8         JMP    MAIN      ;LOOP BACK.

                  10 ****************
16A8:             11 ;SUBROUTINE INPUT
FDED:             12 OUTPUT  EQU    $FDED
16A8:AD 00 C0     13 INPUT   LDA    KYBD      ;READ THE KEYBOARD PORT.
16AB:10 0A        14         BPL    OUT       ;HAS A KEY BEEN PRESSED?
16AD:8D 10 C0     15         STA    $C010     ;YES, CLEAR THE STROBE.
16B0:48           16         PHA              ;SAVE THE ACCUMULATOR ON THE
                                               STACK.
16B1:08           17         PHP              ;SAVE THE P REGISTER ON THE
                                               STACK.
16B2:20 ED FD     18         JSR    OUTPUT    ;ECHO THE CHARACTER TO THE
                                               MONITOR.
16B5:28           19         PLP              ;PULL THE P REGISTER FROM THE
                                               STACK.
16B6:68           20         PLA              ;RESTORE THE ACCUMULATOR.
16B7:60           21 OUT     RTS              ;NO. RETURN TO MAIN PROGRAM.
```

a. Assume the stack pointer if $FF before the JSR INPUT instruction in the main program. What will its value be after execution of the JSR INPUT instruction?

(A subroutine call uses two locations on the stack. After the JSR INPUT instruction the stack pointer will be $FD, pointing to location $01FD, which is the next available location on the stack.)

b. What numbers will be stored in the two stack locations ($01FF and $01FE) used by the JSR INPUT instruction?

(The number $16 will be stored in location $01FF and $A4 will be stored in location $01FE. Refer to the text for an explanation.)

c. What value will the stack pointer have after the PHA and the PHP instructions on lines 16 and 17 are executed?

(Each stack operation instruction reduces the stack pointer by one. After these two instructions are executed the stack pointer will be $FB, pointing to the next available stack location at $01FB.)

d. What number will be stored in location $01FD after the PHA instruction on line 16 is executed?

(Location $01FD will contain the ASCII for the character whose key was pressed.)

e. What is the purpose of the PHP instruction on line 17?

(The subroutine is supposed to return to the calling program with a logic 1 in the N flag—bit seven of the P register—if a key was pressed. The instructions in the OUTPUT subroutine will modify the P register. In order to preserve the status of the N flag during the call of subroutine OUTPUT, the P register is first saved on the stack with the PHP instruction and then restored after the JSR OUTPUT instruction with the PLP instruction.)

f. What value will the stack pointer have after execution of the JSR OUTPUT instruction on line 18?

(The stack pointer will be $F9 directly after the JSR OUTPUT instruction.)

g. How many stack locations have been used by calling the input subroutine with the JSR INPUT instruction on line 7?

(Locations $01FF through $01FA have been used, a total of six locations.)

h. What value will the stack pointer have after execution of the RTS instruction on line 21?

(The stack pointer will be $FF, the same value it had before the call of this subroutine by the main program.)

i. What numbers will be stored in locations $01FB and $01FA during the time when subroutine OUTPUT is being executed?

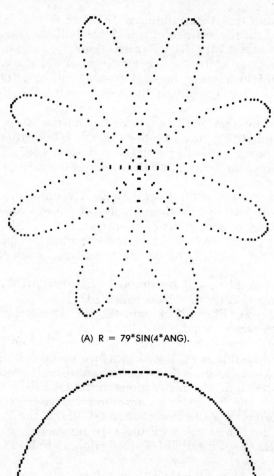

(A) R = 79*SIN(4*ANG).

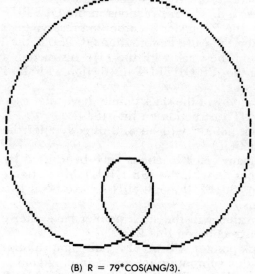

(B) R = 79*COS(ANG/3).

Fig. 7-9. Output of the

Exercise 7–2

The purpose of this exercise is to obtain a thorough under-standing of how $\overline{\text{NMI}}$-type interrupts are handled on the Apple II. You may wish to refer to the discussion in the text to answer the questions.

a. Where is the $\overline{\text{NMI}}$ interrupt vector stored and to what location does it point?

(In any 6502-based system the $\overline{\text{NMI}}$ interrupt vector is stored in locations \$FFFA and \$FFFB. We may use the Apple monitor to examine these locations. Location \$FFFA contains \$FB and location \$FFFB contains \$03. Thus the interrupt vector is \$03FB, the address of the location to which it points.)

b. What instruction is usually the first instruction in an Apple $\overline{\text{NMI}}$ interrupt routine?

(The first instruction in the $\overline{\text{NMI}}$-type interrupt routine is lo-cated at \$03FB. Since there is so little R/W memory space near this address that can be used for programming purposes [page four is the text screen page], one usually places a JMP instruction at \$03FB, where the destination of the jump instruction is a place in R/W memory that has more room for programming space.)

c. Refer to the keyboard interrupt routine in Example 7–8, which is too lengthy to be repeated here. Suppose that the stack pointer is \$FF before the nonmaskable interrupt occurs. What value will it have just before the first instruction in the interrupt routine is executed?

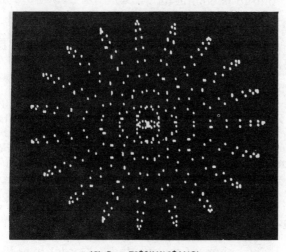

(C) R = 79*SIN(19*ANG).

program in Example 7–11.

(Any interrupt uses at least three locations on the stack, so the stack pointer will be decremented to $FC to point to the next available location.)

d. What numbers are placed on the stack when an interrupt occurs?

(The high-order byte of the address of the instruction following the interrupted instruction is placed in location $01FF, assuming that the value of the stack pointer before the interrupt was $FF. Next, the low-order byte of the address of the instruction following the interrupted instruction is placed on the stack at location $01FE. Finally, the number in the P register at the completion of the interrupted instruction is placed on the stack at location $01FD, and the stack pointer is decremented once more to point to location $01FC.)

e. How many stack locations are used by the routine in Example 7–8?

(The interrupt itself requires three locations. In addition all three registers, A, Y, and X, are saved on the stack, requiring three more locations, giving a total of six locations required by the interrupt routine in Example 7–8.)

f. What will be the value of the stack pointer after the RTI instruction is executed?

(Regardless of the interrupt routine, the stack pointer will have the same value after execution of the routine that it had before the interrupt. In this example it will have the value $FF after the routine is completed.)

Exercise 7–3

This exercise will test your understanding of the $\overline{\text{IRQ}}$-type interrupt structure of the Apple II.

a. Where is the $\overline{\text{IRQ}}$ vector stored, and to what location does it point?

(Use the Apple monitor to examine the locations $FFFE and $FFFF where the interrupt vector is stored. Depending on which model of the Apple you have, the vector will be either $FA40 or $FA86. In either case the vector points to a location in ROM, and the interrupt routines stored in ROM are identical.)

b. If the $\overline{\text{IRQ}}$ routine is in ROM, how can a user provide his or her own routine?

(If you examine the interrupt routine in ROM, you will find that it contains an indirect jump to location $03FE. This means that in locations $03FE and $03FF you must store the starting address of *your* interrupt routine, the low-order byte in location $03FE and the high-order byte in location $03FF.)

c. How many stack locations does an $\overline{\text{IRQ}}$ require?

d. Refer to Example 7–9. How many stack locations will the entire routine require?

(At least seven. It may require more if the output subroutine at location $FDED in the Apple monitor uses the stack to store data or calls subroutines itself.)

e. To transfer your understanding of interrupts from your short-term memory to your long-term memory, without consulting the text write down <u>all</u> of the events that follow either an interrupt request on the $\overline{\text{IRQ}}$ pin or an interrupt request on the $\overline{\text{NMI}}$ pin.

Exercise 7–4

The purpose of this exercise is to bring to your attention some timing considerations involved in processing interrupts. You will want to refer to Example 7–10, which is too long to be repeated here.

a. Approximately how much time does the $\overline{\text{NMI}}$ routine of Example 7–10 require?

(An interrupt occurs 60 times every second. During 59 of those interrupts only 13 instructions are executed. These are the instructions that save the numbers in the registers, decrement the count-to-60 counter, and restore the registers before the final RTI instruction. The interrupt takes 8 clock cycles, and the JMP instruction at $03FB takes 3 clock cycles. The total time for one of these interrupts is approximately 55 clock cycles. A clock cycle on the Apple is less than 1 microsecond, so less than 55 microseconds are required if the hours, minutes, and seconds counters are not incremented. This happens 59 times a second, requiring a total of (approximately) 3250 microseconds each second. If the seconds are incremented, about 50 additional microseconds are required, giving 3300 microseconds as our estimate of the time required for the routine. The time taken to handle minutes and hours is insignificant because it happens so seldom. Thus 3300 microseconds out of the total of 1,000,000 microseconds in a second are required to process the clock routines. This is 3300/1,000,000, which is only 0.33 percent of the time.)

b. Why is this an important question?

(The question is important because time spent in processing the interrupt is always time taken from processing the main program. In this case it is clear that operating a 24-hour clock has a negligible effect on most programs. In other words, you could not possiblynotice the effect of the clock routine on operating the Apple II microcomputer either in the monitor or in BASIC or Pascal.)

Exercise 7–5

This exercise will compare the execution time of a BASIC program with an assembly language program. Refer to Example 7–11 and Example 6–14, the program to plot a point on the hires screen.

a. Estimate the time it takes to execute the PLOT subroutine in Example 6–14.

(This subroutine has 38 instructions that are not in any loop. Making an estimate of approximately 3 clock cycles per instruction, we obtain 114 microseconds. There are seven instructions in a loop that is executed eight times. These 56 instructions we estimate will take 168 clock cycles. The total time of the subroutine is then approximately 282 clock cycles. Let's call this 300 clock cycles.)

b. Load the PLOT subroutine and the program in Example 7–11. Run the program and watch the points as they are plotted. Now start the program again and run it for about 10 seconds. Count the points that were plotted.

(Approximately 75 points were plotted in 10 seconds.)

c. How much time did the subroutine take?

(If 75 points were plotted, then the subroutine was called 75 times. Each time requires about 300 clock cycles, so the subroutine required about 21,500 microseconds, or 0.022 second.)

d. What percentage of the total time to run the program is this?

(About 0.2 percent, so clearly the PLOT subroutine contributes almost nothing to the execution time of the program.)

e. How could you make a better comparison between the time taken to execute a machine language program and a BASIC program?

(Write a BASIC program and a machine language program that accomplish exactly the same objective, then compare their execution times. You may have to put each one in a loop and count the time required to execute the program many times in order to get an easily measurable time interval.)

Exercise 7–6

Some times a number calculated by the main program must be used in a subroutine. There must be some way to *pass the parameter* from the main program to the subroutine. In the text of this chapter it was recommended to use a zero-page memory location (or any memory location) if it was not possible to pass the parameter to the subroutine in one of the registers of the 6502. Some authors suggest using the stack to store parameters used by both the main program and the subroutine. Presumably one would place the parameter on the stack with a PHA instruction in the main program and pull the number off the stack with a PLA instruction in the subroutine. Can you see any problems with this approach? Write a simple program that does this and try to run the program, then try to figure out why it does not work.

(Here is a simple program that describes what is meant.)

```
        LDA #$FF
        PHA
        JSR SUB
        BRK
SUB     PLA
        STA $0000
        RTS
```

CHAPTER 8

Additional Programming Topics

INTRODUCTION

The purpose of this chapter is to collect some programming concepts and routines that the author believes are important to include in this book, but too complex to be introduced at an early stage in your learning process. Because it includes a variety of topics, the chapter may appear to be disjointed, but this effect will not be too disconcerting.

We begin with a complete summary of the addressing modes of the 6502 that will serve as a reference for future programming efforts on your part.

A SUMMARY OF THE ADDRESSING MODES OF THE 6502

Before summarizing the addressing modes in the 6502 instruction set, you are reminded of two definitions. The *operand* of an instruction is the 8-bit number that is the *object* of the instruction. It is the number that is read, stored, rotated, shifted, incremented, compared, ANDed, added, etc. In the case of arithmetic and logical operations, the operand is *one* of the two elements involved in the operation; the other element is already in the accumulator. Loosely speaking, the addressing mode determines where the operand is to be found.

The *operand* can be in the *memory* space of the microprocessor, or it can be in one of the *internal registers* of the 6502. The symbol M is used in the instruction set summary to indicate that the operand is in the memory space. When the operand is in memory, rather than in an internal register of the 6502, then:

- *The symbol ADL represents the low-order byte of the address of the operand.*
- *The symbol ADH represents the high-order byte of the address of the operand.*

Finally, you are reminded that the bracket, "[ ]," notation is read, "the contents of." For example, [ADH-ADL] is the operand.

The Relative Addressing Mode

Relative addressing is only used with branch instructions. Refer to Chapter 3. If the branch condition is met, the second byte of the branch instruction is a twos complement number that is added to the address of the location of the first op code following the branch instruction to calculate the destination of the branch. If the branch condition is not met, then program execution continues with the first operation code following the branch instruction. The destination of the branch is *relative* to the location of the branch instruction. Branches have a maximum value of 127 bytes in the forward direction and 128 bytes in the backward direction.

The Immediate Addressing Mode

The operand in the immediate addressing mode is the second byte of the instruction. See Chapter 2.

The Absolute Addressing Mode

In the absolute addressing mode the ADL and the ADH of the operand are the second and third bytes of the instruction, respectively. See Chapter 2.

The Zero-Page Addressing Mode

In the zero-page addressing mode the second byte of the instruction is the ADL of the operand. The ADH of the operand is $00; thus the operand will always be in page zero of memory.

The Accumulator Addressing Mode

The operand is in the accumulator in this mode. See Chapter 4.

The Implied Addressing Mode

In the implied addressing mode the location of the operand is implied by the instruction. Frequently the operand is in an internal register of the 6502. Otherwise it is in the stack, located in page one of memory. See Chapters 2, 3, 5, and 7.

The Zero-Page Indexed by X Addressing Mode

The ADL of the operand is the sum of the second byte of the instruction and the number in the X register. Any carry from this addition is ignored, so the ADH of the operand will always be $00. See Chapter 6.

The Zero-Page Indexed by Y Addressing Mode

This addressing mode is identical with the zero-page indexed by X mode, except the number in the Y register is added to the second byte of the instruction to give the ADL of the operand. The ADH of the operand is $00.

The Absolute Indexed by X Addressing Mode

In this addressing mode the ADL of the operand is the sum of the number in the X register and the second byte of the instruction. The ADH of the operand is the third byte of the instruction plus any carry from the sum of X and ADL. See Chapter 6.

The Absolute Indexed by Y Addressing Mode

This mode is identical with the absolute indexed by X mode, except the Y register is used as the index.

The Indirect Indexed Addressing Mode

Symbolize the second byte of an instruction using the indirect indexed addressing mode by IAL (Indirect Address Low), a zero-page address. The number in this zero-page location is added to the number in the Y register to give the ADL of the operand. The carry from this sum is added to the number in the zero-page location IAL + 1 to form the ADH of the operand. In symbols,

$$ADL = [IAL] + [Y]$$
$$ADH = [IAL + 1] + C$$
$$operand = [ADH\text{-}ADL]$$

where C represents any carry from the first sum (C is not the value of the carry flag in the P register). See Chapter 6.

The Indexed Indirect Addressing Mode

Symbolize the second byte of an instruction using this mode by IAL. The number in the X register is added to the second byte of the instruction to give a zero-page address that contains the ADL of the operand. The ADH of the operand is found in the next location. In symbols,

$$ADL = [IAL + [X]]$$
$$ADH = [IAL + [X] + 1]$$
$$operand = [ADH\text{-}ADL]$$

where all carrys are ignored. See Chapter 6.

The Indirect Addressing Mode

The second and third bytes of this instruction are the ADL and ADH, respectively, of a location that contains the low-order byte of the destination of the jump (JMP) instruction. The high-order byte of the destination address is in the next location (up) in memory. In symbols,

$$new\ PCL = [ADH\text{-}ADL]$$
$$new\ PCH = [ADH\text{-}ADL + 1]$$

where ADL and ADH symbolize the second and third bytes of the instruction.

ADDING PARITY TO A 7-BIT CHARACTER CODE

This example will illustrate the use of the shift and rotate instructions once again. The information sent over telephone links from one computer to another or between a terminal and a computer is frequently 7-bit ASCII. Refer to Chapter 1 for a brief description of serial and parallel input/output. One way to detect errors in the send/receive process is to make the eighth bit (bit seven) a *parity* bit (see Fig. 1–8). There are two kinds of parity: *even* and *odd*. If even parity is being used, the number of *1s* in the 8-bit word (seven character bits plus one parity bit) is even. If odd parity is being used, the number of 1s sent and received in one word will be odd. *Protocol* is the format of the data being sent and received, and includes, among other things, the specification of even, odd, or no parity. Assume that each 8-bit word sent is to have even parity. The problem is to take a character code in a location symbolized by CHCODE and use bit seven (the eighth bit) to provide even parity. A program that accomplishes this is given in Example 8–1.

Example 8–1. A Program to Provide Even Parity to a 7-Bit Character Code

Object: Write a program that adds a parity bit to a 7-bit code to make an 8-bit word with even parity.

1220:18	6	CLC		;CLEAR THE CARRY FLAG
1221:A2 00	7	LDX	#00	;CLEAR THE X REGISTER TO COUNT ONES.
1223:A0 07	8	LDY	#07	;Y COUNTS THE BITS IN THE CHARACTER.

```
1225:6E FF 03      9  BR1     ROR   CHCODE    ;ROTATE THE CHARACTER RIGHT.
1228:90 01        10          BCC   BR2       ;IF BIT IS ZERO, DON'T COUNT IT.
122A:E8           11          INX             ;IF IT IS ONE, COUNT IT.
122B:88           12  BR2     DEY             ;DECREMENT THE BIT COUNTER.
122C:D0 F7        13          BNE   BR1       ;GET ANOTHER BIT.
122E:6E FF 03     14          ROR   CHCODE    ;ROTATE THE EIGHTH BIT.
1231:8A           15          TXA             ;TRANSFER THE ONE COUNT TO A.
1232:4A           16          LSR   A         ;SHIFT INTO CARRY.
1233:6E FF 03     17          ROR   CHCODE    ;CARRY INTO BIT 7 AS PARITY.
1236:60           18          RTS
```

The program in Example 8–1 rotates the number in CHCODE into the carry flag. Each time a 1 is rotated into the carry flag, the X register is incremented. Thus the X register counts the number of 1s in the character. Seven rotations are required to complete the count, and the Y register keeps track of this. The next rotation, on line 14, rotates the eighth bit into the carry flag. It is this bit we want to modify so the total number of 1s is even. If X contains an odd number, then it has a 1 in bit zero. Transferring it to the accumulator and shifting right puts this 1 in the carry. The last rotation (nine in all), on line 17 of the program, restores the original character, with the proper parity bit in bit seven. If the number in the X register had been even, meaning that the character code already had an even number of 1s, then X would have had a 0 in bit zero. Transferring it to the accumulator and shifting the accumulator in the carry flag would have cleared the carry flag prior to restoring the character, keeping the even parity already present. One final remark about the program in Example 8–1: in order for it to work, the carry flag must be clear at the beginning.

BINARY-TO-BCD AND BCD-TO-BINARY CONVERSIONS

There are numerous applications in which a conversion from binary to binary coded decimal (bcd) or a conversion from bcd to binary is required. Data are frequently input and output in bcd form but must be processed by the program in a binary form, requiring both conversions. The programs listed in this section utilize the algorithms given by John B. Peatman in his book *Microcomputer-Based Design,* Chapter 7 (McGraw-Hill, New York, 1977). There are a number of algorithms for single-digit or single-byte conversions, but Peatman's algorithms are easily extended to two or more bytes.

Consider first the binary-to-bcd conversion. Our objective here is to convert an 8-bit number expressed in binary to a bcd representation. Refer to Table 5–3 to see how each bcd digit is represented. Recall that a byte represents two bcd digits. The first question with which we must deal is the number of memory locations (or bytes) needed to represent the bcd number. The largest number that can be represented by N *binary digits* is $2^N - 1$. For example, the largest 1-bit number is $2^1 - 1$, which is equal to 1. The largest number represented with two bits is $2^2 - 1$, which is 3. The formula for an N-bit number, $2^N - 1$, clearly follows by induction.

On the other hand, the largest number represented with n *decimal digits* is $10^n - 1$. The same kind of inductive reasoning used above will demonstrate the correctness of this formula. For example, the largest 2-digit decimal number is $99 = 10^2 - 1$. Since we wish to be able to represent the same number, both in binary and in bcd, we must have

$$2^N - 1 = 10^n - 1 \qquad (8-1)$$

Some algebraic manipulation of Equation 8–1 yields

$$n = \frac{N \log 2}{\log 10} \qquad (8-2)$$

If $N = 8$, then $n = 2.408$. Since we cannot provide a fractional number of digits, we must make provision for three digits, or two memory locations, if we wish to be able to represent the largest 8-bit binary number. Equation 8–2 can also be used to solve for N, the number of bits required to represent a decimal number with n digits.

Let $b_7, b_6, \ldots, b_0$ represent the bit values (0 or 1) of M, an 8-bit binary number. Then the number is given by the expression

$$M = b_7 2^7 + b_6 2^6 + b_5 2^5 + \cdots + b_1 2^1 + b_0 \qquad (8-3)$$

The binary-to-bcd algorithm depends on the fact that the previous expression may be rewritten to give

$$M = ((((((b_7 2 + b_6)2 + b_5)2 + b_4)2 + b_3)2 + b_2)2 + b_1)2 + b_0$$
$$(8-4)$$

Move b_7 into some memory location. Double this number by adding it to itself *in the decimal mode* (the leftmost "2" in Equation 8–4). Next, add b_6 (the leftmost "+" in Equation 8–4) and double the number again (the second "2" from the left in Equation 8–4). The doubling process is repeated *seven* times, and each of the eight bit values, $b_7, b_6, \ldots, b_0$, are added by moving the bit value into the carry flag and then adding in the decimal mode. It is an elegant algorithm that is easily extended to any N-bit binary number.

The 6502 assembly language implementation of this algorithm is given in Example 8–2. Since three digits are required to represent the largest possible 8-bit number, two locations have been provided for the bcd number, namely BCDLO and BCDHI, the least significant and most significant bytes, respectively. The X register serves as a bit counter. Study the program and notice that the first time through the loop, the b_7 bit is moved into the bcd number. The second time through the loop the number is doubled, and the b_6 bit is added. Six more times through the loop gives a total of seven doublings, and all eight bit values, b_7 through b_0, are added. Observe that the decimal mode flag is set at the beginning so that the addition is performed in the decimal mode. This is the secret to the algorithm. Example 8–2 has been written in the form of a subroutine, and we have chosen to clear the decimal mode flag before returning to the calling program. This procedure is good practice.

Example 8–2. An 8-Bit Binary-to-BCD Conversion Routine

Object: Convert an 8-bit binary number to a 3-digit decimal number.

12F6:F8	8 BCDSUB	SED		;SET THE DECIMAL MODE.
12F7:A9 00	9	LDA	#00	;CLEAR THE BCD LOCATIONS.
12F9:85 01	10	STA	BCDLO	
12FB:85 02	11	STA	BCDHI	
12FD:A2 08	12	LDX	#08	;X WILL BE A BIT COUNTER.
12FF:06 03	13 BR1	ASL	BINUM	;MOVE BINARY NUMBER INTO CARRY.
1301:A5 01	14	LDA	BCDLO	;GET THE LSB OF THE BCD NUMBER.
1303:65 01	15	ADC	BCDLO	;ADD IT TO ITSELF.
1305:85 01	16	STA	BCDLO	;STORE IT. ˙
1307:A5 02	17	LDA	BCDHI	;GET THE MSB OF THE BCD NUMBER.
1309:65 02	18	ADC	BCDHI	;ADD IT TO ITSELF.
130B:85 02	19	STA	BCDHI	;STORE IT.
130D:69 00	20	ADC	#00	;ADD ANY CARRY TO THE ACCUMULATOR.
130F:CA	21	DEX		
1310:D0 ED	22	BNE	BR1	;REPEAT EIGHT TIMES.
1312:D8	23	CLD		;CLEAR THE DECIMAL MODE.
1313:60	24	RTS		;RETURN TO THE CALLING PROGRAM.

We turn next to the bcd-to-binary routine. It is based on a familiar algorithm for converting a base 10 number to a base 2 number. The decimal number is successively divided by 2, and the remainders are noted as either 1s or 0s. The remainder of each successive division gives the next more significant binary digit. Example 8–3 illustrates this process.

The algorithm is simple:

- Divide the bcd number by 2.
- Shift the remainder into the binary number.
- Repeat the above steps until the conversion is complete.

However, division of a bcd number by 2 is not as simple as dividing a binary number by 2. In the latter case you may recall that a single LSR instruction divides a number by 2. This is because the place values or bit weights in an 8-bit binary number are 128, 64, 32, 16, 8, 4, 2, 1. Clearly, shifting such a number to the right divides each bit weight, and hence the number, by 2.

Example 8–3. Decimal-to-Binary Conversion

Object: Convert 59_{10} to a binary number.
Solution: Successively divide 59 by 2, with the divisions beginning from right and proceeding to the left.

$$
\begin{array}{ccccccc}
 & 0 & 1 & 3 & 7 & 14 & 29 \\
 & 2\overline{)1} & 2\overline{)3} & 2\overline{)7} & 2\overline{)14} & 2\overline{)29} & 2\overline{)59} \\
 & 0 & 2 & 6 & 14 & 28 & 58 \\
\hline
59 = & 1 & 1 & 1 & 0 & 1 & 1 & = 11101_2
\end{array}
$$

The bit weights in a bcd number are different. The number 59, for example, is represented by 0101 1001 and the weight of bit four is 10_{10} and the weight of bit six is 40_{10}. In general, the bit weights of an 8-bit bcd number are 80, 40, 20, 10, 8, 4, 2, 1. Suppose a 1 in bit four, with a bit weight of 10, is shifted to a bit three by an LSR or ROR instruction. Clearly, this does not result in a division by 2, although the other bits when shifted do result in division by 2. When a 1 in bit four is shifted to bit three we change a 10 to an 8 rather than a 5. The correction is simple: subtract 3 if the shift right puts a 1 in bit three.

Likewise, if a 1 is shifted right from a bit to the left of bit seven, then we are turning a bit of weight 100 into a bit of weight 80. The cure is simple: subtract $30 if a 1 is shifted into bit seven.

A 6502 assembly language version of this algorithm is listed in Example 8–4 in the form of a subroutine. It will take bcd numbers from 0 to 255 and convert them to a binary number between $00 and $FF. Two locations are used to store the bcd number, BCDLO and BCDHI. If we wanted to convert 255 to a binary number, then 55 would be placed in BCDLO and 02 would be placed in BCDHI before running the program. Note that the subroutine begins by loading $80 into the location for

Example 8-4. A BCD-to-Binary Conversion Subroutine

Object: Convert a bcd number that is 255 or less to a binary number.

1314:A9 50	8 BISUB	LDA	#80	;CLEAR SEVEN BITS OF THE
1316:85 03	9	STA	BINUM	;BINARY NUMBER. BIT 7 = 1.
1318:46 02	10 BR1	LSR	BCDHI	;ROTATE BCDHI INTO BCDLO.
131A:66 01	11	ROR	BCDLO	;REMAINDER INTO CARRY.
131C:66 03	12	ROR	BINUM	;MOVE IT INTO BINUM.
131E:B0 1B	13	BCS	OUT	;ONE IN CARRY SIGNALS THE END.
1320:38	14	SEC		;SET THE CARRY FOR SUBTRACTIONS.
1321:A5 01	15	LDA	BCDLO	;DO WE NEED A FIX?
1323:29 08	16	AND	#08	;CHECK BIT THREE.
1325:F0 06	17	BEQ	BR2	;IT WAS NOT ONE, NO FIX REQUIRED.
1327:A5 01	18	LDA	BCDLO	;FIX REQUIRED. SUBTRACT THREE.
1329:E9 03	19	SBC	#03	
132B:85 01	20	STA	BCDLO	;STORE IT.
132D:A5 01	21 BR2	LDA	BCDLO	;DO WE NEED A FIX ON BIT SEVEN?
132F:29 80	22	AND	#$80	;CHECK IT.
1331:F0 06	23	BEQ	BR3	;IT WAS NOT ONE, NO FIX REQUIRED.
1333:A5 01	24	LDA	BCDLO	;FIX REQUIRED. SUBTRACT THIRTY.
1335:E9 30	25	SBC	#$30	
1337:85 01	26	STA	BCDLO	;STORE IT.
1339:B0 DD	27 BR3	BCS	BR1	;GET MORE BITS.
133B:60	28 OUT	RTS		;RETURN

the binary number (BINUM). As the remainders are shifted into BINUM with a ROR instruction (line 12 in the listing) the "1" that was initially in bit seven of BINUM will eventually be rotated into the carry flag, signaling the end of the conversion that is implemented with the BCS OUT instruction on line 13 of the listing. Observe that if this branch is not taken then the subroutine continues by performing the necessary corrections to the bcd number, as outlined above, and it finally loops back with a BCS BR1 instruction.

An N-BYTE BINARY-TO-BCD CONVERSION ROUTINE

The program in Example 8-5 converts an N-byte binary number to a bcd number. In this example we have chosen N to be four, giving 32 as the maximum number of bits in the binary number to be converted to bcd. Refer to the previous section for an example of an 8-bit conversion program. You must understand how the 8-bit program in Example 8-2 works before studying the program listed in Example 8-5. Both are based on the algorithm that was described in the previous section.

What is the largest number of bcd digits we will require if the

Example 8-5. An N-Byte Binary-to-BCD Conversion Routine

Object: Convert a 32-bit (maximum) binary number to a bcd number.

```
00F0:           3 BCD      EQU   $00F0      ;MOST SIGNIFICANT BYTE OF BCD #.
00E0:           4 BIN      EQU   $00E0      ;MOST SIGNIFICANT BYTE OF
                                            BINARY #.
----- NEXT OBJECT FILE NAME IS EXAMPLE 8-5.
13D0:           5          ORG   $13D0

13D0:           7 ;BINARY-TO-BCD SUBROUTINE
13D0:A9 00      8          LDA   #00        ;CLEAR LOCATIONS FOR BCD #.
13D2:A2 04      9          LDX   #04        ;X + 1 IS # OF BYTES FOR BCD #.
13D4:95 F0     10 LOOP1    STA   BCD,X      ;LOAD WITH ZEROS.
13D6:CA        11          DEX              ;DECREMENT BYTE COUNTER.
13D7:10 FB     12          BPL   LOOP1      ;FINISHED?
13D9:F8        13          SED              ;YES. SET DECIMAL MODE FOR
                                            ADDITIONS.
13DA:A0 20     14          LDY   #$20       ;Y IS NUMBER OF BITS TO BE
                                            CONVERTED.
13DC:A2 03     15 BIGLOOP  LDX   #03        ;X COUNTS BYTES.
13DE:18        16          CLC              ;THIS SET OF INSTRUCTIONS
13DF:36 E0     17 LOOP2    ROL   BIN,X      ;MOVES THE BINARY NUMBER
13E1:CA        18          DEX              ;INTO THE CARRY, ONE BIT
13E2:10 FB     19          BPL   LOOP2      ;AT A TIME.
13E4:A2 04     20          LDX   #04        ;THE NEXT LOOP ADDS THE
13E6:B5 F0     21 LOOP3    LDA   BCD,X      ;BINARY CODED DECIMAL NUMBER
13E8:75 F0     22          ADC   BCD,X      ;TO ITSELF.
13EA:95 F0     23          STA   BCD,X
13EC:CA        24          DEX
13ED:10 F7     25          BPL   LOOP3
13EF:88        26          DEY              ;DECREMENT BIT COUNTER.
13F0:D0 EA     27          BNE   BIGLOOP    ;NO, GET ANOTHER BIT.
13F2:D8        28          CLD              ;YES, THEN GET OUT.
13F3:60        29          RTS
```

largest binary number is a 32-bit number? Equation 8-2 gives the answer 9.63. Therefore we must provide memory space for at least ten digits. This requires five memory locations, since each location stores two digits.

The program in Example 8-5 assumes the binary number is stored in locations $00E0 to $00E3 with the most significant byte in location $00E0. After the conversion the bcd number is in locations $00F0 to $00F4 with the least significant digits in location $00F4.

Study this program in conjunction with the program in Example 8-2. The only difference between the programs is that in the present case we are dealing with a multiple-byte binary number. The X index selects the particular byte being operated on. The BIGLOOP loop in Example 8-5 is the same loop as the BR1 loop in Example 8-2. The smaller loops serve to handle the multibyte numbers.

A BCD-TO-ASCII SUBROUTINE

The program in Example 8–6 takes a 10-digit bcd number and converts each bcd digit to an ASCII character. The ASCII characters are sent to a monitor subroutine to output them to the video monitor screen. Note that a bcd digit may be converted to ASCII by ORing the high-order nibble with $30. The Apple requires that bit seven be set to obtain normal characters (white on black), so an ORA #$80 instruction is included on line 16 of the listing in Example 8–6. Actually, lines 15 and 16 could be combined into a single ORA #$BO instruction, but we wanted to keep the option of using ordinary ASCII in the event the output is to go to another device.

The program works by converting the most significant digit of the bcd number to ASCII, jumping to the output subroutine (COUT) to print the character, and then rotating the bcd

Example 8–6. A BCD-to-ASCII Conversion Program

Object: Convert a 10-digit bcd number to ASCII, then output it with the monitor subroutine, COUT.

00F0:	3 BCD	EQU	$00F0	;MSB OF BCD NUMBER.
FDED:	4 COUT	EQU	$FDED	;MONITOR OUTPUT SUBROUTINE.
----- NEXT OBJECT FILE NAME IS EXAMPLE 8–6.				
13F4:	5 ORG		$13F4	
13F4:	7 ;BCD-TO-ASCII SUBROUTINE			
13F4:A0 0A	8	LDY	#$0A	;Y IS # OF BCD DIGITS.
13F6:A5 F0	9 OUTLOOP	LDA	BCD	;GET MSB OF BCD #.
13F8:29 F0	10	AND	#$F0	;MASK THE LOW NIBBLE.
13FA:4A	11	LSR	A	;MOVE THE HIGH-ORDER NIBBLE
13FB:4A	12	LSR	A	;TO THE LOW-ORDER NIBBLE.
13FC:4A	13	LSR	A	
13FD:4A	14	LSR	A	
13FE:09 30	15	ORA	#$30	;CONVERT TO 7-BIT ASCII.
1400:09 80	16	ORA	#$80	;CONVERT TO APPLE ASCII.
1402:20 ED FD	17	JSR	COUT	;USE APPLE OUTPUT ROUTINE.
1405:98	18	TYA		;SAVE Y IN A.
1406:A0 04	19	LDY	#04	;SHIFT BCD # 4 BITS LEFT.
1408:A2 04	20 LOOP5	LDX	#04	;X+1 IS # OF BYTES IN BCD #.
140A:36 F0	21 LOOP4	ROL	BCD,X	;ROTATE ONE BYTE.
140C:CA	22	DEX		;DO WE NEED TO GET ANOTHER?
140D:10 FB	23	BPL	LOOP4	;YES.
140F:88	24	DEY		;DECREMENT BIT COUNTER.
1410:D0 F6	25	BNE	LOOP5	;FOUR BITS YET?
1412:A8	26	TAY		;YES, SO GET Y BACK.
1413:88	27	DEY		;HAVE ALL THE DIGITS BEEN CONVERTED?
1414:D0 E0	28	BNE	OUTLOOP	;NO, SO CONVERT THE OTHERS.
1416:60	29	RTS		;YES, THEN QUIT.

number four bits to the left so the next-most-significant digit is in the place of the most significant digit. This process is continued until the least significant digit is passed to the output subroutine.

The number initially placed in the Y register (line 8) should be twice the number of locations assigned to the bcd number; that is, Y contains the number of bcd digits to be output. The number of bytes of memory allocated to the bcd number is X + 1. Clearly, these numbers can be easily modified for other applications.

To round out this section a program is included that will input a binary number, convert it to bcd using the program in Example 8–5, and convert the bcd number to ASCII and output it using the program in Example 8–6. This set of routines allows you to convert binary numbers input on the keyboard to bcd numbers that are output on the video monitor. The largest binary number that can be input is \$FFFFFFFF. Be sure to input leading zeros for smaller numbers. For example, to convert \$FFFF to binary, input 00 00 FF FF, and the answer 65535 will appear. The program is listed in Example 8–7. This example makes use of the RDBYTE subroutine which was described in Example 5–20, which is also included in the listing below for your convenience.

Example 8–7. A Program to Input a Binary Number and Output Its BCD Equivalent

```
00F0:           3 BCD     EQU   $00F0
00E0:           4 BIN     EQU   $00E0
1100:           5 RDBYTEE EQU   $1100
13D0:           6 CONV    EQU   $13D0    ;SEE EXAMPLE 8–5.
13F4:           7 OUT     EQU   $13F4    ;SEE EXAMPLE 8–6.
FDED:           8 COUT    EQU   $FDED    ;MONITOR ROUTINE.

----- NEXT OBJECT FILE NAME IS EXAMPLE 8–7A.

15BE:           9         ORG   $15BE

15BE:A2 FC     11         LDX   #$FC
15C0:20 00 11  12 LOOP    JSR   RDBYTE
15C3:95 E4     13         STA   $E4,X
15C5:E8        14         INX
15C6:D0 F8     15         BNE   LOOP
15C8:20 D0 13  16         JSR   CONV
15CB:20 F4 13  17         JSR   OUT
15CE:00        18         BRK

1100:          31 * SUBROUTINE RDBYTE

1100:20 16 11  33         JSR   ASHEX    ;GET NIBBLE.
```

```
1103:0A        34         ASL    A          ;SHIFT TO HIGH NIBBLE.
1104:0A        35         ASL    A
1105:0A        36         ASL    A
1106:0A        37         ASL    A
1107:85 00     38         STA    TEMP       ;STORE NIBBLE.
1109:20 16 11  39         JSR    ASHEX      ;GET THE SECOND NIBBLE.
110C:05 00     40         ORA    TEMP       ;COMBINE WITH FIRST NIBBLE.
110E:85 00     41         STA    TEMP       ;SAVE ENTIRE BYTE.
1110:20 8E FD  42         JSR    CROUT      ;OUTPUT A RETURN.
1113:A5 00     43         LDA    TEMP       ;GET BYTE BACK.
1115:60        44         RTS               ;NO. RETURN.

1116:          46 * ASCII-TO-HEX ROUTINE

1116:20 0C FD  48 ASHEX   JSR    RDKEY      ;GET A CHARACTER.
1119:20 ED FD  49         JSR    COUT       ;DISPLAY IT. EXAMPLE 8-7A
111C:29 7F     50         AND    #$7F       ;MASK BIT 7 OFF.
111E:C9 40     51         CMP    #$40       ;DIGIT OR LETTER?
1120:B0 04     52         BCS    ARND
1122:29 0F     53         AND    #$0F       ;DIGIT, MASK HI-NIBBLE.
1124:10 02     54         BPL    PAST       ;BRANCH PAST LETTER.
1126:E9 37     55 ARND    SBC    #$37       ;LETTER, SUBTRACT $37.
1128:60        56 PAST    RTS               ;RETURN WITH DIGIT IN A.
```

AN N-BYTE BCD-TO-BINARY CONVERSION

Just as Example 8–5 extends the 8-bit binary-to-bcd routine
in Example 8–2 to handle 32 bits, we may extend the bcd-to-
binary conversion subroutine in Example 8–4 to handle larger
numbers.

The program listed in Example 8–8 converts a 6-digit (3-byte)
bcd number to binary. The 6-digit number is stored in locations
$00FC–$00FE with the most significant byte located in $00FC
and the least significant byte located in $00FE. After the con-
version, the most significant byte of the binary number is stored
in location $00F4 and the least significant byte is stored in lo-
cation $00F6. The algorithm is identical with the one described
in connection with Example 8–4. To output the binary number
a 6-digit (3-byte) hexadecimal-to-ASCII conversion routine is
provided in Example 8–9.

As an exercise, write a program similar to the one in Example
8–7 that uses the RDBYTE subroutine to input six bcd digits
and store them in location $00FC–$00FE. Use zero-page indexed addressing, and store the number with the most
significant byte in location $00FC. Combine this with sub-
routine calls to Examples 8–8 and 8–9 to provide a complete
bcd-to-binary conversion routine, complete with keyboard input
and video monitor output.

Example 8-8. An N-Byte BCD-to-Binary Conversion Routine

```
00FF:           3 BCDN    EQU    $00FF    ;BASE ADDRESS OF BCD #.
00F7:           4 BINO    EQU    $00F7    ;BASE ADDRESS OF BINARY #.
00FD:           5 NBYTE   EQU    $FD      ;TWOS COMPLEMENT OF # BYTES

----- NEXT OBJECT FILE NAME IS EXAMPLE 8-8.

1417:           6         ORG    $1417    ;IN THE BCD NUMBER.

1417:           8 ;BCD-TO-BINARY SUBROUTINE
1417:D8         9 CONVERT CLD            ;CLEAR DECIMAL MODE.
1418:A9 00     10         LDA    #00      ;CLEAR LOCATIONS TO HOLD
                                            BINARY #.
141A:A2 FD     11         LDX    #NBYTE   ;X IS BYTE COUNTER.
141C:95 F7     12 LOOPA   STA    BINO,X   ;FILL BINARY # WITH ZEROS.
141E:E8        13         INX
141F:D0 FB     14         BNE    LOOPA
1421:A9 80     15         LDA    #$80
1423:A2 FD     16         LDX    #NBYTE   ;MAKE MOST SIGNIFICANT BIT OF
1425:95 F7     17         STA    BINO,X   ;BINARY NUMBER A ONE.
1427:A2 FD     18 BIGLOOP LDX    #NBYTE
1429:18        19         CLC             ;CLEAR CARRY FOR ROTATE.
142A:76 FF     20 LOOPB   ROR    BCDN,X   ;ROTATE BCD # INTO CARRY
142C:E8        21         INX             ;ONE BIT AT A TIME.
142D:D0 FB     22         BNE    LOOPB
142F:A2 FD     23         LDX    #NBYTE   ;ROTATE LAST CARRY INTO
                                            BINARY #
1431:76 F7     24 LOOPC   ROR    BINO,X   ;ONE BIT AT A TIME.
1433:E8        25         INX
1434:D0 FB     26         BNE    LOOPC
1436:B0 20     27         BCS    OUT      ;IF CARRY IS SET, CONVERSION
                                            COMPLETE.
1438:A2 FD     28         LDX    #NBYTE   ;START CORRECTION TO BCD/2
                                            OPERATION.
143A:38        29         SEC
143B:B5 FF     30 LOOPD   LDA    BCDN,X   ;IF BIT THREE IS SET,
143D:29 08     31         AND    #08      ;THEN SUBTRACT $03.
143F:F0 06     32         BEQ    BR1
1441:B5 FF     33         LDA    BCDN,X
1443:E9 03     34         SBC    #$03
1445:95 FF     35         STA    BCDN,X
1447:B5 FF     36 BR1     LDA    BCDN,X   ;NEXT CHECK BIT SEVEN TO SEE
1449:29 80     37         AND    #$80     ;IF BIT SEVEN IS SET.
144B:F0 06     38         BEQ    BR2      ;IF NOT, DO NOT SUBTRACT.
144D:B5 FF     39         LDA    BCDN,X   ;IF SO, SUBTRACT $30.
144F:E9 30     40         SBC    #$30
1451:95 FF     41         STA    BCDN,X
1453:E8        42 BR2     INX
1454:D0 E5     43         BNE    LOOPD    ;REPEAT FOR ALL BYTES OF THE
                                            BCD #.
1456:F0 CF     44         BEQ    BIGLOOP  ;LOOP BACK FOR ANOTHER BIT.
1458:60        45 OUT     RTS             ;CONVERSION COMPLETE.
```

Example 8–9. An N-Byte Hexadecimal-to-ASCII Conversion Routine

```
FDED:          3 COUT    EQU    $FDED          ;MONITOR OUTPUT ROUTINE.
00F7:          4 BINO    EQU    $00F7          ;BASE ADDRESS OF BINARY #.
00FD:          5 NBYTE   EQU    $FD            ;TWOS COMPLEMENT OF # BYTES
----- NEXT OBJECT FILE NAME IS EXAMPLE 8-9.
1459:          6         ORG    $1459          ;IN THE BCD NUMBER.

1459:          8 ;HEX-TO-ASCII SUBROUTINE
1459:A0 06     9         LDY    #06            ;Y IS # OF HEX DIGITS. 2 TIMES
                                                   # BYTES
145B:A2 FD    10 OUTLOOP LDX   #NBYTE          ;X IS # OF BYTES IN BINARY #.
145D:B5 F7    11         LDA    BINO,X         ;GET THE MOST SIGNIFICANT BYTE.
145F:29 F0    12         AND    #$F0           ;MASK THE LEAST SIGNIFICANT
                                                   NIBBLE.
1461:4A       13         LSR    A              ;SHIFT TO THE LOW-ORDER NIBBLE.
1462:4A       14         LSR    A
1463:4A       15         LSR    A
1464:4A       16         LSR    A
1465:C9 0A    17         CMP    #$0A           ;IS IT A LETTER A-F?
1467:B0 04    18         BCS    BR1            ;YES.
1469:09 30    19         ORA    #$30           ;NO. CONVERT NUMBER TO ASCII.
146B:D0 02    20         BNE    BR2            ;BRANCH AROUND LETTER
                                                   CONVERSION.
146D:69 36    21 BR1     ADC    #$36           ;CONVERTS A-F to ASCII.
146F:09 80    22 BR2     ORA    #$80           ;CHANGE TO APPLE ASCII:BIT 7=1.
1471:20 ED FD 23         JSR    COUT           ;OUTPUT THE CHARACTER.
1474:98       24         TYA                   ;SAVE Y FOR A MOMENT.
1475:A0 04    25         LDY    #04            ;Y WILL COUNT 4 BIT SHIFTS.
1477:A2 02    26 LOOPY   LDX    #02            ;START WITH LSB.
1479:18       27         CLC
147A:36 F4    28 LOOPX   ROL    BINO+NBYTE,X
147C:CA       29         DEX
147D:10 FB    30         BPL    LOOPX
147F:88       31         DEY                   ;FOUR BITS YET?
1480:D0 F5    32         BNE    LOOPY          ;NO, GO BACK AND SHIFT AGAIN.
1482:A8       33         TAY                   ;YES, RESTORE Y.
1483:88       34         DEY                   ;HAVE ALL THE DIGITS BEEN
                                                   CONVERTED?
1484:DO D5    35         BNE    OUTLOOP        ;NO, SO CONVERT ANOTHER.
1486:60       36         TRS                   ;YES, THEN QUIT.
```

SIGNED NUMBER ARITHMETIC

What is a negative number? There seems to be a certain amount of mystery associated with negative numbers. Actually, mathematicians have a very simple definition of a negative number. Suppose m is a whole number $(0, 1, 2, \ldots)$. The *negative* of m, symbolized by $(-m)$, is *defined* as that number which when added to m yields zero. In symbols

$$m + (-m) = 0 \qquad (8\text{--}5)$$

With this definition it is quite simple to prove a theorem showing that subtraction may be accomplished by adding the *negative* of the subtrahend. Here is the theorem.

$$a - m = a + (-m) \qquad (8\text{--}6)$$

Turning our attention to 8-bit binary numbers, we see that there is no way of indicating a minus sign to inform the computer that a number is negative. It is possible, however, to discover a relationship between binary numbers that is identical with Equation 8–5. Now we will verify this.

Suppose M is an 8-bit number. With a few examples you can demonstrate that

$$M + \overline{M} = \$FF \qquad (8\text{--}7)$$

For example, if M = 1100 0101 = $C5 then $\overline{M}$ = 0011 1010 = $3A and $M + \overline{M}$ = 1111 1111 = $FF.

Since adding 1 to $FF gives $00 (with a 1 in the carry flag), we can also state that

$$M + \overline{M} + 1 = \$FF + 1 = 0 \qquad (8\text{--}8)$$

or

$$M + (\overline{M} + 1) = 0 \qquad (8\text{--}9)$$

Refer to Equation 8–5 and observe that Equation 8–9 satisfies the definition of a negative number. That is:

- *The negative of an 8-bit number is found by complementing the number and adding 1.*

The number $(\overline{M} + 1)$ is not usually called the negative of M, although it has the properties of a negative number and it will be used as a negative number. Instead it is called the *twos complement* of M.

Returning to the subtraction theorem expressed by Equation 8–6 we can write an analogous theorem for 8-bit binary numbers, namely,

$$A - M = A + (\overline{M} + 1) \qquad (8\text{--}10)$$

Direct subtraction, indicated by the left-hand member of Equation 8–10 is difficult to implement with the logic circuitry internal to a microprocessor. On the other hand, complementation followed by adding 1 is relatively simple, and microprocessors perform subtraction internally using the right-hand side of Equation 8–10.

Moreover, the "1" in Equation 8–10 can be stored in the

carry flag. To add $(\overline{M} + 1)$ to a number the carry flag could be set followed by the addition of $\overline{M}$. In other words, if the carry flag is *set* then $(\overline{M} + C)$ is the *twos complement* of M. Equation 8–10 can now be modified to read

$$A - M = A + (\overline{M} + C) \qquad (8\text{--}11)$$

Study Equation 8–11 carefully. If C is set, as it should be for a subtraction, then $\overline{C} = 0$. But if $\overline{C} = 0$ then Equation 8–11 could just as well be written

$$A - M - \overline{C} = A + (\overline{M} + C) \qquad (8\text{--}12)$$

Now refer to the instruction set summary and observe that the left-hand member of Equation 8–12 is *identical* with the logical expression for the SBC instruction. The right-hand member of Equation 8–12 is indicative of how the microprocessor actually performs subtraction internally.

In Equation 8–12 observe that if C is set we calculate $A - M$. If C is clear we calculate $A - M$ *with a borrow*.

In the previous paragraphs we have seen how subtraction is performed by a microprocessor and in the process we have seen that the 8-bit number $(\overline{M} + 1)$ *may* be regarded as the negative of the 8-bit number M. In those computer applications that require operations with *signed* numbers, the computer industry has adopted the following convention for 8-bit signed numbers:

- Eight-bit binary numbers represent the decimal integers from -128 to $+127$. Refer to Table 8–1 to observe the pattern of integers, binary numbers, and hexadecimal numbers. Refer to Table 3–1 for the hexadecimal-to-integer conversion for all possible 8-bit numbers. A negative number is the twos complement of the positive number.

- Bit seven is called the *sign bit*. A 1 in bit seven indicates a negative number. A 0 in bit seven indicates a positive number.

With regard to signed hexadecimal representations:

- The numbers \$00 to \$7F represent the nonnegative integers from 0 to 127.
- The numbers \$80 to \$FF represent the negative integers from -128 to -1.

To handle numbers greater than $+127$ and less than -128, two or more bytes are used. Bit seven in the most significant byte remains the sign bit. Thus a 16-bit signed number could have values between $+32,767$ and $-32,768$.

Table 8–1. Twos Complement Representations of Numbers from −128 to +127

Number	Twos Complement	Hexadecimal
+127	0111 1111	$7F
•	•	•
•	•	•
•	•	•
+5	0000 0101	$05
+4	0000 0100	$04
+3	0000 0011	$03
+2	0000 0010	$02
+1	0000 0001	$01
0	0000 0000	$00
−1	1111 1111	$FF
−2	1111 1110	$FE
−3	1111 1101	$FD
−4	1111 1100	$FC
−5	1111 1011	$FB
•	•	•
•	•	•
•	•	•
−128	1000 0000	$80

We pause in this discussion to observe that many micro-computer applications do not require signed numbers. In such applications an 8-bit binary number represents a decimal number between 0 and 255. The *interpretation* of bit seven as a sign bit is *strictly* an *option* of the *programmer*.

Examples 8–10 and 8–11 illustrate some signed number arithmetic operations.

The addition and subtraction programs given in Chapter 5 work for signed numbers as well as whole numbers. The *interpretation of the number as a signed number is made by the programmer*. Having made such an interpretation, the programmer can use the BMI or BPL instructions to test the N flag in the P register to see if the result is positive or negative. Zero is positive in the miniscule mind of the 6502.

Example 8–10. Adding Two Signed Numbers

Object: Perform the addition −21 + 17 = −4 in hexadecimal.
Solution: 21 = $15. Since $15 = 0001 0101, the complement of $15 is 1110 1010 = $EA. The twos complement of $15 is $EA + 1 = $EB. Therefore −21 = $EB. Since 17 = $11, then −21 + 17 = $EB + $11 = $FC. $FC has a 1 in bit seven and its twos complement is $04. Thus the answer is −4, which checks.

Example 8–11. Subtracting Two Signed Numbers

Object: Perform the subtraction −21 − (−32) = 11 in hexadecimal.
Solution: From the previous example, −21 = $EB. Also, 32 = $20, so −32 = $DF + 1 = $E0. Finally, $EB − E0 = $0B = 11, which checks.

A complication arises when numbers are interpreted as signed numbers and addition or subtraction operations are performed. A single example will illustrate this complication. Suppose you add 1 to 127. The result is 1000 0000 in binary, and if this result is considered to be a signed number then there is a 1 in bit seven so the answer is negative (-128 to be exact). This is wrong. What happened was that the sum *overflowed* into the sign bit, giving an incorrect sign. The *overflow flag,* V, in the P register will be set when this happens. The programmer can test this bit after performing a signed number addition or subtraction to check for the overflow condition. The programmer can also *clear* the overflow flag prior to an arithmetic operation with a *CLV instruction.* The overflow flag is tested with the *BVS (branch on overflow set)* and the *BVC (branch on V flag clear)* instructions.

The carry flag, C, has *no meaning* when arithmetic operations are performed on *signed* numbers.

We conclude this discussion of signed number arithmetic by mentioning multiplication and division of signed numbers. Recall that when multiplying or dividing signed numbers, the sign of the result is plus if the signs of the operands are alike; otherwise the sign of the result is minus. The sign of the result can be obtained by masking everything except bit seven of each of the numbers and executing an EOR instruction. If the EOR yields a 1, then the sign of the result is negative; otherwise it is positive. The multiplication or division algorithms usually proceed as follows:

- Perform an EOR with the sign bits of the numbers to determine the sign of the answer.
- Form the twos complement of all negative operands before doing the multiplication or division.
- Perform the multiplication or division with no regard for signs.
- Twos complement the result if the sign of the answer is negative.

It should be clear that the multiplication and division algorithms do not change for signed numbers, and consequently the programs given earlier in this chapter will also work, provided the steps just outlined are taken before performing the operations. A more detailed discussion of signed number arithmetic programs is given by Leo J. Scanlon in *6502 Software Design* (Howard W. Sams & Co., Inc., 1980), page 114.

To operate with rational (fraction) numbers and irrational

numbers *floating-point arithmetic* is used. A discussion of floating-point arithmetic is beyond the scope of this book. A complete set of floating-point routines in 6502 assembly language has been published by Marvin L. De Jong in the March through July issues of *Compute!* magazine. (*Compute!* is published by Small System Services, Inc., P.O. Box 5406, Greensboro, NC 27403, (919) 275–9809.)

EXERCISES

Exercise 8–1

Write a program to add odd parity to the eighth bit of a 7-bit character code.

Exercise 8–2

Test the programs in Examples 8–5, 8–6, and 8–7 to make sure they correctly convert binary numbers to bcd numbers.

Exercise 8–3

Combine the program in Example 8–8 with the program in Example 8–9 with one that you write yourself to give the capability of inputting a bcd number from the keyboard and writing its binary equivalent to the video monitor.

Exercise 8–4

Write single-precision addition, subtraction, multiplication, and division programs that will handle signed numbers. Check your results using Table 3–1. Use the programs in Chapter 5 as a beginning, and use the procedures for handling signed numbers outlined in this chapter. Test for overflow conditions using the V flag in the P register.

CHAPTER 9

Programming with the 6522

OBJECTIVES

At the completion of this chapter you should be able to:

- Understand how the 6522 can be used as an 8-bit input port, an 8-bit output port, or both.
- Program the 6522 to perform simple timing operations including delay loops.
- Use the 6522 to count pulses from external devices, such as voltage-to-frequency converters.
- Understand the various features of the 6522 well enough to use it in your own applications.

INTRODUCTION

The 6522 VIA (versatile interface adapter) is not another microprocessor that you must learn to program. It is one of several integrated circuits designed by the same people who made the 6502, and it is intended to perform input/output and timing/counting functions in 6502-based microcomputer systems. It is called a *family*-type chip because it interfaces very easily to 6502-based systems since it uses the same bus and control signals provided by the 6502 microprocessor. The 6522 VIA, hereinafter called the 6522, gives the microcomputer system two ports that may be configured (programmed) to be either input ports or output ports. Two 16-bit interval timers, one of which can be used to count external pulses, are also provided on the 6522. Although this is a complex chip, we will approach it step by step until you have mastered the most important details of its operation.

Because of its power and versatility, the 6522 has been used in many 6502-based microcomputer systems, but the Apple is an exception. To interface a 6522 to your Apple you can purchase a "6522 Apple II Parallel Interface" board from:

John Bell Engineering, Inc.
P.O. Box 338
Redwood City, CA 94064
(415) 367-1137

This board plugs into any of the peripheral card slots on the Apple. A photograph of the board, showing its two 6522s and the connecting sockets, is given in Fig. 9-1. The jumper wire,

(Courtesy John Bell Engineering, Inc.)

Fig. 9-1. Photograph of the John Bell Engineering 6522 board.

supplied by the user, connects the $\overline{\text{IRQ}}$ output pin on the 6522 to the $\overline{\text{IRQ}}$ line on the Apple microcomputer bus that connects it to the $\overline{\text{IRQ}}$ input pin on the 6502 microprocessor. The i/o ports on the 6522s on the John Bell interface board are connected to 16-pin DIP sockets, also visible in the photograph of Fig. 9–1. The same DIP jumper cable illustrated and used in Chapter 3 is used to connect the 6522 to external circuits on a breadboard. (Refer to the photograph in Fig. 9–22 for details.) In Chapter 10 the 6522 will be used to control an a/d (analog-to-digital) converter and a d/a (digital-to-analog) converter. You may be interested in other details about the John Bell board provided by his documentation. The board comes in kit form or fully assembled. You can also purchase a printed-circuit board with no components on it.

Another option for adding a 6522 to your Apple is to wire-wrap the circuit shown in Fig. 9–2. This circuit is identical with the one used by John Bell Engineering. A Vector 4609 plug-board is recommended for this work. Refer to Appendix B for a description of the Vector plugboard, including photographs.

REVIEW OF INPUT/OUTPUT FUNDAMENTALS

The purpose of an input port is to provide information for the computer from the outside world. This is usually accomplished by an external device, a photocell for example, controlling the voltage level at one of eight pins on an integrated circuit called an *interface adapter* or, more simply, an *input port*. Typically a voltage near 5 volts corresponds to a binary 1, while a voltage near 0 volts corresponds to a binary 0. The integrated circuit that serves as the input port is connected to the data bus and the address bus of the microcomputer. When the address of the input port is placed on the address bus by the 6502, then the input port controls the logic levels on the data bus, and the 6502 *reads* the binary number represented by the voltage levels at the input port. The keyboard on the Apple is an external device that controls the logic levels on the keyboard input port at location $C000. We have used this input port rather frequently in this book.

This mode of operation, in which input ports act like any other memory device in the sense that they supply data to the 6502 only when they are addressed, is called *memory-mapped input*. As far as the 6502 is concerned, an input port is just another location in its address space.

The purpose of an output port is to provide information from the computer to the outside world. An integrated circuit is con-

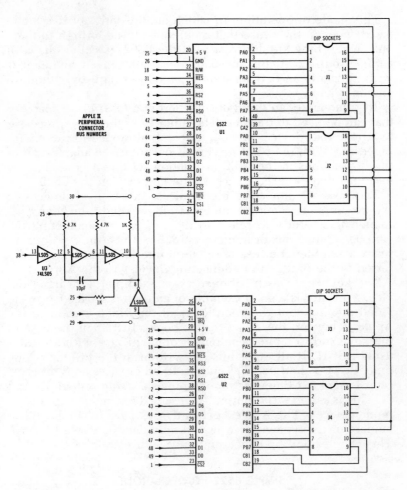

(Courtesy of John Bell Engineering, Inc.)

Fig. 9–2. Circuit diagram of the 6522 board.

nected to the data bus and the address bus, just as in the case of
the input port. This integrated circuit has up to eight pins (typically) each of which may be used to control an external device,
such as a relay or a light-emitting diode (LED). The 6502 *writes*
data to an output port, using an STA instruction for example.
The number stored in the output port controls the voltage levels
on the output pins of the integrated circuit. A binary 0 produces
a voltage level near 0 volts, while a binary 1 produces a voltage
level near 5 volts.

This mode of operation, in which output ports act like memory devices in the sense that a number can be written to them only when they are addressed by the 6502, is called *memory mapped output*. Again, the 6502 does not know whether it is writing data to an R/W location or an output port; only the programmer knows this.

To summarize, an *input/output* port is a *location in memory* that can be used to transfer data either from the microprocessor to an external device, or from an external device to the microprocessor. With the 6522 serving as our interface adapter, all of the instructions in the 6502 instruction set that access memory locations may be used to access the i/o ports on the 6522.

The task of connecting electronic or mechanical devices to the i/o ports of a microcomputer is often called *interfacing*, although this term also refers to the process of connecting the various components of a microcomputer. Since the Apple is already assembled, our use of the term interfacing has usually referred to the problem of connecting devices to the Apple.

The keyboard was mentioned as an example of an input device. A printer is a good example of an output device (so is the video monitor, but the complexity of the video system of the Apple is beyond the scope of this book). Just as in the case of the keyboard, the microcomputer communicates with a printer using ASCII. If all eight bits are written to the printer at one time, this is called *parallel* output. In other cases an 8-bit character is sent out timewise on *one* pin as a *string* of logic 1s and 0s. This is called *serial* output. The same terminology applies to input devices. The Apple keyboard uses *parallel* input, but a modem or teletypewriter would supply data in a *serial* format. This chapter will be concerned only with parallel i/o.

SIMPLE 6522 I/O OPERATIONS

A simplified block diagram of the input/output (i/o) registers of the 6522 is shown in Fig. 9–3. There are two 8-bit i/o ports (or registers), port A and and port B. These ports are accessed in exactly the same way as any other memory locations; that is, they are locations in the address space of the microcomputer. Assume the John Bell card is in peripheral card slot 7 on the Apple. Then the address of port A of 6522 U1 is $C701, and we shall symbolize this location by PAD for "Port A Data." The address of port B (called PBD for "Port B Data") is $C700.

Consult the John Bell Engineering documentation for the corresponding addresses of the i/o ports if the card is placed in another slot in the Apple. In what follows we shall always as-

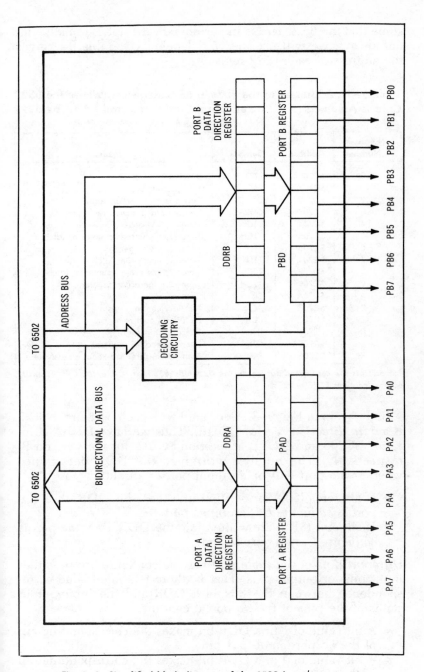

Fig. 9-3. Simplified block diagram of the 6522 input/output ports.

sume that the 6522 card is in peripheral card slot 7. Usually, but not always, we will use the 6522 labeled U1. Table 9–1 gives the address of each 6522 register.

Table 9–1. Addresses of the Sixteen 6522 Registers, Where the 6522 Card Is Assumed to be in Peripheral Card Slot 7 and U1 Is the 6522 Being Used

Register Number	Address	Symbol	Name
0	$C700*	PBD	Input/output port B
1	$C701	PAD	Input/output port A
2	$C702	DDRB	Port B data direction register
3	$C703	DDRA	Port A data direction register
4	$C704	T1CL	Timer 1, low-order counter or latch
5	$C705	T1CH	Timer 1, high-order counter or latch
6	$C706	T1LL	Timer 1, low-order latch
7	$C707	T1LH	Timer 1, high-order latch
8	$C708	T2CL	Timer 2, low-order counter or latch
9	$C709	T2CH	Timer 2, high-order counter
A	$C70A	SR	Shift register
B	$C70B	ACR	Auxiliary control register
C	$C70C	PCR	Peripheral control register
D	$C70D	IFR	Interrupt flag register
E	$C70E	IER	Interrupt enable register
F	$C70F	PAD	Same as register 1 without handshake

*To address the corresponding register on U2, add $80. That is, the 16 registers on U2 occupy locations $C780–$C78F.

Refer again to Fig. 9–3. Associated with each port on the 6522 is a *data direction register* (DDR). Thus we have DDRA at location $C703 and DDRB at location $C702, for ports A and B, respectively. The number written to the DDR determines whether the port will be an input port or an output port.

- If all zeros ($00) are written into the 8-bit DDR, then the port is *configured* as an *input* port.
- If all ones ($FF) are written into the DDR, then the port is *configured* as an *output* port.

Different pins of the *same* port may be configured to be either input pins or output pins. That is, there is a one-to-one correspondence between the bits in a DDR and the input/output status of the pins of the i/o port it controls.

- A bit value of *1* in a DDR bit makes the corresponding pin of the i/o port an *output* pin.
- A bit value of *0* in a DDR bit makes the corresponding pin of the i/o port an input pin.

Example 9–1 illustrates these concepts. In this routine port A is configured as an output port. Pins 7 and 1 of port B are configured as output pins, while pins 1 through 6 of port B are configured as input pins. It is important to realize that *under power-up conditions, or when the computer is reset, the i/o ports on the 6522 will be initialized as input ports*. If the 6522 is interfaced to the input of a 7400 series integrated circuit, then a pin configured as an input pin *appears* to be a logic 1.

Let us continue the i/o port initialization sequence begun in Example 9–1 by setting pins 0 through 3 of port A to logic 1 and setting the other four pins to logic 0. Assume also that pins 7 and 1 of port B are to be initialized to logic 1. Example 9–2 illustrates the additional instructions that must be combined with Example 9–1 to accomplish this.

LOW ORDER BYTE   */ HIGH ORDER BYTE*

Example 9–1. An I/O Port Configuration Routine

Object: Write a routine that makes port A on the 6522 an output port. Make pins 7 and 0 of port B output pins; the other pins of port B should be configured as input pins.

1774:A9 FF	7	LDA	#$FF	;SET UP DDRA TO MAKE
1776:8D 03 C7	8	STA	DDRA	;PORT A AN OUTPUT PORT.
1779:A9 81	9	LDA	#$81	;MAKE PINS SEVEN AND ONE OF PORT B
177B:8D 02 C7	10	STA	DDRB	;OUTPUT PINS.

Example 9–2. A Routine to Initialize the Output Pins

Object: Set pins 7 through 4 of port A to logic 1. Set pins 8 and 1 of port B to logic 1. The two DDRs have been initialized in Example 9–1.

177E:A9 F0	7	LDA	#$F0	;MAKE BITS FOUR-SEVEN LOGIC ONE.
1780:8D 01 C7	8	STA	PAD	;WRITE TO THE OUTPUT PORT.
1783:A9 81	9	LDA	#$81	;MAKE BITS ZERO AND EIGHT EQUAL ONE.
1785:8D 00 C7	10	STA	PBD	;OUTPUT THIS NUMBER TO PORT B.

An extremely simple, but not very useful, task for the computer would be to read an input port and output the same number to an output port. Such a program would allow the user to control eight devices, motors, relays, etc., with eight switch settings. Suppose port A is specified as the output port and port B is specified as the input port. Example 9–3 continues this section on simple i/o by performing the task just outlined. Note again how the data direction registers are initialized, and observe that placing the port-read and port-write instructions in a loop causes the computer to monitor the ports continuously.

Let us consider a few more simple examples of input/output

Example 9–3. A Program to Read an Input Port and Write to an Output Port

Object: Continuously read Port B and write this number to Port A.

```
1788:A9 FF     9          LDA   #$FF       ;MAKE PORT A AN OUTPUT PORT.
178A:8D 03 C7  10         STA   DDRA
178D:A9 00     11         LDA   #$00       ;MAKE PORT B AN INPUT PORT.
178F:8D 02 C7  12         STA   DDRB
1792:AD 00 C7  13  LOOP   LDA   PBD        ;READ PORT B.
1795:8D 01 C7  14         STA   PAD        ;WRITE TO PORT A.
1798:18        15         CLC
1799:90 F7     16         BCC   LOOP       ;LOOP TO DO THIS
                                            CONTINUOUSLY.
```

operations before turning to a more complex description of the 6522. Some devices require an output pulse that triggers them into operation. How could you produce an output pulse on pin 0 of port A, namely PA0? Assume that the shape of the negative pulse is like the one illustrated in Fig. 9–4. First we initialize PA0 to be an output pin and store a logic 1 in bit zero of port A. Thereafter a DEC PAD instruction followed by an INC PAD instruction will produce the desired pulse. Example 9–4 illustrates the program. How long will this pulse be? Since the DEC and INC instructions are being used in the absolute mode, they each take 6 clock cycles. The bit value of PA0 changes during the last cycle of each instruction, so the pulse is 6 clock cycles in duration. For longer pulses put several NOP instructions between the DEC and INC instructions, or put a delay routine between the two instructions.

Certain devices indicate they are *busy* (not ready to accept data or provide data) by holding a pin at logic 1. When they are *ready* the pin is brought to logic 0. Suppose the pin is connected to PB7, pin 7 of port B on the 6522. Write a program that

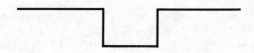

Fig. 9–4. The pulse shape to be produced by the program in Example 9–4.

Example 9–4. A Program to Pulse Pin PA0

Object: Produce a negative pulse on PA0 that is 6 clock cycles in duration.

```
179B:A9 01     7          LDA   #01        ;INITIALIZE PA0 TO BE AN
179D:8D 01 C7  8          STA   PAD        ;OUTPUT PIN AT LOGIC ONE.
17A0:8D 03 C7  9          STA   DDRA
17A3:CE 01 C7  10         DEC   PAD        ;SWITCH PA0 TO LOGIC ZERO.
17A6:EE 01 C7  11         INC   PAD        ;SWITCH PA0 TO LOGIC ONE.
```

waits in a loop until the device is not busy. Example 9–5 is a solution to this demand.

Consider next the program in Example 9–6. Study it and try to understand what it does. Note that it uses port A as an output port, and an INC PAD instruction is placed in a loop. Each of the pins of port A will toggle back and forth between logic 1 and logic 0. The nature of binary counting ensures that PB7 will toggle at half the rate (frequency) of PB6, PB6 will toggle at half the rate of PB5, and so on. You have created eight harmonically related square wave generators. The frequency could be controlled by a delay loop placed within the loop in Example 9–6.

Example 9–5. A Routine to Wait in a Loop Until PB7 Changes to Logic 0

Object: A BUSY signal is applied to PB7. Wait in a loop until the device is not BUSY.

17A9:A9 7F	7		LDA	#$7F	;CLEAR BIT 7 OF DDRB
17AB:2D 02 C7	8		AND	DDRB	;SO PB7 IS AN INPUT PIN.
17AE:8D 02 C7	9		STA	DDRB	
17B1:2C 00 C7	10	LOOP	BIT	PBD	;IS BIT SEVEN AT
17B4:30 FB	11		BMI	LOOP	;LOGIC ONE? YES, WAIT.
17B6:00	12		BRK		;NO, CONTINUE.

Example 9–6. A Program to Toggle All of the Pins of Port A

Object: Produce harmonically related square waves on the pins of port A.

17B7:A9 FF	7		LDA	#$FF	;INITIALIZE PAD TO BE AN
17B9:8D 03 C7	8		STA	DDRA	;OUTPUT PORT.
17BC:EE 01 C7	9	TOGGLE	INC	PAD	;INCREMENT THE NUMBER IN PAD.
17BF:B8	10		CLV		;FORCE A BRANCH.
17C0:50 FA	11		BVC	TOGGLE	

MORE COMPLEX I/O OPERATIONS: A PRINTER INTERFACE

Adhering to our policy of introducing the features of the 6522 as slowly as possible, in this section only two more of the 16 registers of the 6522 will be introduced. We will also discuss how the 6522 can be used to control a printer, and in the process we will observe some additional features of the 6522. The two registers now introduced are the interrupt flag register (IFR) and the peripheral control register (PCR). Refer to Table 9–1 for the addresses of these two registers. The IFR is illustrated in Fig. 9–5[1] and the PCR is illustrated in Fig. 9–6.[1]

---

[1]This figure, and others so noted, were first published by the author in *Micro*, January 1981, page 65. They are reprinted here with permission. *Micro* is published by Micro, Ink, Inc., P.O. Box 6502, Chelmsford, MA 01824. *Micro* is a monthly publication dedicated to the 6502 and the 6809 microprocessors.

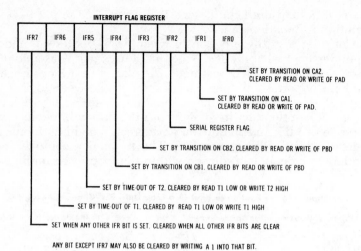

INTERRUPT FLAG REGISTER

| IFR7 | IFR6 | IFR5 | IFR4 | IFR3 | IFR2 | IFR1 | IFR0 |

SET BY TRANSITION ON CA2.
CLEARED BY READ OR WRITE OF PAD

SET BY TRANSITION ON CA1.
CLEARED BY READ OR WRITE OF PAD.

SERIAL REGISTER FLAG

SET BY TRANSITION ON CB2. CLEARED BY READ OR WRITE OF PBD.

SET BY TRANSITION ON CB1. CLEARED BY READ OR WRITE OF PBD

SET BY TIME-OUT OF T2. CLEARED BY READ T1 LOW OR WRITE T2 HIGH

SET BY TIME-OUT OF T1. CLEARED BY READ T1 LOW OR WRITE T1 HIGH

SET WHEN ANY OTHER IFR BIT IS SET. CLEARED WHEN ALL OTHER IFR BITS ARE CLEAR

ANY BIT EXCEPT IFR7 MAY ALSO BE CLEARED BY WRITING A 1 INTO THAT BIT.

(Courtesy Micro[1])

Fig. 9–5. The interrupt flag register (IFR).

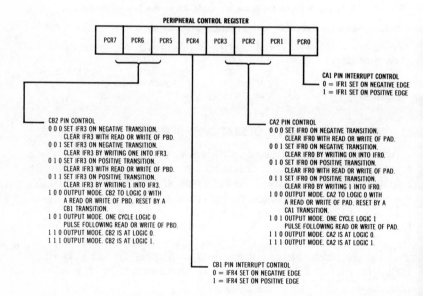

PERIPHERAL CONTROL REGISTER

| PCR7 | PCR6 | PCR5 | PCR4 | PCR3 | PCR2 | PCR1 | PCR0 |

CA1 PIN INTERRUPT CONTROL
0 = IFR1 SET ON NEGATIVE EDGE
1 = IFR1 SET ON POSITIVE EDGE

CB2 PIN CONTROL
0 0 0 SET IFR3 ON NEGATIVE TRANSITION.
  CLEAR IFR3 WITH READ OR WRITE OF PBD.
0 0 1 SET IFR3 ON NEGATIVE TRANSITION.
  CLEAR IFR3 BY WRITING ONE INTO IFR3.
0 1 0 SET IFR3 ON POSITIVE TRANSITION.
  CLEAR IFR3 WITH READ OR WRITE OF PBD.
0 1 1 SET IFR3 ON POSITIVE TRANSITION.
  CLEAR IFR3 BY WRITING 1 INTO IFR3.
1 0 0 OUTPUT MODE. CB2 TO LOGIC 0 WITH
  A READ OR WRITE OF PBD. RESET BY A
  CB1 TRANSITION.
1 0 1 OUTPUT MODE. ONE CYCLE LOGIC 0
  PULSE FOLLOWING READ OR WRITE OF PBD.
1 1 0 OUTPUT MODE. CB2 IS AT LOGIC 0.
1 1 1 OUTPUT MODE. CB2 IS AT LOGIC 1.

CA2 PIN CONTROL
0 0 0 SET IFR0 ON NEGATIVE TRANSITION.
  CLEAR IFR0 WITH READ OR WRITE OF PAD.
0 0 1 SET IFR0 ON NEGATIVE TRANSITION.
  CLEAR IFR0 BY WRITING ON INTO IFR0.
0 1 0 SET IFR0 ON POSITIVE TRANSITION.
  CLEAR IFR0 WITH READ OR WRITE OF PAD.
0 1 1 SET IFR0 ON POSITIVE TRANSITION.
  CLEAR IFR0 BY WRITING 1 INTO IFR0.
1 0 0 OUTPUT MODE. CA2 TO LOGIC 0 WITH
  A READ OR WRITE OF PAD. RESET BY A
  CA1 TRANSITION.
1 0 1 OUTPUT MODE. ONE CYCLE LOGIC 1
  PULSE FOLLOWING READ OR WRITE OF PAD.
1 1 0 OUTPUT MODE. CA2 IS AT LOGIC 0.
1 1 1 OUTPUT MODE. CA2 IS AT LOGIC 1.

CB1 PIN INTERRUPT CONTROL
0 = IFR4 SET ON NEGATIVE EDGE
1 = IFR4 SET ON POSITIVE EDGE

(Courtesy Micro[1])

Fig. 9–6. Determining the function of the control pins by the number stored in the peripheral control register (PCR).

The interrupt flag register is somewhat similar in concept to the status register of the 6502. Each of the eight bits in the IFR is set or cleared by a particular event. For example, refer to Fig. 9–5 to observe that bit one (IFR1) of the IFR is set when a logic level transition occurs on the CA1 pin of the 6522. (One type of transition is illustrated in Fig. 7–6B.) Refer to Fig. 9–2 to identify the CA1 pin.

Fig. 9–5 itemizes the events that set and clear the flags (or bits) in the IFR. Do not try to understand or memorize the entire figure at once. The important idea is that the IFR can be read by the 6502, and the various flag settings or bit values are used to make decisions. After an event has set a flag and the appropriate action has been taken by the microprocessor, then the flag may be cleared by the operation detailed in Fig. 9–5.

Refer next to the peripheral control register illustrated in Fig. 9–6. Again, this figure may seem extremely complex, but perhaps it can be simplified. First observe that four of the eight bits in the PCR are related to the functions of the control pins CA1 and and CA2, while the other four bits have *identical* relationships to the control pins CB1 and CB2. This symmetry reduces the complexity by half.

Focus your attention on the low-order four bits of the PCR diagrammed in Fig. 9–6. Three of the bits, PCR1–PCR3, are related to the functions of CA2, while PCR0 controls the functions of CA1. In particular:

- If PCR0 is *0*, then a *negative transition* (⌐_) on the CA1 pin will *set* bit one (IFR1) in the IFR.
- If PCR0 is *1*, then a *positive transition* (_⌐) on the CA1 pin will *set* bit one (IFR1) in the IFR.

The control pin CA2 has eight possible functions corresponding to the eight combinations of the three bits PCR1–PCR3. We will not discuss each of the possibilities: Fig. 9–6 describes most of them. In our printer interface described below we shall use the "101" mode. In this mode a negative pulse (similar to the one shown in Fig. 9–4) of 1 clock cycle in duration is applied to the CA2 pin following a read or write to port A. The purpose of this will become clear shortly.

In summary, to obtain the desired behavior of the control pins CA1, CA2, CB1, and CB2 on the 6522, a number obtained by studying Fig. 9–6 must be written to the PCR. Clearly, an understanding of the specifications of the particular device being interfaced is also necessary to choose the correct number to write to the PCR.

Since it is impossible to give examples that illustrate all of the possible i/o options involving the control pins on the 6522, the writer decided to illustrate two frequently used input/output operations, namely a keyboard input and a printer output. Of course, your Apple already has a keyboard, but sometime you may wish to add a remote keypad or keyboard. In any case the example is worth studying for its own sake. The printer interface is more complex, so we begin with interfacing a keyboard to a 6522.

It will be assumed that the keyboard is already encoded; that is, pressing a key makes the ASCII representation of the corresponding character available on an 8-pin output device. Refer to Fig. 9–7. Most keyboard encoder integrated circuits, such as the MM5740 used in the Apple, produce a negative strobe when the character code is available at the 8-bit output of the encoder chip. Refer to the simple timing diagram in Fig. 9–8 for the details about the events that follow a key press.

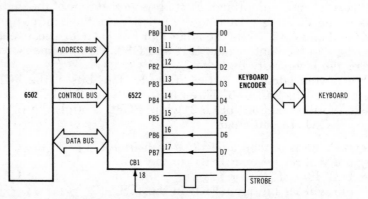

Fig. 9–7. Using the 6522 as a keyboard input port.

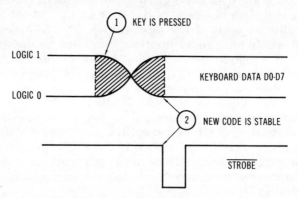

Fig. 9–8. Timing diagram for the data from the keyboard encoder.

We will use port B of the 6522 as the keyboard input port for the microcomputer. The strobe signal will be connected to the CB1 control pin on the 6522. We will load a logic 0 into PCR4 (See Fig. 9–6) so that a negative transition on CB1 (the leading edge of the strobe) sets the IFR4 bit in the interrupt flag register. The necessary steps to initialize the 6522 for these functions are given in Example 9–7. In Example 9–7 the keyboard-read subroutine simply "watches" bit four of the IFR. When it is set, fresh keyboard data is available at port B and the port is read. Reading port B also clears IFR4 so it is ready to signal the next key press. The character code is passed from the subroutine to the main program in the accumulator.

Example 9–7. A Routine to Read a Keyboard Using the 6522

Object: Initialize the 6522 to read a keyboard at port B. Use CB1 as a control pin to detect the keyboard strobe pulse.

```
17C2:            9 ;INITIALIZATION SEQUENCE
17C2:A9 00      10 MAIN    LDA    #$00     ;MAKE PORT B AN INPUT PORT.
17C4:8D 02 C7   11         STA    DDRB
17C7:AD 0C C7   12         LDA    PCR      ;INITIALIZE THE PCR BY CLEARING
17CA:29 EF      13         AND    #$EF     ;BIT 4, PCR4. A NEGATIVE
17CC:8D 0C C7   14         STA    PCR      ;TRANSITION WILL SET IFR4.

                16 ****************************
17CF:           17 ;SUBROUTINE KEYIN
17CF:A9 10      18 KEYIN   LDA    #$10     ;MASK IFR TO ISOLATE IFR4.
17D1:2C 0D C7   19 WAIT    BIT    IFR      ;IS IFR4 SET?
17D4:F0 FB      20         BEQ    WAIT     ;NO, THEN WAIT HERE.
17D6:AD 00 C7   21         LDA    PBD      ;YES, THEN READ PORT AND CLEAR
                                            FLAG.
17D9:60         22         RTS             ;RETURN WITH CODE IN A.
```

The important concept to understand in this keyboard-input example is the use of the control pin CB1 and your ability to *program* the 6522 to control its behavior.

When the personal computer industry was in its infancy, some of the most popular printers were made by Centronics. When the other manufacturers introduced printers they frequently adopted the same interfacing control signals used by Centronics. This type of interface is called "Centronics-compatible interface," or "Centronics-style handshake timing." The 6522 printer interface that we now discuss is a Centronics-compatible interface.

Many printers use only 7-bit character codes, namely 7-bit ASCII. In this case, only seven pins of port B are needed to output the character codes to the printer. There are three control signals used in a printer interface:

- $\overline{\text{DATA STROBE}}$ is a negative pulse ($\overline{\text{⎍}}$) from the 6522 to the printer. It signals the printer that the character code on pins PB0–PB6 is to be printed.
- BUSY is a signal provided by the printer. If BUSY is at logic 1 then the printer is *not* able to read a character.
- $\overline{\text{ACK}}$ is another signal provided by the printer. It *ack*nowledges that the $\overline{\text{DATA STROBE}}$ pulse has been detected *and* the character code has been read.

The timing diagram for these three signals is shown in Fig. 9–9, where the duration of each pulse and the time between pulses depends on the specific equipment. Note that BUSY is normally at logic 0. When the $\overline{\text{DATA STROBE}}$ pulse occurs, BUSY goes to logic 1. If the printer buffer is full, BUSY will stay at logic 1 until more characters can be put into the buffer, then it will return to logic 0. When the $\overline{\text{ACK}}$ pulse is received, the printer has read the character and is ready to accept another character.

An astute reader will detect that there is enough redundancy between BUSY and $\overline{\text{ACK}}$ so that an interface can be constructed that uses either one of these two signals, but not both. Our interface will use only the $\overline{\text{ACK}}$ signal.

The interface circuit is shown in Fig. 9–10. Note that there is

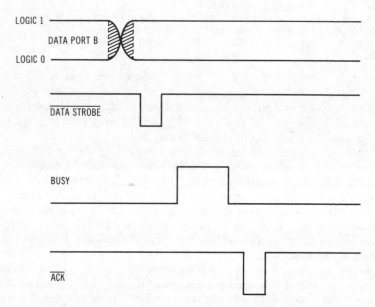

Fig. 9–9. Timing diagram for a Centronics-compatible interface.

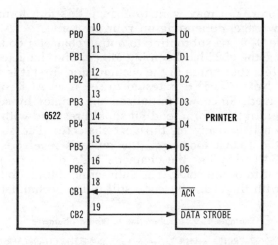

Fig. 9-10. A 6522 interfaced to a printer.

no BUSY signal. Also observe that $\overline{\text{ACK}}$ controls the logic level on the CB1 pin of the 6522, while the CB2 pin of the 6522 is expected to provide the $\overline{\text{DATA STROBE}}$ pulse to the printer. Refer again to Figs. 9-5 and 9-6. We will program the 6522 so that the trailing edge of the $\overline{\text{ACK}}$ pulse sets the IFR4 flag. The 6522 will also be programmed so that writing to PBD produces a pulse on the CB2 pin. Refer to Fig. 9-6 to see that the required number to be stored in the PCR is $B0.

Example 9-8 contains the instructions necessary to initialize the 6522. First port B is configured so that pins PB0-PB6 are output pins. The character code for the printer will appear on these pins. Next, the appropriate bits are set in the PCR so that IFR4 is set on a positive transition on CB1 and a negative pulse occurs on CB2 when a number is written to PBD. Next, the IFR bit four is cleared, in the event that some previous action might have set it. Finally, to get things started a carriage return is sent

Example 9-8. A Program to Initialize the 6522 for the Printer Interface

17DA:A9 7F	9 INITLZ	LDA	#$7F	;MAKE PINS 0–6 OUTPUT PINS.
17DC:8D 02 C7	10	STA	DDRB	
17DF:AD 0C C7	11	LDA	PCR	;INITIALIZE PCR SO CB1 DETECTS
17E2:09 B0	12	ORA	#$B0	;POSITIVE TRANSITION; PULSE
17E4:8D 0C C7	13	STA	PCR	;OUTPUT ON PIN CB2.
17E7:A9 10	14	LDA	#$10	
17E9:8D 0D C7	15	STA	IFR	;CLEAR IFR4, THE CB1 INTERRUPT
				FLAG.
17EC:A9 0D	16	LDA	#$0D	;SEND A CARRIAGE RETURN
17EE:8D 00 C7	17	STA	PBD	;TO THE PRINTER.

to the printer. You may want to change this to a form feed to start a new page, depending on your printer.

Example 9–9 is a subroutine to output character codes to the printer once the 6522 has been initialized. The character code is passed to this subroutine in the accumulator. First it is saved on the stack. Next, the IFR is tested to see if an $\overline{ACK}$ signal has been received. Since we initialized the printer by sending a carriage return (or a form feed), it should respond with an $\overline{ACK}$ pulse when it is ready for the next character. The subroutine waits in the LOAF loop until the pulse is received. Then it clears IFR4 and writes the character code to the printer after retrieving it from the stack. The subroutine returns to the main program with the character code still in the accumulator.

Example 9–9. A Subroutine to Print a Character

```
1801:48          7 PRINT   PHA               ;SAVE THE CHARACTER ON THE
                                              STACK.
1802:A9 10       8 LOAF    LDA   #$10        ;SET UP MASK FOR IFR.
1804:2C 0D C7    9         BIT   IFR         ;IS FLAG SET YET?
1807:F0 F9      10         BEQ   LOAF        ;NO, THEN WAIT HERE.
1809:8D 0D C7   11         STA   IFR         ;YES, THEN CLEAR FLAG,
180C:68         12         PLA               ;GET CHARACTER FROM THE STACK,
180D:8D 00 C7   13         STA   PBD         ;AND PRINT IT.
1810:60         14         RTS
```

Example 9–10 illustrates how these two routines, the initialization routine and the print subroutine, are used with the Apple with a disk operating system. Locations $36 and $37 on the Apple contain a vector to the output routine. In addition to initializing the 6522 the routine in Example 9–10 sets up this vector to point to our printer subroutine, also listed in Example 9–10. The printer subroutine starts at $02EE. Instead of ending with an RTS, the printer subroutine ends with a JMP to the Apple video monitor output subroutine. Thus every character that is printed will also be echoed to the screen. To use the program our DOS (disk operating system) greeting program commands the initialization program to be executed. The greeting program we use is given in Example 9–11.

If you do not have a disk operating system, you can still use the printer. Simply load the program in Example 9–10, change the JMP DOSSYS instruction to a BRK, and execute the program. It will initialize the output vector to point to the printer subroutine, then it will initialize the 6522 and send a carriage return, and then it will return control to the monitor.

We used page two for these routines. Occasionally it may happen that typing in a long string of characters on the

Example 9–10. A Program to Use the Printer Routines on the Apple

```
02CC:A9 EE      9  INITIAL  LDA   #$EE      ;SET UP APPLE OUTPUT REGISTERS
02CE:85 36     10           STA   $36       ;TO POINT TO PRINTER ROUTINE
02D0:A9 02     11           LDA   #$02
02D2:85 37     12           STA   $37
02D4:A9 7F     13           LDA   #$7F      ;INITIALIZE PORT B.
02D6:8D 02 C7  14           STA   DDRB
02D9:AD 0C C7  15           LDA   PCR       ;INITIALIZE PCR.
02DC:09 B0     16           ORA   #$B0
02DE:8D 0C C7  17           STA   PCR
02E1:A9 10     18           LDA   #$10      ;CLEAR IFR4.
02E3:8D 0D C7  19           STA   IFR
02E6:A9 0D     20           LDA   #$0D
02E8:8D 00 C7  21           STA   PBD       ;OUTPUT CARRIAGE RETURN.
02EB:4C EA 03  22           JMP   DOSSYS    ;JUMP TO DISK ROUTINE
02EE:48        23  PRINT    PHA             ;TO EXCHANGE OUTPUT REGISTERS.
02EF:A9 10     24  LOAF     LDA   #$10
02F1:2C 0D C7  25           BIT   IFR
02F4:F0 F9     26           BEQ   LOAF
02F6:8D 0D C7  27           STA   IFR
02F9:68        28           PLA
02FA:8D 00 C7  29           STA   PBD
02FD:4C F0 FD  30           JMP   $FDF0     ;JUMP TO OUTPUT CHARACTER
0300:          31  ;TO THE VIDEO MONITOR.
```

Example 9–11. A GREETING Program that Initializes the Apple for Printer Operation

```
←LIST
 5  REM GREETING PROGRAM
15  PRINT : PRINT : PRINT : PRINT :
21  INPUT "DO YOU WANT THE PRINTER ON? (TYPE Y OR N.) ";A$
22  IF A$ = "Y" THEN 30
23  GOTO 50
30  D$ =CHR$ (4)
40  PRINT D$;"BRUN EXAMPLE 9–10."
50  HOME
60  NEW
70  END
```

keyboard will write over the print program, since page two of
memory is the keyboard input buffer. This event is rare enough
not to be considered an inconvenience.

TIMING AND COUNTING WITH THE 6522

What is an interval timer? In its simplest form it consists of a
memory location (a register in an integrated circuit) in the address space of the microcomputer. A number initially stored in
this register is *decremented*, either by the system clock or by an
external source of pulses, until it decrements *through* zero. At

that instant a flag in another register is set or an interrupt request $\overline{(IRQ)}$ is made, signaling the end of the timing interval. You will soon see how such devices can be used.

The 6522 has one interval timer, called T1, and one counter/timer, called T2. The various timer registers are shown in Fig. 9–11. Also shown in this figure are some additional registers that are related to the timing and counting functions. These registers are detailed in Fig. 9–12[1] and Fig. 9–13[1], and their functions will be explained below. The addresses of the locations of the 16 registers of the 6522 are given in Table 9–1, while additional information about the timer registers is summarized in Table 9–2. Both T1 and T2 are 16-bit devices.

A simple timing operation using T1 would proceed in this way. Two 8-bit numbers are written to T1 using the locations given in Table 9–2. Two successive write operations (STA T1LL and STA T1LH instructions) are needed to load T1. After T1 is loaded, the number in it will be decremented at the system clock rate, 1.023 MHz in the case of the Apple. After the

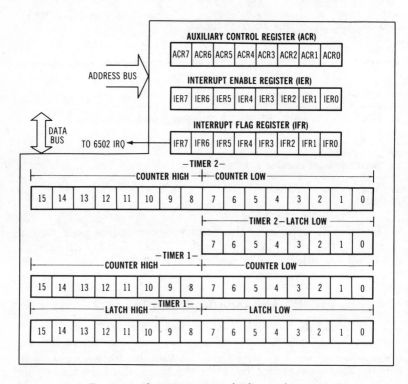

Fig. 9–11. The 6522 registers, latches, and counters.

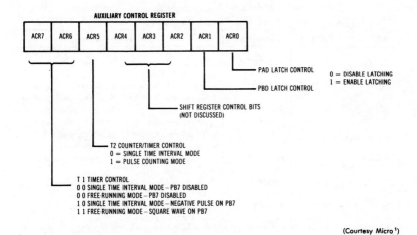

Fig. 9–12. Controlling 6522 functions with the auxiliary control register (ACR).

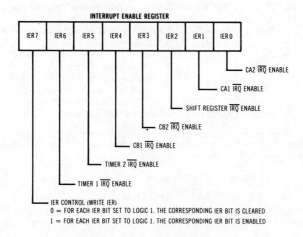

Fig. 9–13. Controlling the $\overline{\text{IRQ}}$ pin on the 6522.

number has decremented through zero; that is, during the clock cycle *after* the number in T1 reaches zero, bit IFR6 in the interrupt flag register (IFR) is set. The setting of the flag signals the completion of the timing interval.

The sequence of events just described is programmed in Example 9–12 and a flowchart of this routine is given in Fig. 9–14. The program illustrates how to implement a simple delay loop of approximately 50,000 clock cycles, using the T1 timer.

Table 9-2. Memory Assignments and Functions of the Timer Registers

Address*	Symbol	Operation	Function
$C704	T1LL	WRITE T1LL	Write an 8-bit number into the low-order byte of the T1 latch.
$C704	T1CL	READ T1CL	Read the contents of the low-order byte of the T1 counter and clear the interrupt flag, IFR6.
$C705	T1LH	WRITE T1LH	Write an 8-bit number into the high-order byte of the T1 latch, transfer the contents of both T1 latches to the T1 counters, clear IFR6, and start the countdown process.
$C705	T1CH	READ T1CH	Read the contents of the high-order byte of the T1 counter.
$C706	T1LL	WRITE T1LL	Write an 8-bit number into the low-order byte of the T1 latch.
$C706	T1LL	READ T1LL	Read the contents of the low-order byte of the T1 latch.
$C707	T1LH	WRITE T1LH	Write an 8-bit number into the high-order byte of the T1 latch and clear IFR6.
$C707	T1LH	READ T1LH	Read the contents of the high-order byte of the T1 latch.
$C708	T2LL	WRITE T2LL	Write an 8-bit number into the low-order byte of the T2 latch.
$C708	T2CL	READ T2CL	Read the contents of the low-order byte of the T2 counter and clear IFR5.
$C709	T2CH	WRITE T2CH	Write an 8-bit number into the high-order byte of the T2 counter, transfer the contents of the low-order byte of the T2 latch to the low-order byte of the T2 counter, clear IFR5, and start the countdown process.
$C709	T2CH	READ T2CH	Read the contents of the high-order byte of the T2 counter.

*The addresses used are those corresponding to the John Bell 6522 card in peripheral card slot 7 on the Apple.

Note in Example 9-12 that the first instruction sets up the auxiliary control register (ACR) so that the T1 timer produces a *single* time-out or flag setting each time it is loaded. Refer to Fig. 9-12 for a complete description of the bits in the ACR that control the functions of T1 and T2. Next T1 is loaded with $C34E. The STA T1LH starts the timer running. When it times out, IFR6 is set, and the program will drop out of the WAIT loop.

If N is the number loaded into the timer, and if the loop time T_L is defined as the time interval from the *completion* of the STA T1LH instruction in Example 9-12 to the *beginning* of the first instruction following the BEQ WAIT instruction, then T_L can be bracketed as follows:

$$(N + 4)T_C \leq T_L \leq (N + 10)T_C$$

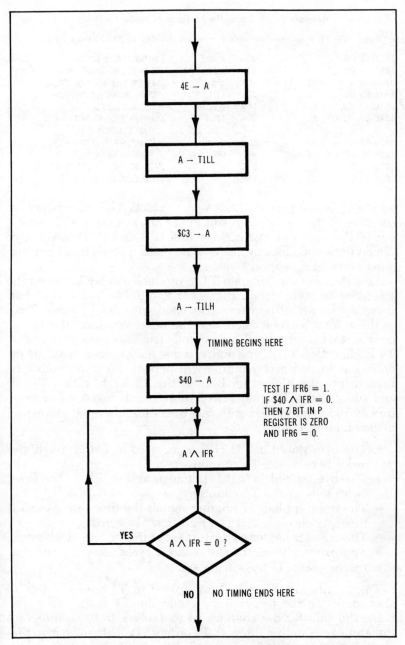

Fig. 9–14. Flowchart of the simple delay loop of Example 9–12, where the symbol ∧ is a logical AND operation.

239

Example 9-12. Using the T1 Timer to Produce a Delay

Object: Use T1 in its one-shot mode to produce a delay of 50,000 clock cycles.

```
1811:A9 00    11         LDA   #$00      ;INITIALIZE T1 TO BE
1813:8D 0B C7 12         STA   ACR       ;IN THE ONE-SHOT MODE.
1816:A9 4F    13         LDA   #$4F      ;SET UP THE TIME INTERVAL
1818:8D 04 C7 14         STA   T1LL      ;TO BE $C34E+1 (50,000)
181B:A9 C3    15         LDA   #$C3      ;CLOCK CYCLES.
181D:8D 05 C7 16         STA   T1LH      ;TIMING BEGINS WITH THIS
                                              INSTRUCTION.
1820:A9 40    17         LDA   #$40      ;SET UP MASK FOR IFR.
1822:2C 0D C7 18 WAIT    BIT   IFR       ;HAS IFR6 BEEN SET?
1825:F0 FB    19         BEQ   WAIT      ;NO, SO WAIT IN THIS LOOP.
1827:00       20         BRK             ;YES, CONTINUE.
```

where T_C is the period of the system clock. The uncertainty in the time of the delay is a result of not knowing where T1 times out in the series of instructions BIT IFR and BEQ WAIT. An uncertainty of 6 clock cycles is of no consequence in all but the most demanding applications.

Now that you can program T1 to produce a delay, consider its operation in more detail. Fig. 9-11 and Table 9-1 reveal that there are four 8-bit registers associated with the T1 timer. Two of these form a 16-bit latch, and the other two form the 16-bit counter that is actually decremented. The low-order byte of the T1 latch, called T1LL and addressed at either location $C704 or $C706, is loaded first. Nothing will happen. Next, a number is loaded into the high-order byte of the T1 latch, called T1LH and addressed at location $C705 or $C707. If register 5 at location $C705 is addressed with this operation, then the following events take place:

- The byte stored in T1LH is transferred to T1CH, the high-order byte of the T1 counter.
- The byte stored in T1LL is transferred to T1CL, the low-order byte of the T1 counter.
- The interrupt flag, IFR6, that signals the time-out of the T1 timer, is cleared; that is, IFR6 is set to zero.
- The counter begins to decrement at the system clock rate.
- Approximately one-half of a clock cycle after the counter reaches zero, IFR6 will be set.

The events just described take place in T1's so-called one-shot mode. In the free-running mode the T1 timer will *automatically* transfer the contents of its *latches* to its *counters* at the end of a counting interval. In order to be able to change the period of the *next* timing interval without affecting the *current* counting-down process, one can load the latches of the T1 timer using registers 6 and 7 addressed at locations $C706 and $C707. Loading the *latches* at these addresses *does not* affect the current timing process, but at the end of the interval the new data in the latches will be transferred to the T1 counters, giving a new timing interval.

The T2 counter/timer does not have this option. Thus only three registers are required, a latch to store the low-order byte for the 16-bit counter/timer while the high-order byte is being written to T2, and the two 8-bit counter registers. Writing to T2CH initiates the counting process. Example 9–13 illustrates how the T2 counter/timer can be used to produce a delay in exactly the same way that T1 was used. Illustrations of T1 in its free-running mode and T2 in its counting mode will follow shortly.

Clearly it is possible to produce a delay either with an interval timer, such as T1 or T2 on the 6522, or with a delay loop similar to the ones we programmed in Chapter 3. What is the advantage of the interval timer? It should be clear that it is easier to program a specific time interval (N clock cycles) with an interval timer than a delay loop. Recall that the delay loop calculations were rather complex. If an error of several clock cycles can be tolerated, then an interval timer can be programmed to produce a delay of N clock cycles simply by loading N into its registers. Another advantage lies in the fact that the computer can be doing something useful during an interval timer implemented delay. Refer to Examples 9–12 and 9–13 and observe that between the instructions that start the timers and the instructions that test for the time-out of the timers one could place other instructions without affecting the operation of the timer or the accuracy of the delay. All that is required is that these instructions take less time than the delay time programmed into the timer. The disadvantage to the interval timer is the additional hardware that is required.

Example 9–13. Using the T2 Counter/Timer to Produce a Delay

Object: Use T2 in its one-shot mode to produce a delay of 0.05 second.

```
1828:A9 00      11        LDA    #$00    ;INITIALIZE T2 TO BE
182A:8D 0B C7   12        STA    ACR     ;AN INTERVAL TIMER:
182D:A9 BE      13        LDA    #$BE    ;SET UP THE TIME INTERVAL
182F:8D 08 C7   14        STA    T2LL    ;TO BE $C7BE+1 CYCLES,
1832:A9 C7      15        LDA    #$C7    ;OR 0.05 SECOND.
1834:8D 09 C7   16        STA    T2CH    ;TIMING BEGINS WITH THIS
                                          INSTRUCTION.
1837:A9 20      17        LDA    #$20    ;SET UP MASK FOR IFR.
1839:2C 0D C7   18 WAIT   BIT    IFR     ;HAS IFR5 BEEN SET?
183C:F0 FB      19        BEQ    WAIT    ;NO, SO WAIT IN THIS LOOP.
183E:60         20        RTS            ;YES, CONTINUE.
```

USING T1 IN ITS FREE-RUNNING MODE

The T1 timer will also run continuously without its latches being reloaded. We will examine this mode and the ability of the T1 timer to generate continuous interrupts that are equally spaced. The program is in Example 9–14. Before this program is described we need to look at the interrupt enable register (IER) illustrated in Fig. 9–13.

Example 9–14. A Program to Demonstrate T1 in its Free-Running Mode

Object: Use the free-running mode of T1 to toggle the Apple speaker and generate a tone.

```
183F:A9 40      11          LDA    #$40     ;INITIALIZE T1 TO RUN FREE,
1841:8D 0B C7   12          STA    ACR      ;GENERATING INTERRUPTS.
1844:A9 C0      13          LDA    #$C0     ;LOAD INTERRUPT ENABLE REGISTER
1846:8D 0E C7   14          STA    IER      ;TO PRODUCE INTERRUPTS
                                                FROM T1.
1849:A9 77      15          LDA    #$77     ;SET UP THE TIME INTERVAL
184B:8D 04 C7   16          STA    T1LL     ;TO PLAY A NOTE NEAR
184E:A9 07      17          LDA    #$07     ;MIDDLE C.
1850:8D 05 C7   18          STA    T1LH     ;TIMING BEGINS WITH THIS
                                                INSTRUCTION.
1853:58         19          CLI             ;ALLOW INTERRUPTS TO START.
1854:18         20          CLC             ;LOOP HERE TO LISTEN TO MUSIC.
1855:90 FE      21  LOITER  BCC    LOITER

1857:           23  ;T1 TIMER INTERRUPT ROUTINE
1857:8D 30 C0   24          STA    $C030    ;TOGGLE THE APPLE SPEAKER.
185A:AD 04 C7   25          LDA    $C704    ;CLEAR THE T1 INTERRUPT FLAG.
185D:A5 45      26          LDA    $45      ;RESTORE THE ACCUMULATOR.
185F:40         27          RTI
1860:           28  ;LOAD INDIRECT JUMP VECTOR FOR
1860:           29  ;APPLE IRQ ROUTINE BEFORE RUNNING.
1860:           30  ;LOAD $57 INTO $03FE.
1860:           31  ;LOAD $18 INTO $03FF.
```

If the $\overline{\text{IRQ}}$ pin on the 6522 VIA is connected to the $\overline{\text{IRQ}}$ pin on the 6502 microprocessor, then the 6522 is capable of producing interrupt requests. When any flag in the interrupt flag register is set, the same event may be used to produce an $\overline{\text{IRQ}}$-type interrupt, if the IER has been properly initialized. Refer to Fig. 9–13. Except for the most significant bit, there is a one-to-one correspondence between the bits in the IER and the IFR. If a bit in the IER is enabled, then when the corresponding flag is set, the $\overline{\text{IRQ}}$ pin will go to logic 0, initiating an interrupt request. For example, if IER6, the T1 interrupt enable bit of the IER, is set, then when the IFR6 flag is set, the $\overline{\text{IRQ}}$ pin on the 6522 goes to logic 0 to request an interrupt.

With T1 in its free-running mode a continuous series of interrupts will be produced. Any task that the microcomputer must perform on a regular basis can be performed in the interrupt routine. In Example 9–14 the speaker on the Apple is toggled in the interrupt routine, producing a tone. Refer to this example to see how the ACR and the IER are initialized. You will also wish to reference Figs. 9–12 and 9–13. Run the program in Example 9–14 to see how it works, but not before loading locations $03FE and $03FF with the starting address of the interrupt routine in Example 9–14.

We can elaborate on the program in Example 9–14 to make sound effects or play a song. To play a note or produce a tone other than the one chosen in Example 9–14, we can make a *note table* consisting of the numbers (each note requires two 8-bit numbers) that must be loaded into T1 to produce the tone that we want. The X index can be used to identify the notes and to access the note table in the absolute indexed addressing mode.

A song is an ordered set of notes (with apologies to all musicians for such an insensitive definition). To play a song we need a *song table* consisting of the set of X indices that identify the notes we wish to play. We will use indirect indexed addressing to access the song table.

Finally, a note must be played for a certain time duration. We can use the T2 timer to provide a delay during which the note will be played. Part of Example 9–13 will be used as a delay subroutine. An "eighth-note" will be one call of the T2 delay subroutine. A "quarter-note" will consist of two calls, and so forth for longer notes. Each number in the *duration table* corresponds to a note in the song table, and each entry contains the number of times the delay subroutine will be called.

Our final composition is given in Example 9–15. This program will play a song. The note table is stored in page $10 and consists of three octaves of notes reasonably close to the equally tempered scale. The note table is given in Chart 9–1. The song table is stored in pages $11 and $12 of memory. The scale may be played with the song table given in Chart 9–2. The duration table is stored in pages $13 and $14 of memory. The longest song that can be played is 512 notes, but that number is easily modified by devoting more memory to the song and duration tables. A duration of $00 ends the song. Study Example 9–15 in connection with the previous examples in this chapter. Actually there are no new concepts introduced in this program, but its use of both timers on the 6522, its use of interrupts, and its use of a variety of the more powerful addressing modes make it a rich example of programming techniques.

Example 9-15. A Program to Play a Song

```
1860:A9 40    *15        LDA  #$40       ;INITIALIZE T1 TO RUN FREE,
1862:8D 0B C7 16         STA  ACR        ;GENERATING INTERRUPTS.
1865:A9 C0    17         LDA  #$C0       ;LOAD INTERRUPT ENABLE REGISTER
1867:8D 0E C7 18         STA  IER        ;TO PRODUCE INTERRUPTS FROM
                                          T1.
186A:A0 00    19         LDY  #00        ;INDIRECT INDEX EQUAL ZERO.
186C:B1 1A    20  LOOP   LDA  (SONG), Y  ;GET NOTE INDEX.
186E:AA       21         TAX             ;USE INDEX TO LOOK UP
186F:BD 00 10 22         LDA  NOTE, X    ;LOW BYTE FOR T1.
1872:8D 04 C7 23         STA  T1LL
1875:BD 24 10 24         LDA  NOTE+$24, X ;GET HIGH BYTE FOR T1.
1878:8D 05 C7 25         STA  T1LH
187B:B1 1C    26         LDA  (DURT), Y  ;GET DURATION OF NOTE.
187D:F0 16    27         BEQ  OUT        ;ZERO DURATION ENDS SONG.
187F:AA       28         TAX
1880:20 2D 18 29  WAIT   JSR  DELAY      ;USE T2 DELAY SUBROUTINE.
1883:CA       30         DEX             ;NUMBER OF DELAYS IS DURATION.
1884:D0 FA    31         BNE  WAIT
1886:E6 1A    32         INC  SONG       ;INCREMENT SONG POINTER.
1888:D0 02    33         BNE  BR1
188A:E6 1B    34         INC  SONG+1     ;GO TO THE NEXT PAGE.
188C:E6 1C    35  BR1    INC  DURT       ;INCREMENT DURATION POINTER.
188E:D0 02    36         BNE  BR2
1890:E6 1D    37         INC  DURT+1     ;GO TO THE NEXT PAGE.
1892:18       38  BR2    CLC
1893:90 D7    39         BCC  LOOP       ;KEEP GETTING NOTES.
1895:00       40  OUT    BRK            ;THE SONG IS OVER.
1896:         41 ;LOAD $57 AND $18 INTO $03FE AND $03FF, RESPECTIVELY.
1896:         42 ;LOAD INTERRUPT ROUTINE FROM EXAMPLE 9-14.
1896:         43 ;INITIALIZE INDIRECT INDEX POINTERS, SONG AND DURT, BY
1896:         44 ;LOADING $00 INTO $001A AND $001C. LOAD $11 INTO $001B
1896:         45 ;AND $13 INTO $001D.
1896:         46 ;LOAD SONG, DURATION, AND NOTE TABLES.
1896:         47 ;LOAD DELAY ROUTINE FROM EXAMPLE 9-13.
```

Chart 9-1. Memory Dump of the Note Table

```
*1000.1047

1000-  EE 18 4D 8E DA 2F 8F F7
1008-  68 E1 61 E9 77 0C A7 47
1010-  ED 98 48 FC B4 70 31 F4
1018-  BC 86 53 23 F6 CC A4 7E
1020-  5A 38 18 FA 0E 0E 0D 0C
1028-  0B 0B 0A 09 09 08 08 07
1030-  07 07 06 06 05 05 05 04
1038-  04 04 04 03 03 03 03 03
1040-  02 02 02 02 02 02 02 01
```

Chart 9–2. Memory Dump of the Song Table

```
*1100.1123

1100-  00 01 02 03 04 05 06 07
1108-  08 09 0A 0B 0C 0E 0F 10
1110-  11 12 13 14 15 16 17 18
1118-  19 1A 1B 1C 1D 1E 1F 20
1120-  21 22 23 24
```

USING T2 TO COUNT PULSES

The T2 counter/timer may be used to count pulses from an external source. This capability allows it to be used in nuclear physics and chemistry experiments, tachometry, and other applications. In fact, in this mode the T2 counter/timer can be used whenever a suitable transducer is available to convert a physical property to a pulse train. Examples include voltage-to-frequency (v/f) converters and temperature-to-frequency (T/f) converters. Pressure and light transducers can be connected to a v/f converter to measure these properties. A common method for integrating a slowly varying voltage, such as the output of a spectrophotometer or a gas chromatograph, is to use a v/f converter to convert the time-varying voltage to a pulse train and then use counting circuitry to add (integrate). The T2 counter/timer can also be used for this purpose. Clearly, the applications that come to the author's mind are related to his previous experience, but undoubtedly you can think of applications of your own.

A simple example of a pulse-counting program is shown in Example 9–16. This program counts 1000 pulses having the pulse shape illustrated in Fig. 9–4. The pulses must be applied to the PB6 pin of the 6522. Furthermore, it is important to know that:

- The 6522 counts logic 0 (negative) pulses.
- The maximum pulse frequency is one-half the clock frequency.
- The flag that signals the end of the count is *set after* the count decrements *through* zero.

The last fact means that if N is the 16-bit number loaded into the counter, then $N + 1$ pulses occur before the flag (IFR5) is set. Study Example 9–16 in connection with Fig. 9–12 to see how T2 is initialized to be in its counting mode. Note that the program simply waits in the BEQ WAIT loop until all 1000 counts have been detected.

Example 9–16. A Program to Demonstrate T2 in Its Counting Mode

Object: Write a routine to count 1000 pulses on T2 before setting its interrupt flag.

1896:A9 20	11		LDA	#20	;INITIALIZE T2 TO BE
1898:8D 0B C7	12		STA	ACR	;IN COUNTING MODE.
189B:A9 E7	13		LDA	#$E7	;SET UP T2 TO COUNT 1000
189D:8D 08 C7	14		STA	T2LL	;PULSES. $03E7 + 1 = 1000.
18A0:A9 03	15		LDA	#$03	
18A2:8D 09 C7	16		STA	T2CH	;COUNTING BEGINS WITH THIS INSTRUCTION
18A5:A9 20	17		LDA	#$20	;SET UP MASK FOR IFR.
18A7:2C 0D C7	18	WAIT	BIT	IFR	;HAS IFR5 BEEN SET?
18AA:F0 FB	19		BEQ	WAIT	;NO, SO WAIT IN THIS LOOP.
18AC:60	20		RTS		;1000 PULSES HAVE BEEN COUNTED.

PRODUCING LONG DELAYS WITH T1 and T2

The longest delay that can be produced with the T1 timer or the T2 counter/timer is 65 536 clock cycles. Longer delays of more than an hour can be programmed using both T1 in its free-running mode and T2 in its counting modes. These topics have already been introduced, but one feature of the T1 timer that is used in this application has not been mentioned. The timing out of the T1 timer can be used to toggle pin PB7; that is, the logic level of PB7 changes whenever T1 decrements through zero. In its free-running mode, the effect of toggling PB7 is to produce a square wave output on PB7 whose period is given by the expression

$$T_p = 2(N + 2)T_C$$

where

T_p is the period of the square wave (the time for one complete cycle),
N is the number loaded into the 16-bit T1 counter register,
T_C is the period of the system clock.

For the Apple, $T_C = 0.977\ 8 \times 10^{-6}$ second.

If the PB7 pin is connected to the PB6 pin and T2 is programmed to count the pulses from PB7, then the time interval (T) between the instruction that initiates the counting (STA T2CH) in T2 and the setting of the T2 interrupt flag (IFR5) is given by the expression

$$T = 2(N_2 + 1)(N_1 + 2)T_C$$

where

N_2 is the 16-bit number in T2
N_1 is the 16-bit number in T1.

The longest delay is about 8.6×10^9 clock cycles, or about 2.3 hours.

A program to produce a delay of approximately 1 hour is given in Example 9–17. The T1 timer is programmed to produce a square wave whose period is 1.0000058×10^{-1} second (the Apple clock is assumed to be operating at a frequency of 1.022714 MHz). This is counted 36,000 times by T2, producing a delay of 1.0000057 hours. The reader should be cautioned about numbers with eight significant figures. The accuracy of these numbers depends exclusively on the accuracy with which the clock frequency of the Apple is known. Errors of several hundred parts per million or several hundredths of 1 percent are not uncommon. The *Apple II Reference Manual* gives only four significant figures. A well-calibrated frequency counter would establish the frequency with greater accuracy. Our numbers are *representative* of the accuracy that *might* be obtainable. In any case the program in Example 9–17 produces a delay of approximately 1 hour.

Example 9–17. A Program That Produces a Long Delay

Object: Write a program that will produce a 1-hour delay.

18AD:A9 E0	13		LDA	#$E0	;INITIALIZE T1 TO TOGGLE PB7 IN ITS
18AF:8D 0B C7	14		STA	ACR	;FREE-RUNNING MODE. T2 COUNTS PULSES.
18B2:A9 BE	15		LDA	#$BE	;T1 WILL PRODUCE A PERIOD OF
18B4:8D 04 C7	16		STA	T1LL	;2($C7BE + 2) CLOCK CYCLES.
18B7:A9 C7	17		LDA	#$C7	;$C7BE + 2 = 51,136.
18B9:8D 05 C7	18		STA	T1LH	;START T1 RUNNING THE SQUARE WAVE.
18BC:A9 9F	19		LDA	#$9F	;SET UP T2 TO COUNT $8C9F + 1 PULSES
18BE:8D 08 C7	20		STA	T2LL	;BEFORE TIMING OUT.
18C1:A9 8C	21		LDA	#$8C	;$8C9F + 1 = 36,000.
18C3:8D 09 C7	22		STA	T2CH	;START COUNTING.
18C6:A9 20	23		LDA	#$20	;SET UP MASK FOR IFR5.
18C8:2C 0D C7	24	WAIT	BIT	IFR	;HAS FLAG BEEN SET?
18CB:F0 FB	25		BEQ	WAIT	;NO, SO WAIT HERE FOR AN HOUR OR SO.
18CD:60	26		RTS		;YES, AN HOUR IS UP. RETURN.

A PRECISION TIMER

Another example of a program that uses both the T2 counter/timer in its counting mode and the T1 timer in its free-running mode is given in Example 9–18. This is a versatile program with numerous applications. The program *measures* the time required for N events to occur. Since the frequency, *f*, of a periodic phenomenon is defined as the number of cycles (events) per unit time, the program may be *used* to measure frequencies. The program can also be *used* to make precise time measurements. The time between two events (the start and end of a race, for example) can be measured. The precision of the measurement is approximately ±50 microseconds.

Example 9–18. A Precision Timing Program

Object: Measure the time for N pulses from an external pulse source.

```
                16 ****************
1900:           17 ;INTERRUPT ROUTINE
1900:E6 1D      18          INC   TIME        ;INCREMENT A TWO-BYTE
1902:D0 02      19          BNE   BR1         ;COUNTER FOR EACH
1904:E6 1E      20          INC   TIME+1      ;T1 INTERRUPT.
1906:AD 04 C7   21 BR1      LDA   T1CL        ;CLEAR T1 INTERRUPT FLAG.
1909:A5 45      22          LDA   $45         :RESTORE ACCUMULATOR.
190B:40         23          RTI

                25 ****************
190C:           26 ;BASIC SUBROUTINE
190C:D8         27          CLD               ;CLEAR THE DECIMAL MODE.
190D:A2 FF      28          LDX   #$FF
190F:A9 60      29          LDA   #$60        ;SET UP T1 TO RUN FREE
1911:8D 0B C7   30          STA   ACR         ;AND T2 TO COUNT PULSES.
1914:A9 FE      31          LDA   #$FE        ;SET UP THE T1 TIMER
1916:8D 06 C7   32          STA   T1LL        ;WITH $FFFE.
1919:A9 C0      33          LDA   #$C0        ;ENABLE IRQ FROM T1.
191B:8D 0E C7   34          STA   IER
191E:A9 00      35          LDA   #00         ;CLEAR TWO-BYTE
1920:85 1D      36          STA   TIME        ;INTERRUPT COUNTER.
1922:85 1E      37          STA   TIME+1
1924:8D 08 C7   38          STA   T2CL        ;START WITH 0 IN T2 TO
1927:8D 09 C7   39          STA   T2CH        ;DETECT THE ZEROTH EVENT.
192A:A9 20      40          LDA   #$20        :SET UP MASK TO TEST T2
192C:2C 0D C7   41 WAIT     BIT   IFR         ;INTERRUPT FLAG, IFR5.
192F:F0 FB      42          BEQ   WAIT        ;WAIT FOR ZEROTH EVENT.
1931:8E 05 C7   43          STX   T1CH        ;START THE TIMER.
1934:58         44          CLI               ;MAKE SURE IRQ IS NOT MASKED.
1935:A5 19      45          LDA   NUMB        ;RELOAD T2 WITH
1937:8D 08 C7   46          STA   T2CL        ;NUMBER OF EVENTS.
193A:A5 1A      47          LDA   NUMB+1
193C:8D 09 C7   48          STA   T2CH
193F:A9 20      49          LDA   #$20        ;SET UP MASK FOR IFR5,
1941:2C 0D C7   50 LOAF     BIT   IFR         ;THE T2 FLAG.
1944:F0 FB      51          BEQ   LOAF        ;WAIT FOR ALL THE EVENTS.
1946:AC 04 C7   52          LDY   T1CL        ;READ THE LOW BYTE OF T1.
1949:AE 05 C7   53          LDX   T1CH        ;READ THE HIGH BYTE OF T1.
194C:78         54          SEI               ;MASK INTERRUPTS.
```

194D:C0 04	55		CPY	#04	;ADJUST FOR READING HIGH BYTE AFTER
194F:B0 10	56		BCS	ARND	;READING THE LOW BYTE.
1951:E8	57		INX		;MAKE CORRECTION TO THE HIGH BYTE.
1952:D0 0D	58		BNE	ARND	;DOES INTERRUPT COUNTER NEED
1954:38	59		SEC		;CORRECTION? YES, DECREMENT IT
1955:A5 1D	60		LDA	TIME	;BY SUBTRACTING ONE.
1957:E9 01	61		SBC	#01	
1959:85 1D	62		STA	TIME	
195B:A5 1E	63		LDA	TIME+1	
195D:E9 00	64		SBC	#00	
195F:85 1E	65		STA	TIME+1	
1961:84 1B	66	ARND	STY	TIME-2	;STORE LOW BYTE.
1963:86 1C	67		STX	TIME-1	;STORE HIGH BYTE.
1965:A9 FE	68		LDA	#$FE	;FIND THE LOW COUNT.
1967:E5 1B	69		SBC	TIME-2	
1969:85 1B	70		STA	TIME-2	;STORE IT.
196B:A9 FF	71		LDA	#$FF	;FIND THE HIGH COUNT.
196D:E5 1C	72		SBC	TIME-1	
196F:85 1C	73		STA	TIME-1	;STORE IT.
1971:60	74		RTS		
1972:	75	;LOAD $03FE AND $03FF WITH $00 AND			
1972:	76	;$19, RESPECTIVELY, TO PRODUCE THE			
1972:	77	;INDIRECT JUMP IN THE IRQ ROUTINE.			

Although the precision timing routine listed in Example 9-18 might be used in a machine-language environment, we have chosen to call it from a BASIC program in order to simplify the calculations. This BASIC program is listed in Example 9-19. Study the listing of the BASIC program and you will understand our reasons for using a high-level language to call the precision timing routine.

Example 9-19. A BASIC Program to Call the Precision Timer Routine

```
1 REM PRECISION TIMER PROGRAM
20 PRINT "INPUT THE NUMBER OF EVENTS."
25 PRINT "THIS NUMBER MUST BE LESS THAN 65537."
30 INPUT N
35 N = N - 1
36 REM POKE N INTO TWO LOCATIONS.
40 NHI = INT (N / 256)
45 POKE 26,NHI
50 NLO = (N / 256 - NHI) * 256
55 POKE 25, NLO
56 REM SET UP JUMP VECTOR.
60 POKE 10,76: POKE 11, 12: POKE 12,25
64 REM CALL PRECISION TIMER SUB ROUTINE.
65 Z = USR (0)
69 REM CONVERT NUMBER OF CLOCK CYCLES FROM HEXADECIMAL TO DECIMAL.
70 A = PEEK (27)
75 B = 256 * PEEK (28) + A
80 C = 65536 * PEEK (29) + B
```

```
81 C = C / 1022714
82 REM CLOCK FREQUENCY = 1.022714 MHZ.
85 D = (16777216 / 1022714) * PEEK (30)
90 T = D + C
100 PERIOD = T / (N +1)
110 F = 1 / PERIOD
120 PRINT "THE PERIOD IS ";PERIOD;" SECONDS."
130 PRINT "THE FREQUENCY IS ";F;" HERTZ."
140 GOTO 65
```

Because the T2 counter/timer counts negative pulses, the *events* to be timed must each produce a negative pulse. Refer to Fig. 9–15 for an illustration of two possible waveshapes that can be applied to the PB6 pin of the 6522 in conunction with the program. The pulse widths must be at least 500 nanoseconds and N cannot exceed 65,536. The pulses need not be regularly spaced; in the case of nuclear counting applications they would not be so spaced. Also refer to the flowchart of the program that is drawn in Fig. 9–16. Study these figures in conjunction with the comments listed in Example 9–18 and Example 9–19 for a detailed understanding of what the program does and how it works.

Refer to Fig. 9–15. The so-called zeroth pulse initiates the timing process. If a race were being timed, pulling the trigger on the starting gun should also produce a negative pulse on the PB6 pin. Still using the race as an example, the first event shown in Fig. 9–15 would be the end of the race and this would end the timing measurement. In this example $N = 1$. The number of events, N, is an input parameter in Examples 9–18 and 9–19.

To measure the frequency of some periodic phenomenon, it

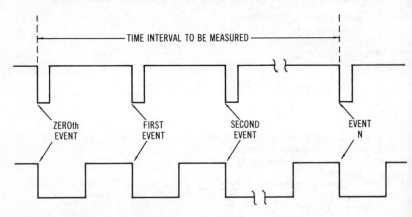

Fig. 9–15. Timing diagram for the precision timing program.

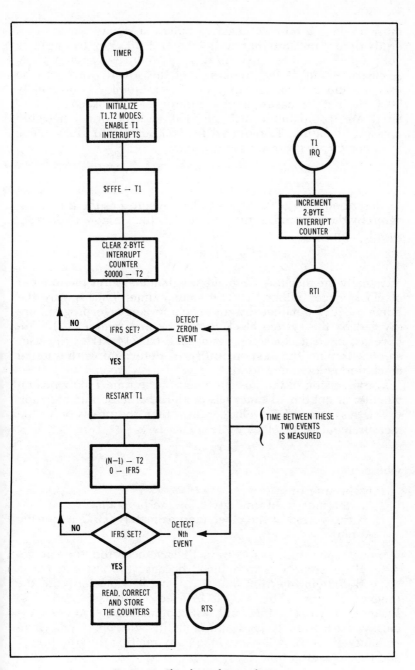

Fig. 9-16. Flowchart of Example 9-18.

must produce a train of negative pulses, a square wave, or an equivalent function that will trigger PB6. For example, a voltage-to-frequency converter usually produces a square wave. A measurement of the frequency of the square wave can be used to find the voltage. Suppose the frequency is nominally 5000 Hz and a measurement of approximately 1 second is desired. We would input an N of 5000, and the program would measure the time, T, required for 5000 cycles to elapse. The frequency, f, is given by the equation

$$f = \frac{N}{T}$$

As described, $N = 5000$ so $f = 5000/T$, where T is the time measured by the program. If the *period, P,* is the variable to be measured, then

$$P = \frac{1}{f} = \frac{T}{N}$$

Actually the machine language program measures the number of clock cycles rather than the actual time. This is why the "time" values obtained by the machine language program are divided by the system clock frequency in Example 9–19. We have assumed a clock frequency of 1.022714 MHz; the user should assume the responsibility of determining the actual clock frequency being used.

The precision of the measurement of the time T depends on whether or not the T1 timer has produced at least one interrupt. If T is less than 65,536 clock cycles, then the precision of the measurement is ±7 clock cycles. That is,

$$T = T_m \pm 7T_C$$

where

T is the true time,

T_m is the measured time given by the program,

T_C is the period of the clock (approximately 0.977 μs for the Apple).

If one or more interrupts from T1 have occurred, then an additional uncertainty is introduced because the last event may occur during an interrupt, but it will not be detected until the program returns to the BEQ LOAF loop in lines 50 and 51 in Example 9–18. The interrupt lasts approximately 55 clock cycles (worst case analysis). Combining this with the previous uncertainty gives the following inequality relating the true time T and the measured time T_m:

$$T_m - 7T_C \leq T \leq T_m + 62T_C$$

If the best estimate of the true time is the *average* of the extremes, then we obtain

$$T = (T_m + 28T_C) \pm 34T_C$$

In the BASIC program we have chosen not to include the correction of $28T_C$. In any case the "worst" measurement will be within 62 clock cycles of the true time. The accuracy of the system clock should also be taken into account if you are doing research-grade work with this program.

USING THE PRECISION TIMER PROGRAM

In this section we will outline several applications of the precision timing and counting program described in the previous section.

Frequency Counting

To use the program as a frequency counter, simply load the programs in Examples 9–18 and 9–19, load the interrupt routine indirect jump vector at $03FE and $03FF with $00 and $19, respectively, and run the BASIC program in Example 9–19. You must enter the number of pulses you wish to count to make a determination of the frequency, and the source of the pulses must be connected to the PB6 pin on the 6522 (this is pin 16 on the 6522, and on the John Bell 6522 card it is pin 7 on J2). The pulse source must produce square wave pulses that jump between 0 and 5 volts. Applying a sine wave to the 74LS14 Schmitt trigger or the 555 timer circuit described by Berlin[2] will convert a sine wave to a square wave. Suppose you enter 10,000 when the program asks for the number of pulses you wish to count. Then it will measure the time it takes for 10,000 pulses to occur and output the pulse frequency. Refer to line 130 in Example 9–19. You may wish to remove line 120 if your only purpose is to measure frequency. As far as the uncertainty of the result is concerned, the relative error in the frequency measurement is identical with the relative error in the time measurement, and this has been discussed in the previous section. Greater precision is obtained by counting more pulses, but of course this requires a sacrifice in time.

Implementing a Stopwatch

In order to make simple stopwatch-type timing measurement, you must enter the number 1 when the program asks for how

---

[2]Berlin, Howard M., *The 555 Timer Applications Sourcebook, With Experiments*, Indianapolis: Howard W. Sams, & Co., Inc., 1976, p. 13.

many pulses are to be counted, corresponding to the single pulse that ends the event. The program then prints the time between the pulse that started the event and the pulse that ended the event. Refer again to Fig. 9–15. A suitable source of starting and stopping pulses is described by Fig. 9–17. A mechanical push-button switch with both normally open (no) and normally closed (nc) contacts is connected to the 74LS00 cross-coupled NAND gate circuit. Each time the switch is connected to the no position a pulse occurs on the PB6 pin. The first pulse initiates the timing sequence, the next terminates it. You may wish to eliminate line 130 from the program in Example 9–19 and modify line 120 to reflect the nature of your measurement.

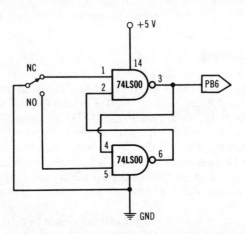

Fig. 9–17. A circuit to debounce a push-button switch for stopwatch operation.

Measuring Temperature

To measure temperature we combine the circuit in Fig. 9–18 with a modified version of the program in Example 9–19. The modified program is shown in Example 9–20. It simply converts the frequency of the pulses from an Analog Devices AD537 T/f converter to kelvins and then to Fahrenheit degrees. The temperature is rounded to the nearest degree.

A word about the AD537 integrated circuit may be necessary. Analog Devices (Route 1 Industrial Park, P.O. Box 280, Norwood, Massachusetts 02062, (617)–329–4700) makes several of the integrated circuits that we will use in this book. See Chapter 10, where an a/d converter and a d/a converter are described. Since they require a $50 minimum order, you may wish to order the AD537, AD570, and the AD558 all at once, which should bring your order to the $50 minimum. Their integrated circuits

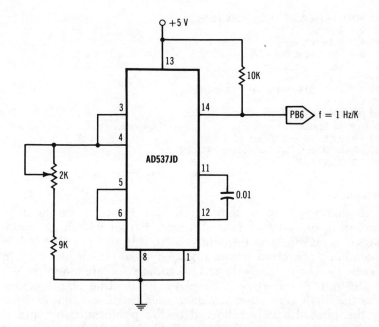

Fig. 9–18. A temperature-to-frequency converter using the Analog Devices AD537.

have been chosen for use in this book because they require an absolute minimum of external wiring and components, making it easier for the novice to breadboard or construct the circuits. Other T/f, a/d, and d/a converters may also be used, however, and National Semiconductor and Motorola also make these integrated circuits. The AD537 integrated circuit may also be used as a voltage-to-frequency converter to measure voltages in conjunction with our precision timer program. Be sure to request a specification sheet when you order the part, because it contains a great deal of information, such as how to use the AD537 in a remote location with a two-wire interface.

Example 9–20. A Program to Measure Temperature

```
 1 REM TEMPERATURE MEASUREMENT
20 PRINT "INPUT THE NUMBER OF EVENTS."
25 PRINT "THIS NUMBER MUST BE LESS THAN 65537."
30 INPUT N
35 N = N − 1
40 NHI = INT (N / 256)
45 POKE 26,NHI
50 NLO = (N / 256 − NHI) * 256
55 POKE 25,NLO
```

```
 60 POKE 10,76: POKE 11,12: POKE 12,25
 65 Z = USR (0)
 70 A = PEEK (27)
 75 B = 256 * PEEK (28) + A
 80 C = 65536 * PEEK (29) + B
 81 C = C / 1022714
 85 D = (16777216 / 1022714) * PEEK (30)
 90 T = D + C
100 PERIOD = T / (N + 1)
110 F = 1 / PERIOD
120 F = 9 / 5 * (F − 273.1) + 32
130 PRINT INT (F + .5);" DEGREES FAHRENHEIT."
140 GOTO 65
```

Tachometry

Another application of the precision timing program is in measuring the rotation rate of a gear, fan, or wheel. Although magnetic pickups are frequently used, it is also possible to use photodiode-phototransistor arrays. A typical circuit is shown in Fig. 9–19. The photodiode and phototransistor are mounted in a single unit. A reflective surface on the rotating object passes near the diode-transistor pair once each rotation. Light emitted by the photodiode is reflected to the phototransistor and it conducts. The voltage across the 25-kilohm potentiometer rises during each light pulse that is reflected. The 74C14 Schmitt trigger cleans up the rather noisy waveform from the phototransistor, producing a clean negative pulse for each pass of the reflecting surface. These pulses are counted and timed by the BASIC program in Example 9–19, and the rotation rate is the same as the frequency of the pulses.

If a piece of paper that had alternate dark and light strips on it were passed near the photodiode-phototransistor array, the pulse train appearing on the PB6 output would be directly related to the *velocity* of the paper. Thus the circuit of Fig. 9–19 is capable of measuring linear velocity as well as regular velocity.

The 25-kilohm resistor is adjusted to give the best pulse response, which depends on the ambient light conditions and the proximity of the reflecting surface that produces the pulse. An oscilloscope is extremely useful for making the initial adjustments.

Other Applications

Clearly there are a number of applications that are too complex to be described in this book, but they are worth mentioning. Geiger-Mueller (G-M) tubes, scintillation detectors, photoresistors, and photomultipliers are frequently used to produce

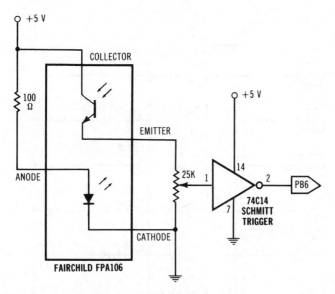

Fig. 9–19. Tachometer circuit.

pulses to be counted. The microcomputer can be programmed to measure the half-life of a radioactive source by interfacing a G-M tube or a scintillation detector to the 6522. By programming various delays, the user can measure the activity of a radioactive substance at various times over a period of hours, days, or even years. The Apple can be programmed to do pulse height analysis as well. The various pressure and temperature transducers now available make the Apple a valuable research tool in a laboratory as well as a personal computer.

EXERCISES

Exercise 9–1

  a. The purpose of this exercise is to familiarize yourself with the input/output ports on the 6522. To minimize the amount of wiring we will only use six bits of each of the 8-bit ports on the 6522. A circuit diagram of the output port is shown in Fig. 9–20. It is designed to light an LED (light-emitting diode) when a "1" is written to the corresponding bit; otherwise the LED does not light. The circuit diagram of the input port is shown in Fig. 9–21. The switch settings control the logic levels on the six input pins, PB0–PB5. When a switch is open the bit value is 1 (due to the nature of the 6522 integrated circuit). When a switch is closed, the bit value is 0.

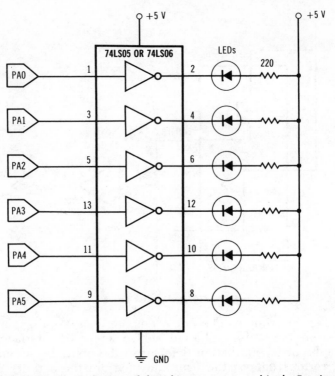

Fig. 9–20. Circuit diagram of the 6-bit output port used in the Exercises.

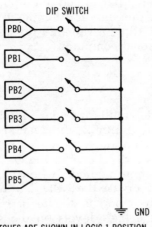

Fig. 9–21. Circuit diagram of the 6-bit input port.

SWITCHES ARE SHOWN IN LOGIC 1 POSITION

The writer mounted both of these circuits on the breadboard shown in the photograph in Fig. 9–22. This picture should give

Fig. 9–22. Photograph of the 6-bit i/o ports.

you a good idea of how to mount the components. Since we are using the John Bell Engineering 6522 board in peripheral card slot seven, two DIP jumpers were used to connect the circuit on the breadboard to the John Bell board. Port A is accessed at socket J1 on the John Bell board and port B is accessed at the J2 socket. The DIP jumpers, each 2 feet long, are also shown in Fig. 9–22.

Breadboard these circuits, recheck all your wiring, then connect your circuit to the John Bell board or your own wire-wrapped circuit board.

b. Apply power to the Apple. What are the conditions of the LEDs when power is applied?

(The LEDs should all be on. During power-up conditions or RESET the 6522 ports are initialized to be input ports. In the input condition they appear to be at logic 1 as far as the 74LS05 is concerned. This is simply a result of how 74LS00-series chips are designed.)

c. Use the monitor to configure port A as an output port. Write $FF to $C703, the address of the data direction register of port A. What is the status of the LEDs after this operation?

(The writer observed that several were turned on, while the others were off. The data in the output register, PAD, is random when power is applied, and the status of the LEDs reflects this randomness.)

d. Use the monitor to write various numbers to port A, PAD, at location $C701. Try the following numbers: $00, $01, $02, $04, $08, $10, and $20. What do you observe?

(The number $00 should turn all the lights off. The remaining numbers should light the LEDs in sequence.)

e. How would you light LEDs 0–3?

(Write $0F to port A using the monitor.)

f. Experiment with various numbers until you have convinced yourself that you understand the operation of the output port.

g. Write a short program that will initialize PA0–PA5 to be output pins and light diodes 1 and 5. An answer is given below.

```
1774:A9 3F    9         LDA    #$3F
1775:8D 03 C7 10         STA    DDRA
1779:A9 22    11         LDA    #$22
177B:8D 01 C7 12         STA    PAD
```

h. Run your program. You may wish to end it with a BRK instruction. Then try different numbers in the second byte of the program until you are sure you can turn any LED on or off.

Exercise 9–2

a. Next we will experiment with the input port. Set the switches on the 6-bit input port to some number; that is, turn some of the switches to a logic 1 value and the others to a logic 0 value.

b. Use the monitor to read port B at location $C700. The number you read should reflect the settings of the switches.

c. Set the switches to another number, and use the monitor to read port B. Which switch sets what bit?

d. Why are bits seven and six always 1?

(PB7 and PB6 are not connected to a switch. In this situation they "float" at logic 1.)

Exercise 9–3

a. This exercise will give you some additional experience with the input/output circuits. Load the program in Example 9–3. It is listed here for your convenience.

```
1788:A9 FF     9         LDA    #$FF     ;MAKE PORT A AN OUTPUT PORT.
178A:8D 03 C7 10         STA    DDRA
178D:A9 00    11         LDA    #$00     ;MAKE PORT B AN INPUT PORT.
178F:8D 02 C7 12         STA    DDRB
1792:AD 00 C7 13 LOOP    LDA    PBD      ;READ PORT B.
1795:8D 01 C7 14         STA    PAD      ;WRITE TO PORT A.
1798:18       15         CLC
1799:90 F7    16         BCC    LOOP     ;LOOP TO DO THIS CONTINUOUSLY.
```

b. Run the program. Experiment with the switch settings. What do you observe?

(You should observe that the switches of the input port control the LEDs in the sense that if a switch is on, the corresponding LED is on; otherwise it is off.)

Exercise 9-4

a. The next few exercises will help you to become familiar with the 6522 timers. Load the program in Example 9-14. It is rather lengthy, so it will not be repeated here.

b. Be sure the indirect jump vector in the Apple $\overline{\text{IRQ}}$ routine is loaded. That is, put $57 into location $03FE and put $18 into location $03FF.

c. Run the program in Example 9-14. What do you observe? (You should hear a tone on the Apple speaker.)

d. Experiment with different numbers in the T1 latches. That is, change the bytes at locations $184A and $184F in the program, then rerun it. What is the highest frequency you can hear? What is the lowest?

Exercise 9-5

a. Load the program in Example 9-15. The indirect jump vector is the same for this example, so you need not reload it unless you have turned the power off.

b. Load memory with the numbers in Charts 9-1, 9-2, and 9-3.

c. Run the program. You should hear the scale being played with a variety of note durations.

d. Write your own song or sound effects. Can you reproduce the sound of a racing car shifting gears? A wolf whistle or a siren?

Chart 9-3. Memory Dump of the Duration Table

```
*1300.1324

1300-  01 02 04 08 10 20 10 08
1308-  04 02 01 02 04 08 10 20
1310-  10 08 04 02 01 02 04 08
1318-  10 20 10 08 04 02 01 02
1320-  04 08 10 20 00
```

Exercise 9-6

a. Load the program in Example 9-16. A slightly modified listing is given below.

```
1896:A9 20      11        LDA    #$20      ;INITIALIZE T2 TO BE
1898:8D 0B C7   12        STA    ACR       ;IN COUNTING MODE.
189B:A9 0A      13        LDA    #$0A
189D:8D 08 C7   14        STA    T2LL
18A0:A9 03      15        LDA    #$03
18A2:8D 09 C7   16        STA    T2CH      ;COUNTING BEGINS WITH THIS
                                             INSTRUCTION.
18A5:A9 20      17        LDA    #$20      ;SET UP MASK FOR IFR.
18A7:2C 0D C7   18 WAIT   BIT    IFR       ;HAS IFR5 BEEN SET?
18AA:F0 FB      19        BEQ    WAIT      ;NO, SO WAIT IN THIS LOOP.
18AC:00         20        BRK
```

b. Breadboard the circuit to debounce a switch shown in Fig.
9–17. Connect it to the PB6 input using a DIP jumper from the
J2 socket on the John Bell 6522 board.

c. The circuit in Fig. 9–17 will be used to produce pulses to
be counted by T2 with the program listed above. Each time the
button on the push-button switch is pushed, a negative pulse is
generated.

d. Run the program listed above. Note that $0A is loaded into
the T2LL and $00 is loaded into the T2CH, so the program is
set to count ten pulses. What do you expect will happen after
you push the button ten times?

(After ten pulses the BRK instruction is encountered, and
program control returns to the monitor. You should hear the bell
and see the contents of the 6502 registers displayed.)

e. Try it. What do you observe?

(Although all of the 6522 specification sheets claim that the
T2 flag will be set after counting N pulses, where N is the
number loaded into T2, all of the author's experiments have
shown that $N + 1$ pulses are required; that is, the counter must
count *through* zero, not *to* zero, in order to set IFR5. In other
words, you will probably have to push the button eleven times
in order to observe the BRK instruction.)

f. Try some other numbers to experiment with the program
and the circuit.

Exercise 9–7

a. Load the program in Example 9–17. Replace the RTS instruction at the end of the program with a BRK instruction.

b. Connect PB7 to PB6 using the DIP jumper to a breadboard, and a single wire between the PB7 pin and the PB6 pin.

c. Run the program at the beginning of an hour on your clock,
or better yet, using radio station WWV. Loaf for an hour while
your program is running. Near the end of the hour get ready for
the program to end. How close to an hour was the programmed
delay?

Exercise 9–8

   a. Load the program in Example 9–18. Breadboard the circuit in Fig. 9–17 that will be used to make a stopwatch circuit. Make the connection to PB6.

   b. Load the BASIC program in Example 9–19.

   c. Run the BASIC program. When it requests the number of events, enter the number 1.

   e. When you are ready to time something, like how fast you can count to ten, press the stopwatch button. When you are finished counting, press it again. You should observe that the time is displayed on the screen as a "PERIOD." You may wish to delete the "FREQUENCY" printout since it has no meaning in this context, and you may wish to change "PERIOD" to "TIME."

   f. Connect a square wave generator to PB6. Set it for 1000 Hz. Now run the program in Example 9–19 again. Enter 1000 for N. You should observe a print statement about once every second listing the frequency as 1000 Hz and the period as 0.001 second.

   g. If you have a high-precision 100-kilohertz clock, use it to check the precision of your program. Adjust the number we have given for the clock frequency so that you obtain the correct answer for your 100-kHz standard.

   h. Breadboard the temperature-to-frequency converter shown in Fig. 9–18. A photograph is given in Fig. 9–23. Replace the program in Example 9–19 with the program in Example 9–20. Run the program.

   i. With the program running, adjust the potentiometer to give the correct temperature. This is the only adjustment that is required. You now have a system to measure temperature. An N of 1000–10,000 gives reasonably spaced readouts. What is the smallest value of N that gives consistent temperature readings?

   (The writer found that even with N = 1 he obtained consistent results.)

Exercise 9–9

   Consider this project. Instead of measuring the time between two pulses or the time for N pulses to occur, which was the objective of the program in Example 9–18, suppose we wish to measure the duration of one pulse, say a negative pulse. How would the program in Example 9–18 be modified to do this?

   (This is a project for you, so the complete answer will not be given. A hint, however, may be in order. Instead of using T2, apply the pulse to CB1. Program CB1 to set its interrupt flag, IFR4, on a negative transition. When this transition is detected,

Fig. 9–23. Photograph of the temperature-to-frequency converter circuit.

then start T1 running, just as in Example 9–18. Now reprogram CB1 to set its interrupt flag on a positive transition, and end the timing, just as in Example 9–18, when the positive transition occurs. The remaining details are left as a challenge to you. You can use the BASIC program in Example 9–19 to drive your assembly language program, provided that you locate it in the same place as the program in Example 9–18. You can test it with the stopwatch circuit in Fig. 9–17. What is the shortest duration that you can hold the push button down?)

CHAPTER 10

Applications

INTRODUCTION

The obvious reason for learning to program a computer is so you can make it perform some task (a computer to mow the lawn or shovel snow would be a real breakthrough for mankind). If the task is producing mailing labels, solving equations, or keeping track of your inventory for example, then a language such as BASIC is suitable. If the task involves controlling a machine or a process, then the microcomputer is functioning as a *controller*, and frequently machine language must be used because of its speed of execution. Another application where machine language is essential is in high-speed data acquisition, transmission, or output.

In this chapter we will discuss a very simple application in which the computer functions as a controller. Also illustrated are some high-speed data handling techniques involving an a/d (analog-to-digital) converter and a d/a (digital-to-analog) converter. We begin with an application that allows the computer to control a radio transmitter to send Morse code. The program about to be described will, of course, be most appealing to amateur radio operators. However, it illustrates several important programming concepts that may be worth examining even if you do not participate in amateur radio.

A PROGRAM TO TRANSMIT MORSE CODE

Background Information

Morse code consists of dots and dashes interspersed with spaces. To the radio operator the dots and dashes are perceived as tones and the spaces are perceived as the absence of a tone. A dot is distinguised from a dash by its duration, a dash being three times the length of a dot. The Morse code dots and dashes will be called *elements*. The space between two elements is called an *element space*. A collection of elements and element spaces forms a *character*. A character may be a letter from the alphabet, a number, or a punctuation mark. Characters are separated by *character spaces*. A group of characters separated only by character spaces is called a *word*. Words are separated by *word spaces*. The single feature that distinguishes between dot/dash elements or between the three types of spaces (element, character, and word spaces) is the *duration*. Of course, an element is distinguished from space by the fact that a tone is *on* for an element and *off* for a space. Table 10-1 summarizes the various durations or lengths of the code components, assuming the basic unit of measurement is one dot time.

Table 10-1. Morse Code Duration Table

Component	Duration
Dot	1T
Dash	3T
Element space	1T
Character space	3T
Word space	7T

Another parameter that is important to this background material is the *code speed*. Clearly, if the *ratios* of the durations of the elements and spaces are preserved while each is shortened, then more of them can be transmitted in a given time interval, resulting in a greater code speed. Just as in typing, code speed is usually described in units of *words per minute* (wpm). For our purposes it is more useful to have the actual dot time, *T*, corresponding to a code speed, *S*. The required relation is

$$T = \frac{1200}{S} \text{ milliseconds} \qquad (10-1)$$

It will be even more useful to have the dot time expressed in clock cycles on the Apple because the system clock will determine the length of the various code components. Call *N* the number of clock cycles in one dot time. Using a clock frequency of 1.023 MHz gives

$$N = \frac{1,227,600}{S} \text{ clock cycles} \qquad (10-2)$$

where *S* is the code speed in words per minute.

Specifications

One of the most important tasks in programming is to *specify* carefully the various functions of the program. The specification stage of writing a program is probably the most important stage. What do we want this program to accomplish?

- Characters input from the Apple keyboard are to be translated to Morse code.
- The output of the computer will drive a relay that will be closed (on) during an element and open (off) during a space. The relay is used to key a transmitter.

These are rather simple specifications and they will require elaboration. However, the output is relatively simple; all that is required is a 1-bit output port to drive the relay. One of the annunciator outputs on the Apple game i/o connector will work quite nicely. A circuit diagram is shown in Fig. 10–1, and with it the electronics portion of the design is completed. When the annunciator is in its logic 0 state the relay is turned on. Otherwise it is open, or off.

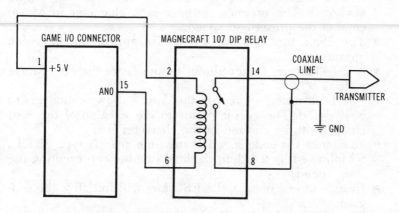

Fig. 10–1. Interface for the Morse code send program.

Generating specifications means asking yourself questions about what you want the program to do. How will the code speed be determined? Should the input be buffered? That is, should the ASCII characters that are input from the keyboard be stored in R/W memory until they can be sent as Morse code? A buffer allows the operator to "type ahead" of the Morse code. Should it be possible to backspace or delete to remove a character that was erroneously entered? All of these questions, and others, should be answered during the specification stage.

A professional approach to programming requires that you devote a great deal of time to the specification stage of the design and less time to actual programming. On the other hand, when programming for fun, even professionals frequently start writing the program with a vague idea of what they want the program to accomplish. The former approach requires discipline and motivation (usually financial). The latter approach, in which a program "evolves," is a more relaxed but far less efficient one. Pick the one that is appropriate to your circumstances.

Program Features

The features of the program that follow evolved from the specification stage of the design:

- When execution begins, a 2-digit decimal number representing the code speed must be entered from the keyboard. This number must be between 05 and 99.
- After the code speed is entered, you send code by typing letters, numbers, or punctuations marks from the Apple keyboard. The program outputs each character in Morse code at the prescribed speed.
- The characters that are typed also appear on the video monitor.
- A 256-character buffer allows typing faster than the Morse code is sent.
- The backspace (←) key on the Apple allows characters to be deleted. The cursor points to the location of the next character to be entered in the character string.
- To change the code speed at any time, merely type "CTRL S" followed by a 2-digit decimal number representing the code speed.
- In case of emergency, the ESC key will initialize the program.
- The CTRL R key may be used to send the program to another routine, and the CTRL T key may be used to return to the transmitting routine.

The Subroutines

The program to transmit Morse code is divided into three parts:

- A set of subroutines including a timing loop, a send subroutine that does the actual conversion of ASCII to Morse code, and a subroutine to calculate the parameters for the code speed.

- An interrupt routine that scans the keyboard for a key depression. If an alphanumeric character is entered then it is stored in the buffer. If a control character is entered, the appropriate action is taken or the character is ignored.
- A main program that calls the subroutines. Its main function is to scan the buffer to see if a character is to be sent. It will send characters until the buffer is empty.

We begin the description of the program with a listing and a brief description of the subroutines.

The subroutine listings are given in Example 10–1. The purpose of each of the subroutines will be described in turn. Subroutine TIMER in lines 18–34 of Example 10–1 produces a delay of one dot time. It is a simple nested delay loop of the kind described in Chapter 3. Including the JSR instruction needed to call the subroutine and the RTS instruction, the number, N_D, of clock cycles this subroutine takes is given by the expression:

$$N_D = 43 + 5N_x + 1284(N_y - 1) \qquad (10–3)$$

where

N_x is the number loaded from the location labeled LOBYTE,
N_y is the number loaded from the location labeled HIBYTE.

Subroutine CNTSPD calculates the numbers to be stored in these two locations once the code speed has been entered on the keyboard. Subroutine CNTSPD is the last subroutine listed in Example 10–1.

Example 10–1. Subroutines for the Morse Code Send Program

```
SOURCE FILE: CODE SUBROUTINES
0000:       1 LOBYTE  EQU  $0000      ;LOW-ORDER BYTE FOR TIMER.
0001:       2 HIBYTE  EQU  $0001      ;HI-ORDER BYTE FOR TIMER.
0002:       3 DVSRLO  EQU  $0002      ;LOW-ORDER BYTE OF DIVISOR.
0003:       4 DVSRMI  EQU  $0003
0004:       5 DVSRHI  EQU  $0004
0005:       6 DVNDLO  EQU  $0005      ;LOW-ORDER BYTE OF DIVIDEND.
0006:       7 DVNDMI  EQU  $0006
0007:       8 DVNDHI  EQU  $0007
0008:       9 REMLO   EQU  $0008      ;LOW-ORDER BYTE OF REMAINDER.
0009:      10 REMMI   EQU  $0009
000A:      11 REMHI   EQU  $000A
000B:      12 SPEED   EQU  $000B      ;BCD VALUE OF CODE SPEED.
000C:      13 BISPED  EQU  $000C      ;BINARY VALUE OF CODE SPEED.
000D:      14 FIFO    EQU  $000D
0800:      15 CODE    EQU  $0800
```

------NEXT OBJECT FILE NAME IS CODE SUBROUTINES.

```
2000:              16              ORG    $2000
2000:              17 ;SUBROUTINE TIMER
2000:48            18 TIMER  PHA                ;SAVE A ON THE STACK.
2001:8A            19        TXA                ;SAVE X
2002:48            20        PHA                ;ON STACK.
2003:98            21        TYA                ;SAVE Y
2004:48            22        PHA                ;ON THE STACK.
2005:A6 00         23        LDX    LOBYTE      ;LO-ORDER BYTE INTO TIMING
                                                    LOOP.
2007:A4 01         24        LDY    HIBYTE      ;HI-ORDER BYTE INTO TIMING
                                                    LOOP.
2009:CA            25 TMLOOP DEX
200A:D0 FD         26        BNE    TMLOOP
200C:88            27        DEY
200D:D0 FA         28        BNE    TMLOOP      ;BOTH TIMING LOOPS COMPLETE?
200F:68            29        PLA                ;GET Y
2010:A8            30        TAY                ;FROM THE STACK.
2011:68            31        PLA                ;GET X
2012:AA            32        TAX                ;FROM STACK.
2013:68            33        PLA                ;GET A FROM STACK.
2014:60            34        RTS                ;RETURN TO CALLING PROGRAM.

                   36 ***************************
2015:              37 ;SUBROUTINE SEND
2015:A0 00         38 SEND   LDY    #00         ;CLEAR Y FOR INDIRECT INDEXED
                                                    LOAD.
2017:B1 0D         39        LDA    (FIFO),Y    ;GET CHARACTER FROM THE TABLE.
2019:E6 0D         40        INC    FIFO        ;INCREMENT FIFO POINTER.
201B:AA            41        TAX                ;CHARACTER BECOMES INDEX.
201C:BD 00 08      42        LDA    CODE,X      ;GET MORSE CODE CHARACTER.
201F:F0 26         43        BEQ    WDSPCE      ;SEND A WORD SPACE.
2021:0A            44 REST   ASL    A           ;SHIFT CODE INTO CARRY FLAG.
2022:F0 1A         45        BEQ    CHSPCE      ;CHARACTER FINISHED. SEND
                                                    SPACE.
2024:B0 14         46        BCS    DASH        ;SEND A DASH IF CARRY IS SET.
2026:A2 01         47        LDX    #01         ;X COUNTS # OF TIMER CALLS.
2028:8D 58 C0      48 DOT    STA    $C058       ;ANNUNCIATOR TO LOGIC ZERO
202B:20 00 20      49 MORE   JSR    TIMER       ;FOR ONE DOT TIME.
202E:CA            50        DEX
202F:D0 FA         51        BNE    MORE
2031:8D 59 C0      52        STA    $C059       ;ANNUNCIATOR TO LOGIC ONE.
2034:20 00 20      53        JSR    TIMER       ;ADD AN ELEMENT SPACE.
2037:B8            54        CLV                ;BRANCH BACK TO GET THE
2038:50 E7         55        BVC    REST        ;REST OF THE CHARACTER.
203A:A2 03         56 DASH   LDX    #03         ;SEND THREE DOTS.
203C:D0 EA         57        BNE    DOT
203E:A2 02         58 CHSPCE LDX    #02         ;SEND A CHARACTER SPACE.
2040:20 00 20      59 SPACE  JSR    TIMER
2043:CA            60        DEX
2044:D0 FA         61        BNE    SPACE       ;MORE SPACE.
2046:60            62        RTS
2047:A2 04         63 WDSPCE LDX    #04
2049:D0 F5         64        BNE    SPACE

                   66 ***************************
```

```
204B:                  67 ;SUBROUTINE BCD-TO-BINARY
204B:A9 80             68 CONVERTLDA    #$80        ;THIS ROUTINE CONVERTS
204D:85 0C             69        STA    BISPED      ;THE BCD VALUE OF
204F:46 0B             70 RB1    LSR    SPEED       ;CODE SPEED TO
2051:66 0C             71        ROR    BISPED      ;A BINARY NUMBER.
2053:B0 0F             72        BCS    BR3
2055:38                73        SEC
2056:A5 0B             74        LDA    SPEED
2058:29 08             75        AND    #08
205A:F0 06             76        BEQ    BR2
205C:A5 0B             77        LDA    SPEED
205E:E9 03             78        SBC    #03
2060:85 0B             79        STA    SPEED
2062:B0 EB             80 BR2    BCS    BR1
2064:60                81 BR3    RTS

                       83 ***************************
2065:                  84 ;SUBROUTINE DIVIDE
2065:A9 00             85 DIVIDE LDA    #00         ;THIS ROUTINE PERFORMS
2067:85 08             86        STA    REMLO       ;THE 24-BIT DIVISION
2069:85 09             87        STA    REMMI       ;FOR THE CODE SPEED
206B:85 0A             88        STA    REMHI       ;CALCULATION.
206D:A2 18             89        LDX    #$18        ;24-BIT DIVISION.
206F:06 05             90        ASL    DVNDLO
2071:26 06             91        ROL    DVNDMI
2073:26 07             92        ROL    DVNDHI
2075:26 08             93 BR4    ROL    REMLO
2077:26 09             94        ROL    REMMI
2079:26 0A             95        ROL    REMHI
207B:A5 08             96        LDA    REMLO
207D:C5 02             97        CMP    DVSRLO
207F:A5 09             98        LDA    REMMI
2081:E5 03             99        SBC    DVSRMI
2083:A5 0A            100        LDA    REMHI
2085:E5 04            101        SBC    DVSRHI
2087:90 12            102        BCC    BR5
2089:A5 08            103        LDA    REMLO
208B:E5 02            104        SBC    DVSRLO
208D:85 08            105        STA    REMLO
208F:A5 09            106        LDA    REMMI
2091:E5 03            107        SBC    DVSRMI
2093:85 09            108        STA    REMMI
2095:A5 0A            109        LDA    REMHI
2097:E5 04            110        SBC    DVSRHI
2099:85 0A            111        STA    REMHI
209B:26 05            112 BR5    ROL    DVNDLO
209D:26 06            113        ROL    DVNDMI
209F:26 07            114        ROL    DVNDHI
20A1:CA               115        DEX
20A2:D0 D1            116        BNE    BR4
20A4:60               117        RTS

20A5:                 119 ;SUBROUTINE RDBYTE
                      120 ***************************
000C:                 121 TEMP   EQU    $000C       ;TEMPORARY STORAGE LOCATION.
```

```
FD8E:           122 CROUT   EQU    $FD8E        ;CARRIAGE RETURN.
FD0C:           123 RDKEY   EQU    $FD0C        ;READ KEYBOARD.
FDED:           124 COUT    EQU    $FDED        ;OUTPUT SUBROUTINE.
20A5:20 BB 20   125 RDBYTE  JSR    ASHEX        ;GET NIBBLE.
20A8:0A         126         ASL    A            ;SHIFT TO HIGH NIBBLE.
20A9:0A         127         ASL    A
20AA:0A         128         ASL    A
20AB:0A         129         ASL    A
20AC:85 0C      130         STA    TEMP         ;STORE NIBBLE.
20AE:20 BB 20   131         JSR    ASHEX        ;GET THE SECOND NIBBLE.
20B1:05 0C      132         ORA    TEMP         ;COMBINE WITH FIRST NIBBLE.
20B3:85 0C      133         STA    TEMP         ;SAVE ENTIRE BYTE.
20B5:20 8E FD   134         JSR    CROUT        ;OUTPUT A RETURN.
20B8:A5 0C      135         LDA    TEMP         ;GET BYTE BACK.
20BA:60         136         RTS                 ;NO. RETURN.

20BB:           138 ;ASCII-TO-HEX ROUTINE
                139 ***************************
20BB:20 0C FD   140 ASHEX   JSR    RDKEY        ;GET A CHARACTER.
20BE:20 ED FD   141         JSR    COUT         ;DISPLAY IT.
20C1:29 7F      142         AND    #$7F         ;MASK BIT 7 OFF.
20C3:C9 40      143         CMP    #$40         ;DIGIT OR LETTER?
20C5:B0 04      144         BCS    ARND
20C7:29 0F      145         AND    #$0F         ;DIGIT, MASK HI-NIBBLE.
20C9:10 02      146         BPL    PAST         ;BRANCH PAST LETTER.
20CB:E9 37      147 ARND    SBC    #$37         ;LETTER, SUBTRACT $37.
20CD:60         148 PAST    RTS                 ;RETURN WITH DIGIT IN A.

20CE:           150 ;SUBROUTINE CNTSPD
                151 ***************************
20CE:20 A5 20   152 CNTSPD  JSR    RDBYTE       ;GET A 2-DIGIT BCD NUMBER FROM
20D1:85 0B      153         STA    SPEED        ;THE KEYBOARD AND
20D3:20 4B 20   154         JSR    CONVERT      ;CONVERT IT TO BINARY.
20D6:A9 12      155         LDA    #$12         ;FIND NUMBER OF CLOCK CYCLES
20D8:85 07      156         STA    DVNDHI       ;IN ONE DOT TIME.
20DA:A9 BB      157         LDA    #$BB         ;$12BB50=1,227,600.
20DC:85 06      158         STA    DVNDMI       ;#CYCLES = 1,227,600/SPEED.
20DE:A9 50      159         LDA    #$50
20E0:85 05      160         STA    DVNDLO
20E2:A9 00      161         LDA    #$00
20E4:85 03      162         STA    DVSRMI
20E6:85 04      163         STA    DVSRHI
20E8:A5 0C      164         LDA    BISPED       ;DIVIDE 1,227,600 BY
20EA:85 02      165         STA    DVSRLO       ;CODE SPEED.
20EC:20 65 20   166         JSR    DIVIDE
20EF:A9 04      167         LDA    #04          ;$0504 = 1284.
20F1:85 02      168         STA    DVSRLO       ;HI-BYTE IN TIMER
20F3:A9 05      169         LDA    #05          ;IS # CYCLES DIVIDED BY
20F5:85 03      170         STA    DVSRMI       ;1284.
20F7:A9 00      171         LDA    #00
20F9:85 04      172         STA    DVSRHI
20FB:20 65 20   173         JSR    DIVIDE       ;FIND HI-BYTE FOR TIMER.
20FE:A5 05      174         LDA    DVNDLO
2100:85 01      175         STA    HIBYTE
2102:E6 01      176         INC    HIBYTE
```

```
2104:A5 08    177    LDA    REMLO    ;REMAINDER OF THIS DIVISION
2106:85 05    178    STA    DVNDLO   ;WILL BE DIVIDED BY
2108:A5 09    179    LDA    REMMI    ;FIVE TO FIND THE LO-BYTE
210A:85 06    180    STA    DVNDMI   ;FOR THE TIMER SUBROUTINE.
210C:A5 0A    181    LDA    REMHI
210E:85 07    182    STA    DVNDHI
2110:A9 00    183    LDA    #00
2112:85 03    184    STA    DVSRMI
2114:85 04    185    STA    DVSRHI
2116:A9 05    186    LDA    #05      ;DIVIDE BY FIVE.
2118:85 02    187    STA    DVSRLO
211A:20 65 20 188    JSR    DIVIDE
211D:A5 05    189    LDA    DVNDLO
211F:85 00    190    STA    LOBYTE   ;RESULT INTO LO-BYTE FOR
2121:60       191    RTS             ;TIMER SUBROUTINE.
```

***SUCCESSFUL ASSEMBLY: NO ERRORS

Subroutine SEND converts the ASCII characters found in the buffer to Morse code. Refer to Chapter 6 to refresh your memory on the procedure for using indexed addressing to convert ASCII to Morse code. The address of the character buffer is stored in FIFO and FIFO + 1. Indirect indexed addressing is used to access the character buffer. Page $09 of memory was used for the character buffer. The first action of the SEND subroutine is to fetch an ASCII character from the buffer. Then it increments the number that points to the next location in the buffer. The character is transferred to the X index register to fetch the corresponding Morse code character that is stored in a table in page $08 of memory. Chart 10-1 is the complete ASCII-to-Morse code lookup table. Refer again to Chapter 6 for a complete description of the conversion process.

The next task of the subroutine is to take the Morse representation of a character and transform it into the appropriate set of dots and dashes, followed by a character space. The steps required to take the Morse representation of the character in the accumulator and transform it into dots, dashes, and spaces are outlined in Chart 10-2, the SEND algorithm. Study this chart in connection with the comments in the listing in Example 10-1.

The remaining subroutines have been described in one form or another in previous chapters. This book will merely explain their function in the context of this application rather than explain each one in detail. Subroutine BCD-TO-BINARY converts the 2-digit bcd number entered for the code speed to a binary number. This is required in order to perform the division outlined in Equation 10-2.

Subroutine DIVIDE performs this division. Since the dividend in Equation 10-2 is 1,227,600, at least 23 bits are required

Chart 10–1. ASCII-to-Morse Code Lookup Table

```
*0988080. 087FF

0880-   00  00  00  00  00  00  00  CE
0888-   00  00  00  00  CE  8C  56  94
0890-   FC  7C  3C  1C  0C  04  84  C4
0898-   E4  F4  16  32  00  8C  00  32
08A0-   00  60  88  A8  90  40  28  D0
08A8-   08  20  16  32  CE  8C  56  94
08B0-   FC  7C  3C  1C  0C  04  84  C4
08B8-   E4  F4  16  32  20  8C  20  32
08C0-   00  60  88  A8  90  40  28  D0
08C8-   08  20  78  B0  48  E0  A0  F0
08D0-   68  D8  50  10  C0  30  18  70
08D8-   98  B8  C8  00  00  00  00  00
08E0-   00  00  00  00  00  00  00  00
08E8-   00  00  00  00  00  00  00  00
08F0-   00  00  00  00  00  00  00  00
08F8-   00  00  00  00  00  00  00  00
```

since $1,227,600 = \$12BB50$. It is more convenient to use 3 bytes or 24 bits. Subroutine DIVIDE is also used to determine the numbers to be used in the timing loops. Refer to Equation 10–3. To determine N_y the number, N_D, of clock cycles in one dot is first divided by 1284. This result is incremented by one and the result is stored in HIBYTE, where it will become N_y in the timing loop. The remainder from this division is divided by 5 to yield N_x. It is stored in LOBYTE to be used by the timing subroutine. All of these calculations take place in the last subroutine in Example 10–1.

Subroutine RDBYTE fetches two digits from the keyboard, converts them from ASCII to bcd digits, and stores them in location $000B, SPEED. This subroutine calls an ASCII-to-HEX subroutine, lines 140–148. Subroutine RDBYTE is only used to input the speed in words per minute. The interrupt routine, described below, handles the input functions of the characters to be converted to Morse code and the control characters.

Finally, subroutine CNTSPD performs the speed conversions described above. It calls most of the subroutines just described in order to convert the code speed entered from the keyboard to the numbers in HIBYTE and LOBYTE that control the timing loop. This completes our discussion of the subroutines.

Chart 10-2. The SEND Algorithm

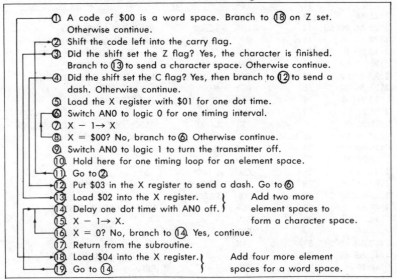

1. A code of $00 is a word space. Branch to ⑱ on Z set. Otherwise continue.
2. Shift the code left into the carry flag.
3. Did the shift set the Z flag? Yes, the character is finished. Branch to ⑬ to send a character space. Otherwise continue.
4. Did the shift set the C flag? Yes, then branch to ⑫ to send a dash. Otherwise continue.
5. Load the X register with $01 for one dot time.
6. Switch AN0 to logic 0 for one timing interval.
7. X − 1 → X
8. X = $00? No, branch to ⑥ Otherwise continue.
9. Switch AN0 to logic 1 to turn the transmitter off.
10. Hold here for one timing loop for an element space.
11. Go to ②
12. Put $03 in the X register to send a dash. Go to ⑥
13. Load $02 into the X register. ⎫ Add two more
14. Delay one dot time with AN0 off. ⎬ element spaces to
15. X − 1 → X. ⎭ form a character space.
16. X = 0? No, branch to ⑭. Yes, continue.
17. Return from the subroutine.
18. Load $04 into the X register. ⎫ Add four more element
19. Go to ⑭. ⎬ spaces for a word space.

The Interrupt Routine

The interrupt routine is listed in Example 10-2 and a flow-chart of its essential features is given in Fig. 10-2. The principal function of the interrupt routine is to read the Apple keyboard. Why use interrupts for this purpose? The main task of the microcomputer is to send the Morse code characters. If the computer must *wait* for a key to be pressed before sending a character, then you can only input the characters from the keyboard as fast as they are to be sent. On the other hand, in the interrupt mode, the microcomputer continues to send code, and you can type ahead. The interrupt routine takes so little time that fetching a character and storing it in the buffer cannot be discerned in listening to the Morse code character string.

Example 10-2. Interrupt Routine for the Code Program

```
SOURCE FILE: INTERRUPT ROUTINE
000D:          1 FIFO     EQU    $000D
0010:          2 PNTR     EQU    $0010
20CE:          3 CNTSPD   EQU    $20CE      ;SUBROUTINE TO SET SPEED.
FDED:          4 COUT     EQU    $FDED
----NEXT OBJECT FILE NAME IS INTERRUPT ROUTINE.
2122:          5          ORG    $2122

2122:          7 ;INTERRUPT ROUTINE
               8 ***************************
2122:8A        9          TXA               ;SAVE THE X AND Y REGISTERS
```

```
2123:48          10         PHA                        ;ON THE STACK.
2124:98          11         TYA
2125:48          12         PHA
2126:AD 00 C0    13         LDA    $C000              ;READ THE KEYBOARD.
2129:10 1A       14         BPL    OUT                ;BRANCH TO END IF NO KEY.
212B:8D 10 C0    15         STA    $C010              ;KEY PRESSED. CLEAR STROBE.
212E:C9 A0       16         CMP    #$A0               ;IS IT A CHARACTER?
2130:90 1D       17         BCC    CONTROL            ;NO, IT'S A CONTROL CODE.
2132:A0 00       18         LDY    #00                ;YES, SO PUT IT IN
2134:91 10       19         STA    (PNTR),Y           ;THE FIFO MEMORY.
2136:E6 10       20         INC    PNTR
2138:20 ED FD    21 BACK    JSR    COUT               ;ALSO, OUTPUT THE CHARACTER.
213B:A4 24       22 HERE    LDY    $24                ;ADVANCE THE FLASHING
213D:B1 28       23         LDA    ($28),Y            ;CURSOR.
213F:29 3F       24         AND    #$3F
2141:09 40       25         ORA    #$40
2143:91 28       26         STA    ($28),Y
2145:AD 04 C7    27 OUT     LDA    $C704
2148:68          28         PLA                        ;RESTORE THE REGISTERS.
2149:A8          29         TAY
214A:68          30         PLA
214B:AA          31         TAX
214C:A5 45       32         LDA    $45                ;GET THE ACCUMULATOR.
214E:40          33         RTI                        ;RETURN.
214F:C9 93       34 CONTROL CMP    #$93               ;CONTROL S?
2151:D0 06       35         BNE    NEXT1              ;NO.
2153:20 CE 20    36         JSR    CNTSPD             ;YES, SET SPEED.
2156:18          37         CLC                        ;THEN GET OUT.
2157:90 EC       38         BCC    OUT
2159:C9 88       39 NEXT1   CMP    #$88               ;DELETE KEY?
215B:D0 0E       40         BNE    NEXT2              ;NO.
215D:20 ED FD    41         JSR    COUT               ;YES, DELETE FROM SCREEN.
2160:A5 10       42         LDA    PNTR               ;ALSO DECREMENT POINTER
2162:C5 0D       43         CMP    FIFO               ;TO CURRENT FIFO LOCATION.
2164:F0 DF       44         BEQ    OUT
2166:C6 10       45         DEC    PNTR
2168:B8          46         CLV                        ;THEN GET OUT.
2169:50 D0       47         BVC    HERE
216B:C9 9B       48 NEXT2   CMP    #$9B               ;ESCAPE? PANIC?
216D:D0 03       49         BNE    NEXT3              ;NO.
216F:4C 00 22    50         JMP    $2200              ;YES. RESTART THE PROGRAM.
2172:C9 8D       51 NEXT3   CMP    #$8D               ;CARRIAGE RETURN.
2174:D0 02       52         BNE    NEXT4
2176:F0 C0       53         BEQ    BACK
2178:C9 92       54 NEXT4   CMP    #$92               ;"CTRL R" KEY?
217A:D0 03       55         BNE    NEXT5
217C:4C 50 22    56         JMP    $2250              ;JUMP TO ANOTHER ROUTINE.
217F:C9 94       57 NEXT5   CMP    #$94               ;"CTRL T" KEY?
2181:D0 C2       58         BNE    OUT                ;NO, THEN RETURN FROM
                                                       INTERRUPT.
2183:4C 3E 22    59         JMP    $223E              ;START SENDING CODE.
```

*** SUCCESSFUL ASSEMBLY: NO ERRORS

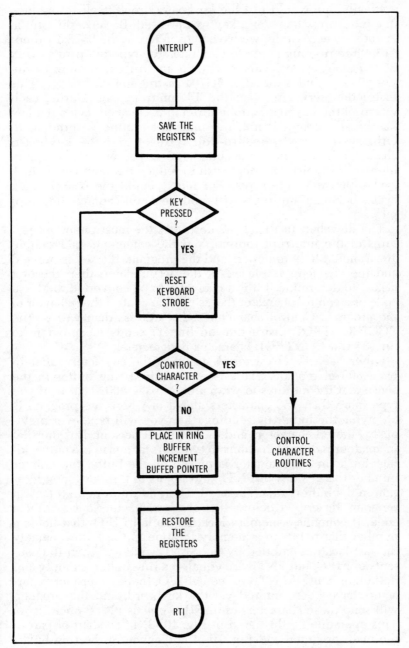

Fig. 10-2. The interrupt routine for the Morse code program.

277

Ideally one would use the keyboard strobe itself to produce one interrupt whenever a key was pressed. Because this strobe is not very accessible, we have chosen to use the 6522 T1 timer in its free-running mode to generate $\overline{\text{IRQ}}$-type interrupts every 65,537 clock cycles. This is why the interrupt routine in Example 10–2 includes an LDA $C704 instruction on line 27. This instruction serves to clear the T1 interrupt flag. During each interrupt the keyboard strobe flip-flop is checked to see if a key has been pressed. If not, the interrupt routine is terminated. Otherwise the strobe flip-flop is reset and the keyboard character is now in the accumulator. If you are an extremely high-speed typist, you may wish to reduce the number of clock cycles between interrupts. For most people the 65,537 clock cycles between interrupts will produce a rapid enough interrupt rate.

The flowchart in Fig. 10–2 describes the most important features of the interrupt routine, and the comments in Example 10–2 should help to understand the program. If a key is pressed and the character is placed in the accumulator, then the first task is to determine if it is a character to be converted to Morse code or a control character that is used to control the behavior of the program. Control character codes are less than $A0, so the BCC CONTROL instruction on line 17 sends the program to line 34 if a CONTROL character is detected.

Otherwise, the character is stored in the character buffer in page $09 of memory. This is essentially a ring buffer in the sense that it continues to wrap around page $09. That is, if you type more than 256 characters ahead of where the program is emptying the buffer by sending, then you will type over previously entered characters and they will not be sent. It is unusual in amateur radio applications to type this far ahead of your sending. Each time a character is placed on the buffer the pointer number that resides in PNTR and points to the next open location in the buffer is incremented. There is a routine in the main program, described below, that sends characters out as Morse code. It contains a memory location, called FIFO, that holds a number that points to a memory location in the buffer, namely the last location emptied by the SEND routine. When the contents of FIFO and PNTR are equal, the ring buffer is empty and nothing is sent. If PNTR exceeds FIFO, then one or more characters have been entered via the keyboard, and the program will send these characters until FIFO equals PNTR once again. This operation is illustrated in Fig. 10–3, a flowchart of part of the main program, and Fig. 10–4, a diagram of the ring buffer concept.

To keep the flowchart in Fig. 10–2 simple we do not consider any details related to the display of the characters as they are entered. This operation consists of a subroutine call to the monitor's COUT display subroutine. The function of the control characters is self-explanatory once the program comments are studied. We turn next to the main program.

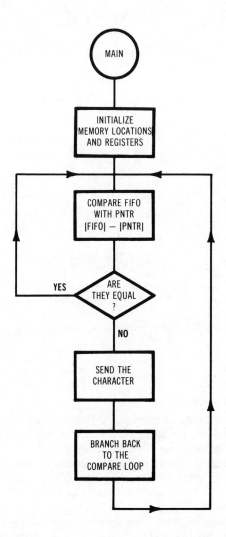

Fig. 10–3. Simplified flowchart of the main program in which the location FIFO is incremented when a character is converted to Morse code.

279

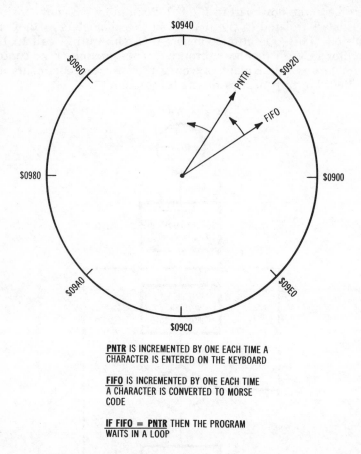

PNTR IS INCREMENTED BY ONE EACH TIME A
CHARACTER IS ENTERED ON THE KEYBOARD

FIFO IS INCREMENTED BY ONE EACH TIME
A CHARACTER IS CONVERTED TO MORSE
CODE

IF FIFO = PNTR THEN THE PROGRAM
WAITS IN A LOOP

Fig. 10–4. The ring buffer used to store the characters to be converted to Morse code.

The Main Code Program

The main program of the Morse Code Send Program is listed in Example 10–3. It begins by turning the annunciator to its logic 1 position to make sure the transmitter is off (the relay in Fig. 10–1 is open). Then various memory locations, such as the buffer pointers, are initialized. Timer T1 is started in its free-running mode, the screen is cleared, and the code speed calculations are made. The interrupt flag is cleared, and then the program is ready to start. The most important parts of the main code program are described by the flowchart in Fig. 10–3. Study it in connection with the comments and you will surely understand how it works.

Example 10-3. Main Program for the Morse Code Program

SOURCE FILE: MAIN CODE PROGRAM

```
000D:           1 FIFO    EQU    $000D
0010:           2 PNTR    EQU    $0010
FC58:           3 HOME    EQU    $FC58    ;MONITOR ROUTINE TO CLEAR THE
                                              SCREEN.
2015:           4 SEND    EQU    $2015
20CE:           5 CNTSPD  EQU    $20CE
C704:           6 T1LL    EQU    $C704
C705:           7 T1LH    EQU    $C705
C70B:           8 ACR     EQU    $C70B
C70E:           9 IER     EQU    $C70E
```

-----NEXT OBJECT FILE NAME IS MAIN CODE PROGRAM.

```
2200:          10         ORG    $2200
2200:78        11         SEI
2201:8D 59 C0  12         STA    $C059    ;ANNUNCIATOR TO LOGIC ONE.
2204:D8        13         CLD
2205:A9 FF     14         LDA    #$FF     ;SET UP TIMER TO GIVE
2207:8D 04 C7  15         STA    T1LL     ;INTERRUPTS EVERY 65537
220A:A9 FF     16         LDA    #$FF     ;CLOCK CYCLES.
220C:8D 05 C7  17         STA    T1LH
220F:AD 0B C7  18         LDA    ACR      ;PUT T1 IN FREE-RUNNING MODE.
2212:09 40     19         ORA    #$40
2214:8D 0B C7  20         STA    ACR
2217:AD 0E C7  21         LDA    IER      ;ENABLE INTERRUPTS FROM T1.
221A:09 C0     22         ORA    #$C0
221C:8D 0E C7  23         STA    IER
221F:20 58 FC  24         JSR    HOME     ;CLEAR THE SCREEN.
2222:20 CE 20  25         JSR    CNTSPD
2225:A9 21     26         LDA    #$21     ;SET UP INTERRUPT VECTOR.
2227:8D FF 03  27         STA    $03FF
222A:A9 22     28         LDA    #$22
222C:8D FE 03  29         STA    $03FE
222F:A9 00     30         LDA    #$00
2231:85 0D     31         STA    FIFO     ;SET UP INDIRECT INDEXED
                                              POINTERS.
2233:85 10     32         STA    PNTR
2235:A9 09     33         LDA    #09
2237:85 0E     34         STA    FIFO+1
2239:85 11     35         STA    PNTR+1
223B:A0 00     36         LDY    #00
223D:58        37         CLI             ;ALLOW INTERRUPTS.
223E:A5 0D     38 BR6     LDA    FIFO     ;IS FIFO DIFFERENT
2240:C5 10     39         CMP    PNTR     ;FROM POINTER?
2242:F0 FA     40         BEQ    BR6      ;NO, WAIT HERE FOR A NEW
                                              CHARACTER.
2244:20 15 20  41         JSR    SEND     ;YES, THEN SEND A CHARACTER.
2247:B8        42         CLV             ;FORCE A BRANCH BACK.
2248:50 F4     43         BVC    BR6
```

*** SUCCESSFUL ASSEMBLY: NO ERRORS

This completes the description of this application. Once you have the program loaded and the interface constructed you can test the operation by placing an ohmmeter across the relay contacts that normally go to the transmitter. At slow enough speeds you should be able to detect the correct characters being sent. Be sure not to forget to load the lookup table in Chart 10–1.

If you do not have a 6522 available to produce interrupts, use the technique outlined in Chapter 7 to produce $\overline{\text{NMI}}$-type interrupts. See Fig. 7–8. Also, load location $03FB-03FD with $4C, $22, and $21 to produce a jump to the interrupt routine. A 60-Hz interrupt rate will work very nicely.

A MORSE CODE RECEIVE ROUTINE*

For the sake of completeness and for your entertainment, included in this chapter is a program that will *receive* Morse code. It is listed in Example 10–4, and a circuit to interface the microcomputer to a communications receiver is given in Fig. 10–5. The Morse code receive routine may be accessed from the Morse code send program in Examples 10–1 to 10–3 by loading both programs and pressing the CTRL R key. You can return to the send program by pressing the CTRL T key. The union of the two programs makes a complete send/receive package for the Apple.

Example 10–4. A Morse Code Receive Routine

```
SOURCE FILE: APPLECODE
C784:        1 T1L       EQU   $C784
C785:        2 T1H       EQU   $C785
FDF0:        3 COUT      EQU   $FDF0
0E80:        4 TAB       EQU   $0E80
C788:        5 T2CL      EQU   $C788
C78B:        6 ACR       EQU   $C78B
C78D:        7 IFR       EQU   $C78D
00B1:        8 CHAR      EQU   $00B1
00B2:        9 SPACE     EQU   $00B2
00B3:       10 MARK      EQU   $00B3
00B4:       11 DOT       EQU   $00B4
00B5:       12 HALFDOT   EQU   $00B5
00B6:       13 THFTDOT   EQU   $00B6
00B7:       14 DDOT      EQU   $00B7
00B8:       15 FDOT      EQU   $00B8
00B9:       16 STORE     EQU   $00B9
00BA:       17 TEMP      EQU   $00BA
-----NEXT OBJECT FILE NAME IS APPLECODE.
```

---

*For a more complete description of this program see "An Improved Morse Code Receive Routine and Interface," *Micro*, No. 29, October 1980, p. 23.

```
2250:           18        ORG    $2250
2250:D8         19 START  CLD
2251:A9 20      20        LDA    #$20      ;SET UP T2 TO COUNT PULSES.
2253:8D 8B C7   21        STA    ACR       ;INITIALIZATION SEQUENCE.
2256:A9 0E      22        LDA    #$0E
2258:85 B4      23        STA    DOT
225A:85 B3      24        STA    MARK
225C:78         25        SEI
225D:20 03 23   26        JSR    CAL
2260:A9 01      27        LDA    #$01
2262:85 B1      28        STA    CHAR
2264:20 D2 22   29        JSR    TIMER     ;START RECEIVING CODE.
2267:A9 00      30 STATE1 LDA    #$00      ;IN STATE 1 THE PROGRAM
2269:85 B2      31 RPT    STA    SPACE     ;WAITS UNTIL A TONE AT
226B:85 B3      32        STA    MARK      ;LEAST ¾ DOT LENGTH
226D:20 E2 22   33 CNT    JSR    COUNT     ;HAS BEEN DETECTED.
2270:A5 B3      34        LDA    MARK      ;THEN IT JUMPS TO STATE 2.
2272:C5 B6      35        CMP    THFTDOT
2274:B0 08      36        BCS    STATE2
2276:A5 B2      37        LDA    SPACE
2278:C5 B4      38        CMP    DOT
227A:B0 EB      39        BCS    STATE1
227C:90 EF      40        BCC    CNT
227E:A9 00      41 STATE2 LDA    #$00      ;IN STATE 2 A TONE IS BEING
2280:85 B2      42        STA    SPACE     ;COUNTED. WHEN THE TONE ENDS
2282:20 E2 22   43 MORE   JSR    COUNT     ;THE PROGRAM CONTINUES
2285:A5 B2      44        LDA    SPACE     ;IN THIS STATE UNTIL
2287:C5 B5      45        CMP    HALFDOT   ;A SPACE HAS BEEN
2289:90 F7      46        BCC    MORE      ;DETECTED.
228B:06 B1      47 STATE3 ASL    CHAR      ;IN STATE 3 A DECISION
228D:A5 B3      48        LDA    MARK      ;IS MADE TO SEE IF
228F:C5 B7      49        CMP    DDOT      ;THE ELEMENT WAS A DOT
2291:90 0C      50        BCC    ARND      ;OR A DASH.
2293:E6 B1      51        INC    CHAR      ;THE CHARACTER REGISTER
2295:4A         52        LSR    A         ;IS UPDATED.
2296:4A         53        LSR    A
2297:85 B3      54        STA    MARK
2299:4A         55        LSR    A
229A:18         56        CLC
229B:65 B3      57        ADC    MARK
229D:85 B3      58        STA    MARK
229F:20 03 23   59 ARND   JSR    CAL       ;JUMP TO AUTOMATIC
22A2:A9 00      60        LDA    #$00      ;CALIBRATION ROUTINE.
22A4:85 B3      61        STA    MARK
22A6:20 E2 22   62 LOAF   JSR    COUNT
22A9:A5 B3      63        LDA    MARK
22AB:C5 B6      64        CMP    THFTDOT   ;WAIT FOR ANOTHER ELEMENT.
22AD:B0 CF      65        BCS    STATE2    ;BACK TO STATE 2.
22AF:A5 B2      66        LDA    SPACE     ;WAIT FOR A CHARACTER SPACE.
22B1:C5 B7      67        CMP    DDOT
22B3:90 F1      68        BCC    LOAF
22B5:20 29 23   69        JSR    OUTPUT    ;OUTPUT THE CHARACTER.
22B8:A9 01      70        LDA    #$01
22BA:85 B1      71        STA    CHAR      ;RESET THE CHARACTER
22BC:20 E2 22   72 LOITER JSR    COUNT     ;REGISTER. WAIT
```

22BF:A5 B3	73		LDA	MARK	;FOR MARK OR A WORDSPACE.
22C1:C5 B6	74		CMP	THFTDOT	
22C3:B0 B9	75		BCS	STATE2	
22C5:A5 B2	76		LDA	SPACE	
22C7:C5 B8	77		CMP	FDOT	
22C9:90 F1	78		BCC	LOITER	
22CB:20 29 23	79		JSR	OUTPUT	;OUTPUT THE SPACE.
22CE:A9 00	80		LDA	#$00	
22D0:F0 97	81		BEQ	RPT	
22D2:A9 52	82	TIMER	LDA	#$52	;SUBROUTINE TIMER.
22D4:8D 84 C7	83		STA	T1L	
22D7:A9 05	84		LDA	#$05	
22D9:8D 85 C7	85		STA	T1H	
22DC:AD 88 C7	86		LDA	T2CL	
22DF:85 B9	87		STA	STORE	
22E1:60	88		RTS		
22E2:58	89	COUNT	CLI		;SUBROUTINE TO COUNT
22E3:78	90		SEI		;PULSES FROM THE
22E4:2C 8D C7	91	WAIT	BIT	IFR	;RECEIVER.
22E7:50 FB	92		BVC	WAIT	
22E9:38	93		SEC		
22EA:A5 B9	94		LDA	STORE	
22EC:ED 88 C7	95		SBC	T2CL	
22EF:85 BA	96		STA	TEMP	
22F1:20 D2 22	97		JSR	TIMER	
22F4:A5 BA	98		LDA	TEMP	
22F6:F0 08	99		BEQ	AHED	
22F8:18	100		CLC		
22F9:65 B3	101		ADC	MARK	
22FB:85 B3	102		STA	MARK	
22FD:18	103		CLC		
22FE:90 02	104		BCC	DETOUR	
2300:E6 B2	105	AHED	INC	SPACE	
2302:60	106	DETOUR	RTS		
2303:A5 B4	107	CAL	LDA	DOT	;CALIBRATION SUBROUTINE.
2305:06 B4	108		ASL	DOT	
2307:65 B4	109		ADC	DOT	
2309:65 B3	110		ADC	MARK	
230B:4A	111		LSR	A	
230C:4A	112		LSR	A	
230D:C9 0F	113		CMP	#$0F	
230F:B0 02	114		BCS	SKIP	
2311:A9 0F	115		LDA	#$0F	
2313:85 B4	116	SKIP	STA	DOT	
2315:0A	117		ASL	A	
2316:85 B7	118		STA	DDOT	
2318:0A	119		ASL	A	
2319:18	120		CLC		
231A:65 B4	121		ADC	DOT	
231C:85 B8	122		STA	FDOT	
231E:A5 B4	123		LDA	DOT	
2320:4A	124		LSR	A	
2321:85 B5	125		STA	HALFDOT	
2323:4A	126		LSR	A	
2324:65 B5	127		ADC	HALFDOT	

```
2326:85 B6      128        STA    THFTDOT
2328:60         129        RTS
2329:A5 B1      130 OUTPUT LDA    CHAR        ;OUTPUT SUBROUTINE.
232B:A8         131        TAY
232C:B9 80 0E   132        LDA    TAB,Y
232F:09 80      133        ORA    #$80
2331:20 F0 FD   134        JSR    COUT
2334:60         135        RTS
```

*** SUCCESSFUL ASSEMBLY: NO ERRORS

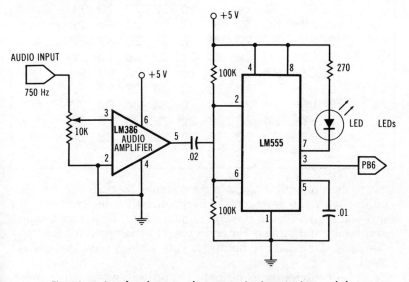

Fig. 10–5. Interface between the communications receiver and the microcomputer for the Morse code receive routine.

Although this book will not devote any space to explaining how the program works, here are some instructions relating to its use. Connect the interface circuit to the audio output of your transmitter. For best reception a good narrow-band (250 Hz or less) filter centered on 750 Hz is required. Do not expect good results with a cheap receiver. Adjust the audio level of your receiver to a comfortable listening level, and then adjust the 10-kilohm potentiometer in the interface circuit so that the LED blinks on and off in unison with the incoming code. The 555 timer in Fig. 10–5 acts as a Schmitt trigger and is intended to discriminate against low-level noise. Adjust the gain so that the LED flashes only occasionally with noise spikes or static crashes.

Load the Morse-to-ASCII conversion table in Chart 10–3, load the program in Example 10–4, and start it running. It is

Chart 10–3. Morse Code-to-ASCII Lookup Table

```
*0E80.0EF3

0E80-  20 20 45 54 49 41 4E 4D
0E88-  53 55 52 57 44 4B 47 4F
0E90-  48 56 46 20 4C 20 50 4A
0E98-  42 58 43 59 5A 51 20 20
0EA0-  35 34 20 33 20 20 20 32
0EA8-  20 20 20 20 20 20 20 31
0EB0-  36 3D 2F 20 20 20 20 20
0EB8-  37 20 20 20 38 20 39 30
0EC0-  20 20 20 20 20 20 20 20
0EC8-  20 20 20 20 3F 20 20 20
0ED0-  20 20 20 20 20 2E 20 20
0ED8-  20 20 20 20 20 20 20 20
0EE0-  20 20 20 20 20 20 20 20
0EE8-  20 20 20 20 20 20 20 20
0EF0-  20 20 20 2C
```

best to begin with a good strong signal so that you become familiar with the program. Experiment with the gain settings until you are receiving the code quite nicely. Note that the program tracks and adjusts for code speed variations, but this may take several characters before it gets locked onto the correct speed.

The best advice is to be patient and willing to experiment. Once you have discovered the best gain settings you will find that it is a good program for code reception. Of course, there is no computer that can compete with the human mind/human ear combination. Do not expect the program to perform well under crowded band conditions, in the presence of static, with weak signals, or with an operator who does not send good code. The program performs best with an operator using a keyboard to send code at 30–60 wpm.

One final note: the program assumes the tone coming from the receiver is 750 Hz and it is important to adjust the receiver for this frequency. If the bandpass of your receiver is centered at another frequency, then you should modify the timing loop in lines 82–85 of the listing. The T1 timer should be loaded so that it times out once every period of the tone that you are receiving. For a 750-Hz tone this is 1.333 ms. The number to be loaded into the T1 timer is $1,023,000/f$, where f is the frequency of the tone. Be sure to convert this number to hexadecimal.

The use of a computer to convert Morse code to alphanumeric symbols on the video monitor is a challenging problem. The basic problem is the detection of a signal in the presence of noise and interference. The human brain is rather remarkable in its ability to do this. The program in Example 10–4 is suggested as a first step in the direction of better programs to accomplish the same task. Take this program and this interface as a challenge to write and construct better ones.

AN APPLICATION USING AN A/D CONVERTER

The next application to be described is a digital storage oscilloscope that can be constructed with two integrated circuits and the John Bell Engineering 6522 board (or a 6522 board of your own construction). When operating at its fastest rate, the program and circuit are capable of sampling a time-varying voltage at a rate of one sample every 31 microseconds. Of course, the sampling rate may be reduced as much as is necessary for your applications. The voltage waveform is displayed on the video monitor after it is converted and stored in memory. The program and the interface could be used, for example, to study nerve potentials as a function of time since these potentials vary rather slowly. With a suitable detector the program and interface could be used to make and store electrocardiograms. When sampling at its fastest rate, the system is capable of sampling speech waveforms, which when "played back" through a d/a converter are recognizable.

The analog-to-digital converter that was chosen for this application was an Analog Devices AD570. It is a compromise between speed and cost; that is, there are faster, more expensive a/d converters and there are slower but less expensive a/d converters. One advantage of the AD570 is that it interfaces easily and requires few or no external components. In order to minimize the conversion time, our interface circuit makes use of an additional integrated circuit, a 74LS00 NAND gate, but it is possible to construct an interface with no external components. This feature makes wire-wrapping or breadboarding the a/d converter an easy task. The AD570 can be upgraded to an AD571, a pin-for-pin compatible 10-bit converter. The AD570 is an 8-bit converter; that is, the analog voltage at its input is converted to an 8-bit number on its eight output pins. An 8-bit conversion gives a precision of one part in 256, or about 0.4 percent, which is comparable to the precision with which a dot may be placed on the Apple hires screen.

The interface circuit is shown in Fig. 10–6. The 6522 used for

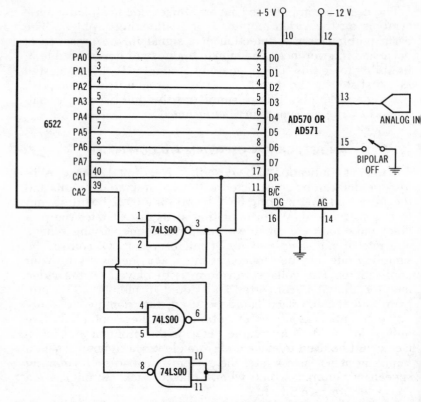

Fig. 10–6. The 6522 to AD570 analog-to-digital converter interface.

all of our programs was the No. 2 6522 on the John Bell Engineering Parallel Interface Board mounted in slot 7 of the Apple. You can also build your own interface on a breadboard similar to the one in the photograph in Fig. 10–7. The author's approach was to use a DIP jumper, described earlier, to connect the 6522 to a breadboard. Note that the AD570 requires a −12-V supply. The Apple provides −12 V on pin 33 of each peripheral card slot. The author soldered a short piece of wire-wrap wire from the pin 33 pad on the John Bell 6522 board to an unused pin, pin 13, on the J3 socket on the John Bell board. The DIP jumper then provides all data, control, and power lines that are necessary to operate the AD570. Pin diagrams of the AD570 and the 74LS00 are given in Appendix C. With the bipolar switch open, voltages between −5 V and +5 V are converted to a bi-nary number between $00 (−5 V) and $FF (+5 V). Zero volts gives a binary number of $80. With the bipolar mode switch

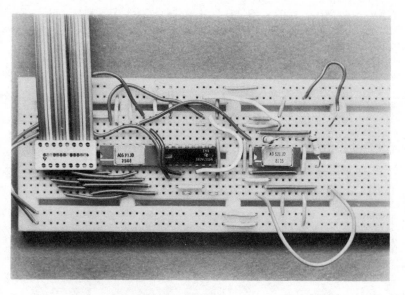

Fig. 10–7. The AD570 a/d converter circuit on a breadboard.

closed, voltages between 0 volts and 10 volts are converted to binary numbers between $00 and $FF. When you order an AD570 from Analog Devices, Route 1 Industrial Park, P.O. Box 280, Norwood, MA 02062, be sure to request a specification sheet.

Continue to refer to Fig. 10–6. The PA0–PA7 pins of the 6522 are used to read the 8-bit number from the AD570 with an LDA PAD instruction. The CA1 and CA2 pins are used to control the AD570. A negative pulse on the CA2 pin produces a positive pulse on the blank and convert (B/$\overline{\text{C}}$) pin on the AD570. The trailing edge of the pulse on the B/$\overline{\text{C}}$ pin initiates the conversion, which will take approximately 25 to 30 microseconds. At the end of that time interval the $\overline{\text{DR}}$ (data ready) pin on the AD570 goes to logic 0, signaling the 6522 that the conversion data is ready at pins D0–D7. Another conversion is initiated by producing another pulse on the CA2 pin. The specifications of the AD570 require that the B/$\overline{\text{C}}$ pin be in its logic 1 state for at least 2 microseconds before a conversion is started by bringing this pin to logic 0. The function of the cross-coupled NAND gate circuit is to produce the necessary pulse width on the B/$\overline{\text{C}}$ pin.

To illustrate how the AD570 is controlled with a program, a simple one-conversion program is listed in Example 10–5. The 6522 is programmed to produce a 1 clock cycle pulse on the

CA2 pin following a "read" of port A (PAD). It is also programmed so that a negative transition on CA1 sets the flag in bit one of the interrupt flag register (IFR). Thus a conversion is initiated by an LDA PAD instruction. When the IFR2 flag goes to logic 1 the conversion is complete, and the datum may be read with an LDA PAD instruction. Note that this initiates a second conversion, which is of no interest to us in Example 10-5. You should understand this program before continuing, because the basic idea will be used in all subsequent a/d conversion routines described here.

Example 10-5. A Program to Perform a Single A/D Conversion

```
1970:A9 0A      7           LDA   #$0A      ;INITIALIZE PCR TO
1972:8D 8C C7   8           STA   PCR       ;PULSE CA2 TO START A
1975:AD 81 C7   9           LDA   PAD       ;CONVERSION.
1978:A9 02      10 BACK      LDA   #02       ;SET UP MASK FOR IFR1.
197A:2C 8D C7   11 WAIT      BIT   IFR       ;IS THE CONVERSION COMPLETE?
197D:F0 FB      12           BEQ   WAIT      ;NO, THEN WAIT.
197F:AD 81 C7   13           LDA   PAD       ;YES, READ DATA.
1982:60         14           RTS
```

The next step in the elaboration or sophistication of our a/d conversion techniques is listed in Example 10-6. It is very similar to Example 10-5 except that the conversion instructions have been placed in a loop that repeats itself 256 times, each time placing the conversion data in a different location in page $0F of R/W memory.

Example 10-6. A Program to Perform 256 Conversions

```
1983:A2 00      8           LDX   #00       ;CLEAR X.
1985:A9 0A      9           LDA   #$0A      ;INITIALIZE PCR TO
1987:8D 8C C7   10          STA   PCR       ;PULSE CA2.
198A:AD 81 C7   11          LDA   PAD       ;START A CONVERSION.
198D:A9 02      12 BACK      LDA   #02       ;SET UP MASK.
198F:2C 8D C7   13 WAIT      BIT   IFR       ;CONVERSION COMPLETE.
1992:F0 FB      14          BEQ   WAIT      ;NO, THEN WAIT.
1994:AD 81 C7   15          LDA   PAD       ;YES, READ DATA.
1997:9D 00 0F   16          STA   TABLE,X   ;STORE IT IN A TABLE.
199A:E8         17          INX             ;GET MORE DATA.
199B:D0 F0      18          BNE   BACK      ;256 POINTS?
199D:00         19          BRK             ;YES, THEN QUIT.
```

To test the performance of this routine the author connected a signal generator to the input of the AD570 and ran the program. Next the data were displayed on the video monitor using Examples 6-15, 6-16, and 6-18. Finally, he used a graphics package that he purchased with his printer to transfer the picture on the screen to a printed output. The results are shown in Fig. 10-8 and Fig. 10-9. In Fig. 10-8 are the results of convert-

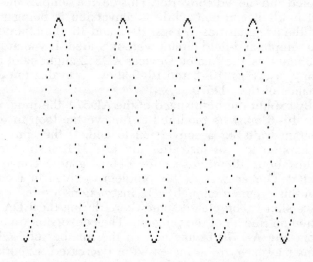

Fig. 10–8. Results obtained from converting a 500-Hz analog sine waveform to digital, where the program in Example 10–6 was used to collect the data.

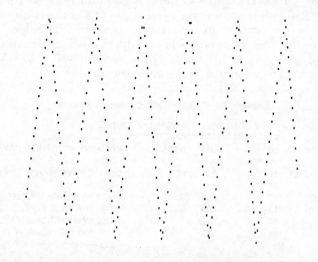

Fig. 10–9. Results obtained from converting a 700-Hz triangular waveform to digital, where the program in Example 10–6 was used to collect the data.

ing a 500-Hz sine waveform voltage to 256 numbers and then graphing the numbers. In Fig. 10–9 a 700-Hz triangular waveform was sampled. In critical applications a sample-and-hold integrated circuit would be placed between the voltage to be sampled and the a/d converter. This device samples the voltage and holds it constant while a conversion is being made. Some of the irregularities in Figs. 10–8 and 10–9 might not appear if a sample-and-hold circuit were included. If you are concerned about this, the Analog Devices AD582 might be of interest. In any case Figs. 10–8 and 10–9 allow an evaluation of the performance of the AD570.

To fully exploit the high speed of the AD570, the program in Example 10–6 must be modified to remove the loop in which the program waits for a conversion to end. If the conversion should happen to end just after the BIT IFR instruction, it would be about 10 microseconds before a new conversion would start. Our answer to this problem is given in Example 10–7. In this program enough NOP instructions are inserted so the conversion is completed somewhere during the LDA PAD instruction on line 28 of the program. The conversion time may vary from one AD570 to another, so the number of NOP instructions may have to be increased or decreased. Experiment with the program until reliable data are obtained with the fewest number of NOP instructions. A result obtained from sampling a 1000-Hz sine waveform is given in Fig. 10–10. Note that the 256 points span eight cycles, giving a conversion rate of about one conversion every 31 microseconds. The loop that produces the 256 conversions is exactly 32 clock cycles in duration and, given that the Apple clock frequency is 1.023 MHz, we obtain a loop time of 31.28 microseconds.

Example 10–7. A Fast A/D Conversion Routine

199E:	8	;FAST ONE-PAGE CONVERSION ROUTINE.			
	9	******************************			
199E:A9 0A	10		LDA	#$0A	;INITIALIZE PCR. PULSE CA2, IFR1 SET
19A0:8D 8C C7	11		STA	PCR	;ON NEGATIVE TRANSITION ON CA1.
19A3:A2 00	12		LDX	#00	;START WITH INDEX AT ZERO.
19A5:AD 81 C7	13		LDA	PAD	;START THE FIRST CONVERSION.
19A8:EA	14		NOP		;THESE INSTRUCTIONS WASTE TIME
19A9:EA	15		NOP		;UNTIL THE CONVERSION IS COMPLETE.
19AA:EA	16		NOP		
19AB:EA	17		NOP		
19AC:EA	18		NOP		
19AD:EA	19 BACK		NOP		
19AE:EA	20		NOP		
19AF:EA	21		NOP		
19B0:EA	22		NOP		
19B1:EA	23		NOP		
19B2:EA	24		NOP		

```
19B3:EA        25        NOP
19B4:EA        26        NOP
19B5:EA        27        NOP
19B6:AD 81 C7  28 HERE   LDA   PAD       ;READ THE CONVERTER AND
19B9:9D 00 0F  29        STA   TABLE,X   ;START ANOTHER, STORE DATUM.
19BC:E8        30        INX
19BD:D0 EE     31        BNE   BACK      ;GET 256 CONVERSIONS.
19BF:60        32        RTS             ;QUIT.
```

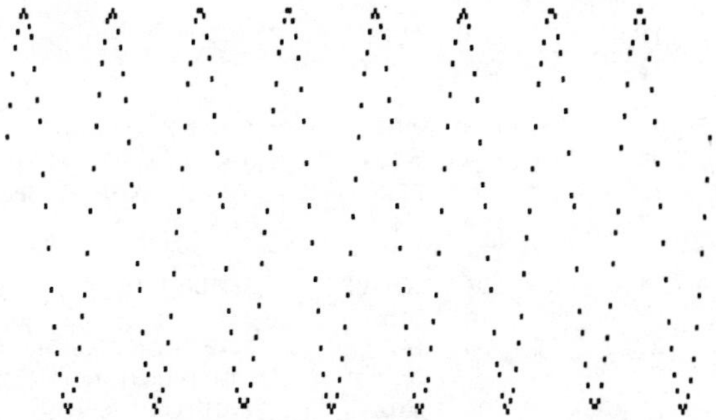

Fig. 10–10. The 256 points on a 1000-Hz sine function obtained with the program in Example 10–7.

The next improvement in the direction of realizing a real-time data acquisition and display system is the inclusion of a means to control the time interval between analog-to-digital conversions. This allows the user to adjust the sampling rate to match the waveform to be observed. Another feature included in this next level of sophistication is "level triggering." That is, the program waits in a loop until a preassigned voltage level is exceeded before beginning its task of sampling 256 points on the waveform. Primitive triggering schemes are available in the most inexpensive oscilloscopes, so this method was included here. With some programming effort it is possible to implement slope triggering or some other elegant triggering procedure. The improvements are given in the program listed in Example 10–8. Locations LOTIME and HITIME contain the numbers to be stored in the T1 timer on the 6522 that determine the time interval between samples. Timer T1 is initialized to operate in its free-running mode, so the time interval between samples remains constant. This program is the heart of the storage oscilloscope. The comments in Example 10–8, coupled with the previous programs, should allow you to understand how it operates.

The storage oscilloscope is now very easy to complete. It re-

Example 10–8. Data Logging with Triggering and Timing

```
00F2:          2 LOTIME    EQU    $F2          ;CONTAINS LO-BYTE FOR TIMER.
00F1:          3 HITIME    EQU    $F1          ;CONTAINS HI-BYTE FOR TIMER.
00F0:          4 TRIG      EQU    $F0          ;CONTAINS TRIGGER LEVEL.
0F00:          5 TABLE     EQU    $0F00        ;TABLE FOR DATA.
C781:          6 PAD       EQU    $C781        ;CONVERTER PORT.
C784:          7 T1LL      EQU    $C784
C785:          8 T1LH      EQU    $C785
C78B:          9 ACR       EQU    $C78B
C78C:         10 PCR       EQU    $C78C
C78D:         11 IFR       EQU    $C78D
19C0:         12           ORG    $19C0

19C0:A2 00    14           LDX    #00          ;CLEAR X.
19C2:A9 0A    15           LDA    #$0A         ;INITIALIZE PCR. PULSE CA2.
19C4:8D 8C C7 16           STA    PCR          ;IFR1 SET WITH PULSE ON CA1.
19C7:A9 40    17           LDA    #$40         ;T1 RUNS FREE.
19C9:8D 8B C7 18           STA    ACR
19CC:A5 F2    19           LDA    LOTIME       ;SET UP T1LL.
19CE:8D 84 C7 20           STA    T1LL
19D1:AD 81 C7 21           LDA    PAD          ;START CONVERSION. THESE
                                                  INSTRUCTIONS
19D4:A9 02    22 BACK      LDA    #02          ;WAIT FOR THE VOLTAGE TO EXCEED
19D6:2C 8D C7 23 WAIT      BIT    IFR          ;A PREASSIGNED
19D9:F0 FB    24           BEQ    WAIT
19DB:AD 81 C7 25           LDA    PAD          ;TRIGGER LEVEL.
19DE:C5 F0    26           CMP    TRIG         ;DOES IT EXCEED TRIGGER LEVEL?
19E0:90 F2    27           BCC    BACK         ;NO SO WAIT UNTIL IT DOES.
19E2:A5 F1    28           LDA    HITIME       ;START TIMING.
19E4:8D 85 C7 29           STA    T1LH
19E7:A9 02    30 MORE      LDA    #02          ;WAIT FOR THE CONVERSION.
19E9:2C 8D C7 31 PAUSE     BIT    IFR
19EC:F0 FB    32           BEQ    PAUSE        ;CONVERSION FINISHED?
19EE:2C 8D C7 33 HOLD      BIT    IFR          ;YES, WAIT FOR TIMER.
19F1:50 FB    34           BVC    HOLD
19F3:AD 81 C7 35           LDA    PAD          ;READ & START CONVERTER.
19F6:9D 00 0F 36           STA    TABLE,X      ;STORE THE LAST RESULT.
19F9:AD 84 C7 37           LDA    T1LL         ;CLEAR IFR5 FOR TIMER.
19FC:E8       38           INX
19FD:D0 E8    39           BNE    MORE         ;GET THE REMAINING POINTS.
19FF:60       40           RTS
```

quires a subroutine call to the routine in Example 6–18. Refer
to this example and note that it plots the contents of page $0F of
memory using the PLOT routine in Example 6–16, and the
routine to clear the hires screen in Example 6–15. After using
the routine in Example 10–8, complete with timing and triggering, to obtain 256 points on some waveform, it plots the data on
the hires screen. The program then waits for a key to be pressed
before it gets another 256 points to graph. The necessary subroutine calls are given in the listing in Example 10–9. Of
course, if you want the greatest possible sampling rate, use the

sampling routine in Example 10–7 rather than the one in Example 10–8. Fig. 10–11 illustrates the results obtained by sampling the output of an electric guitar directly after a string was plucked. The tone control filtered out most of the high frequencies. The waveform generated by a freshly plucked guitar string is rich in harmonics, which is obvious from Fig. 10–11. After a short period, the waveform becomes much more sinusoidal.

Example 10–9. The Storage Oscilloscope Program

```
152E:          2 GRAPH1   EQU   $152E
153A:          3 GRAPH2   EQU   $153A
19C0:          4 ATOD     EQU   $19C0
1A00:          5          ORG   $1A00
1A00:20 2E 15  6          JSR   GRAPH1   ;SUBROUTINE IN EXAMPLE 6–18.
1A03:20 C0 19  7 AGAIN    JSR   ATOD     ;SUBROUTINE IN EXAMPLE 10–8.
1A06:20 3A 15  8          JSR   GRAPH2   ;SUBROUTINE IN EXAMPLE 6–18.
1A09:AD 00 C0  9 WAIT     LDA   $C000    ;READ KEYBOARD.
1A0C:10 FB     10         BPL   WAIT     ;WAIT FOR KEY.
1A0E:AD 10 C0  11         LDA   $C010    ;RESET KEYBOARD FLIP-FLOP.
1A11:4C 03 1A  12         JMP   AGAIN    ;GET ANOTHER SET OF DATA.
1A14:          13 ;SUBROUTINES GRAPH1 AND GRAPH2 CALL SUBROUTINES
1A14:          14 ;IN EXAMPLES 6–15 AND 6–16.
```

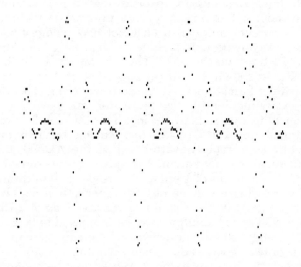

Fig. 10–11. Using the a/d converter to sample the output of an electric guitar.

The input impedance of the AD570 is only about 5 kilohms. Because of this it may be necessary to buffer the input with an amplifier. An amplifier is also useful for detecting and sampling small signals, from a guitar pickup, for example. We use the

AD521 amplifier; a circuit diagram is shown in Fig. 10–12. In this figure the gain is set by adjusting R and it may vary from 0.1 to 1000.

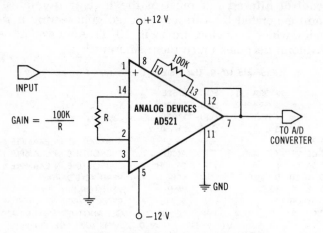

Fig. 10–12. Preamplifier circuit for the AD570.

It is frequently necessary to measure and record more than 256 conversions. For this purpose a program is included that will fill an integer number of pages of R/W memory with data from the a/d converter. It includes a time delay implemented with the T1 timer on the 6522. The program is listed in Example 10–10. As shown, it will fill pages $08 through $0F (eight pages) with information from the a/d converter. The program may be easily modified to use more storage.

We conclude this section by looking at a simple circuit for measuring temperature in kelvins. Analog Devices makes a temperature-to-current converter, called the AD590, that will sink 1 microampere per kelvin. A simple circuit is shown in Fig. 10–13. With a current of 1 microampere per kelvin through the 10-kilohm resistor, a voltage of 0.01 V per kelvin may be measured across it. At 0° Celsius, this gives a voltage of 2.732 volts (°C = K − 273.2). (The output may be increased to 0.02 volt per kelvin by using a 20-kilohm resistor. The precision of the output voltage is only as good as the precision of this resistor.) Because of its low input impedance, the AD570 cannot be connected directly across the 10-kilohm resistor in Fig. 10–13. Instead, use the AD521 amplifier operating with unit gain. This circuit is given in Fig. 10–12. Connect the output of the AD521 amplifier to the AD570 analog-to-digital converter. The program in Example 10–10 can be used to log 2048 temperature measurements.

```
00FD:        2 LOTIME   EQU  $FD           ;CONTAINS LO-BYTE FOR TIMER.
00FE:        3 HITIME   EQU  $FE           ;CONTAINS HI-BYTE FOR TIMER.
00FB:        4 IAL      EQU  $FB
0008:        5 LOPAGE   EQU  $08
000F:        6 HIPAGE   EQU  $0F
C781:        7 PAD      EQU  $C781         ;CONVERTER PORT.
C784:        8 T1LL     EQU  $C784
C785:        9 T1LH     EQU  $C785
C78B:       10 ACR      EQU  $C78B
C78C:       11 PCR      EQU  $C78C
C78D:       12 IFR      EQU  $C78D
1A12:       13          ORG  $1A12

1A12:A2 00  15          LDX  #00           ;INITIALIZE LOCATIONS USED
1A14:86 FB  16          STX  IAL           ;FOR THE INDIRECT INDEXED
1A16:A2 08  17          LDX  #LOPAGE       ;ADDRESSING MODE.
1A18:86 FC  18          STX  IAL+1
1A1A:A2 0F  19          LDX  #HIPAGE
1A1C:A0 00  20          LDY  #00
1A1E:A9 0A  21          LDA  #$0A          ;INITIALIZE PCR. PULSE CA2.
1A20:8D 8C C7 22        STA  PCR           ;IFR1 SET WITH PULSE ON CA1.
1A23:A9 40  23          LDA  #$40          ;T1 RUNS FREE.
1A25:8D 8B C7 24        STA  ACR
1A28:A5 FD  25          LDA  LOTIME        ;SET UP T1LL.
1A2A:8D 84 C7 26        STA  T1LL
1A2D:AD 81 C7 27        LDA  PAD           ;START CONVERSION. THESE
                                             INSTRUCTIONS
1A30:A5 FE  28          LDA  HITIME        ;START TIMING.
1A32:8D 85 C7 29        STA  T1LH
1A35:A9 02  30 MORE     LDA  #02           ;WAIT FOR THE CONVERSION.
1A37:2C 8D C7 31 PAUSE  BIT  IFR
1A3A:F0 FB  32          BEQ  PAUSE         ;CONVERSION FINISHED?
1A3C:2C 8D C7 33 HOLD   BIT  IFR           ;YES, WAIT FOR TIMER.
1A3F:50 FB  34          BVC  HOLD
1A41:AD 81 C7 35        LDA  PAD           ;READ & START CONVERTER.
1A44:91 FB  36          STA  (IAL),Y       ;STORE THE LAST DATUM.
1A46:AD 84 C7 37        LDA  T1LL          ;CLEAR IFR5.
1A49:C8     38          INY
1A4A:D0 E9  39          BNE  MORE          ;PAGE FILLED?
1A4C:E6 FC  40          INC  IAL+1         ;YES, INCREMENT THE PAGE
1A4E:E4 FC  41          CPX  IAL+1         ;NUMBER.
1A50:B0 E3  42          BCS  MORE          ;ALL PAGES FILLED?
1A52:60     43          RTS                ;YES, THEN RETURN.
```

INTERFACING A DIGITAL-TO-ANALOG CONVERTER

The last project described in this chapter uses the Analog Devices AD558 d/a (digital-to-analog) converter. A d/a converter (dac) converts a number to a voltage or current proportional to the number. In the case of the AD558 an 8-bit number is converted to a voltage between 0 and 10 volts, in the sense that the number $00 corresponds to 0 volts and the number $FF corre-

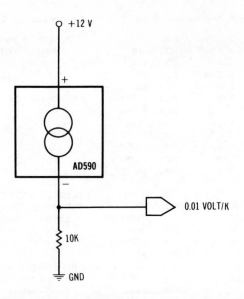

+12 V

+

AD590

−

0.01 VOLT/K

10K

GND

Fig. 10–13. Using the AD590 temperature-to-current transducer.

sponds to 10 volts. The AD558 is also capable of operating over the voltage range from 0 to 2.55 volts so that the voltage out is exactly 0.01N, where N is the binary number written to the d/a converter.

Again, this particular device was chosen because of its simplicity. No external components are required. When used with the 6522, only the eight lines of a port need be connected to the eight data pins of the AD558. A circuit diagram is shown in Fig. 10–14. In this figure the AD558 is shown configured to operate from 0 to 10 volts output. As in the previous examples this circuit was breadboarded on a protoboard and connected to the John Bell Engineering 6522 board with a DIP jumper. The following example programs assume that the AD558 is interfaced to the J4 (port B) socket. A short jumper was soldered between pin 15 of J4 and the 12-volt line on the board to provide a 12-volt supply for the AD558. It can also be operated at $V_{CC} = 5$ volts if it is configured to be in its 0- to 2.55-volt range. In the 0- to 10-volt mode, pins 14 (SELECT) and 13 are connected. In the 0- to 2.55-volt range, pins 14 and 15 are connected. Be sure to get a specification sheet when you order the chip.

This section will differ from the previous sections in this chapter in the sense that a complete real-time control applica-

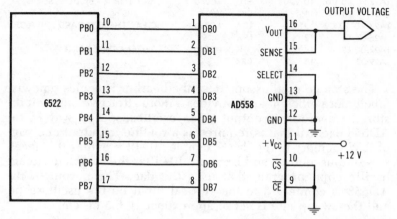

Fig. 10–14. Interfacing the 6522 to an AD558 d/a converter.

tion is not offered. Instead, we will study several examples that illustrate how the AD558 may be used. We begin by running a test program to see if the dac is working. Breadboard the circuit given in Fig. 10–14. Load the program in Example 10–11. Connect a voltmeter to the dac output, pin 16. It should read 10 volts before the program is executed. Start the program. The program begins by loading the dac with the number $00. This should bring the dac output to 0 volts. Each time a key on the Apple is pressed, the number stored in the dac is incremented by one. This should result in a voltage increase of about 0.04 volt. If the dac is operating in its 0- to 2.55-volt range, each step should increment the voltage by 0.01 volt. The author used a BK digital vom to measure the voltages. On the 0- to 10-volt range of the dac he obtained 0.00 volts with $00 stored in the dac port, 5.01 volts with $80 stored in the dac port, and 9.98 volts with $FF stored in the DAC port. Using the 0- to 2.55-volt range, he measured 0 volts corresponding to the binary number zero, 1.28 volts when he wrote the number $80 to the dac, and writing $FF to the dac gave a voltage of 2.56 volts. The errors were, therefore, always less than 0.02 volt, and it is not clear whether the voltmeter or the dac produced the error.

Example 10–11. A Program to Test the AD558 D/A Converter

```
1A14:A9 FF      6           LDA   #$FF     ;CONFIGURE PORT B AS AN 8-BIT
1A16:8D 82 C7   7           STA   DDRB     ;OUTPUT PORT TO CONTROL THE
                                            DAC.
1A19:A2 00      8           LDX   #00      ;INITIALIZE X.
1A1B:8E 80 C7   9 LOOPX     STX   PBD      ;OUTPUT THE NUMBER IN X TO THE
                                            DAC.
```

```
1A1E:2C 00 C0   10 WAIT    BIT   $C000    ;WAIT FOR A KEY DEPRESSION.
1A21:10 FB      11         BPL   WAIT
1A23:AD 10 C0   12         LDA   $C010    ;CLEAR THE KEYBOARD FLIP-FLOP.
1A26:E8         13         INX
1A27:D0 F2      14         BNE   LOOPX    ;GET ANOTHER POINT.
1A29:00         15         BRK
```

The storage oscilloscope described earlier becomes timewise much more efficient and provides a more attractive output if the stored waveform is output to an oscilloscope by way of the AD558 dac. All that is required is a routine to output one page of R/W memory to the dac. Example 10–12 provides the necessary output routine, and Example 10–13 is the complete storage oscilloscope program that uses the dac. The output of the AD558 is connected to the vertical input on the oscilloscope, and the sweep rate is set to approximately 0.5 ms/cm.

Example 10–12. A Routine to Output One Page of Data to the AD558

```
1A2A:A9 FF      7          LDA   #$FF     ;CONFIGURE PORT B AS AN 8-BIT
1A2C:8D 82 C7   8          STA   DDRB     ;OUTPUT PORT TO CONTROL THE
                                            DAC.
1A2F:A2 00      9          LDX   #00      ;INITIALIZE X.
1A31:BD 00 0F   10 LOOPX   LDA   TABLE,X  ;FETCH A NUMBER FROM THE
                                            TABLE.
1A34:8D 80 C7   11         STA   PBD      ;OUTPUT IT TO THE DAC.
1A37:E8         12         INX
1A38:D0 F7      13         BNE   LOOPX
1A3A:00         14         BRK
```

Example 10–13. The Storage Scope Modified to Use an Oscilloscope

```
00FD:           2 LOTIME   EQU   $FD      ;CONTAINS LO-BYTE FOR TIMER.
00FE:           3 HITIME   EQU   $FE      ;CONTAINS HI-BYTE FOR TIMER.
00FC:           4 TRIG     EQU   $FC      ;CONTAINS TRIGGER LEVEL.
0F00:           5 TABLE    EQU   $0F00    ;TABLE FOR DATA.
C780:           6 PBD      EQU   $C780    ;DAC LOCATION.
C782:           7 DDRB     EQU   $C782    ;PORT B DATA DIRECTION
                                            REGISTER.
C781:           8 PAD      EQU   $C781    ;CONVERTER PORT.
C784:           9 T1LL     EQU   $C784
C785:           10 T1LH    EQU   $C785
C78B:           11 ACR     EQU   $C78B
C78C:           12 PCR     EQU   $C78C
C78D:           13 IFR     EQU   $C78D
1A3D:           14         ORG   $1A3D

1A3D:A2 00      16         LDX   #00      ;CLEAR X.
1A3F:A9 0A      17         LDA   #$0A     ;INITIALIZE PCR. PULSE CA2.
1A41:8D 8C C7   18         STA   PCR      ;IFR1 SET WITH PULSE ON CA1.
1A44:A9 40      19         LDA   #$40     ;T1 RUNS FREE.
1A46:8D 8B C7   20         STA   ACR
1A49:A9 FF      21         LDA   #$FF     ;SET UP PORT B TO BE AN OUTPUT
```

```
1A4B:8D 82 C7   22        STA    DDRB       ;PORT FOR THE AD558 D/A
                                             CONVERTER.
1A4E:A5 FD      23        LDA    LOTIME     ;SET UP T1LL.
1A50:8D 84 C7   24        STA    T1LL
1A53:AD 81 C7   25 AGAIN  LDA    PAD        ;START CONVERSION. THESE
                                             INSTRUCTIONS
1A56:A9 02      26 BACK   LDA    #02        ;WAIT FOR THE VOLTAGE TO
                                             EXCEED
1A58:2C 8D C7   27 WAIT   BIT    IFR        ;A PREASSIGNED
1A5B:F0 FB      28        BEQ    WAIT
1A5D:AD 81 C7   29        LDA    PAD        ;TRIGGER LEVEL.
1A60:C5 FC      30        CMP    TRIG       ;DOES IT EXCEED TRIGGER LEVEL?
1A62:90 F2      31        BCC    BACK       ;NO SO WAIT UNTIL IT DOES.
1A64:A5 FE      32        LDA    HITIME     ;START TIMING.
1A66:8D 85 C7   33        STA    T1LH
1A69:A9 02      34 MORE   LAD    #02        ;WAIT FOR THE CONVERSION.
1A6B:2C 8D C7   35 PAUSE  BIT    IFR
1A6E:F0 FB      36        BEQ    PAUSE      ;CONVERSION FINISHED?
1A70:2C 8D C7   37 HOLD   BIT    IFR        ;YES, WAIT FOR TIMER.
1A73:50 FB      38        BVC    HOLD
1A75:AD 81 C7   39        LDA    PAD        ;READ & START CONVERTER.
1A78:9D 00 0F   40        STA    TABLE,X    ;STORE THE LAST RESULT.
1A7B:8D 80 C7   41        STA    PBD
1A7E:AD 84 C7   42        LDA    T1LL       ;CLEAR IFR5 FOR TIMER.
1A81:E8         43        INX
1A82:D0 E5      44        BNE    MORE       ;GET THE REMAINING POINTS.
1A84:BD 00 0F   45 LOOPX  LDA    TABLE,X    ;GET A NUMBER.
1A87:8D 80 C7   46        STA    PBD        ;OUTPUT IT TO THE DAC.
1A8A:E8         47        INX
1A8B:D0 F7      48        BNE    LOOPX
1A8D:2C 00 C0   49        BIT    $C000      ;CHECK FOR A KEY DOWN.
1A90:10 F2      50        BPL    LOOPX      ;OUTPUT THE TABLE AGAIN.
1A92:8D 10 C0   51        STA    $C010      ;CLEAR KEYBOARD FLIP-FLOP.
1A95:30 BC      52        BMI    AGAIN
```

The function of the dac in this case is to provide a Y-axis deflection while the internal circuitry of the oscilloscope provides the deflection along the X-axis. Because a table can be written to the dac much faster than it can be plotted on the Apple video monitor screen, this version of the storage oscilloscope has more versatility and does not flicker. A photograph of the output of the dac displayed on an oscilloscope is shown in Fig. 10–15. On the other hand, if you do not have an oscilloscope, then the Apple hires version of the storage scope must suffice.

The dac can also be used to output a table of data to an X-Y plotter. Of course, since mechanical devices respond much less quickly than electronic devices, the data must be output at a much slower rate. Also, the X-Y plotter will require another dac to provide the X-coordinate deflection. This can be accomplished with the program in Example 10–12 by inserting an

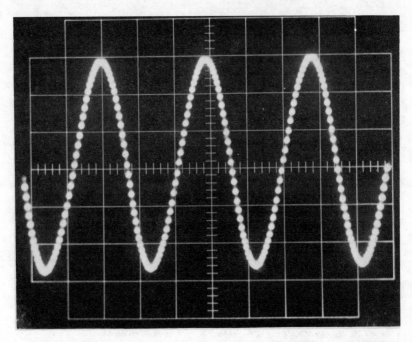

Fig. 10–15. Photograph of a sine function written to the AD558 dac and output to an oscilloscope.

STX PAD just before the INX instruction, provided another dac is connected to port A. The X register stores the X-coordinate, while the accumulator is used to obtain the Y value from the table and plot it at each of the 256 X values. A suitable delay loop must be inserted to slow down the process until the mechanical motions of the X-Y plotter can be accommodated.

The AD558 d/a converter can also be used to measure voltages. A circuit diagram to illustrate how this can be accomplished is given in Fig. 10–16 and a program to make the measurement is given in Example 10–14. A photograph of this circuit mounted on a breadboard is shown in Fig. 10–17. The 10-kilohm potentiometer in Fig. 10–16 is intended to represent a voltage somewhere between 0 and 10 volts that is to be measured. The actual voltage may be produced by the temperature-to-voltage circuit in Fig. 10–13 or any other voltage. The author used the AD558 to measure the voltage output of a National Semiconductor LX1601A pressure transducer in order to implement a digital barometer.

The LM311 is a voltage comparator. When the voltage at pin

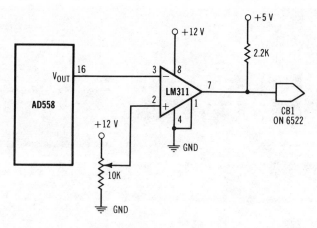

Fig. 10–16. Using the AD558 d/a converter to measure voltage.

Example 10–14. A Program to Measure Voltage Using the AD558 D/A Converter

1A97:A9 FF	7		LDA	#$FF	;CONFIGURE PORT B AS AN 8-BIT
1A99:8D 82 C7	8		STA	DDRB	;OUTPUT PORT TO CONTROL THE DAC.
1A9C:A2 FF	9 START		LDX	#$FF	;INITIALIZE X.
1A9E:E8	10 RAMP		INX		;INCREMENT X
1A9F:8E 80 C7	11		STX	PBD	;OUTPUT IT TO THE DAC.
1AA2:A9 10	12		LDA	#$10	;CHECK THE CB1 FLAG, IFR4.
1AA4:2C 8D C7	13		BIT	IFR	;IS IT SET?
1AA7:F0 F5	14		BEQ	RAMP	;NO, TRY ANOTHER X.
1AA9:8A	15		TXA		;YES, TRANSFER X TO A.
1AAA:20 DA FD	16		JSR	$FDDA	;OUTPUT THE CHARACTER.
1AAD:20 8E FD	17		JSR	$FD8E	;OUTPUT A CARRIAGE RETURN.
1AB0:4C 9C 1A	18		JMP	START	

3 exceeds the voltage at pin 2 then the output voltage at pin 7 drops to zero. The program in Example 10–14 increments the voltage at pin 3 in steps of 0.04 volt using the AD558 dac. When the voltage output of the AD558 exceeds the voltage to be measured, then the negative transition on the CB1 pin of the 6522 sets bit four (IFR4) in the interrupt flag register. The program in Example 10–14 outputs the number that was written to the dac to produce this voltage. The program then repeats itself. Note that the program outputs a number, N, to the video monitor. The voltage, V, is given by the expression

$$V = \frac{10N}{255}$$

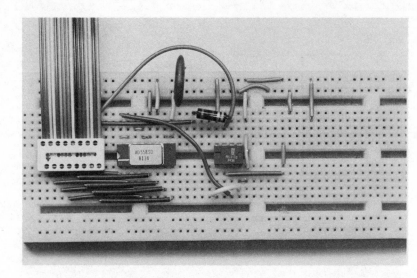

Fig. 10–17. A photograph of the AD558 d/a converter circuit on a breadboard.

where N is the number written to the dac. The true voltage will be less than 0.04 volt less than V. It would be convenient to call the routine in Example 10–14 from a BASIC program and do the binary-to-decimal conversion with BASIC.

This section would not be complete without noting that d/a converters are used extensively in music synthesis applications. In its simplest form, computer music is generated by writing the contents of a waveform table to a dac that is connected to an amplifier and a speaker. The desired waveform, calculated using Fourier analysis techniques, is stored in a table. The pitch and the timbre of the note can be completely controlled by the programmer, allowing a tremendous variety of sounds, including complex chords, to be synthesized. A second dac can be used to control the attack-sustain-decay envelope for each musical note, allowing almost complete real-time control of the important musical parameters. The chief limitation of these techniques is the speed of the microprocessor, which has the effect of limiting the bandwidth of the sound. Nevertheless, the results are impressive. For additional information on 6502-related music synthesis techniques and software, write Micro Technology Unlimited, 2806 Hillsborough Street, P.O. Box 12106, Raleigh, NC 27605.

We conclude this chapter and this book with an illustration of one of the most sophisticated real-time control and data acquisition systems known to computer scientists. It is shown in the photograph in Fig. 10–18. It was running at a reduced clock rate when the photograph was taken, and two of its light transducers are in a logic 0 condition. Its two sound transducers appear to be operating, as well as its strange-chemical detector. It is a "beast" to program, and it rarely does what you want it to do. Originally programmed in machine language, it has primitive speech recognition circuits that allow it to be partially controlled with a user-friendly, high-level language. It features an extremely sophisticated nth-generation molecular-electronics processor that makes current VLSI techniques obsolete. This system is legendary for its ability to operate in severe environments and it uses naturally occurring energy sources. The entire system should be the subject of intense interest to computer scientists for many years to come.

Fig. 10–18. Photograph of an extremely sophisticated real-time control and data acquisition system.

Decimal, Binary, and Hexadecimal Number Systems

OBJECTIVES

At the completion of this appendix you should be able to:

- Understand and define the terms number, face value, place value, base, bit, byte, and nibble.
- Understand that numbers are used to indicate quantity, to indicate order, or to indicate codes for various operations.
- Convert binary numbers to decimal numbers and decimal numbers to binary numbers.
- Convert hexadecimal numbers to binary numbers and binary numbers to hexadecimal numbers.

INTRODUCTION

Microprocessors use binary numbers to control internal operations, to communicate with other components in the microcomputer system, and to exchange information with peripheral devices. On the other hand, devices that humans use to input information to a microcomputer and devices that display information output by the microcomputer frequently use hexadecimal numbers. Hexadecimal numbers are representations of binary numbers that provide human beings with readily recognized symbols that aid in handling binary numbers. These facts justify competency in dealing with binary and hexadecimal numbers.

NUMBERS

Numbers are used in the following ways:

- Numbers are used to indicate *quantity*. This is the use with which we are most familiar.
- Numbers are used to indicate *order*. For example, the order in which a mechanical device is assembled is specified by numbers.
- Numbers are used as *names* or *codes*. Your social security number is a code which identifies you.

Sometimes numbers are used in several of these ways. The page numbers of a book *order* the pages, *name* the pages, and indicate the *quantity* of pages.

You will see that a microcomputer uses numbers in each of these three ways.

- A "smart" blood pressure monitor measures a signal and displays a number representing the blood pressure of a patient.
- A microcomputer program is executed one step at a time, and the order is determined by a number stored in the *program counter*.
- All microprocessor instructions have *code numbers*. The number 69 sent to the 6502 microprocessor will cause it to execute an addition operation.
- The memory locations in a microcomputer are ordered and named by a number called the *address* of the location.

A *number* is a sequence of digits. In the familiar decimal (base-10) system, the ten *decimal digits* are 0, 1, 2, . . . , 9. The binary number system (base-two) uses only two *binary digits*, namely 0 and 1. The words *binary digit* are frequently contracted to form the word *bit*. (If the same thing were done with decimal digits we would have *dits*, while hexadecimal digits would be *hits*.) The hexadecimal system (base 16) requires sixteen different hexadecimal digits. They are 0, 1, 2, . . . , 9, A, B, C, D, E, and F. Perhaps a better choice could have been made for the last six digits, but these are the ones commonly used.

DECIMAL NUMBERS

In order to understand binary and hexadecimal numbers it will be helpful to dissect a familiar decimal number. Taking the number 1939 as an example, we obtain the following diagram.

```
        ┌──── Digit Number 3
       ┌─── Digit Number 2
      ┌── Digit Number 1
     ┌─ Digit Number 0
 1 9 3 9 = 1000 + 900 + 30 + 9
```

$$= (1 \times 1000) + (9 \times 100) + (3 \times 10) + (9 \times 1)$$

FACE VALUES / PLACE VALUES

$$= (1 \times 10^3) + (9 \times 10^2) + (3 \times 10^1) + (9 \times 10^0)$$

DIGIT NUMBERS / BASE = 10

Referring to the preceding diagram, each decimal digit has a *face value*, the meaning of which is acquired from experience and memorization at an early age. There are 10 different face values in a base-10 system. Each decimal digit has a *digit number* or *place* in the decimal number which determines its *place value*. The place value of digit number 0 is $10^0 = 1$; the place value of digit number 1 is $10^1 = 10$. Place values of successive digits are $10^2 = 100$, $10^3 = 1000$, and so on. The place value is equal to the *base* raised to a power equal to the digit number.

BINARY NUMBERS

Binary numbers are constructed the same way as decimal numbers except the base is two and only two face values, 0 and 1, are required. Each binary digit is called a bit. The place values are $2^0 = 1$, $2^1 = 2$, $2^2 = 4$, $2^3 = 8$, and $2^4 = 16$, corresponding to bit numbers 0, 1, 2, 3, and 4, respectively. Table A-1 lists powers of 2.

Table A-1. A Table of Powers of 2

		$2^0 = 1$	
$2^1 = 2$	$2^5 = 32$	$2^9 = 512$	$2^{13} = 8192$
$2^2 = 4$	$2^6 = 64$	$2^{10} = 1024$	$2^{14} = 16384$
$2^3 = 8$	$2^7 = 128$	$2^{11} = 2048$	$2^{15} = 32768$
$2^4 = 16$	$2^8 = 256$	$2^{12} = 4096$	$2^{16} = 65536$

To illustrate these ideas and to show you how a binary number may be converted to a decimal number, the binary number 1101 is expanded in a way similar to the decimal number expansion above.

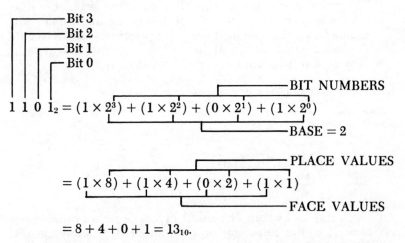

$$1\ 1\ 0\ 1_2 = (1 \times 2^3) + (1 \times 2^2) + (0 \times 2^1) + (1 \times 2^0)$$

$$= (1 \times 8) + (1 \times 4) + (0 \times 2) + (1 \times 1)$$

$$= 8 + 4 + 0 + 1 = 13_{10}.$$

The subscripts "2" and "10" are used to indicate the base of the number unless the base is obvious from the context of the discussion. The expansion diagram for the number 1101_2 also suggests how binary numbers may be converted to decimal numbers. Multiply the face value (either 1 or 0, so the multiplication is easy) by the place value of each bit and add the results. The place values are 2^n, where n is the bit number. The place value for bits numbered 0–16 may be obtained from Table A–1. Example A–1 gives another base 2 to base 10 conversion.

Example A–1. Conversion of 10100010_2 to Base 10

$$10100010_2 = (1 \times 2^7) + (0 \times 2^6) + (1 \times 2^5) + (0 \times 2^4)$$
$$+ (0 \times 2^3) + (0 \times 2^2) + (1 \times 2^1) + (0 \times 2^0)$$
$$= 128 + 32 + 2$$
$$= 162_{10}$$

Sometimes it is simpler to organize your work from the smallest place value, or *least significant bit* (the bit on the extreme right), to the largest place value, or *most significant bit* (the bit on the extreme left). Thus

$$1100_2 = (0 \times 1) + (0 \times 2) + (1 \times 4) + (1 \times 8) = 4 + 8 = 12_{10}$$

There are several techniques to convert a decimal number to a binary number. Here is a simple one; Example A-2 illustrates it.

- To find the highest place value that has a face value of 1 (that is, the most significant nonzero bit), find the largest power of 2 which will divide the number. Place a 1 in this bit position and note the remainder of the division.
- The remainder of the first result is then divided by the next largest power of 2. If it will not divide the first remainder, then a 0 is put in the next lower bit position. Otherwise, a 1 is placed in this bit position, and the remainder is noted.
- Repeat step two until you finish by dividing by 1.

Example A–2. Conversion of 233_{10} to Base 2

Clearly the largest power of two which will divide 233 is $2^7 = 128$. The process now proceeds as follows:

$$
\begin{array}{cccccccc}
1 & 1 & 1 & 0 & 1 & 0 & 0 & 1 \\
128\overline{)233} & 64\overline{)105} & 32\overline{)41} & 16\overline{)9} & 8\overline{)9} & 4\overline{)1} & 2\overline{)1} & 1\overline{)1} = 11101001_2 \\
\underline{128} & \underline{64} & \underline{32} & & \underline{8} & & & \underline{1} \\
105 & 41 & 9 & & 1 & & & 0
\end{array}
$$

Although this looks complicated, it proceeds rather quickly because most of the steps can be done mentally. In any case, it will be easier to handle binary numbers in terms of their hexadecimal representations as you shall see in a subsequent section.

BITS, BYTES, AND NIBBLES

Numbers used to express quantity are usually of *variable* length; they have no leading zeros to take up "unused" places. Numbers used as codes, zip codes for example, are usually *fixed* in length and often have leading zeros. All numbers used by a microprocessor are fixed in length regardless of whether they are used to express quantity, determine order, or represent a code. If a binary number represents quantity, the leading zeros are disregarded.

The fixed length of the numbers which the 6502 microprocessor regards as *data* is eight bits. An 8-bit number is called a *byte*. The number 7_{10} is represented as shown in Example A–3.

Example A–3. How the Number 7_{10} Is Represented by a Byte of Data

Data Byte	0	0	0	0	0	1	1	1	$= 7_{10}$
Data Bit Designations	D7	D6	D5	D4	D3	D2	D1	D0	

The 6502 microprocessor also *names* and *orders* 65536 different locations in memory with a 16-bit fixed length binary number called an *address*. The number 1020_{10} representing location 1020_{10} in memory is represented as an address as shown in Example A-4.

The 16-bit address number is frequently referred to in terms of two bytes. The low-order byte, or *address low* (ADL) as it is sometimes called, is the eight bits on the top while the high-order byte, or *address high* (ADH) as it is sometimes called, is the eight bits on the bottom.

Example A–4. How the Address 1020_{10} is Represented by a 16-Bit Binary Address

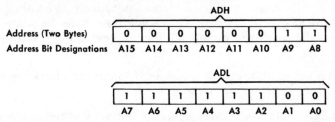

A 4-bit binary number is sometimes called a *nibble*. This is a useful idea when representing binary numbers by means of hexadecimal digits. A byte consists of a high-order nibble and a low-order nibble.

HEXADECIMAL NUMBERS

The sixteen hexadecimal digits and their decimal and binary equivalents are given in Table A-2. The subscripts 16, 10, and 2 are omitted.

Table A-2. Decimal, Binary, and Hexadecimal Equivalents

Decimal Number	Binary Number	Hexadecimal Number
0	0000	0
1	0001	1
2	0010	2
3	0011	3
4	0100	4
5	0101	5
6	0110	6
7	0111	7
8	1000	8
9	1001	9
10	1010	A
11	1011	B
12	1100	C
13	1101	D
14	1110	E
15	1111	F
16	10000	10

Notice that one hexadecimal digit represents four binary digits or one nibble. This fact provides the most convenient way to convert from binary numbers to hexadecimal numbers and vice versa.

Once the table has been committed to memory, the conversion process is as follows:

- Divide the binary number into groups of nibbles, starting from the least significant bit.
- Mentally convert each nibble to a hexadecimal number and write it down. (This process sometimes calls for a mental translation of the binary number to decimal and a translation of the decimal number to hexadecimal.)

Examples A–5 and A–6 illustrate how binary numbers are converted into hexadecimal numbers.

Example A–5. Conversion of Binary Numbers 01010101_2, 00000101_2, 10101111_2, and 11111110_2 Into Hexadecimal Numbers

$$01010101_2 = 0101\ 0101 = 55_{16}$$
$$10101111_2 = 1010\ 1111 = AF_{16}$$
$$00000101_2 = 0000\ 0101 = 05_{16}$$
$$11111110_2 = 1111\ 1110 = FE_{16}$$

Example A–6. Conversion of Binary Numbers 1001111100011100_2 and 0100010111011011_2 Into Hexadecimal Numbers

$$1001111100011100_2 = 1001\ 1111\ 0001\ 1100 = 9F1C_{16}$$
$$0100010111011011_2 = 0100\ 0101\ 1101\ 1011 = 45DB_{16}$$

The reverse process, converting from hexadecimal to binary, is done in a similar way.

- Divide the hexadecimal number into separate digits.
- Mentally convert each hexadecimal digit into a binary nibble.

Example A–7 illustrates the process.

Example A–7. Conversion of $3D_{16}$ and $FC83_{16}$ Into Binary Numbers

$$3D_{16} = 0011\ 1101 = 00111101_2$$
$$FC83_{16} = 1111\ 1100\ 1000\ 0011 = 1111110010000011_2$$

By now it should be easy for the reader to understand that hexadecimal numbers represent 8-bit and 16-bit binary numbers more efficiently than decimal numbers. Practice will produce the familiarity required for rapid calculations. A table of binary to hexadecimal to decimal conversions is provided in Table A–3.

Table A–3. Binary to Hexadecimal to Decimal Conversions

Binary Number				Hexadecimal Number	Decimal Number
			0001 NIBBLE	01	1
			0010 "	02	2
			0011 "	03	3
			0100 "	04	4
			0101 "	05	5
			0110 "	06	6
			0111 "	07	7
			1000 "	08	8
		0001	0000 BYTE	10	16
		0010	0000 "	20	32
		0100	0000 "	40	64
		1000	0000 "	80	128
		1000	1000 "	88	136
		1000	1100 "	8C	140
		1100	1100 "	CC	208
		1111	1111 "	FF	255
	0001	0000	0000 3 NIBBLES	0100	256
	0010	0000	0000 "	0200	512
	0011	0000	0000 "	0300	768
	0011	1111	1111 "	03FF	1023
	0100	0000	0000 "	0400	1024
	1000	0000	0000 "	0800	2048
0001	0000	0000	0000 2 BYTES	1000	4096
0001	1111	1111	1111 "	1FFF	8191
0010	0000	0000	0000 "	2000	8192
0011	1111	1111	1111 "	3FFF	16383
0100	0000	0000	0000 "	4000	16384
0101	1111	1111	1111 "	5FFF	24575
0110	0000	0000	0000 "	6000	24576
0111	1111	1111	1111 "	7FFF	32767
1000	0000	0000	0000 "	8000	32768
1001	1111	1111	1111 "	9FFF	40959
1010	0000	0000	0000 "	A000	40960
1011	1111	1111	1111 "	BFFF	49151
1100	0000	0000	0000 "	C000	49152
1101	1111	1111	1111 "	DFFF	57343
1110	0000	0000	0000 "	E000	57344
1111	1111	1111	1111 "	FFFF	65535

It might be added that hexadecimal numbers are frequently called "hex" numbers, and sometimes the suffix "H" is attached to indicate the hexadecimal representation. The notation used in this book to indicate hexadecimal numbers is a "$" prefix. That is, 36_{16} = \$36 and $7FFC_{16}$ = \$7FFC. This is the most common practice among 6502 users, perhaps to make them feel wealthy. Readers who were not previously familiar with hexadecimal and binary numbers are urged to try the exercises at the end of this appendix.

1. Identify the digit number of the digit 5 in the number 25033. If this a base 10 number what is the place value of the 5? Would the face value be changed if this were a base 16 number? Would the place value be changed if this were a base 16 number?

2. What is the place value of a digit in the nth place of a number written in base b?

3. Give examples of how numbers are used to indicate quantity, to indicate order, and as codes or names.

4. Convert the following decimal numbers to binary numbers: 17, 31, 64, 65, 127, 255, and 365.

5. Convert the following binary numbers to decimal numbers:

10110110	11110000
00010010	11111111
01000000	01010101
10000001	00110011

6. Convert the decimal numbers in Problem 4 to hexadecimal numbers. Use the binary results you obtained by doing Problem 4. Also convert the binary numbers in Problem 5 to hexadecimal numbers.

7. How many different 4-bit numbers or nibbles are there? 8-bit numbers? 16-bit numbers?

8. Define *number, bit, byte,* and *nibble.*

EXERCISE ANSWERS

1. The digit number of 5 is 3. (Digit numbers start with 0 on the right and increase to the left.) Its place value is $10^3 = 1000$ if the base is 10. Face values are the same in numbers of any base, provided that face value exists. For example, there is no face value of 5 in the binary number system. If the base of the number were 16 then the place value of the digit 5 would be $16^3 = 4096_{10}$.
2. The general formula for the place value of a digit in the nth place of a number written in base b is b^n.
3. The number of words on this page is a quantity. If the Kansas

City Royals are in second place, the 2 is used as an indication of order. The ASCII for the letter A is 41_{16}. Thus A is represented by the code number 41_{16}.
4. $17 = 10001_2$, $31 = 11111_2$, $64 = 1000000_2$, $65 = 1000001_2$, $127 = 1111111_2$, $255 = 11111111_2$, $365 = 101101101_2$.
5. $10110110 = 182_{10} = B6_{16}$ $11110000 = 240_{10} = F0_{16}$
   $00010010 = 34_{10} = 12_{16}$ $11111111 = 255_{10} = FF_{16}$
   $01000000 = 64_{10} = 40_{16}$ $01010101 = 85_{10} = 55_{16}$
   $10000001 = 129_{10} = 81_{16}$ $00110011 = 51_{10} = 33_{16}$
6. Some of the answers are given in Problem 5. The conversions from Problem 4 are $10001 = 11_{16}$, $11111 = 1F_{16}$, $1000000 = 40_{16}$, $1000001 = 41_{16}$, $1111111 = 7F_{16}$, $11111111 = FF_{16}$, and $101101101 = 16D_{16}$.
7. Notice that there are two different 1-bit numbers, four different 2-bit numbers, eight different 3-bit numbers and sixteen different 4-bit numbers. Thus, there are sixteen different nibbles. Using induction, if the number of bits in a number is n, then the number of different n-bit numbers is 2^n. Thus, there are $2^8 = 256$ different bytes or 8-bit numbers and $2^{16} = 65,536$ different 16-bit numbers. These answers may be verified with the table.
8. A number is a sequence of digits. A bit is a binary digit. A byte is an 8-bit binary number, and a nibble is a 4-bit binary number. Leading zeros are permitted.

Additional Circuits and Programs

A SINGLE-STEP CIRCUIT AND PROGRAM

One of the more useful aids in debugging assembly language programs is the ability to *single-step,* that is, execute the program one instruction at a time. It is also useful to be able to see the contents of each of the 6502's internal registers after the execution of each instruction.

If you have Integer BASIC and ROM, then you have the ability to single-step through a program. However, the Apple II Plus with Applesoft BASIC does not have any single-step capability. Craig Peterson has written a "Step and Trace for the Apple II Plus" routine that can be found in *Micro,* No. 30, November 1980, page 61. Both of these single-step programs have one disadvantage. If your program in R/W memory calls a monitor subroutine, the single-step mode will cause it to single-step through the monitor routine. This can take a lot of time, and although there may be some educational value in single-stepping through a monitor routine, these routines certainly do not have to be debugged.

We use a different approach here. Our routine makes use of interrupts (see Chapter 7 for a complete discussion of interrupts). After each instruction is executed the program being studied is interrupted and the contents of the various registers are displayed on the screen of the video monitor. Pressing any key on the keyboard allows the next instruction to be executed. The circuit that is used to produce the interrupts only will cause an interrupt when an op code located between $1000 and $1FFF is fetched. Consequently, programs at other locations, such as the monitor, will not be interrupted.

The Single-Step Circuit

The circuit is shown in Fig. B–1. It is a very simple circuit that is intended to be mounted on a peripheral card that fits into any of the eight peripheral card slots inside the Apple. The author suggests using the Vector 4609 Plugboard (Vector Electronic Company, Inc., 12460 Gladstone Ave., Sylmar, CA 91342, Telephone (213) 365–9661). See Fig. B–2 for a photograph of this card. All of the components for this project are available from Priority One Electronics, 9161C Deering Ave., Chatsworth, CA 91311, Telephone (213) 709–5464, as well as a number of other electronic parts supply houses. You will need the following parts:

- One 4609 Vector plugboard.
- Two 16-pin wire-wrap DIP sockets and one 14-pin wire-wrap DIP socket.
- A 74LS00 and a 74LS85 integrated circuit.
- An 8-contact DIP switch.
- Soldering and wire-wrap equipment.

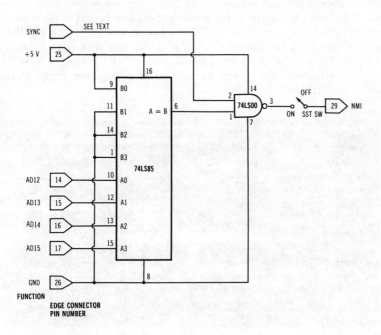

Fig. B–1. Single-step circuit diagram.

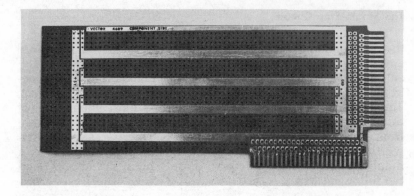

Fig. B−2. Photograph of the Vector 4609 plugboard.

You will also need either some experience with wiring circuits or some help from someone with such experience.

Wire the circuit shown in Fig. B−1. Pin diagrams for the various integrated circuits are shown in Appendix C. Refer to the photograph in Fig. B−3 to see how the author mounted the components on the board. Note that there is enough space for several other projects to be mounted on the board. The pins on the edge connector of the 4609 card correspond to the numbering of the pins on the card slots and the pin numbers given in Fig. B−1. See Fig. B−4 for a photograph that illustrates how the author attached the wires to the edge connector pads of the 4609 plugboard.

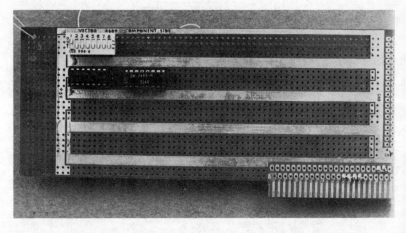

Fig. B−3. Photograph of the single-step circuit components.

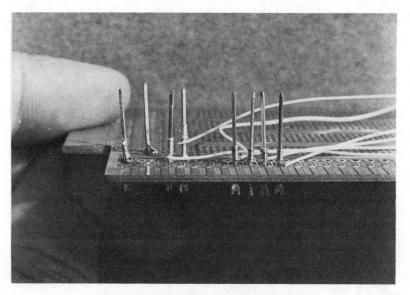

Fig. B-4. Detail of the wire-wrap approach.

The wire from the SYNC pin (7) on the 6502 to the input of the 74LS00 requires special attention. The designers of the Apple did not distribute the 6502 SYNC signal to the peripheral connectors, so you will need to make a special connection. Connect an 8-inch (20-cm) piece of 30-gauge wire (ordinary wire-wrap wire) to pin 2 of the 74LS00 NAND gate. Leave the other end free until the circuit is completely wired and ready for testing. When you are ready to install the plugboard, open up the Apple and remove any circuit boards in the peripheral connectors that may interfere with the following operation. Using a small screwdriver or an IC extractor, pry up the 6502 so that the pins on the right-hand side of the computer are free from the socket, while those on the left-hand side of the computer are only partly free. The idea is to have pin 7 just clear of the socket. Locate pin 7 on the 6502 and the socket and insert the free end of the 8-inch (20-cm) wire (with about 1/8 inch, or 3.2 mm, of insulation stripped from the end) into the pin 7 socket. While holding the wire in place, carefully push down the 6502 so that pin 7 holds the wire in place. Pull gently on the wire to make sure it will not spring loose, and make sure the 6502 is firmly seated in its socket. Now install the single-step circuit board in any of the slots and replace any other boards that were removed. Put the single-step switch in the OFF position. Your Apple will now operate normally.

The Single-Step Routine

To operate in the single-step mode, load the program in Example B-1. Next, load the NMI jump vector at locations $03FB-$03FD with the numbers $4C, $00, $80, which will result in a JMP to the single-step program located at $8000. The single-step program may be located anywhere except between $1000 and $1FFF, in which case it would attempt to single-step through itself (which might be intriguing, but not useful). Regardless of where it is located, the NMI jump vector in locations $03FB-$03FD must contain a JMP instruction to the first address in the program. Failure to have this will cause considerable grief in debugging the program.

Example B-1. A Single-Step Routine for the Apple

SOURCE FILE: SINGLE-STEP

```
0045:           3 AREG    EQU   $0045
0048:           4 PREG    EQU   $0048
003A:           5 PCL     EQU   $003A
003B:           6 PCH     EQU   $003B
0046:           7 XREG    EQU   $0046
0047:           8 YREG    EQU   $0047
0049:           9 SREG    EQU   $0049
C000:          10 KYBD    EQU   $C000
C010:          11 STROBE  EQU   $C010
FDDA:          12 PRBYTE  EQU   $FDDA
F948:          13 PRBLNK  EQU   $F948
FD8B:          14 CROUT1  EQU   $FD8B
FAD7:          15 REGDSP  EQU   $FAD7
0024:          16 CURSHO  EQU   $0024
0025:          17 CURSVT  EQU   $0025
-----NEXT OBJECT FILE NAME IS SINGLE STEP PROGRAM
8000:          18         ORG   $8000

8000:85 45     20         STA   AREG    ;SAVE A.
8002:68        21         PLA           ;PULL P OFF STACK.
8003:85 48     22         STA   PREG    ;SAVE P.
8005:68        23         PLA           ;PULL PCL OFF STACK.
8006:85 3A     24         STA   PCL     ;SAVE IT.
8008:68        25         PLA           ;PULL PCH OFF STACK.
8009:85 3B     26         STA   PCH     ;SAVE IT.
800B:84 47     27         STY   XREG    ;SAVE Y.
800D:86 46     28         STX   XREG    ;SAVE X.
800F:BA        29         TSX           ;STACK POINTER TO X
8010:86 49     30         STX   SREG    ;SAVE S.
8012:A9 00     31         LDA   #00     ;HOME CURSOR.
8014:85 24     32         STA   CURSHO  ;HORIZONTAL POSITION.
8016:85 25     33         STA   CURSVT  ;VERTICAL POSITION.
8018:A2 17     34         LDX   #$17    ;CLEAR SCREEN.
801A:20 8B FD  35 BR3     JSR   CROUT1
```

```
801D:CA            36        DEX
801E:10 FA         37        BPL    BR3
8020:A9 00         38        LDA    #00
8022:85 24         39        STA    CURSHO
8024:85 25         40        STA    CURSVT
8026:A5 3B         41        LDA    PCH          ;GET PCH.
8028:20 DA FD      42        JSR    PRBYTE       ;PRINT IT.
802B:A5 3A         43        LDA    PCL          ;GET PCL.
802D:20 DA FD      44        JSR    PRBYTE       ;PRINT IT.
8030:A0 00         45        LDY    #00          ;CLEAR Y.
8032:20 48 F9      46        JSR    PRBLNK       ;PRINT BLANKS.
8035:B1 3B         47        LDA    (PCH),Y      ;GET OP CODE.
8037:20 DA FD      48        JSR    PRBYTE       ;PRINT IT.
803A:20 D7 FA      49        JSR    REGDSP       ;DISPLAY THE REGISTERS.
803D:A9 C3         50        LDA    #$C3         ;ASCII C.
803F:8D 67 07      51        STA    $0767        ;DISPLAY IT.
8042:8D 51 07      52        STA    $0751
8045:A9 DA         53        LDA    #$DA         ;ASCII Z.
8047:8D 66 07      54        STA    $0766        ;DISPLAY IT.
804A:A9 C9         55        LDA    #$C9         ;ASCII I.
804C:8D 65 07      56        STA    $0765        ;DISPLAY IT.
804F:A9 C4         57        LDA    #$C4         ;ASCII D.
8051:8D 64 07      58        STA    $0764        ;DISPLAY IT.
8054:A9 C2         59        LDA    #$C2         ;ASCII B.
8056:8D 63 07      60        STA    $0763        ;DISPLAY IT.
8059:A9 A0         61        LDA    #$A0         ;ASCII SPACE.
805B:8D 62 07      62        STA    $0762        ;DISPLAY IT.
805E:A9 D6         63        LDA    #$D6         ;ASCII V.
8060:8D 61 07      64        STA    $0761        ;DISPLAY IT.
8063:A9 CE         65        LDA    #$CE         ;ASCII N.
8065:8D 60 07      66        STA    $0760        ;DISPLAY IT.
8068:A5 45         67        LDA    AREG         ;GET A.
806A:48            68        PHA                 ;SAVE IT.
806B:A2 07         69        LDX    #07          ;DISPLAY IT.
806D:66 45         70 BACK   ROR    AREG
806F:A9 00         71        LDA    #00
8071:69 B0         72        ADC    #$B0
8073:9D F0 07      73        STA    $07F0,X
8076:CA            74        DEX
8077:10 F4         75        BPL    BACK
8079:68            76        PLA
807A:85 45         77        STA    AREG
807C:A2 07         78        LDX    #07
807E:A5 48         79        LDA    PREG         ;GET P.
8080:48            80        PHA                 ;SAVE IT.
8081:66 48         81 BR1    ROR    PREG         ;ONE BIT AT A TIME.
8083:A9 00         82        LDA    #00          ;CONVERT TO ASCII.
8085:69 B0         83        ADC    #$B0
8087:9D E0 07      84        STA    $07E0,X      ;OUTPUT IT TO THE SCREEN.
808A:CA            85        DEX                 ;GET ANOTHER BIT.
808B:10 F4         86        BPL    BR1
808D:68            87        PLA                 ;GET P BACK.
808E:85 48         88        STA    PREG         ;RESTORE IT.
8090:A9 D0         89        LDA    #$D0         ;ASCII P.
8092:8D 50 07      90        STA    $0750        ;DISPLAY IT.
```

8095:8D 58 07	91	STA	$0758	
8098:A9 CF	92	LDA	#$CF	;ASCII O.
809A:8D 57 07	93	STA	$0757	;DISPLAY IT.
809D:A9 C1	94	LDA	#$C1	;ASCII A.
809F:8D 70 07	95	STA	$0770	;DISPLAY IT.
80A2:AD 00 C0	96 BR2	LDA	KYBD	;WAIT FOR KEYBOARD.
80A5:10 FB	97	BPL	BR2	
80A7:8D 10 C0	98	STA	STROBE	;CLEAR STROBE.
80AA:A6 49	99	LDX	SREG	;RESTORE THE REGISTERS.
80AC:9A	100	TXS		
80AD:A4 47	101	LDY	YREG	
80AF:A6 46	102	LDX	XREG	
80B1:A5 3B	103	LDA	PCH	
80B3:48	104	PHA		
80B4:A5 3A	105	LDA	PCL	
80B6:48	106	PHA		
80B7:A5 48	107	LDA	PREG	
80B9:48	108	PHA		
80BA:A5 45	109	LDA	AREG	
80BC:40	110	RTI		;RETURN TO THE PROGRAM.

Load a program in the memory space between $1000 and $1FFF; you might start with the programs in Examples 2–5 to 2–9. Run the program to make sure it is working. Next put the single-step switch in the ON position and restart the program. You should see the contents of the registers displayed near the top of the video monitor screen. Near the bottom of the screen you will see the program counter contents, namely the address of the op code of the *next* instruction to be executed. You will also see the next op code, and a display of the number in the P register and the accumulator expressed in binary. Pressing any key on the keyboard will cause the next instruction in the program to be executed.

You should quit single-stepping when you reach a BRK op code in a program. To get out of the single-step mode, simply put the single-step switch in the OFF position, then press a key on the keyboard.

The program in Example B-1 is simply an NMI-type interrupt routine. One interrupt is produced by the circuit each time an instruction is executed. The program merely displays the contents of the various registers, either by using a monitor subroutine, or with a routine included in the program. Chart B-1 is a hexadecimal dump of the program for your convenience in loading it.

Circuit Operation

A brief explanation of the circuit follows. The 6502 knows when it is fetching an op code, and the SYNC output goes to logic 1 during an op-code fetch. This signal is NANDed with a

```
*8000.80BC
8000-  85 45 68 85 48 68 85 3A
8008-  68 85 3B 84 47 86 46 BA
8010-  86 49 A9 00 85 24 85 25
8018-  A2 17 20 8B FD CA 10 FA
8020-  A9 00 85 24 85 25 A5 3B
8028-  20 DA FD A5 3A 20 DA FD
8030-  A0 00 20 48 F9 B1 3B 20
8038-  DA FD 20 D7 FA A9 C3 8D
8040-  67 07 8D 51 07 A9 DA 8D
8048-  66 07 A9 C9 8D 65 07 A9
8050-  C4 8D 64 07 A9 C2 8D 63
8058-  07 A9 A0 8D 62 07 A9 D6
8060-  8D 61 07 A9 CE 8D 60 07
8068-  A5 45 48 A2 07 66 45 A9
8070-  00 69 B0 9D F0 07 CA 10
8078-  F4 68 85 45 A2 07 A5 48
8080-  48 66 48 A9 00 69 B0 9D
8088-  E0 07 CA 10 F4 68 85 48
8090-  A9 D0 8D 50 07 8D 58 07
8098-  A9 CF 8D 57 07 A9 C1 8D
80A0-  70 07 AD 00 C0 10 FB 8D
80A8-  10 C0 A6 49 9A A4 47 A6
80B0-  46 A5 3B 48 A5 3A 48 A5
80B8-  48 48 A5 45 40
```

signal from the 74LS85 4-bit comparator to produce a negative transition at the output of the 74LS00 NAND gate whenever the output of the 74LS85 is at logic 1 *and* the SYNC signal makes a transition to logic 1 (at the beginning of an op-code fetch cycle). The negative transition on the output of the NAND gate produces an NMI interrupt, which in turn causes the microprocessor to execute the single-step program. After it returns from the interrupt it continues to process the program that was interrupted.

When is the output of the 74LS85 at logic 1? Note that the output we are discussing is the so-called A=B output. When the four A inputs have the same logic levels as the four B inputs, then the A=B output goes to logic 1. The four A inputs are connected to address lines AD15, AD14, AD13, and AD12, the high-order nibble of the address on the address bus. The *corre-*

sponding B inputs are hard-wired (permanently connected) to logic levels of 0, 0, 0, and 1, respectively. Thus the A=B output will be at logic 1 only when the high-order nibble of the address is $1, that is, for addresses $1000 through $1FFF. Only programs in this memory range are capable of being single-stepped. Note that any program can be moved to these locations to be tested and then moved back to the locations where you want it to be stored. Note also that you cannot single-step through monitor programs: they will be executed at normal speeds.

Use of Single-Stepping

Single-step capability is very useful for debugging programs as well as having educational value when used to study programs. You are urged to provide yourself with this capability either by using the single-step mode in Integer BASIC, the single-step circuit and program just described, or the program given in the reference above. Another approach is to use *single-cycle* execution in which each instruction is executed one cycle at a time. John Bell Engineering provides this option in the form of a card that plugs into one of the peripheral card slots. Sixteen LEDs display the logic levels on the address bus and eight LEDs display the logic levels on the data bus. Although execution proceeds more slowly when executing one cycle at a time, there is great educational value in studying the behavior of the microcomputer system in this mode. Write for more details (John Bell Engineering, P.O. Box 338, Redwood City, CA 94064, (415) 367–1137).

THE COMPUTER ASSISTED LEARNING (CAL) PROGRAM

A listing of the computer program that was used to demonstrate the logic instructions, the rotate and shift instructions, and the arithmetic instructions is listed in Example B–2. A hexadecimal memory dump of the program is given in Chart B–2. Several of the routines were discussed in the text, and the program will not be discussed further. The comments should be sufficient to understand its operation, once you have a fundamental grasp of assembly language programming.

Example B–2. The Computer Assisted Learning (CAL) Program

SOURCE FILE: EXAMPLE B-2

```
0000:           2 TEMP    EQU  $0000        ;TEMPORARY STORAGE LOCATION.
FD8E:           3 CROUT   EQU  $FD8E        ;CARRIAGE RETURN.
FD0C:           4 RDKEY   EQU  $FD0C        ;READ KEYBOARD.
FC58:           5 HOME    EQU  $FC58        ;SUBROUTINE TO CLEAR THE
                                               SCREEN.
1100:           6 RDBYTE  EQU  $1100        ;SUBROUTINE TO GET A BYTE.
FDED:           7 COUT    EQU  $FDED        ;OUTPUT SUBROUTINE.
0048:           8 PREG    EQU  $0048
0045:           9 AREG    EQU  $0045
-----NEXT OBJECT FILE NAME IS EXAMPLE B-2.
1100:          10         ORG  $1100

1100:          12 * SUBROUTINE RDBYTE

1100:20 16 11  14         JSR  ASHEX       ;GET NIBBLE.
1103:0A        15         ASL  A           ;SHIFT TO HIGH NIBBLE.
1104:0A        16         ASL  A
1105:0A        17         ASL  A
1106:0A        18         ASL  A
1107:85 00     19         STA  TEMP        ;STORE NIBBLE.
1109:20 16 11  20         JSR  ASHEX       ;GET THE SECOND NIBBLE.
110C:05 00     21         ORA  TEMP        ;COMBINE WITH FIRST NIBBLE.
110E:85 00     22         STA  TEMP        ;SAVE ENTIRE BYTE.
1110:20 8E FD  23         JSR  CROUT       ;OUTPUT A RETURN.
1113:A5 00     24         LDA  TEMP        ;GET BYTE BACK.
1115:60        25         RTS              ;NO. RETURN.

1116:          27 * ASCII-TO-HEX ROUTINE

1116:20 0C FD  29 ASHEX   JSR  RDKEY       ;GET A CHARACTER.
1119:20 ED FD  30         JSR  COUT        ;DISPLAY IT.
111C:29 7F     31         AND  #$7F        ;MASK BIT 7 OFF.
111E:C9 40     32         CMP  #$40        ;DIGIT OR LETTER?
1120:B0 04     33         BCS  ARND
1122:29 0F     34         AND  #$0F        ;DIGIT, MASK HI-NIBBLE.
1124:10 02     35         BPL  PAST        ;BRANCH PAST LETTER.
1126:E9 37     36 ARND    SBC  #$37        ;LETTER, SUBTRACT $37.
1128:60        37 PAST    RTS              ;RETURN WITH DIGIT IN A.
1129:          39 * SUBROUTINE DISPLAY

1129:85 45     41 DISPLAY STA  AREG        ;SAVE A.
112B:48        42         PHA              ;SAVE A ON THE STACK.
112C:08        43         PHP              ;PUT P ON THE STACK.
112D:08        44         PHP
112E:68        45         PLA
112F:85 48     46         STA  PREG
1131:8A        47         TXA
1132:48        48         PHA              ;SAVE X ON THE STACK.
1133:A2 07     49         LDX  #07
```

```
1135:66 45      50 BR2      ROR     AREG        ;ROTATE A CONTENTS INTO CARRY.
1137:A9 00      51          LDA     #00
1139:69 B0      52          ADC     #$B0        ;CONVERT BIT TQ ASCII.
113B:9D 10 05   53          STA     $0510,X
113E:CA         54          DEX
113F:10 F4      55          BPL     BR2
1141:66 48      56          ROR     PREG
1143:A9 00      57          LDA     #00
1145:69 B0      58          ADC     #$B0
1147:8D 0E 05   59          STA     $050E
114A:68         60          PLA                 ;GET X FROM THE STACK.
114B:AA         61          TAX
114C:28         62          PLP                 ;GET P FROM THE STACK.
114D:68         63          PLA                 ;GET A FROM THE STACK.
114E:60         64          RTS                 ;RETURN TO CALLING PROGRAM.

114F:           66 ;* SUBROUTINE GETBYTS

0001:           68 OPA      EQU     $0001
0002:           69 OPB      EQU     $0002
0003:           70 RESULT   EQU     $03
114F:20 58 FC   71 GETBYTS  JSR     HOME        ;HOME THE CURSOR.
1152:20 00 11   72          JSR     RDBYTE      ;GET THE FIRST NUMBER.
1155:85 01      73          STA     OPA         ;STORE IT.
1157:20 00 11   74          JSR     RDBYTE      ;GET THE SECOND NUMBER.
115A:85 02      75          STA     OPB         ;STORE IT.
115C:60         76          RTS

115D:           78 ;* SUBROUTINE TEST

115D:20 29 11   80 TEST     JSR     DISPLAY     ;DISPLAY THE RESULT.
1160:20 00 11   81 AGAIN    JSR     RDBYTE      ;GET THE ANSWER.
1163:45 03      82          EOR     RESULT      ;IS IT EQUAL TO THE RESULT?
1165:D0 F9      83          BNE     AGAIN       ;NO, THEN TRY AGAIN.
1167:60         84          RTS
```

*** SUCCESSFUL ASSEMBLY: NO ERRORS

Chart B-2. A Memory Dump of the CAL Program
Used in Chapters 4 and 5

```
*1100.1167
1100-  20 16 11 0A 0A 0A 0A 85
1108-  00 20 16 11 05 00 85 00
1110-  20 8E FD A5 00 60 20 0C
1118-  FD 20 ED FD 29 7F C9 40
1120-  B0 04 29 0F 10 02 E9 37
1128-  60 85 45 48 08 08 68 85
1130-  48 8A 48 A2 07 66 45 A9
1138-  00 69 B0 9D 10 05 CA 10
1140-  F4 66 48 A9 00 69 B0 8D
1148-  0E 05 68 AA 28 68 60 20
1150-  58 FC 20 00 11 85 01 20
1158-  00 11 85 02 60 20 29 11
1160-  20 00 11 45 03 D0 F9 60
```

APPENDIX C

Pin Diagrams of Some Integrated Circuits

CONNECTION DIAGRAM
(TOP VIEW)

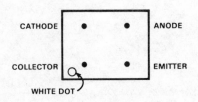

(Courtesy Fairchild Camera and Instrument Corp.)

Fig. C–1. FPA 106.

(Courtesy Rockwell International)

Fig. C–2. R6522.

328

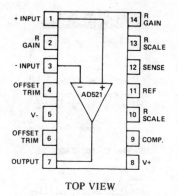

TOP VIEW

(Courtesy Analog Devices, Inc.)

Fig. C-3. AD521.

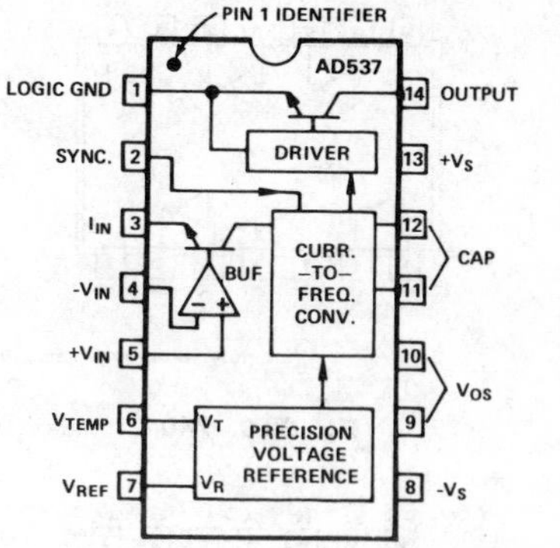

(Courtesy Analog Devices, Inc.)

Fig. C-4. AD537.

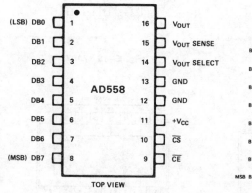

TOP VIEW

(Courtesy Analog Devices, Inc.)

Fig. C-5. AD558.

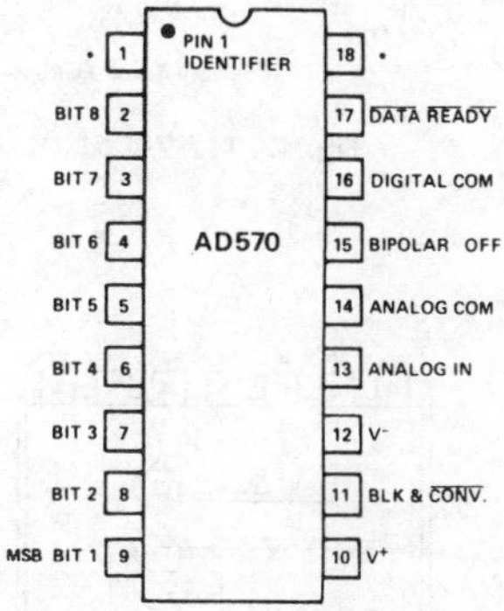

(Courtesy Analog Devices, Inc.)

Fig. C-6. AD570.

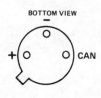

(Courtesy Analog Devices, Inc.)

Fig. C-7. AD590.

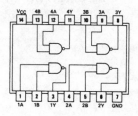

(Courtesy Texas Instruments, Inc.)

Fig. C-8. 7400.

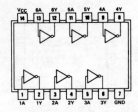

(Courtesy Texas Instruments, Inc.)

Fig. C–9. 7404.

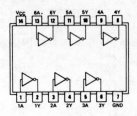

(Courtesy Texas Instruments, Inc.)

Fig. C–10. 7405.

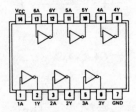

(Courtesy Texas Instruments, Inc.)

Fig. C–11. 7406.

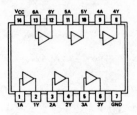

(Courtesy Texas Instruments, Inc.)

Fig. C–12. 7407.

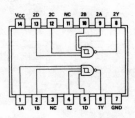

(Courtesy Texas Instruments, Inc.)

Fig. C–13. 7413.

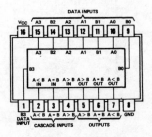

(Courtesy Texas Instruments, Inc.)

Fig. C–14. 7485.

Index

READER SERVICE CARD

To better serve you, the reader, please take a moment to fill out this card, or a copy of it, for us. Not only will you be kept up to date on the Blacksburg Series books, but as an extra bonus, **we will randomly select five cards every month, from all of the cards sent to us during the previous month. The names that are drawn will win, absolutely free, a book from the Blacksburg Continuing Education Series.** Therefore, make sure to indicate your choice in the space provided below. For a complete listing of all the books to choose from, refer to the inside front cover of this book. Please, one card per person. Give everyone a chance.

In order to find out who has won a book in your area, call (703) 953-1861 anytime during the night or weekend. When you do call, an answering machine will let you know the monthly winners. Too good to be true? Just give us a call. Good luck.

If I win, please send me a copy of:

_____

I understand that this book will be sent to me absolutely free, if my card is selected.

For our information, how about telling us a little about yourself. We are interested in your occupation, how and where you normally purchase books and the books that you would like to see in the Blacksburg Series. We are also interested in finding authors for the series, so if you have a book idea, write to The Blacksburg Group, Inc., P.O. Box 242, Blacksburg, VA 24060 and ask for an Author Packet. We are also interested in TRS-80, APPLE, OSI and PET BASIC programs.

My occupation is _____

I buy books through/from _____

Would you buy books through the mail? _____

I'd like to see a book about _____

Name _____

Address _____

City _____

State _____ Zip _____

MAIL TO: BOOKS, BOX 715, BLACKSBURG, VA 24060
!!!!!PLEASE PRINT!!!!!

21894